Cole's Funny Picture Book No. 1

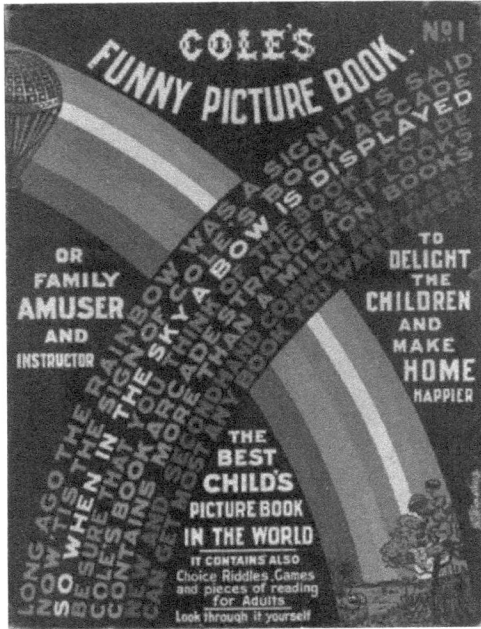

by

Edward William Cole

Contents

COLE'S Funny Picture Book No. 1

Or Family Amuser And Instructor;
To Delight The Children And Make Home Happier;
The Best Child's Picture Book In All The World.

It Contains Also Choice Riddles, Games
and pieces of reading for Adults.
Look through it yourself.

Long ago the Rainbow was a Sign it is said,
Now 'tis the Sign of Cole's Book Arcade.
So, when in the sky a bow is displayed,
Be sure that you think of the Book Arcade.
Cole's Book Arcade strange as it looks,
Contains more than a million books.
New and second-hand, common and rare,
Can get most any book you want there.

[*] BIBLIOGRAPHICAL NOTE: The reprintings of this book since Cole's death in 1918 have involved very few changes, and in most cases it has been bibliographically misleading to term them "editions". Undoubtedly, somewhere in the past, the distinction between a "printing" and an "edition" has not been understood. However, with due cognisance of the irregularity, the practice of giving each reprint a new edition number accompanied by a running sales total is being maintained for statistical interest.

Edward William Cole

Born Woodchurch, Kent, England
4th January, 1832

Died Essendon, Victoria, Australia
16th December, 1918

Australia Is The Best Country On Earth
Australia a Grand Country

I think that Australia, for its size, is, all-round, the best country in the world. It's climate is pleasant and health-giving. It has no desolating blizzards, no frost bites, and few sunstrokes. In edible produce, for both size and quality, it stands very high, if not the highest. I have been in many lands, but never saw a country supply such a variety of products as Australia does— potatoes, onions, cabbages, carrots, peas, beans and scores of other vegetables in abundance. In fruits it produces apples, pears, plums, peaches, oranges, grapes, and Northern Australia also produces all the tropical fruits in abundance wherever cultivated. In corn Australia produces superior wheat, oats, barley, maize and all other kinds in abundance, especially when scientifically irrigated. As a milk, butter and meat country, it is one of the best in the world. It is the largest and best wool-producing country in the world. It contains the largest area in the world especially suitable for growing cotton, the most extensively-used clothing material. Flowers grow luxuriantly and beautifully whenever cultivated and watered. A few years ago when writing on the "White Australia" question, I stated that with high culture, water irrigation, and scientific irrigation, Australia was capable of supporting 400 millions of inhabitants. A high literary authority, in reviewing the book, remarked that this seemed like a "gross exaggeration"; but probably he had not thought so much on the subject as I had.

I will here concisely state the principle reasons for my opinion. The great want of Australia, to make it amazingly fruitful, is the complete conservation of water and it's scientific application to the soil. Water, warmth, and soil will grow anything in Australia, if rationally managed. Australia has abundance of water now running to waste. On thousands of house-roofs water enough is caught for the domestic use of the respective families. Over large areas of the country there are 30 inches of rainfall, and the average rainfall over vast areas is 24 inches, and could be made much greater by cultivation. Four-fifths of this water now runs to waste. Again surface-parched Australia has vast areas of underground water which only require to be tapped and brought to the surface, to irrigate and fertilise the soil.

Australia is also a country where timber grows well and fast, if planted in trenched ground and slightly irrigated. Hundreds of straight trees can be grown upon an acre of land if they are first planted thickly and some gradually thinned out. Many kinds of trees will grow upon very poor soil if they are properly planted and irrigated, as the bulk of their sustenance is derived from the air. One more remark about trees and their possibilities as food providers. Wherever any kind of tree will grow some kind of fruit tree will grow. There are hundreds of millions of gum trees growing in Australia. Where every one of these trees is, some kind of fruit tree would grow if properly planted and looked after.

Again, to utilise Australia to it's full extent the

3

whole world should be sought through for the best plants and trees of every kind, and only the very best grown, and those in situations and soil best adapted for them.

One argument against Australia is that much of its surface is sandy, but experiments and developments in various countries show that the planting of marram grass, lupins, and other plants ties even the drifting sand together and gradually, through their decay, turns the sandy wastes into fertile soil. Besides, science can, in many other ways, utilise the elements in the air to enrich the soil.

Australia's Mineral Resources

It has been objected that in the above epitome no mention is made of the great mineral wealth of Australia. The reason is that minerals, exceedingly useful as they are in the arts, are not absolutely necessary (with the exception perhaps of iron) to the feeding, clothing, and housing of mankind. Vast multitudes have lived without them; but it may be remarked that Australia is a country very rich in minerals; some hold it the richest in the world. It possesses immense deposits of iron not yet utilised, and the most extensive gold-fields yet discovered. Australia and Tasmania have, according to the latest estimate of our Commonwealth Statistician, produced minerals to the value of £660,252,694— comprising in round numbers, Gold £474,000,000; Tin £24,000,000; and other kinds £8,000,000. The bulk of the above has been produced during the last 60 years, in a population rising from about 300,000 to 4,000,000 and it forecasts how vast the mineral-producing future of Australia is likely to be. Altogether Australia is a country as highly favoured by nature as any other of equal size upon earth, for the bountiful production of useful animals, vegetables, minerals, and men.

The Best Country On Earth—
Unknown Australia

"'If we Australians took as much trouble to prepare for our summer as the Canadians take to forestall their winter, Australia would be THE MOST PROSPEROUS COUNTRY ON EARTH.'

The speaker was the Rev. A. R. Edgar, head of the Central Mission, Melbourne.

"'After circling the globe, then, you are still satisfied that Australia is not a bad country to live in?'

"'The best,' said Mr Edgar, emphatically. 'I have no hesitation in saying that Canada and America are not to be compared with Australia. Unfortunately, England doesn't know it. Australia herself doesn't half realise it, and as for America and Canada, they haven't the remotest ghost of a notion of it. In England they learn with regrettable slowness, and their knowledge is scanty indeed; but across the Atlantic the ignorance is deplorable. "Australia?" says the Canadian. "Oh yes! Let's see, that's the place where it's always droughty—yes, yes, to be sure, the place where y' can't get a drink of water." He laughs at the idea of Australia producing as much wool and wheat as Canada, and bluntly tells you there's no country on the face of the planet can grow wheat and wool like his. But the fact is, there isn't a bit of territory fit to compare with the Western District of Victoria, for example, and conditions are infinitely harder for the agriculturist than in Australia. Canada's western district is icebound in winter, and her eastern lands are strewn over with great boulders, between which the plough works laboriously in and out'."—From the "New Idea."

I often feel for the dweller in Canada; for notwithstanding his beautiful spring and autumn he has six months of ice and snow and freezing winds, and I feel selfishly grateful that my lot is cast in more genial Australia.

Let us well ponder Mr. Edgar's concise and forcible statement: "If we Australians took as much trouble to prepare for our summer as the Canadians take to fore-stall their winter, Australia would be the most prosperous country on earth."

This is quite true. The Canadian must thoughtfully and rationally prepare for his winter, or he would freeze and starve. We have no frigid climate to prepare against, but we have possible drought, and our first and greatest consideration should be the conservation of water for irrigation.

This water conservation is exceedingly important thing. Men do not think, and the waste is enormous. When the rain falls it runs into the gully, from the gully to the creek, from the creek to the river, from the river into the sea; and then in the dry season water is deplorably scarce.

I once asked a young squatter from the New South Wales side of the Murray "Have you got a garden?" He answered: "No: it is too dry up our way!" I said, "How do you get water for domestic purposes?" He answered, "We catch it off the roof; we catch it in 11 tanks and are never out of a supply." I asked, "How large an area have all your roofs put together?" He answered, "I think about 20 feet by 100 feet." This would be about a twentieth of an acre. Now just reflect! One acre of rainfall would supply, if caught, 20 establishments like that squatter's home, for the rain would fall fairly alike over that part of the country. A rainfall of 30 inches over an acre of ground measures about 680,000 gallons and weighs about 3000 tons, the bulk of which is allowed to run away every year!

A gentleman said to me the other day, "Since the water was brought to Coolgardie and Kalgoorlie, under Sir John Forrest's great scheme, they have very beautiful gardens right along the line of supply. Wherever the water touches the land the vegetation is splendid, and, what is more, the evaporation is bringing heavier rainfall." Of course, wherever cultivation and irrigation are carried on, more evaporation takes place, and, in most cases, causes additional rainfall.

When I affirmed that Australia was capable of supporting 400 millions of people I did not mean Australia as we now have it, but as it might be, and probably will be, when water is carefully conserved and its soil scientifically irrigated and cultivated.

E.W. Cole

I'M JOHNNY SMITH

I Want Cole's Funny Picture Book
JOHNNY SMITH'S GOT ONE

I've Got Cole's Funny Picture Book
I'M SO GLAD

This Is The Funniest Picture Book In The World For Children

If you search through the World you will not get a book that will so please a child, if you pay £100 or even £1000 for it. To parents, Grandparents, Uncles, Aunts, and Friends—Every Good Child should be given one of these Books for being Good. Every Bad Child should be given one to try to make it Good.

TIRED AND GOING TO BED

A Piece of Poetry for Mother and Father to Read

I suppose if all the children,
 Who have lived through ages long,
Were collected and inspected
 They would make a wondrous throng.

Oh the babble of the Babel!
 Oh, the flutter and the fuss;
To begin with Cain and Abel,
 And to finish up with us!

Some have never laughed nor spoken,
 Never used their rosy feet;
Some have even flown to heaven,
 Ere they knew that earth was sweet.

And indeed, I wonder whether,
  If we reckon every birth,
And bring such a flock together,
  There is room for them on earth.

Think of all the men and women
  Who are now and who have been;
Every nation since creation
  That this world of ours has seen.

And of all of them not any
  But was once a baby small;
While of children, oh, how many
  Never have grown up at all.

GETTING UP AS HAPPY AS LARKS

Who will wash their smiling faces?
  Who their saucy ears will box?
Who will dress them and caress them?
  Who will darn their little socks?

Where are arms enough to hold them?
  Hands to pat each smiling head?
Who will praise them? who will scold them?
  Who will pack them off to bed?

Little happy Christian children,
  Little savage children too,
In all stages of all ages,
  That our planet ever knew;

Little princes and princesses,
  Little beggars, wan and faint—
Some in very handsome dresses,
  Naked some, bedaubed with paint.

Only think of the confusion
  Such a motley crowd would make;
And the clatter of their chatter,
  And the things that they won't break

Oh the babble of the Babel!
  Oh, the flutter and the fuss;
To begin with Cain and Abel,
  And to finish up with us!

Children's Rhymes

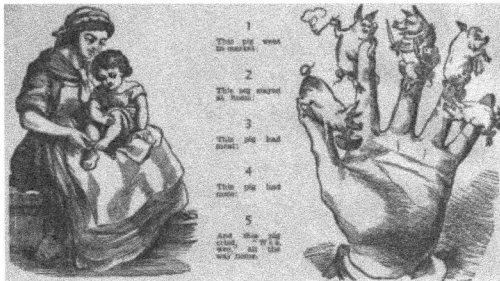

1. This pig went to market:
2. This pig stayed at home:
3. This pig had meat:
4. This pig had none:
5. And this pig cried, "Wee, wee," all the way home.

Game of Child's Features

Here sits the Lord Mayor! (forehead)
Here sits his two men! (eyes)
Here sits the cock! (right cheek)
Here sits the hen! (left cheek)
Here sit the little chickens! (tip of nose)
Here they run in; (mouth)
Chinchopper, chinchopper,
Chinchopper, chin! (chuck the chin)

Face Game

Ring the bell! (giving its hair a pull)
Knock at the door! (tapping its forehead)
Draw the latch! (pulling up it's nose)
And walk in! (putting finger in mouth)

Face Game

(Eye) Bo Peeper! (Nose) Nose dreeper!
  (Chin) Chinchopper!
  (Teeth) White Lopper!
(Mouth) little gap! (Tongue) and red rag!

Game on the Toes

1. Let us go to the wood, says this pig;
2. What to do there? says that pig;
3. Too look for my mother, says this pig;
4. What to do with her? says that pig;
5. Kiss her to death, says this pig.

Going to Market

To market, to market, to buy a fat pig;
Home again, home again, jiggety-jig.
To market, to market, to buy a fat hog;
Home again, home again, joggety-jog.

Baby Riding

Ride baby, ride, pretty baby shall ride,
And have a little puppy-dog tied to her side.
And a little pussy-cat tied to the other,
And away she shall ride to see her grand-mother,
To see her grandmother.

Ride a Cock-Horse

Ride a cock-horse to banbury-cross,
  To see what Tommy can buy;
A penny white loaf, a penny white cake,
  And a two-penny apple pie.
Ride a cock-horse to banbury-cross,
  To see a young lady on a white horse,
Rings on her fingers, and bells on her toes,
  And so she makes music wherever she goes.

Baby Riding

This is the way the ladies ride;
  Tre, tre, tree,
This is the way the ladies ride;
  Tre, tre, tree.
This is the way the gentlemen ride;
  Gallop-a-gallop-a-trot!
This is the way the gentlemen ride;
  Gallop-a-gallop-a-trot!
This is the way the farmers ride;
  Hobbledy-hobbledy-hoy!
This is the way the farmers ride;
  Hobbledy-hobbledy-hoy!

Clap Hands

Clap hands, clap hands,
  Till father comes home;
For father's got money,
  But mother's got none.

When Dad Comes Home

You shall have an apple,
  You shall have a plum,
You shall have a rattle,
  When your dad comes home.

Pat-A-Cake

Pat-a-cake, pat-a-cake, baker's man!
So I will, master, as fast as I can,
Pat it, and prick it, and mark it with T,
Put it in the oven for Tommy and me.

Come, Butter, Come

Churn, butter, churn! come, butter, come!
  Peter stands at the gate,
  Waiting for a butter cake;
Come, butter, come!

Baby Crying

When Jacky's a very good boy,
  He shall have cakes and a custard;
But when he does nothing but cry,
  He shall have nothing but mustard.

Hickup, go away.

Hickup, hickup, go away!
Come again another day:
Hickup, hickup, when I bake,
I'll give to you a butter-cake.

Dance, Baby.

Dance, little baby, dance up high,
Never mind, baby, mother is nigh;
Crow and caper, caper and crow—
There, little baby, there you go!
Up to the ceiling, down to the ground,
Backwards and forwards, round and round.
Dance, little baby, and mother will sing!
Merrily, merrily, ding, dong, ding!

Dance, Little Baby.

Dance to your daddy,
My little babby,
Dance to your daddy,
My little lamb.
You shall have a fishy

In a little dishy;
You shall have a fishy
When the boat comes in.

Danty Baby Diddy.

Danty baby diddy,
What can a mammy do wid'e,
　But sit in a lap,
　And give 'un a pap?
Sing danty baby diddy.

Hush-a-bye Baa Lamb.

Hush-a-bye, a baa lamb,
　Hush-a-by a milk cow,
You shall have a little stick
　To beat the naughty bow-wow.

Bye, Baby Bunting.

Bye, baby bunting,
Daddy's gone a hunting,
To get a little rabbit skin
To wrap a baby bunting in.

Hush-a-bye Baby.

Hush-a-bye baby, on the tree top,
When the wind blows, the cradle will rock;
When the bough breaks, the cradle will fall;
Down will come baby, bough, cradle, and all.

Hush-a-bye baby, Daddy is near:
Mammy's a lady, and that's very clear.

Rock-a-bye Baby.

Rock-a-bye baby, thy cradle is green;
Father's a nobleman, mother's a queen;
And Betty's a lady, and wears a gold ring,
And Johnny's a drummer, and drums for the king.

Kissing Baby.

My dear cockadoodle, my jewel, my joy,
My darling, my honey, my pretty, sweet boy;
Before I do rock thee with soft lullaby,
Give me thy dear lips to be kiss'd, kiss'd, kiss'd.

Good-night Baby

Baby, baby, lay your head
On your pretty cradle bed;
Shut your eye-peeps, now the day
And the light are gone away;
All the clothes are tucked in tight,
Little baby, dear, good night.

Lie still with Daddy.

Hush thee, my babby,
Lie still with thy daddy,
Thy mammy has gone to the mill,
To grind thee some wheat,
To make thee some meat,
And so, my babby, lie still.

17

Monkey feeding Baby.

Oh, my lady! my lady! my lady!
Here's that funny monkey
Has put on your night-cap,
And is feeding
The baby! the baby! the baby!

Baby getting up

Baby, baby ope your eye,
For the sun is in the sky,
And he's peeping once again
Through the pretty window pane:
Little baby, do not keep
Any longer fast asleep.

Washing Baby's Hands

Wash hands, wash,
  Daddy's gone to plough;
If you want your hands wash'd,
  Have them washed now.

Combing Baby's Hair

Comb hair, comb,
  Daddy's gone to plough;
If you want your hair comb'd
  Have it combed now.

Baby Brother

My pretty baby-brother
  Is six months old to-day,
And though he cannot speak,
  He knows whate'er I say.

Whenever I come near,
  He crows for very joy;
And dearly do I love him,
  The darling baby-boy.

Baby

He opens his mouth when he kisses you;
He cries very loud when he misses you;
He says "Boo! boo! boo!" for "How-do-you-do?"
And he strokes down your face when he's loving you.

Learning to walk alone

Come, my darling, come away,
Take a pretty walk to-day;
Run along, and never fear,
I'll take care of baby dear;
Up and down with little feet,
That's the way to walk, my sweet.

See-Saw

See-saw sacradown,
Which is the way to London town,
One foot up is the other down,
That is the way to London town.

Naughty Baby

Baby, baby Charlie,
  Naughty in his play,
Slapping little Annie,
  Pushing her away.

Patting with his soft hands,
  Laughing in his fun;
Slapping with such good-will,
  That the tear-drops run.

Do not cry, dear Annie,
  Wipe away the tear;
Keep away from Charlie,
  Do not come so near,

Or his little hands will
  Pull your curly hair;
Peep at baby, Annie—

Peep behind the chair.

Kiss the baby, darling,
  Kiss the little one;
He is only playing,
  In his baby fun.

Tom Thumb's Alphabet

A was an archer, who shot at a frog;
B was a butcher, who had a great dog;
C was a captain, all covered with lace;
D was a drunkard, and had a red face;
E was an esquire, with pride on his brow;
F was a farmer, who followed the plough;
G was a gamer, who had but ill luck;
H was a hunter, and hunted a buck;
I was an innkeeper, who loved to bouse;
J was a joiner, and built up a house;
K was King William, once governed this land;
L was a lady, who had a white hand;
M was a miser, and hoarded up gold:
N was a nobleman, gallant and bold;
O was an oyster girl, and went about town;
P was a parson, and wore a black gown;
Q was a queen, who wore a silk slip;
R was a robber, and wanted a whip;
S was a sailor, and spent all he got;
T was a tinker, and mended a pot;
U was an usurer, a miserable elf;
V was a vintner, who drank all himself;
W was a watchman, and guarded the door;
X was expensive, and so became poor;
Y was a youth, that did not love school;
Z was a Zany, a poor harmless fool;

Sing a Song-a-Sixpence

Sing a song-a-sixpence,
  A pocket full of rye;
Four-and-twenty blackbirds
  Baked in a pie;
When the pie was opened
  The birds began to sing:
Was that not a dainty dish
  To set before the king?
The king was in his counting-house,
  Counting out his money,
The queen was in the parlour,
  Eating bread and honey;
The maid was in the garden,
  Hanging out the clothes;
Down came a blackbird,
  And snapt off her nose.

Old Chairs to Mend

If I'd as much money as I could spend,
I never would cry old chairs to mend;
Old chairs to mend, old chairs to mend;
I never would cry old chairs to mend.
If I'd as much money as I could tell,
I never would cry old clothes to sell;
Old clothes to sell, old clothes to sell;
I never would cry old clothes to sell.

Dad's gane to Ploo

Cock-a-doodle-doo,
My dad's gane to ploo;
Mammy's lost her pudding-poke
And knows not what to do.

Hot Cross Buns

Hot-cross buns! Hot-cross buns!
One a penny, two a penny,
  Hot-cross buns!
Hot-cross buns! Hot-cross buns!
If you have no daughters,
  Give them to your sons.

Rabbit Pie

Rabbit, rabbit, rabbit-pie!
Come, my ladies, come and buy;
Else your babies they will cry.

A—Apple-Pie

A apple pie;
B bit it;
C cut it;
D danced for it;

E eat it;
F fought for it;
G got it;
H had it;
I ignored it;
J jumped for it;
K kept it;
L longed for it;
M mourned for it;
N nodded at it;
O opened it;
P peeped in it;
Q quartered it;
R ran for it;
S stole it;
T took it;
U uncovered it;
V viewed it;
W wanted it;
X ax'ed for it;
Y yawned for it:
Z cried, "Zounds! let's eat it up."

Three Men in a Tub

Rub a dub, dub,
Three men in a tub;
And who do you think they were?
The butcher, the baker, the candlestick maker,
They all came out of a rotten potato.

Dinner

Hey ding a ding, what shall I sing?
How many holes in a skimmer?
Four-and-twenty, my stomach is empty;

Pray mamma, give me some dinner.

The Barber

Barber, barber, shave a pig,
How many hairs will make a wig?
"Four-and-twenty, that's enough,"
Give the barber a pinch of snuff.

Punch and Judy

Punch and Judy fought for a pie;
Punch gave Judy a blow on the eye.

Pease Pudding

Pease pudding hot,
  Pease pudding cold,
Pease pudding in the pot,
  Nine days old.

Porridge

A little bit of powdered beef,
  And a great net of cabbage,
The best meal I have to-day
  Is a good bowl of porridge.

Shaving

The barber shaved the mason,
As I suppose cut of his nose,
And popp'd it in a basin.

Captain Duck

I saw a ship a-sailing,
  A-sailing on the sea;
And, oh! it was all laden
  With pretty things for thee.
There were comfits in the cabin,
  And apples in the holds;
The sails were made of silk,
  And the masts were made of gold.
The four-and-twenty sailors
  That stood between the decks,
Were four-and-twenty white mice,
  With chains about their necks.
The captain was a duck,
  With a packet on his back;
And when the ship began to move,
  The captain said "Quack quack!"

Little Tee Wee

Little Tee Wee' he went to sea
In an open boat; and while afloat
The little boat bended,
And my story's ended.

Jack be Quick

Jack be nimble, and Jack be quick;
And Jack jump over the candle-stick.

Jack Sprat

Jack Sprat had a cat,
It had but one ear;
It went to buy butter
When butter was dear.

Jack Horner

Little Jack Horner sat in the corner,
Eating a Christmas Pie;
He put in his thumb, and he took out a plum,
And said, "What a good boy am I!"

Tom Tucker

Little Tom Tucker
Sings for his supper;
What shall he eat?
White bread and butter.
How shall he cut it
Without e'er a knife?
How will he be married
Without e'er a wife?

27

Georgie Porgie

Georgie Porgie, pudding and pie,
Kissed the girls and made them cry.
When the girls came out to play
Georgie Porgie ran away.

See-Saw

See-saw, Margery Daw,
Little Jacky shall have a new master;
Little Jacky shall have but a penny a day,
Because he can't work any faster.

Little Lad

Little lad, little lad, where wast thou born?
Far off in Lancashire, under a thorn,
Where they sup sour milk in a ram's horn.

Jack-a-Dandy

Handy Spandy, Jack-a-dandy,
Loved plum-cake and sugar-candy;
He bought some at a grocer's shop,
And out he came, hop, hop, hop.

My Son John

Deedle, deedle, dumpling, my son John
Went to bed with his stockings on;
One shoe off, the other shoe on.
Deedle, deedle, dumpling, my son John

Jack and Jill

Jack and Jill went up the hill,
  To fetch a pail of water;
Jack fell down and broke his crown,
  And Jill came tumbling after.

Who Can Draw Best

Willie drew a little pig,
Harry drew a mouse,
Tommy drew a ladder tall
Leaning on a house.

Baa, Baa Black Sheep

Baa, baa, black sheep,
  Have you any wool?
Yes, marry have I,
  Three bags full:
One for my master,
  And one for my dame,
But none for the little boy
  Who cries in the lane.

Hey diddle diddle

Hey diddle diddle, the cat and the fiddle,
The cow jumped over the moon;
The little dog laughed to see such sport,
And the dish ran after the spoon.

The Quaker's Version

"Hey! diddle diddle,
The cat and the fiddle,
The cow jumped under the moon;
The little dog barked
to see such sport
And the cat ran after the spoon!" [*]

[*] Our friend, the Quaker, holds that the last verse is the proper one, as it is the truest; but the wonderful is taken out of it, and children, accordingly, prefer the first. There is nothing wonderful in the cow jumping "under" the moon, but there is in the cow jumping "over" the moon, so with the black-birds baked in a pie. It is the fact of their singing when the pie is opened that pleases the children—'twas the wonder of the thing; so with the

freaks of Mother Hubbard's Dog, etc. In nearly all nursery rhymes it is the ludicrous and wonderful that arrests
the attention and pleases.
E. W. Cole

Frightened Boy

There was a little boy, went into a barn,
  And lay down on some hay;
An owl came out, and flew about,
  And the little boy ran away.

Frightened Boys

Tweedle-dum and tweedle-dee
  Resolved to have a battle,
For tweedle-dum said tweedle-dee
  Had spoiled his nice new rattle.
Just then flew by a monstrous crow,
  As big as a tar-barrel,
Which frightened both the heroes so,
  They quite forgot their quarrel.

Baked in a Pie

Baby and I
Were baked in a pie,
The gravy was wonderful hot;
We had nothing to pay
To the baker that day
And so we crept out of the pot.

Maid not at Home

High diddle doubt, my candle's out,
My little maid is not at home;
Saddle my hog, and bridle my dog,
And fetch my little maid home.

Dame not at Home

Rowsty dowt, my fire's all out,
My little dame is not at home;
I'll saddle my goose and bridle my hen,
And fetch my little dame home again;
Home she came, tritty trot;
And asked for the porridge she left in the pot.

All in the Dumps

We're all in the dumps,
For diamonds are trumps;
The kittens are gone to St. Paul's!
The babies are bit,
The moon's in a fit,
And the houses are built without walls.

Hot Rolls

Blow, wind, blow! and go, mill, go!
That the miller may grind his corn;
That the baker may take it,
And into rolls make it,
And send us some hot in the morn.
Rosemary green,
And lavender blue,

Thyme and sweet marjoram,
  Hyssop and rue.

Bed Time

Come, let's to bed, says Sleepy-head
  Tarry a while says Slow;
Put on the pot, says Greedy-Jock,
  Let's sup before we go.

Go to Bed First

Go to bed first,
A golden purse;
Go to bed second,
A golden Pheasant;
Go to bed third,
A golden bird.

Morals

The three Cry-Babies

Cry-Baby Belle

Cry-baby Belle
  Is always in tears
Nothing you can give her can ease her!
  Sugar and spice,
  And everything nice,
Kisses and cakes will not please her.

  She'll cry if she happens
  To get a slight fall,
She'll cry if the naughty boys tease her;
  She'll cry for a spoon,
  And she'll cry for the moon;
So there's no use in trying to please her.

  If the food set before her
  Don't happen to suit—
Oh, then just as loud as she's able,

This cry-baby Belle
Will set up a yell,
And scare all the folks at the table.

If she wants to go out
In the street she will cry;
If she wants to come in how she screeches!
For nothing at all
She will set up and bawl,
Unmindful of comforting speeches,

She screams in the morning
Because she's not dress'd;
And at night when they want to undress her
More loudly she'll roar,
And roll over the floor
As if she had pains to distress her.

She cries when she's sick,
And she cries when she's well,
And often cries when she's sleeping,
So that heavy and red,
And most out of her head
Are her eyes, on account of such weeping.

She always is fretful,
Unhappy, and cross,
No matter what she may be doing,
And cry-baby Belle
Pleases nobody well
Because of her constant boo-hooing.

For a Naughty Little Girl

My sweet little girl should be careful and mild,
And should not be fretful, and cry!
Oh! why is this passion? remember, my child,

God sees you, who lives in the sky.

That dear little face, which I like so to kiss,
  How frightful and sad it appears!
Do you think I can love you, so naughty as this,
  Or kiss you so wetted with tears?

Remember, tho' God is in heaven, my love,
  He sees you within and without,
And he always looks down from His glory above,
  To notice what you are about.

If I am not with you, or if it be dark,
  And nobody is in the way,
His eye is as able your doings to mark,
  In the night as it is in the day.

Then dry up your tears, and look smiling again
  And never do things that are wrong;
For I'm sure you must feel it a terrible pain,
  To be naughty, and crying so long.

Paulina Pry

    Paulina Pry
      Would eat nothing but pie;
    Pie was her daily diet;
      Apple or plum,
      She must have some
    Or else she wouldn't be quiet.

      She would not eat
      Any bread or meat,
    Though plenty of these were handy,
      But would pout and cry
      For a piece of pie,
    Or a stick of sugar-candy.

They heard her cry
In the Land of Pie,
And sent her dozens and dozens,
Both tender and tough,
Till she'd had more than enough
For her sisters, her aunts and her cousins.

Tearful Annie

Poor little Annie, you will find,
Is very gentle, good, and kind,
But soon a a fault appears.
The slightest thing will give her pain,
Her feelings she can ne'er restrain,
But gives way to her tears.

The other day when Ferdinand—
And if you search throughout the land,
No nicer boy you'll find—
Said something which he never meant
To cause the slightest discontent,
For hours she sobbed and whined.

Her father grieved, said: "This must cease
We never have a moment's peace,
She cries both day and night."
A portrait painter then he paid,
To paint his little tearful maid,
Crying with all her might.

He set to work that very day,
Directly he received his pay;
The picture soon was done.
Yes, there she was, all sobs and sighs,
Large tear-drops streaming from her eyes.
"How like!" said every one.

It was in truth a great success;

COLE

Quite perfect, neither more nor less;
Her father was so glad.
He hung the portrait in her room;
It filled her with the deepest gloom;
She felt annoyed and sad.

With every relative who came,
And saw the picture, 'twas the same,
All startled with affright.
Uncles, and aunts, and cousins too,
Found it so striking, life-like, true
That soon they took to flight.

Annie not long could this endure;
It brought about a speedy cure,
She ceased to cry and moan.
Her father ceased to scold and frown,
He had the picture taken down,
And in the garret thrown.

Tearful Annie's Likeness

Our Christmas Hamper.

Hattie's Birthday

Oh! This is a happy, beautiful world!
  My heart is light and gay;
The birds in the trees sing blithely to me
  And I'm six years old to-day.

Yes, six, and father has bought me a book,
  And mother, the sweetest doll,
All dressed in white with blue eyes bright,
  And the nicest hat and shawl.

My kitty sat quietly near the fire
  As Dolly and I came by;
Miss Dolly bowed, and pussy meowed,
  And opened her yellow eye.

Ah me! if Kit could only talk,
  And Dolly could but chat,
We'd social be as any three—

Talk, sing, and all of that.

I dressed all up in grandma's cap,
  And put on her glasses too;
"Why, Grandma!" I said, as I looked at myself,
  "I'm almost as old as you."

My mother softly kissed my cheek,
  And then she blessed me too,
Praying that I, as years went by,
  Might be as good and true.

My birthday song is a merry one,
  And my heart is warm and light;
Kind father, mother, and dear grandma,
  Sweet dolly and pussy, good night.

Youth and Age

A funny thing I heard to-day,
  I might as well relate.
Our Lil is six, and little May
  Still lacks a month of eight.

And, through the open play-room door,
  I heard the elder say:
"Lil, run downstairs and get my doll;
  Go quick, now—right away!"

And Lillie said—(and I agreed
  That May was hardly fair):—
"You might say 'please,' or go yourself—
  I didn't leave it there."

"But, Lillie," urged the elder one,
  "Your little legs, you know,
Are younger than mine are, child,
  And so you ought to go!"

Children

"I would not be a girl," said Jack,
  "Because they have no fun;
They cannot go a-fishing, nor
  A-shooting with a gun;
They cannot climb up trees for fruit,
  Nor bathe without a bathing dress,
Which is no fun at all."

"I would not be a boy," said May,
  "For boys are nasty things,
With pockets filled with hooks and knives,
  And nails, and tops and strings
And when a boy becomes a man,
  He's got to buy girls rings;"

A Lost Child

"I'm losted! Could you find me, please?"
  Poor little frightened baby!
The wind had tossed her golden fleece,
The stones had scratched her dimpled knees,
I stooped and lifted her with ease,
  And softly whispered "Maybe."

"Tell me your name, my little maid:
  I can't find you without it."
"My name is Shiny-eyes," she said,
"Yes; but your last name?" She shook her head:
"Up to my house 'ey never said
  A single word about it."

"But, dear," I said, "what is your name?"
  "Why, didn't you hear me told you?
Dust Shiny-eyes." A bright thought came:

"Yes, when you're good. But when they blame
You little one,—is it just the same
  When mamma has to scold you?"

"My mamma never scolds," she moans,
  A little blush ensuing,
"'Cept when I've been a-frowing stones;
And then she says (the culprit owns),—
Mehitabel Sapphira Jones.
  What has you been a-doing?"

Anna E. Burnham

Little Mary

Here stands little, little Mary,
With her face of winning grace,
Chattering tongue that runs apace,
  And her ways contrary

Who so gay as Mary?
With her laughs of rippling glee
Brimming o'er with melody,—
  Bonny, blithesome Mary.

Household pet is Mary—
Such a merry, joyous sprite,
Filling all our home with light—
  Pretty winsome Mary!

Mischief-loving Mary,
Busy as the busiest bee,
Full of sunshine, life, and glee
  Is our heart's sweet Mary!

Girl and Angel

As Peter sat at Heaven's gate
  A maiden sought permission,
And begged of him, if not too late,
  To give her free admission.

"What claim hast thou to enter here?"
  He cried with earnest mien.
"Please sir," said she, 'twixt hope and fear,
  "I'm only just sixteen!"

"Enough," the hoary guardian said,
  And the gate wide open threw.
"That is the age when every maid
  Is girl and angel too."

Our Country Cousin.

Girl Who Wouldn't Go to Bed

Once I knew a little girl,
  Who wouldn't go to bed,
And in the morning always had
  A very sleepy head.

At night she'd stop upon the stairs,
  And hold the railings tight
Then with a puff she'd try to blow
  Out Mary Ann's rushlight.

The bed at last they tuck'd her in,
  The light she vow'd to keep;
Left in the dark she roar'd and cried;
  Till tired she went to sleep.

Little Girl that Beat her Sister

Go, go, my naughty girl, and kiss
  Your little sister dear;
I must not have such things as this,
  Nor noisy quarrels here.

What! little children scold and fight
  Who ought to be so mild;
Oh! Mary, 'tis a shocking sight
  To see an angry child.

I can't imagine for my part,
  The reason of your folly,
As if she did you any hurt
  By playing with your dolly.

Children Should not Quarrel

Let dogs delight to bark an bite,
  For God hath made them so;
Let bears and lions growl and fight:
  For 'tis their nature to.

But children you should never let
  Such angry passions rise;
Your little hands were never made
  To tear each other's eyes.

The Sulky Girl

Why is Mary standing there,
  Leaning down upon the chair,
With pouting lip and frowning brow?
  I wonder what's the matter now.

Come here, my dear, and tell me true,
  Is it because I spoke to you
About what you just now had done,
  That you are such a naughty one?

When, then, indeed, I'm grieved to see
  That you can so ill-tempered be:
You make your faults a great deal worse
  By being sulky and perverse.

Oh! how much better it appears,
  To see you melting into tears,
And then to hear you humbly say,
  "I'll not do so another day!"

The Little Girl that did not Like to be Washed

What! cry when I wash you! not love to be clean?
There, go and be dirty, unfit to be seen;
And till you leave off, and I see you have smiled,
I'll not take the trouble to wash such a child.

The Girl who Sucked her Fingers

A little girl, named Mary Kate,
　Whom you may have chance to see,
Would have been loved by small and great,
But for one thing, which I'll relate;
　So listen now to me.

A silly habit she's acquired
　Of putting in her mouth,
The pretty fingers of her hand,
And sucking them, for hours she'd stand,
　In a manner most uncouth.

Her play-companions used to laugh,
　And jeeringly would say,
"Oh, pray bring Mary Kate some crumbs,
Poor thing! she's dining off her thumbs,
　She'll eat them all away."

Girl Stealing Treacle

Girl Stealing Treacle

This is Nelly Pilfer;
 I'll tell you what she earned
By stealing off the treacle
 When Mary's back was turned.

They caught the greedy Nelly
 With treacle on her hand,
They put her in the corner,
 And there they made her stand.

The Girl who Soiled her Clothes

Little Polly Flinders,
Sat among the cinders,

Warming her pretty toes;
Her mother came and caught her,
And scolded her little daughter,
For spoiling her nice new clothes.

The Greedy Little Girl

I knew a greedy little girl,
Who all day long did roar;
Whatever toys were given her,
She always wanted more.

Five dolls she had—one was black,
A ball and battledore,
But held them all so very tight,
The roar'd and scream'd for more.

Now this was wicked of the child,
As everyone must own;
So for the whole of one long day
They shut her up alone.

The Girl Who Played with Fire

Mamma, a little girl I met,
Had such a scar, I can't forget!
All down her arms and neck and face;
I could not bear to see the place.

Poor little girl! and don't you know
The shocking trick that made her so?
'Twas all because she went and did
A thing her mother had forbid.

For once, when nobody was by her,
This silly child would play with fire;

And long before her mother came,
Her pinafore was all in flame.

In vain she tried to put it out,
Till all her clothes were burnt about;
And then she suffer'd ten times more,
All over with a dreadful sore.

For many months before 'twas cured,
Both day and night the pain endured;
And still you see, when passing by her,
How sad it is to play with fire.

Little Miss Consequence

Little Miss Consequence strutted about,
  Turned up her nose, pointed her toes,
And thought herself quite a grand person, no doubt.
Gave herself airs; took many cares,
  To appear old; was haughty and cold.
She spoke to the servants like a dog or a cat
And fussed about this, and fussed about that.

The Vulgar Little Lady

"But, mamma, now," said Charlotte, "pray don't you believe
  That I'm better than Jenny my nurse?
Only see my red shoes, and the lace on my sleeve;
  Her clothes are a thousand times worse.

"I ride in my coach, and have nothing to do.
  And the country folks stare at me so;
And nobody dares to control me but you,
  Because I'm a lady, you know.

"Then servants are vulgar and I am genteel;

So, really, 'tis out of the way,
To think that I should not be better a deal
  Than maids, and such people as they."

"Gentility, Charlotte," her mother replied,
  "Belongs to no station or place;
And nothing's so vulgar as folly and pride,
  Though dressed in red slippers and lace.

"Not all the fine things that fine ladies possess
  Should teach them the poor to despise;
For 'tis in good manners, and not in good dress,
  That the truest gentility lies."

Girl Who Wouldn't be Dressed

Naughty, Dirty Girl

Peggy Won't

"I won't be dressed, I won't, I won't!"
  Cried Peggy one morn to mamma.
"Very well, dear," was quietly said,
  "I'll teach you how silly you are."

Peggy then frowned and set her lips
  Expecting a kiss as of old,
But mother had gravely walked away,
  And Peggy was getting so cold.

The minutes passed, and Peggy sighed,
  For thoughts of her breakfast arose,
And "Mammy, dear," she loudly wept,
  While stamping her bare little toes.

Then mother came, and firmly said,
  "I'm taking you, dear, at your word;
'I won't be dressed—I won't, I won't!'

51

Has many times lately been heard.

"So now to bed, my little maid,
 For you *will not* be dressed to-day;
Then Peggy will be taught to think
 Before acting in such a way."

Oh, for the tears that Peggy shed!
 But now every morn, I am told,
A wee young maid is quietly dressed,
 And is always as good as gold.

Meddlesome Matty

One ugly trick has often spoiled
 The sweetest and the best;
Matilda, though a pleasant child,
 One ugly trick possessed,
Which, like a cloud before the skies,
Hid all her better qualities.

Sometimes she'd lift the teapot lid
 To peep at what was in it;
Or tilt the kettle, if you did
 But turn your back a minute.
In vain you told her not to touch—
Her trick of meddling grew so much.

Her grandma went out one day,
 And by mistake she laid
Her spectacles and snuff-box gay
 Too near the little maid;
"Ah! well," thought she, "I'll try them on,
As soon as grandmamma is gone,"

Forthwith she placed upon her nose
 The glasses large and wide;
And looking round, as I suppose,
 The snuff box she too spied:

"Oh! what a pretty box is that;
I'll open it." said little Matt.

"I know grandmamma would say,
  'Don't meddle with it, dear;'
But then she's far enough away,
  And no one else is near;
Besides, what can there be amiss
In opening such a box as this?"

So thumb and finger went to work
  To move the stubborn lid;
And presently a mighty jerk
  The mighty mischief did;
For all at once, ah! woeful case,
  The snuff came puffing in her face.

Poor eyes, and nose, and mouth beside,
  A dismal sight presented;
In vain, as bitterly she cried,
  Her folly she repented.
In vain she ran about for ease;
She could do nothing now but sneeze.

She dashed the spectacles away,
  To wipe her tingling eyes;
And as in twenty bits they lay,
  Her grandmamma she spies.
"Heyday! and what's the matter now?"
Says grandmamma, with lifted brow.

Matilda, smarting with the pain,
  And tingling still and sore,
Made many a promise to refrain
  From meddling evermore.
And 'tis a fact, as I have heard,
She ever since has kept her word.

COLE

The Girl who Spilled the Ink

"Oh! Lucy! Fanny! Make haste here!
Mamma will be so vexed, I fear,
  For I've upset the ink!
See, on my frock and pinafore,
Such great black stains! And there are more
  Upon my socks, I think."

And Lucy cries, with open eyes,
And hands extended in surprise,
  "Oh, naughty Mary Ann,
Those stains can never be washed out;
Whatever have you been about?
  Look at her, sister Fan!"

Mamma comes in: "Heyday! what's this?
Why, Mary Ann, I told you, Miss,
  The inkstand ne'er to move;
And little girls who won't obey,
And mind each word their parents say,
  Good people ne'er will love."

The Naughty Girl

A naughty girl had got no toy,
  And didn't know what to do,
So she rumpled her frock
And tore her sock,
  And tried to eat her shoe.

The Girl who was Always Tasting

Little Miss Baster, of Sunnyside,
  Was known as a taster, far and wide;
Picking and licking, spying and prying,

54

Each bottle and dish with her fingers trying.
Dangerous practice! dreadful little fact is!
Once almost poisoned, and very near dying.
  Little Miss Baster, of Sunnyside,
  Has got some poison in paper tied;
Harmless she deems it, yes, she must taste,
Like sugar seems it, ah! but 'tis paste.
Rat's-bane, the mixture. Oh! woe the day!
Run for the doctor, bid him not stay.
Dreadful her anguish—nearly she died,
Did little Miss Baster, of Sunnyside.

Children Stealing Jam.

Children Stealing Jam

Four naughty little children thought
  Some jam they'd try and steal;
But see how nicely they were caught
  With a crash that made them squeal.

Their mother who was just next door,

And heard the horrid noise,
Came in and shook those naughty girls,
And whipped those naughty boys.

Sally, the Lazy Girl

Her sister would come to the bedside and call,
  "Do you mean to sleep here all the day?"
I saw Kitty Miles up two hours ago,
  A-washing and working away.

"The water is boiling, the table is spread,
  Your father is just at the door;
If you are not quick, we shall eat all the bread,
  And you will not find any more."

Then Sally sat up and half opened her eyes,
  And gave both a grunt and a groan;
And yawning she said, in a quarrelsome voice,
  "I wish you would let me alone."

But though she was lazy, she always could eat,
  And wished for a plentiful share,
So tumbled her clothes on, and smeared her white face,
  Forgetting her hands and her hair.

Her frock was all crumpled and twisted away,
  Her hair was entangled and wild,
Her stockings were down and her shoes were untied,
  She looked a most slovenly child.

She sauntered about till the old village clock
  Had sounded and then died away,
Before she put on her torn bonnet and went
  To school without further delay.

But soon as she came to the little cake shop,
  She loitered with lingering eyes,

Just wishing that she had a penny to spend,
  For one of the pretty jam pies.

Again she went on, and she loitered again
  In the same foolish way as before,
And the clock in the school was just warning for ten,
  As she lifted the latch of the door.

The governess frowned as she went to her place,
  She had often so spoken in vain,
And now only said, with a sorrowful sigh,
  "There's Sally the latest again!"

She hated her reading, and never would write,
  She neither could cypher nor sew,
And little girls whispered, "We never will be
  So silly as Miss Sally Slow."

Girl who Wouldn't Comb her Hair

I tell you of a little girl, who would herself have been,
  As pretty a young lady as ever could be seen,
But that about her little head she had no cleanly care.
  And never, never could be made to brush and comb her hair.
        She would have been a pretty child,
          But, oh! she was a fright—
        She looked just like a girl that's wild,
          Yes, quite as ugly, quite;
        She looked just like a girl that's wild—
          A frightful ugly sight.

The Nasty, Cross Girls

    The school was closed one afternoon,
      And all the girls were gone;

57

And some walked on alone.

Some plucked the flowers upon the banks,
  Some chatted very fast,
And some were talking secretly,
  And whispered as you passed.

And if, perchance, a girl came near,
  Then one of these would say,
"Don't listen to our secrets, Miss,
  You'll please to go away."

As Nelly White ran home from school,
  Her work-bag in her hand,
She chanced to pass near Lucy Bell,
  And her friend Susan Brand.

"We don't want you," said Lucy Bell,
  "You little tiresome chit;
Our secrets are not meant for you,
  You little tell-tale-tit."

Then both girls cried, "Tell-tale-tit,"
  And pushed her roughly by;
Poor Nelly said, "I'm no such thing,"
  And then began to cry.

I'm Governess

Now children dear, you all come near
And do not make a noise;
But listen here, just take and clear
That desk of all those toys.

For now I'm Governess you'll find,
That its myself will make you mind;
So Alice Brown you do your sum,

And Betty Snooks don't look so glum.

And Sarah White sit down at once,
And Susan Black you are a dunce,
And Annie Grey you needn't think
I didn't see you spill the ink.

And find your thimble Maggie More,
And mind your sewing Jennie Shore;
And Linda Cole you know 'tis wrong
To make a stitch two inches long.

And you Kate Ross, stop pinching there,
Don't scratch! nor pull your sister's hair;
And you, you naughty Lucy Moyes,
Must not be talking to the boys.

And Bridget Mace don't make that face;
And Norah Finn keep your tongue in.
Don't be a Tom-boy Emma Pyke,
You really must act lady-like.

Now I want all good children in my school,
Don't want a single dunce, bad girl or fool,

So I will kindly ask you to be brave,
And try to very, very well behave.

Yes all be good and learn your lessons well,
And then I'll ring the little bell to tell
That school is over for the day,
And you can all run out to play.

Little Governess

Little Nellie Nipkin, brisk, and clean, and neat,
Keeps a little baby-school in the village street;
Teaches little pupils all that she can find,
And keeps a little birch that teaches them to mind.

My Mamma's Maid

Dingty diddledy, My mamma's maid,
She stole oranges, I'm afraid;
Some in her pockets, some in her sleeve,
She stole oranges, I believe.

Tangle Pate

There was a girl, named tanglepate,
    She lived—I won't say where—
Who was not willing any one
    Should comb or curl her hair.

She cried and made a dreadful fuss,
    At morning, noon, or night,
And did not seem at all ashamed
    Of looking like a fright.

Her hair stood out around her head

Just like a lion's mane,
And she was scolded, coaxed, and teased
  About it—but in vain.

It caught on buttons, hooks, and boughs
  As here and there she rushed,
And yet she would not consent
  To have it combed or brushed.

And so she fell asleep one day
  Within the woods, and there
Two birdies came and built a nest
  Amid her tangled hair.

A Careless Girl

I know a very careless girl,
Her hair is always out of curl,
In rags and tatters are her clothes,
And she's a fright, you may suppose.

Her skirts she catches on a nail,
And leaves behind and ugly trail;
Her sashes always are untied,
Her dresses always gaping wide.

'Tis her delight to tear and rend,
She does not like to patch or mend,
And 'tis no wonder that she goes
So out at elbows and at toes.

Naughty Girl

The naughty girl
  Never minds mamma,
Always says, "I won't!"

To dear papa!
Makes a great deal of noise
  About the house.
When her mother wants her
  As still as a mouse.

She pinches the cat,
  She pulls her tail;
And takes the bird-cage
  Down from the nail;
Teases her brothers,
  And spoils her hair,
And reproved says,
  "I don't care!"

She worries poor grandma,
  Makes baby cry;
She cannot please him,
  And I know why:—
She lets him lie
  In the crib and moan,
While she is amusing
  Herself alone.

At school she forgets
  What the teacher said,
Sits idly leaning her hands
  On her head;
She never learns
  The task that's given,
And cannot tell even
  Seven times seven.

At table she's careless,
  And spills her drink,
Can never be taught
  To "stop and think;"
Gets down from the table
  And goes to play,
To do the same over

Another day.

Mopy Maria

Mopy Maria
Would sit by the fire,
It seemed to be
Her greatest desire;
Bent and bowed
As if wrapped in a shroud,
And her face as black
As a thunder-cloud.

She filled the room
So full of gloom,
The place was as
Dismal as a tomb;
And few would admire
Her, or desire
To spend much time
With Mopy Maria,

She moped and pined
Yet no-one could find
That any trouble
Disturbed her mind;
Nor reasons good
Why she should brood
An such a
Ridiculous attitude.

It wasn't her style
To laugh and smile
She didn't think
It was worth her while;
So dull and flat
She daily sat
Like a Chinese idol,

Or worse than that,

If the children came
To propose a game
Of any sort,
It was all the same;
She wouldn't play,
She wouldn't be gay,
But sat and pouted
The livelong day.

Her face grew thin;
And at length her chin
Grew long and sharp;
Oh! as sharp as a pin!
And one windy day
She blew away
Like a great big kite
That had gone astray.

The winds were high,
And she had to fly
Away at their bidding;
It made her cry;
But she couldn't get higher
Than the tall church spire,
So there she stuck—
Poor Mopy Maria!

Disobedient May

Naughty May will not obey,
But will always have her way
Every moment of the day.

If you say do this, or that,
She will be amazed thereat,

Show her claws like any cat.

O she is a naughty child!
Very fond of running wild,
Never gentle, meek, or mild.

Some fine day, I don't know when—
She'll be popp'd in piggy's pen,
And be most unhappy then.

Pigs are stubborn things indeed,
Will not go as you would lead,
Never words of counsel heed.

And pig-headed folks are they
Who will always have their way,
Spite of anything you say.

Sluttishness

Oh! Mary, my mary,
 Why, where is your dolly?
Look here, I protest, on the floor:
 To leave her about
 In the dirt so is folly,
You ought to be trusted no more.

 I thought you were pleas'd.
 And receiv'd her quite gladly,
When on your birthday she came home;
 Did I ever suppose
 You would use her so sadly,
And strew her things over the room?

 Her bonnet of straw
 You once thought a great matter,
And tied it so pretty and neat;
 Now see how 'tis crumpled,

No trencher is flatter,
It grieves your mamma thus to see't.

Suppose (you're my Dolly,
You know, little daughter,
Whom I love to dress neat, and see good),
Suppose in my care of you,
I were to falter,
And let you get dirty and rude!

But Dolly's mere wood,
You are flesh and bone living,
And deserves better treatment and care;
That is true, my sweet girl,
'Tis the reason I'm giving
This lesson so sharp and severe.

'Tis not for the Dolly
I'm anxious and fearful,
Tho' she cost too much to be spoil'd;
I'm afraid lest yourself
Should get sluttish, not careful,
And that were a sad thing, my child.

Jane, who Bit her Nails

When I was living down in Wales,
I knew a girl who bit her nails;
Her finger-ends became so sore,
The blood flowed from them to the floor.

The more she bit the more they bled,
Until upon herself she fed;
And as she nibbled day by day,
The fingers slowly wore away.

See, here she is: she sadly stands
With only stumps instead of hands;

The silly girl can never play,
Yet she was cautioned every day.

Her father said, "You naughty thing,
Some wooden fingers I must bring,
And try to get them fastened to
Your hands with little bits of glue."

Poking Fun

When little Lizzie came across
  A birdie, or a chick,
A duckling, or a gosling,
  she would poke it with a stick.

She chased the dog, she chased the cat,
  But when she saw a mouse
She gave a scream so very loud
  It echoed through the house.

She poked the turtles and the frogs
  And thought it was fine fun,
But when the geese poked out their necks
  At her, she had to run.

One day she chanced to find a hive
  With not a bee about,
And said, "Is any one at home?
  "I'll very soon find out!"

And so she did. As soon as she
  Had poked her stick inside,
The bees flew out and stung her so
  She very nearly died.

The Pin

"Dear me! what signifies a pin,
  Wedg'd in a rotten board?
I'm certain that I won't begin,
  At ten years old, to hoard!
I never will be called a miser;
That I'm determined," said Eliza.

So onward tripped the little maid,
  And left the pin behind,
Which very snug and quiet lay,
  To its hard fate resign'd;
Nor did she think (a careless chit)
'Twas worth her while to stoop for it.

Next day a party was to ride
  To see an air balloon;
And all the company beside
  Were dressed and ready soon:
But she a woful case was in,
For want of just a single pin.

In vain her eager eyes she brings
  To ev'ry darksome crack,
There was not one! and yet her things
  Were dropping off her back.
She cut her pincushion in two,
But no, not one had slidden through.

At last, as hunting on the floor,
  Over a crack she lay,
The carriage rattled to the door,
  Then rattled fast away:
But poor Eliza was not in,
For want of just a single pin.

There's hardly anything so small,
  So trifling or so mean,
That we may never want at all,

For service unforseen;
And wilful waste, depend upon't
Brings, almost always, woful want!

Ann Taylor

Stupid Jane

Oh! she was such a stupid Jane,
  They tried in vain
  To make things plain,
But she would ask and ask again,
As if there wasn't any brain
Inside the head of stupid Jane.

If she was set to do a task,
So many questions she would ask,
'Twas easier far her teachers said
To do the work themselves instead,
Than try to make her understand
The lesson she had in hand.

If on an errand told to go,
And cautioned to do thus and so,
Turn here and there along the way,
Oh! Jane was sure to go astray;
For she hade such a crooked pate,
She could not do an errand straight.

She did not care for books or toys,
She could not play with girls or boys;
Because so oft she blocked their games,
They used to call her dreadful names,
And in loud, angry tones complain,
"Oh, what a horrid, Stupid Jane!"

Brought to the parlour nicely drest
To be presented to a guest,

With finger in her mouth she'd stand
And stare about on every hand,
Nor answer by a single word,
Nor even act as if she heard.

Oh! she was such a stupid Jane,
  They tried in vain
  To make things plain,
But she would ask and ask again,
As if there wasn't any brain
Inside the head of stupid Jane.

Little Girl who wouldn't eat Crusts

The awfullest times that ever could be
They had with a bad little girl of Dundee,
  Who never would finish her crust
    In vain they besought her,
    And patiently taught her
    And told her she must.
    Her grandma would coax,
    And so would the folks,
    And tell her the sinning
    Of such a beginning.
    But no, she wouldn't.
    She couldn't, she shouldn't,
    She'd have them to know—
    So they might as well go.
And what do you think came to pass?
This little girl of Dundee, alas!
Who wouldn't take crusts the regular way,
Sat down to a feast one summer's day;
And what did the people that little girl give?
Why, a dish of bread pudding—as sure as I live!

Pouting Polly

Polly was a little girl,
  Pretty as a posy;
Rather straight, and rather tall;
  Very round and rosy.

Other little girls and boys
  Always were delighted,
So if to pretty Polly's house
  They had been invited.

There they'd romp, and have great fun,
  Frolicking and shouting;
But alas! they soon would find
  Pretty Polly pouting!

What had any one done?
  How had they displeased her?
Was she sad or mad because
  Johnny Dean had teased her?

Why are you so cross and glum
  When the rest are jolly?
With your under-lip thrust out,
  Tell us, pouting Polly!

Polly loves to have her way;
  Ah! no one can doubt it;
And whenever she's displeased
  She will pout about it.

Such a funny under-lip!
  You would like to grab it,
So that little Polly might
  Break this naughty habit.

In the house or out-of-doors,
  Little Polly Horner
You will find a dozen times

Pouting in a corner.

Once, when in the garden she
  Stood thus melancholy,
On her under-lip a bee
  Stung Miss Pouting Polly.

Then she danced, and then she screamed;
  People heard her yelling
Half-a-mile or more away,
  While her lip was swelling.

Oh, it swelled, and swelled, and swelled,
  Like a great big blister,
And the pain was very great
  Where the bee had kissed her.

Many days she kept her bed;
  And there is no doubting
That the sorry little maid
  Had her fill of pouting.

For the buzzing busy-bee
  Cured her of her folly;
And the remedy will cure
  Any pouting Polly.

Untidy Emily

Oh, here's a sad picture!
  Pray carefully look!
As sad as was ever
  Yet seen in a book.

'Tis Emily's portrait:
  Not at all flattered.
Slovenly, dirty, untidy,

And tattered.

Her mother implores her,
  Again and again,
To make herself tidy;
  But all is in vain.

Her trimmings are torn;
  There's a hole in her dress;
Another, still larger;
  Her shoes in a mess;

Stockings down, buttons missing;
  Shabby old hat,
Not for worlds would I
  Wear it, battered and flat.

Her mother does nothing
  But patch, darn and mend,
Till, saddened and weary,
  She says, "This must end.

"All, all is in vain.
  And now, happen what may,
I can do nothing more;
  So go your own way."

A terrible thing
  Very soon now befell,
Oh, horror! I shudder
  The story to tell.

This girl ran quite wild;
  Till at last she became
All tatters and rags,
  With no feeling of shame.

A man, who was passing,
  Then took her one day,
And in his field placed her,

To scare birds away.

She is still standing there;
  Stands there day and night.
The sparrows fly round her,
  And cry in affright:

"Look at this dreadful thing!
  Take care now, take care!
Beware of the scarecrow!
  Beware, now, beware!"

There she is!!—that's her!!!

Verse & Story

The Shadows

"Mamma! I see something
  Quite dark on the wall;—
It moves up and down,
  And it looks very strange!
Sometimes it is large,
  And sometimes it is small;
Pray, tell me what it is,
  And why does it change?"

"It is Mamma's shadow
  That puzzles you so,
And there is your own
  Close beside it, my love!
Now run round the room,
  It will go where you go;
It rests where you sit,
  When you rise it will move.

"These wonderful shadows
  Are caused by the light
From fire and from candles
  Upon us that falls;
If we were not here,
  All that place would be bright,
But light can't shine
  Through us to lighten the wall.

"And when you are out
  Some fine day in the sun,

I'll take you where shadows
  Of apple-trees lie;
And houses and cottages too—
  Every one
Repose on their shadows
  Beneath the bright sky.

"Now hold up your mouth,
  And give me a sweet kiss;
Our shadows kiss too!—
  Don't you see it quite plain?"
"O yes! and I thank you
  For telling me this,
I'll not be afraid
  Of a shadow again."

Mary Lundie

Girl in Disgrace—Her Dog is Sorry

Another Naughty Girl

Little Bo-Peep

Little Bo-Peep has lost her sheep,
  And can't tell where to find them;
Leave them alone, and they'll come home
  And bring their tails behind them.

Little Bo-Peep fell fast asleep,
  And dreamed she heard them bleating,
But when she awoke, 'twas all a joke—
  Alas! they still were fleeting.

Then up she took her little crook,
  Determined for to find them;
She found them, indeed, bit it made her heart bleed,
  They'd left their tails behind them.

It happened one day, as Bo-Peep did stray

77

Over the meadows hard by,
That there she espied their tails side by side,
All hung on a tree to dry.

She heaved a sigh, and gave by-and-by
Each careless sheep a banging;
And as for the rest, she thought it was best
Just to leave their tails a-hanging.

Mary's Little Lamb

Mary had a little lamb
Whose fleece was white as snow,
And everywhere that Mary went
That Lamb it would not go;

So Mary took that little Lamb
And put it on the spit,
And soon it was so nicely done
She ate it every bit.

Pemmy

Pemmy was a pretty girl,
But Fanny was a better;
Pemmy look'd like any churl,
When little Fanny let her.

Pemmy had a pretty nose,
But Fanny had a better;
Pemmy oft would come to blows,
But Fanny would not let her.

Pemmy had a pretty song,
But Fanny had a better;
Pemmy would sing all day long,

But Fanny would not let her.

Little Husband

I had a little husband,
  No bigger than my thumb;
I put him in a pint pot,
  And there I bid him drum.

I bought a little horse,
  That galloped up and down;
I bridled him, and saddled him,
  And sent him out of town.

I gave him some garters,
  To garter up his hose,
And a little handkerchief,
  To wipe his pretty nose.

My Dolly

I have a little doll, I take care of her clothes;
She has soft flaxen hair, and her name is Rose.
She has pretty blue eyes, and a very small nose,
And a funny little mouth, and her name is Rose.

Tommy Snooks

As Tommy Snooks and Bessy Brooks
  Were walking out one Sunday,
Says Tommy Snooks to Bessy Brooks,
  "To-morrow will be Monday."

Little Betty Blue

Little Betty Blue, lost her left shoe,
  What can little Betty do?
Give her another, to match the other,
  And then she may walk in two.

Cross Patch

Cross patch, draw the latch,
  Sit by the fire and spin;
Take a cup, and drink it up,
  Then call your neighbours in.

Jumping Joan

Hinx, minx! the old witch winks,
  The fat begins to fry;
There's nobody at home but jumping Joan,
  Father, mother, and I.

Princess Lost Her Shoe

Doodle, doodle, doo,
The Princess lost her shoe;
  Her highness hopp'd
  The fiddler stopp'd
Not knowing what to do.

Hobble Gobble

The girl in the lane that couldn't speak plain,
  Cried "Gobble, gobble, gobble;"
The man on the hill that couldn't stand still,
  Went "Hobble, hobble, hobble."

Our Girl's Rabbits

Mary, Kate, and Maria went down as agreed,
To the hutch in the garden, the rabbits to feed;
There was the mother, a steady old bunny,
Moving her nose in a manner so funny.

A young rabbit also, tho' seeming to dose,
Kept munching his breakfast and moving his nose;
Mary, Kate, and Maria gave the rabbits some food,
And lovingly stroked them because they were good.

Little Red Riding Hood

Once upon a time there was a dear little girl whose mother made her a scarlet cloak with a hood to tie over her pretty head; so people called her (as a pet name) "Little Red Riding-Hood." One day her mother tied on her cloak and hood and said,

"I wish you to go to-day, my darling, to see your grandmamma, and take her a present of some butter, fresh eggs, a pot of honey, and a little cake with my love."

Little Red Riding-Hood loved her grandmother, and was very glad to go. So she ran gaily through the wood, gathering wild flowers and gambolling among the ferns as she went; and the birds all sang their sweetest songs to her, and the bluebells nodded their pretty heads, for everything loved the gentle child.

By and by a great hungry Wolf came up to her. He wished to eat her up, but as he heard the woodman Hugh's axe at work close by, he was afraid to touch her, for fear she should cry out and he should get killed. So he only asked her where she was going. Little Red Riding-Hood innocently told him (for she did not know he was a wicked Wolf) that she was going to visit her grandmother, who lived in a cottage on the other side of the wood. Then the Wolf made haste, and ran through the wood, and came to the cottage of which the child had told him. He tapped at the door.

"Who's there?" asked the old woman, who lay sick in bed.

"It is Little Red Riding-Hood, Grandmamma," answered the Wolf in a squeaky tone, to imitate the voice of her grandchild.

"Pull the string, and the latch will come up," said the old lady, "for I am ill and cannot open the door."

The cruel Wolf did so, and, jumping on the bed, ate the poor grandmother up.

Then he put on her night-cap and got into bed. By and by Little Red Riding-Hood, who had lingered gathering flowers as she came along, and so was much later than the Wolf, knocked at the door.

"Who's there?" asked the Wolf, mimicking her grandmother's voice.

"It is Little Red Riding-Hood, dear Grandmamma," said the child.

"Pull the string and the latch will come up," said the Wolf.

So Red Riding-Hood came in, and the Wolf told her to put down her basket, and come and sit on the bed. When Little Red Riding-Hood drew back the curtain and saw the Wolf, she began to be rather frightened and said,

"Dear Grandmamma, what great eyes you have got!"

"All the better to see you with, my dear," said the Wolf, who liked a grim joke.

"And what a large nose you have, Grandmamma!" cried the child.

"All the better to smell you with, my dear."

"And, oh! Grandmamma, what long white teeth you have!"

Alas! she reminded the greedy Wolf of eating.

"All the better to eat you with!" he growled; and, jumping out of bed, sprang at Red Riding-Hood.

But just at that moment Hugh the woodman, who had seen the sweet child go by, and had followed her, because he knew there was a Wolf prowling about the forest, burst the door open, and killed the wicked animal with his good axe. Little Red Riding-Hood clung round his neck and thanked him, and cried for joy; and Hugh took her home to her mother; and after that she was never allowed to walk in the greenwood by herself.

It was said at first that the Wolf had eaten the child, but that was not the case; and everybody was glad to hear that the first report was not correct, and that the Wolf had not really killed Little Red Riding-Hood.

Little Miss Jewel

Little Miss Jewel
Sat on a stool,
Eating of curds and whey;
There came a little spider
Who sat down beside her,
And frightened Miss Jewel away.

Little Girl

Little girl, little girl, where have you been;
Gathering Roses to give to the Queen.
Little girl, little girl, what gave she you?
She gave me a diamond as big as my shoe.

Little Betty Blue

Little Betty Blue lost her pretty shoe;
What can Little Betty do?
Give her another, to match the other,
And then she can walk in two.

I'm Grandmamma

Last night when I was in bed,
  Such fun it seemed to me;
I dreamt that I was Grandmamma,
  And Grandmamma was me.

But she was such a tiny girl,
  And dressed in baby clothes;
And I thought I smacked her face, because
  She wouldn't blow her nose.

An I went walking up the street,
  And she ran by my side;
And because I walked too quick for her,

My goodness, hoe she cried.

And after tea I washed her face;
  And when her prayers were said,
I blew the candle out, and left
  Poor Grandmamma in bed.

The Babes In The Wood

A long time ago there lived in an old mansion in the country a rich gentleman and his wife, who had two dear little children, of whom they were very fond. Sad to relate, the gentleman and lady were both taken ill, and, feeling they were about to die, sent for the uncle of the children, and begged him to take care of them till they were old enough to inherit the estates.

Now this uncle was a bad and cruel man, who wanted to take the house, the estates, and the money for himself,—so after the death of the parents he began to think how he could best get rid of the children. For some time he kept them till he claimed for them all the goods that should have been theirs. At last he sent for two robbers, who had once been his companions, and showing them the boy and girl, who were at play, offered them a large sum of money to carry them away and never let him see them more.

One of the two robbers began coaxing the little boy and girl, and asking them if they would not like to go out for a nice ride in the woods, each of them on a big horse. The boy said he should if his sister might go too, and the girl said she should not be afraid if her brother went with her. So the two robbers enticed them away from the house, and, mounting their horses, went off into the woods, much to the delight of the children, who were pleased with the great trees, the bright flowers, and the singing of the birds.

Now, one of these men was not so bad and cruel as the other, and he would not consent to kill the poor little creatures, as the other had threatened he would do. He said that they should be left in the woods to stray about, and perhaps they might then escape. This led to a great quarrel between the two, and at last the cruel one jumped off his horse, saying he would kill them, let who would stand in the way. Upon this the other drew his sword to protect the children, and after a fierce fight succeeded in killing his companion.

But though he had saved them from being murdered, he was afraid to take them back or convey them out of the wood, so he pointed out a path, telling them to walk straight on and he would come back to them when he had bought some bread for their supper; he rode away and left them there all alone, with only the trees, and birds and flowers. They loved each other so dearly, and were so bold and happy, that they were not much afraid though they were both very hungry.

The two children soon got out of the path, which led into the thickest part of the wood, and then they wandered farther and farther into the thicket till they were both sadly tired, but they found some wild berries, nuts and fruits, and began to eat them to satisfy their hunger. The dark night came on and the robber did not return. They were cold, and still very hungry, and the boy went about looking for fresh fruit for his sister, and tried to comfort her as they lay down to sleep on the soft moss under the trees.

The next day, and the next, they roamed about, but there was nothing to eat but wild fruits; and they lived on them till they grew so weak that they could not go far from the tree where they had made a little bed of grass and weeds. There they laid down as the shades of night fell upon them, and in the morning they were both in heaven, for they died there in the forest, and as the sun shone upon their little pale faces, the robins and other birds came and covered their bodies with leaves, and so died and were buried the poor Babes in the Wood.

Cinderella

Cinderella's mother died while she was a very little child, leaving her to the care of her father and her step-sisters, who were very much older than herself; for Cinderella's father had been twice married, and her mother was his second wife. Now, Cinderella's sisters did not love her, and were very unkind to her. As she grew older they made her work as a servant, and even sift the cinders: on which account they used to call her in mockery "Cinderella." It was not her real name, but she became afterwards so well known by it that her proper one has been forgotten.

She was a sweet tempered, good girl, however, and everybody except her cruel sisters loved her. It happened, when Cinderella was about seventeen years old, that the King of that country gave a ball, to which all the ladies of the land, and among the rest the young girl's sisters were invited. So they made her dress them for this ball, but never thought of allowing her to go.

"I wish you would take me to the ball with you, sisters," said Cinderella, meekly.

"Take you, indeed!" answered the elder sister with a sneer, "it is no place for a cinder-sifter: stay at home and do your work."

When they were gone, Cinderella, whose heart was sad, sat down and cried; but as she sorrowful, thinking of the unkindness of her sisters, a voice called to her from the garden, and she went to see who was there. It was her godmother, a good old Fairy.

"Do not cry, Cinderella," she said; "you also shall go to the ball, because you are a kind, good girl. Bring me a large pumpkin."

Cinderella obeyed, and the fairy touched it with her wand, turned it into a grand coach. Then she turned a rat into a coach-man, and some mice into footmen; and touching Cinderella with her wand, the poor girl's rags became a rich dress trimmed with costly lace and jewels, and her old shoes became a charming pair of glass slippers, which looked like diamonds. The fairy told her to go to the ball and enjoy herself, but to be sure and leave the ball-room before the clock struck eleven. "If you do not," she said, "your fine clothes will all turn to rags again.

So Cinderella got into the coach, and drove off with her six footmen behind, very splendid to behold, and arrived at the King's Court, where she was received with delight. She was the most beautiful young lady at the ball, and the Prince would dance with no one else. But she made haste to leave before the hour fixed and had time to undress before her sisters came home. They told her a beautiful Princess had been at the ball, with whom the Prince was delighted. They did not know it was Cinderella herself.

Three times Cinderella went to royal balls in this manner, but the third time she forgot the Fairy's command, and heard eleven o'clock strike. She darted out of the ball-room and ran down stairs in a great hurry. But her dress all turned to rags before she left the palace and she lost one of her glass slippers. The Prince sought for her everywhere, but the guard said no one had passed the gate but a poor beggar girl. However, the prince found the slipper, and in order to discover where Cinderella was gone, he had it proclaimed that he would marry the lady who could put on the glass slipper. All the ladies tried to wear the glass slipper in vain, Cinderella's sisters also, but when their young sister begged to be allowed to try it also, it was found to fit her exactly, and to the Prince's delight, she drew the fellow slipper from her pocket, and he knew at once that she was his beautiful partner at the ball. So she was married to the Prince, and the children strewed roses in their path as they came out of church.

Cinderella forgave her sisters, and was so kind to them that she made them truly sorry for their past cruelty and injustice.

The Three Bears

Once upon a time three bears lived in a nice little house in a great forest.

There was Father Bear, Mother Bear, and Baby Bear.

They had each a bed to sleep in, a chair to sit on, and a basin and a spoon for eating porridge, which was their favourite food.

One morning the three bears went to take a walk before breakfast; but before they went out they poured the hot porridge into their basins, that it might get cool by the time they came back. Mr and Mrs Bear walked arm-in-arm, and Baby Bear ran by their side. Now, there lived in that same forest a sweet little girl who was called Golden Hair. She, also, was walking that morning in the wood, and happening to pass by the bear's house, and seeing the window open, she peeped in.

There was no one to be seen, but three basins of steaming hot porridge all ready to be eaten, seemed to say "Come in and have some breakfast." So Golden Hair went in and tasted the porridge in all the basins, then she sat down in Baby Bear's chair, and took up his spoon, and ate up all his porridge. Now this was very wrong. A tiny bear is only a tiny bear, still he has the right to keep his own things. But Golden Hair didn't know any better.

Unluckily, Baby Bear's chair was too small for her, and she broke the seat and fell through, basin and all.

Then Golden Hair went upstairs, and there she saw three beds all in a row. Golden Hair lay down on Father Bear's bed first, but that was too long for her, then she lay down on Mother Bear's bed, and that was too wide for her, last of all she lay down on Baby Bear's bed, and there she fell asleep, for she was tired.

By-and-by the bears came home, and Old Father Bear looked at his chair, and growled:

"Somebody has been here!"

Mother Bear growled more softly:

"Somebody has been here!"

Baby Bear, seeing his chair broken, squeeled out "Somebody has been here, and broken my chair right through!"

Then they went to the table, and looked at their porridge, and Father Bear Growled:

"Who has touched my basin?"

And Mother Bear growled:

"Who has touched my basin?"

And Baby Bear squeaked:

"Somebody has broken mine and eaten up all my porridge!"

They went upstairs and Father Bear growled:

"Who has been lying on my bed?"

And Mother Bear growled:

"Who has been lying on my bed?"

And Baby Bear squeaked out:

"O! here is a little girl in my bed; and it must be she who has eaten my breakfast and broken my chair and basin!"

Then Father Bear growled:

"Let us eat her up!"

Then Mother Bear growled:

"Let us eat her up!"

And Tiny Bear squeaked:
"Let us eat her up!"

But the noise they made awoke Golden Hair; she startled out of bed (on the opposite side) and jumped out of the window. The three bears all jumped out after her, but they fell one on the top of the other, and rolled over and over, and while they were picking themselves up, little Golden Hair ran home, and they were not able to catch her.

Bluebeard

Once there lived in a lovely castle a very rich man called Bluebeard. A short distance off lived an old gentleman with two lovely daughters, named Fatima and Annie. Bluebeard visited their house, and at length proposed to Fatima, was accepted by her, and they were married with great splendour. He took her home with him to his castle, and permitted her sister Annie to reside with her for company for a time.

She lived very happily in her new home, her new husband was very kind to her, and allowed her to have everything she wished for, but one day he suddenly told her that business called him away from home, that he should be away some days, and handed her the keys to his wardrobe, treasures, and all parts of the castle, he also gave her one key of a small closet, and told her that she might unlock every door in the castle, but not the closet door, for if she did so, she should not live an hour longer. He then left home fondly kissing her at the door.

Her sister and herself returned into the castle, and enjoyed themselves in unlocking room after room, looking over the curiosities, treasures, &c, until Annie became tired and lay down to rest on a rich sofa, and fell asleep. Fatima, as soon as she saw that her sister was asleep, felt a womanly curiosity, an irresistible temptation to unlock the forbidden closet, and take a peep.

She tripped lightly up to the door, turned the key in

the lock, pushed the door open, and, oh! horror! there were five or six dead ladies lying in the closet, with their marriage rings on their fingers. She at once concluded that they were Bluebeard's previous wives, she let the key drop in her fright into the blood on the floor, she picked it up and attempted to wipe it, but the blood would not come off. She awoke her sister, and they both tried, but they could not get it off, and gave it up in despair.

Just then Bluebeard suddenly returned, and asked his wife if she could please to hand him the keys. She trembling did so. He said "How came the blood on the closet key? You have disobeyed me, and shall die at once."

She begged a few minutes to say her prayers and just as he was going to chop her head off, her two brothers arrived at the castle, burst open the door, killed the cruel wretch, and rescued their sisters.

Our three little Belles.

My Girl

A little corner with it's crib.
A little mug, a spoon, a bib,
A little tooth so pearly white,
A little rubber-ring to bite.

A little plate all lettered round,
A little rattle to resound,

A little creeping—see! she stands!
A little step 'twixt outstretched hands.

A little doll with flaxen hair.
A little willow rocking chair,
A little dress of richest hue,
A little pair of gaiters blue.

A little school day after day,
A little "schoolma'am" to obey,
A little study—soon 'tis past—
A little graduate at last.

A little muff for wintry weather,
A little jockey-hat and feather,
A little sac with funny pockets,
A little chain, a ring, and lockets.

A little while to dance and bow,
A little escort homeward now,
A little party somewhat late,
A little lingering at the gate.

A little walk in leafy June,
A little talk while shines the moon,
A little reference to papa,
A little planning with mamma.

A little ceremony grave,
A little struggle to be brave,
A little cottage on the lawn,
A little kiss—my girl was gone!

Good and Bad

There was a little girl,
And she had a little curl
Right in the middle of her forehead

When she was good
She was very good,
But when she was bad, she was horrible.

My little Daughter's Shoes

Two little rough-worn, stubbed shoes
  A plump, well-trodden pair;
With striped stockings thrust within,
  Lie just beside my chair.

Of very homely fabric they,
  A hole is in each toe,
They might have cost, when they were new,
  Some fifty cents or so.

And yet this little, worn-out pair
  Is richer far too me
Than all the jewelled sandals are
  Of Eastern luxury.

This mottled leather, cracked with use,
  Is satin in my sight;
These little tarnished buttons shine
  With all a diamond's light.

Search through the wardrobe of the world!
  You shall not find me there
So rarely made, so richly wrought,
  So glorious a pair.

And why? Because they tell of her,
  Now sound asleep above,
Whose form is moving beauty, and
  Whose heart is beating love.

They tell me of her merry laugh;
  Her rich, whole-hearted glee;

Her gentleness, her innocence,
  And infant purity.

They tell me that her wavering steps
  Will long demand my aid;
For the old road of human life
  Is very roughly laid.

High hills and swift descents abound;
  And, on so rude a way,
Feet that can wear these coverings
  Would surely go astray.

Sweet little girl! be mine the task
  Thy feeble steps to tend!
To be thy guide, thy counsellor,
  Thy playmate and thy friend!

And when my steps shall faltering grow,
  And thine be firm and strong,
Thy strength shell lead my tottering age
  In cheerful peace along.

The Old Cradle

And this was your cradle?
  Why, surely, my Jenny,
Such slender dimensions
  Go somewhat to show
You were a delightfully
  Small picaninny
Some nineteen or twenty
  Short summers ago.

Your baby-day flowed
  In a much troubled channel;
I see you as then
  In your impotent strife,

A tight little bundle
  Of wailing and flannel,
Perplexed with that
  Newly-found fardel called Life,

To hint at an infantine
  Frailty is scandal;
Let bygones be bygones—
  And somebody knows
It was bliss such a baby
  To dance and to dandle,
Your cheeks were so velvet,
  So rosy your toes.

Ay, here is your cradle,
  And Hope, a bright spirit,
With love now is watching
  Beside it, I know.
They guard the small nest
  You yourself did inherit
Some nineteen or twenty
  Short summers ago.

It is Hope gilds the future—
  Love welcomes it smiling;
Thus wags this old world,
  Therefore stay not to ask,
"My future bids fair,
  Is my future beguiling?"
If masked, still it pleases—
  Then raise not the mask.

Is life a poor coil
  Some would gladly be doffing?
He is riding post-haste
  Who their wrongs will adjust;
For at most 'tis a footstep
  From cradle to coffin—
From a spoonful of pap

To a mouthful of dust.

Then smile as your future
  Is smiling, my Jenny!
Tho' blossoms of promise
  Are lost in the rose,
I still see the face
  Of my small picaninny
Unchang'd, for these cheeks
  Are as blooming as those.

Ay, here is your cradle!
  Much, much to my liking,
Though nineteen or twenty
  Long winters have sped;
But, hark! as I'm talking
  There's six o'clock striking,
It is time Jennie's baby
  Should be in its bed.

Frederick Locker

A Little Goose

The chill November day was done,
  The working world home a-faring,
The wind came roaring through the streets,
  And set the gas lamps flaring.

And hopelessly and aimlessly
  The seared old leaves were flying,
When, mingled with the sighing wind,
  I heard a small voice crying,

And shivering on the corner stood
  A child of four or over;
No hat nor cloak her small soft arms

Or wind-blown curls to cover.

Her dimpled face was stained with tears;
  Her round blue eyes ran over;
She crushed within her wee, cold hands
  A bunch of faded clover.

And one hand round her treasures,
  While she slipped in mine the other,
Half-scared, half-confidential, said
  "Oh! please, I want my mother."

"Tell me your street name and number, pet;
  Don't cry, I'll take you to it,"
Sobbing, she answered, "I forget—
  The organ made me do it."

"He came and played at Miller's steps;
  The monkey took the money;
And so I followed down the street,
  That monkey was so funny.

I've walked about a *hundred hours*,
  From one street to another;
The monkey's gone; I've spoiled my flowers:
  Oh! please, I want my mother."

"But what's your mother's name?
  And what's the street? now think a minute."
"My mother's name is mamma dear,
  The street—I can't begin it."

"But what is strange about the house,
  Or new—not like the others?"
I guess you mean my trundle bed—
  Mine and my little brother's.

Oh! dear, I ought to be at home,
  to help him say his prayers;
He's such a baby, he forgets,

98

And we are both such players.

"And there's a bar between, to keep
  From pitching on each other;
For Harry rolls when he's asleep—
  Oh! dear, I want my mother."

The sky grew stormy, people passed,
  All muffled, homeward faring;
"You'll have to spend the night with me,"
  I said at last, despairing.

I spied a ribbon about her neck.
  "What ribbon's this, my blossom?"
"Why, don't you know?" she smiling asked,
  And drew it from her bosom.

A card with number, street, and name!
  My eyes astonished, met it.
"For," said the little one, "you see
  I might some tome forget it.

And so I wear a little thing
  That tells you all about it;
For mother says she's very sure
  I might get lost without it.

Eliza S. Turner

The Playmates.

Girls

There's the pretty girl,
  And the witty girl,
And the girl that bangs her hair;
  The girl that's a flirt,
  And the girl that is pert,
And the girl with the baby stare.

There's the dowdy girl,
  And the rowdy girl,
And the girl that's always late;
  There's the girl of style,
  And the girl of wile,
And the girl with the mincing gaits

There's the tender girl,
  And the well-read girl,
And the girl with the sense of duty
  There's the dainty girl
  And the fainty girl

And the girl that has no beauty.

There's the lazy girl,
And the daisy girl,
And the girl that has two faces;
There's the girl that's shy,
And the girl that's fly
And the girl that bets on races

There are many others,
Oh! men and brothers,
Than are named in this narration.
There are girls *and* girls,
Yet they're all of them pearls,
Quite the best sorts in creation.

Girl's Names

There is a strange deformity
  Combined with countless graces,
As often in the ladies' names,
  As in the ladies faces;
Some names fit for every age,
  Some only fit for youth;
Some passing sweet and musical,
  Some horribly uncouth;
Some fit for dames of loftiest grades,
Some only fit for scullery maids
Ann is too plain and common,
  And Nancy sounds but ill;
Yet Anna is endurable,
  And Annie better still,
There is a grace in Charlotte,
  In Eleanor a state,
An elegance in Isabel,
  A haughtiness in Kate;
And Sarah is sedate and neat,
And Ellen innocent and sweet

Matilda has a sickly sound,
  Fit for a nurse's trade;
Sophie is effeminate,
  And Esther sage and staid;
Elizabeth's a matchless name,
  Fit for a queen to wear
In castle, cottage, hut, or hall—
  A name beyond compare;
And Bess, and Bessie follow well,
But Betsy is detestable.
Maria is too forward,
  And Gertrude is too gruff,
Yet, coupled with a pretty face,
  Is pretty name enough'
And Adelaide is fanciful,
  And Laura is too fine,
But Emily is beautiful,
  And Mary is divine
Maud only suits a high-born dame,
  And Fanny is a baby name
Eliza is not very choice,
  Jane is too blunt and Bold,
And Martha somewhat sorrowful,
  And Lucy proud and cold;
Amelia is too light and gay,
  Fit for only a flirt;
And Caroline is vain and shy,
  And Flora smart and pert;
Louisa is too soft and sleek
But Alice—gentle, chaste and meek
And Harriet is confiding,
  And Clara grave and mild.
And Emma is affectionate,
  And Janet arch and wild!
And Patience is expressive,
  And Grace is cold and rare,
And Hannah warm and dutiful,
  And Margaret frank and fair
And Faith, and Hope and Charity
Are heavenly names for sisters three.

Sarah

Oh, Sarah mine, hark to my song
  Your slumbers soft invading.
For here beneath your window-sill
  I come a-Sarah-nading.

You know my fond heart beats for you
  In tenderest adoration,
And then, you know, I long to have
  You be my own Sal-vation.

The day's not far when you'll be mine—
  The thought makes my soul merry;
You'll be the pride of all my life,
  But not my adver-Sarey.

The tender fates shall crown your lot,
  And sweet contentment parcel;
And while you're just the world to me,
  Love will be univer-Sal.

With bridal altar draped with flowers
  And everything so tony,
In crowded church we will be wed
  With lots of Sarah-money.

There's nothing I'll not do for you
  Till life comes to an end, dear.
I'd brave the battles of the world
  And fight a Sara-cen, dear.

I must to sleep, Sal, soda you,
  For here I must not dally,
For that bull-dog I hear, like me,
  Is bound to have a Sally.

Several Kinds of Girls

A good girl to have—Sal Vation.
A disagreeable girl—Anna Mosity.
A fighting girl—Hittie Magginn.
Not a Christian girl—Hettie Rodoxy.
A sweet girl—Carrie Mel.
A pleasant girl—Jennie Rosity.
A sick girl—Sallie Vate.
A smooth girl—Amelia Ration.
A seedy girl—Cora Ander.
One of the best girls—Ella Gant.
A clear case of girl—E. Lucy Date.
A geometrical girl—Rhoda Dendron.
A musical girl—Sarah Nade.
A profound girl—Mettie Physics.
A star girl—Meta Oric.
A clinging girl—Jessie Mine.
A nervous girl—Hester Ical.
A muscular girl—Callie Sthenici.
A lively girl—Anna Mation.
An uncertain girl—Eva Nescent.
A sad girl—Ella G.
A serene girl—Molly Fy.
A great big girl—Ella Phant.
A warlike girl—Millie Tary.
The best girl of all—Your Own.

A Puzzle—The Dog and Cat Show—Where are the Cats?
Your bold, naughty brother will show you.

Jumping-Jennie

Jennie has a jumping-rope
  As slender as a whip.
And all about the street and house
  She'd skip, and skip, and skip.

She knocked the vases from the shelf,
  Upset the stools and chairs,
And one unlucky day, alas!
  Went headlong down the stairs.

Against the wall, against the door
  Her head she often bumped,
And stumbled here, and stumbled there,
  Yet still she jumped, and jumped.

She jumped so high, she jumped so hard,
  That—so the story goes—
She wore her shoes and stockings out,
  Likewise her heels and toes.

I Don't Care

Matilda was a pretty girl,
  And she had flaxen hair;
And yet she used those naughty words
  "I'm sure I do not care."

She once her lessons would not learn,
  But talk'd about the fair,
And lost her tickets, but she said,
  "I'm sure I do not care."

As she advanced to riper years,
  I'm sorry to declare,
She still preserved those naughty words,
  "I'm sure I do not care."

She grew a woman, and for life
  'Twas time she should prepare,
But still she said "there's time enough,
  If not, I do not care."

Duties neglected, warnings spurn'd,
  Her mother in despair;
And though she saw the evil done,
  She said, "I do not care."

Still on she went from bad to worse,
  She spurned her father's prayer;
Who feared she'd find an awful end,
  Because she would not care.

Afflictions came, and death in view,
  Which filled her with despair;
Her God neglected, and she feared
  For her He would not care.

Could you have then Matilda seen,
  Or heard her broken prayer,
She urged her friends never to use

Those awful words—Don't Care.

Little Miss Meddlesome

Little Miss Meddlesome
  Scattering crumbs,
Into the library
  Noisily comes—
Twirls off her apron,
  Tilts open some books,
And into a work-basket
  Rummaging, looks.

Out goes the spools spinning
  Over the floor,
Beeswax and needle-case
  Stepped out before;
She tosses the tape-rule
  And plays with the floss,
And says to herself,
  "Now won't mamma be cross!"

Little Miss Meddlesome
  Climbs to the shelf,
Since no-one is looking,
  And mischievous elf,
Pulls down the fine vases,
  The cuckoo-clock stops,
And sprinkles the carpet
  With damaging drops.

She turns over the ottoman,
  Frightens the bird,
And sees that the chairs
  In a medley are stirred;
Then creeps on the sofa,
  And, all in a heap,
Drops out of her

Frolicsome mischief asleep.

But here comes the nurse,
  Who is shaking her head,
And frowns at the mischief
  Asleep on her bed.
But let's hope when Miss Meddlesome's
  Slumber is o'er,
She may wake from good dreams
  And do mischief no more.

Careless Matilda

"Again, Matilda,
  Is your work astray,
Your thimble is gone!
  Your scissors, where are they?

Your needles, pins, your thread,
  And tapes all lost—
Your housewife here,
  And there your work-bag tost.

Fie, fie, my child!
  Indeed this will not do,
Your hair uncomb'd,
  Your frock in tatters too;

I'm now resolv'd
  No more delays to grant,
This day I'll send you
  To your stern old aunt."

In vain Matilda wept,
  Repented, pray'd,
In vain a promise
  Of amendment made.

Arriv'd at Austere Hall,
  Matilda sigh'd.
By Lady Rigid,
  When severely eyed.

"You read, and write,
  And work well, as I'm told,
Are gentle, kind, good-natur'd,
  Far from bold.

But very careless,
  Negligent, and wild—
When you leave me,
  You'll be a different child."

The little girl
  Next morn a favour asks:
"I wish to take a walk,"
  "Go learn your tasks,"

The lady harsh replies,
  "Nor cry nor whine.
Your room you leave not
  Till you're call'd to dine."

As thus Matilda sat,
  O'erwhelm'd with shame,
A dame appear'd,
  Disorder was her name.

Her hair and dress neglected,
  Soil'd her face,
She squinted leer'd,
  And hobbled in her pace.

"Here, child," she said,
  "My mistress sends you this,
A bag of silks—
  A flow'r not work'd amiss—

A polyanthus bright,
  And wondrous gay;
You'll copy it by noon,
  She bade me say."
Disorder grinn'd,
  Then shuffling walk'd away.

Entangled were
  The silks of every hue,
Confus'd and mix'd
  Were shades of pink, green, blue;

She took a thread,
  Compar'd it with the flow'r;
"To finish this is
  Not within my pow'r.

Well-order'd silks
  Had Lady Rigid sent,
I might have work'd,
  If such was her intent."

She sigh'd, and melted
  Into sobs and tears,
She hears a noise
  And at the door appears

A pretty maiden, clean,
  Well-dress'd, and neat
Her voice was soft,
  Her looks sedate, yet sweet.

"My name is Order,
  Do not cry my love;
Attend to me,
  And thus you may improve."

She took the silks,
  And drew out shade for shade,
In sep'rate skeins,

Each hue with care she laid;
Then smiling kindly,
  Left the little maid.

Matilda now resumed
  Her sweet employ,
And sees the flow'r complete—
  How great her joy.

She leaves the room,
  "I've done my task," she cries.
But soon her harshness
  The lady look'd
With disbelieving eyes,
  Chang'd to glad surprise.

"Why this is well!
  A very pretty flow'r,
Work'd clean, exact,
 And done within the hour!

And now amuse yourself,
  Ride, walk or play."
Thus passed Matilda
  This much-dreaded day.

At all her tasks
  Disorder would attend
At all her tasks
  Still Order stood her friend.

With tears and sighs
  Her studies oft began,
These into smiles
  Were changed by Order's plan;

No longer Lady Rigid
  Seem'd severe,
Her looks the negligent

Alone need fear.

And when the day
  The wish'd-for day is come
When young Matilda's
  Suffer'd to go home:

"You quit me, child,
  But oft to mind recall
The time you spent
  With me at Austere Hall.

And now, my dear,
  I'll give you one of these,
Your servant she will be;
  Take which you please."

"From me," Disorder asked,
  "Old friend, why start?"
Matilda clasped
  Sweet Order to her heart.
"My dearest girl," she cried,
  "We'll never part."

Forty Little School Girls

Forty little school girls, running, but not flirty;
Ten ran into Cole's Book Arcade,
And then there were but thirty.

Thirty little school girls swimming the river Plenty;
Ten swam into Cole's Book Arcade,
And then there were but twenty.

Twenty little school girls jumping in velveteen;
One jumped into Cole's Book Arcade,
And then there were nineteen.

Nineteen little school girls going out a-skating;
One skated into Cole's Book Arcade,
And then there were but eighteen.

Eighteen little school girls dancing with the queen;
One danced into Cole's Book Arcade,

COLE

And then there were seventeen.

Seventeen little school girls driving a bullock team;
One drove into Cole's Book Arcade,
And then there were sixteen.

Sixteen little school girls creeping out unseen;
One crept into Cole's Book Arcade,
And then there were fifteen.

Fifteen little school girls hopping on the green;
One hopped into Cole's Book Arcade,
And then there were fourteen.

Fourteen little schoolgirls floating down a stream;
One floated into Cole's Book Arcade,
And then there were thirteen.

Thirteen little school girls leaping out to delve;
One leaped into Cole's Book Arcade,
And then there were but twelve.

Twelve little school girls racing out for leaven;
One raced into Cole's Book Arcade,
And then there were eleven.

Eleven little school girls dodging a lion when—
One dodged into Cole's Book Arcade,
And then there were but ten.

Ten little school girls, all skipping in a line;
One skipped into Cole's Book Arcade,
And then there were but nine.

Nine little school girls swinging on a gate;
One swung into Cole's Book Arcade,
And then there were but eight.

Eight little school girls, trying to fly to heaven;
One flew into Cole's Book Arcade,

And then there were but seven.

Seven little school girls tripping out for sticks;
One tripped into Cole's Book Arcade,
And then there were but six.

Six little school girls, going for a dive;
One dived into Cole's Book Arcade,
And then there were but five.

Five little school girls, sailing to explore;
One sailed into Cole's Book Arcade,
And then there were but four.

Four little school girls steaming on the sea;
One steamed into Cole's Book Arcade,
And then there were but three.

Three little school girls, riding on a moo;
One rode into Cole's Book Arcade,
And then there were but two.

Two little school girls, sliding about for fun;
One slid into Cole's Book Arcade,
And then there was but one.

One little school girl, the nicest, last and best,
She walked into Cole's Book Arcade,
And read books with all the rest.
The following is the way that each girl went into Cole's Book Arcade:
                    Ada ran into it.
                    Agnes ran into it.
                    Alice ran into it.
                    Amy ran into it.
                    Annie ran into it.
                    Angelina ran into it.
                    Bessie ran into it.
                    Bridget ran into it.
                    Carrie ran into it.
                    Clara ran into it.

Edith swam into it.
Eliza swam into it.
Emily swam into it.
Emma swam into it.
Fanny swam into it.
Florence swam into it.
Hannah swam into it.
Harriet swam into it.
Jane swam into it.
Jessie swam into it.
Kate jumped into it.
Lillie skated into it.
Lizzie danced into it.
Lottie drove into it.
Louisa crept into it.
Lucy hopped into it.
Mary floated into it.
Martha leaped into it.
Matilda raced into it.
Maggie dodged into it.
Maria skipped into it.
Mabel swung into it.
Maude flew into it.
May tripped into it.
Minnie dived into it.
Nellie sailed into it.
Olive steamed into it.
Rose rode into it.
Sarah slid into it.
Tottie walked into it.

N.B.—Any little girl is invited to walk, run, jump, dance, skip, hop, swim, fly, or come into Cole's Book Arcade in any way she chooses, the same as the Forty Little School Girls.

Story Of The Funny Monkeys

Once there was a funny old monkey—and this old monkey had six young monkeys. There was one white monkey, and one black monkey, and one yellow monkey, and one red monkey, and one blue monkey, and one green monkey; and the white monkey's name was Linda, and the black monkey's name was Eddie, and the yellow monkey's name was Vally, and the red monkey's name was Ruby, and the blue monkey's name was Pearl, and the green Monkey's name was Ivy Diamond. And the white monkey liked apples, and the black monkey liked grapes, and the yellow monkey liked cherries, and the red monkey liked strawberries, and the blue monkey liked oranges, and the green monkey liked nuts, and that's all about these FUNNY MONKEYS. The names of any children can be told in this story instead of Linda, Eddie, Vally, Ruby, Pearl, and Diamond.

117

My Five Sisters.

Maidenhood

Maiden! with the meek, brown eyes,
In whose orbs a shadow lies,
Like a dusk in evening skies!

Thou, whose locks outshine the sun,
Golden tresses, wreathed in one,
As the braided streamlets run!

Standing, with reluctant feet,
Where the brook and river meet!
Womanhood and childhood fleet!

Gazing, with a timid glance,
On the brooklet's swift advance,
On the river's broad expanse!

Deep and still, that gliding stream
Beautiful to thee must seem,

As the river of a dream.

Then why pause with indecision,
When bright angels in thy vision
Beckon thee to fields of Elysian?

Seest thou shadows sailing by,
As the dove, with startled eye,
Sees the falcon's shadow fly?

Hearest thou voices on the shore,
That our ears perceive no more,
Deafen'd by the cataract's roar?

O, thou child of many prayers!
Life hath quicksands—Life hath snares!
Care and age come unawares!

Like the swell of some sweet tune,
Morning rises into noon,
May glides onward into June

Childhood is the bough where slumber'd
Birds and blossoms many-number'd—
Age, that bough with snows encumber'd

Gather, then each flower that grows,
When the young heart overflows,
To embalm that tent of snows

Bear a lily in thy hand;
Gates of brass cannot withstand
One touch of that magic wand

Bear, through sorrow, wrong, and ruth,
In thy heart the dew of youth,
On thy lips the smile of truth.

Oh! that dew, like balm, shall steal
Into wounds, that cannot heal,

119

Even as sleep our eyes doth seal:

And that smile, like sunshine, dart
Into many a sunless heart,
For a smile of God thou art.

Longfellow

Girls that are in Demand

The girls that are wanted are good girls—
  Good from the heart to the lips;
Pure as the lily is white and pure,
  From it's heart to its sweet leaf tips.
The girls that are wanted are home girls—
  Girls that are a mother's right hand,
That fathers and brothers can trust to,
  And the little ones understand.

The girls that are fair on the hearthstone,
  And pleasant when nobody sees;
Kind and sweet to their own folks,
  Ready and anxious to please.
The girls that are wanted are wise girls,
  That know what to do and to say;
That drive with a smile and soft word
  The wrath of the household away.

The girls that are wanted are girls of sense,
  Whom fashion can never deceive;
Who can follow whatever is pretty,
  And dare what is silly to leave.
The girls that are wanted are careful girls,
  Who count what a thing will cost.
Who use with a prudent generous hand,
  But see that nothing is lost.

The girls that are wanted are girls with hearts,

They are wanted for mothers and wives,
Wanted to cradle in loving arms
The strongest and frailest lives.
The clever, the witty, the brilliant girl,
There are few who can understand,
But, oh! for the wise, loving home girls
There's a constant steady demand.

Girl's Names

Francis, is "unrestrained and free;"
  Bertha, "pellucid, purely bright;"
Clara, "clear" as the crystal sea;
  Lucy, a star of radiant "light;"
Catherine, is "pure" as mountain air;
  Barbara, cometh "from afar;"
Mabel, is "like a lily fair;"
  Henrietta, a soft, sweet "star;"
Felicia, is a "happy girl;"
  Matilda, is a "lady true;"
Margaret, is a shining "pearl;"
  Rebecca, "with the faithful few;"
Susan, is a "lily white;"
  Jane has the "willow's" curve and grace;
Cecilia, dear, is "dim of sight;"
  Sophia, shows "wisdom" on her face;
Constance, is firm and "resolute;"
  Grace, a delicious "favour meet;"
Charlotte, "noble, of good repute;"
  Harriet, a fine "odour sweet;"
Isabella, is "a lady rare;"
  Lucinda, "constant" as the day;
Maria, means a "lady fair;"
  Abigail, "joyful as the May;"
Elizabeth, "an oath of trust;"
  Adeline, "nice princess, proud;"
Agatha, "is truly good and just;"
  Leila, "a joy of love avowed;"
Jemima, "a soft sound in air;"
  Caroline, "a sweet spirit, hale;"

121

Cornelia, "harmonious and fair;"
  Selina, "a sweet nightingale;"
Lydia, "a refreshing well;"
  Judith, "a song of sacred praise;"
Julia, "a jewel none excel;"
  Priscilla, "ancient of days."

Kate

There's something in the name of Kate
  Which many will condemn;
But listen now while I relate
  The traits of some of them.

There's deli-Kate, a modest dame,
  She's worthy of your love!
She's nice and beautiful a flame,
  And gentle as a dove,

Communi-Kate's intelligent,
  As we may well suppose;
Her fruitful mind is ever bent
  On telling all she knows.

There's intri-Kate, she's so obscure
  'Tis hard to find her out;
For she is often very sure
  To put your wits to rout.

Prevari-Kate's a surly maid,
  She's sure to have her way;
The cavilling, contrary jade,
  Objects to all you say.

There's alter-Kate, a perfect pest;
  Much given to dispute;
Her prattling tongue can never rest,

You cannot her refute.

Then dislo-Kate, is quite a fret,
  Who fails to gain her point;
Her case is quite unfortunate
  And sorely out of joint.

Equivo-Kate no one will woo—
  The thing would be absurd.
She is so faithless and untrue,
  You cannot take her word.

There's vindi-Kate, she's good and true,
  And strives with all her might
Her duty faithfully to do
  And battles for the right.

There's rusti-Kate, a country lass,
  Quite fond of rural scenes;
She likes to ramble through the grass
  And through the evergreens.

Of all the maidens you can find,
  There's none like edu-Kate;
Because she elevates the mind
  And aims at something great.

My Five Cousins.

COLE'S ELECTRO-MICRO SCOLDING MACHINE FOR SCOLDING NAUGHTY GIRLS.

Coles Electro-micro Scolding Machine For Scolding Naughty Girls

Cole's Electro-micro Scolding Machine is a combination of three instruments, the Phonograph, the Microphone, and the Wonderphone.

The Phonograph is an instrument that will preserve

words for any length of time. Any person can speak, sing, whistle, or scold into a Phonograph, and months or years afterwards by simply turning a handle the same sounds can be reproduced a dozen, a hundred, or a thousand times in the exact voice of the person who spoke them in; so that if a man or a woman, who is a great scold, speak some good, loud, severe scolding into a Phonograph, the mildest teacher can then scold her pupils, or the kindest mother her children, just by turning the handle.

The Microphone is an instrument that magnifies sound in the same way as a microscope magnifies objects; a very powerful microphone magnifies the sound of a fly walking into a loud tramping footstep, the tick of a watch into a deafening clatter, and a whisper into a loud shout. Take a Microphone, then properly affix it to the Phonograph described above, and you have a good Scolding Machine; turn the handle, and as the Phonograph gives out the scoldings, the microphone part magnifies them so loudly that they are heard for a considerable distance.

The Wonderphone (Cole's own secret) is another remarkable instrument; it will cause sound to travel very distinctly, but frightfully and equally loud, for forty miles in all directions; by attaching this powerful instrument to the combination of the other two, Cole's Electro-micro Scolding Machine is formed—and which is the first Scolding Machine ever invented. If the machine is already *charged* by having had some scolding spoken, or even whispered into it, give the handle a turn, and forty miles to the east, forty miles to the west, forty to the north, forty to the south, forty up in the sky, and down in the mines forty miles deep, in fact forty miles in every direction, everybody can clearly hear every word being said to the girl being scolded. Suppose for instance, Hannah Maria Smith had done something wrong in school, the schoolmistress could give the handle of the machine a turn, and it would scold her so loudly that her mother, and father, and brothers, and sisters, and uncles, and aunts, and friends, and those she didn't like would all hear her scolded. The machine can be charged

125

on the instant by anyone scolding into it. In fact the whole value of Cole's Scolding Machine lies in its power to repeat out exceedingly loud whatever is spoken into it.

If the schoolmistress chooses she can put the scolding into verse, so that all who hear it in the forty miles around, can more easily remember it. The machine that I have before me now, was charged this morning for an aristocratic school and speaks as follows:—Silence!! Attention!!!

Ada Alice Arabella Angelina Andal,
Why do you talk for ever, such a tittle-tattling scandal?
Betsy Bertha Bridget Belinda Bowing,
Will you be quiet and go on with your sewing?
Cora Caroline Christina Clarinda Clare,
Now do look in the glass at your untidy hair.
Dorah Dinah Dorothy Dorinda Dresson,
You really must get on with your short drawing lesson.
Edith Ellen Evelina Elizabeth Eadle,
This makes this day your nineteenth broken needle.
Fanny Florence Frederica Florinda Flynn,
How cruel of you to prick Jane with a pin.
Grace Gertrude Genevieve Georgina Grimble,
You careless girl to lose your silver thimble.
Hilda Hanna Harriet Henrietta Hawker,
You really are a most inveterate talker.
Ida Izod Irene Isabella Inching,
You spiteful—stop that scratching and pinching.
Jane Julia Josephine Jemima Jesson,
Sit down at once and learn your music lesson.
Kate Kester Katrina Kathleen Kent,
You're vulgar, saucy, rude and insolent.
Lizzie Letitia Lucretia Lorinda Loeries,
You're the champion of the world for telling stories.
Maud Mary Martha Matilda Moyes,
Sends letters to, and flirts with, naughty boys.
Nancy Nelly Ninette Naomi Nations,
Shame of you to talk 'gainst other girls' relations.
Olive Osberta Orphelia Octavia O'Dyke,
Your conduct is outrageous and unladylike.
Polly Patience Prudence Paulina Pitt,

You really are our champion tell-tale-tit.
Quilla Quintina Quinburga Quendrida Quirk,
How very, very, dirty you have made your fancy-work.
Rose Ruth Rachel Rebecca Ritting,
Now stop that crying and get on with your knitting.
Sarah Sophia Selina Susannah Stacies,
Don't spoil your face by making those grimaces.
Tilda Theresa Tabitha Theodora Tapping,
You'd gain the prize if one was given for slapping.
Una Ursula Urica Urania Urls,
You'd gain the prize for teasing little girls.
Venus Violet Victoria Veronica Vo-shi,
Just learn your task and put away that crochet.
Wilmett Walberg Winefride Wilhelmina Wriggling,
Now once for all do stop that stupid giggling.
Xenodice Xanthippe Xanthisa Xenophona X-cess,
You think and talk of nothing else but dress! dress!
Yana Yulga Yapeena Yestina Young,
Will you behave yourself and just draw in your tongue.
And lastly and worst of all, you,
Zoe Zora Zillah Zenobia Zeen,
How dare you! how dare you!! yes, how dare you!!!
Sneer at the boy's new whipping Machine.

Notice To The Public

If a schoolmistress chooses to live a hundred or
a thousand miles away from her school, she can use the
Scolding Machine by means of a *Telephone* attached
thereto.

One great advantage of the Electro-micro Scolding Machine is, that after it has been in use a short time
the girls will all have been shamed into good behaviour;
but the Machine will not become useless, as it can,
without a farthing outlay, be turned into a Praising Machine, for it can be made to praise in a gentle voice as
well as scold in a harsh one. In fact, as said above it will
repeat in exact tones, anything that is recited, preached,
sung, whistled, whispered, shouted, scolded or praised

into it—and any of which will be heard for forty miles around.

Cole can supply Scolding Machines from £5 to £50. A very good one (The Excelsior), price £10, can be charged in one minute, and set going like a musical box, and will sing, whistle, recite, preach, or scold away for a full hour without stopping. Cole would particularly recommend this one to the ladies, it would make a fine ornament for their own table.

Final Notice Extraordinary—If the champion male scold of the world, and the champion female scold of the world, will call on Professor Cole, at the Book Arcade, Melbourne, he will give them both good wages, and find them constant employment at charging Scolding Machines. If any wife has got the champion male scold for a husband, she will please to let me know. If any husband has got the champion female scold for a wife, he will please to let me know—£10 bonus for information in each case.

E.W. Cole

Jenny Lee

An orphan child was Jenny Lee;
  Her father, he was dead.
And very hard her mother worked;
  To get the children bread.

In winter time, she often rose
  Long ere the day was light,
And left her orphan family,
  Till dark again at night.

And she would always say to Jane,
  Before she went away;
"Be sure you mind the little ones,

And don't go out to play.

"Keep baby quiet in his bed,
  As long as he will lie;
Then take him up, and dance him well,
  Don't leave him there to cry.

"And don't let little Christopher,
  Get down into the street,
For fear he meets an accident
  Beneath the horse's feet.

"And mind about the fire, child,
  And keep a tidy floor;
We never need be dirty, Jane,
  Although we may be poor.

"Good-by my precious comforter,
  For all the neighbours say,
That I can trust my little maid,
  Whenever I'm away."

Then Jenny she was quite as proud
  As England's noble Queen,
And she resolved to do the work,
  And keep the dwelling clean.

She did not stop to waste her time,
  But very brisk was she,
And worked as hard and cheerfully
  As any busy bee.

If down upon the cottage floor
  Her little brother fell,
She stroked the places tenderly,
  And kissed and made them well.

And when the little babe was cross,
  As little babes will be,
She nursed and danced it merrily,

129

And fed it on her knee.

But when they both were safe in bed,
  She neatly swept the hearth,
And waited until her mother's step
  Came sounding up the path.

Then open flew the cottage door,
  The weary mother smiled.
"Ah! Jenny dear, what should I do,
  Without my precious child!"

Work Before Play

"Mother has sent me to the well,
  To fetch a jug of water,
And I am very glad to be
  A useful little daughter;
That's why I cannot play
  With you and Mary Ann to-day.

"Some afternoon I'll come with you,
  And make you wreaths and posies;
I know a place where blue-bells grow,
  And daisies and primroses;
But not to-day, for I must go
  And help my mother, dears, you know.

"She says, that I am nearly eight,
  So I can fill the kettle,
And sweep the room and clean the grate,
  And even scrub a little;
Oh! I'm so very glad to be
  A little useful girl, you see.

"So Johnny, do not ask to-day—
  Perhaps I'll come to morrow;
But you'd not wish me now to stay,

And give my mother sorrow.
When she can spare me, she will say,
'Now, Susan, you may go and play.'"

Lucy Gray

Oft I had heard of Lucy Gray;
  And, when I crossed the wild,
I managed to see at break of day
  The solitary child.

No mate, no comrade Lucy knew;
  She dwelt on a wide moor,—
The sweetest thing that ever grew
  Besides a human door!

You yet may spy the fawn at play,
  The hare upon the green;
But the sweet face of Lucy Gray

Will never more be seen.

"To-night will be a stormy night—
  You to the town must go;
And take a lantern, child, to light
  Your mother through the snow."

"That, father, will I gladly do!
  'Tis scarcely afternoon—
The minster-clock has just struck two,
  And yonder is the moon."

At this the father raised his book
  And snapped a faggot band;
He piled his work,—and Lucy took
  The lantern in her hand.

Not blither is the mountain roe;
  With many a wanton stroke
Her feet disperse the powdery snow,
  That rises up like smoke.

The storm came on before it's time;
  She wandered up and down;
And many a hill did Lucy climb,
  But never reached the town.

The wretched parents all that night
  Went shouting far and wide,
But there was neither sound or sight
  To serve them for a guide.

At day-break on a hill they stood
  That overlooked the moor;
And thence they saw the bridge of wood
  A furlong from their door.

And, turning homeward, now they cried
  "In heaven we shall meet!"
When in the snow the mother spied

The print of Lucy's feet.

Then downwards from the steep hill's edge
  They tracked the footmarks small;
And through the broken hawthorn edge,
  And by the long stone wall.

And then an open field they crossed—
  The marks were still the same;
They tracked them on, nor ever lost;
  And to the bridge they came.

They followed from the snowy bank
  The footmarks, one by one,
Into the middle of the plank;
  And further there were none!

Yet some maintain that to this day
  She is a living child;
That you may see sweet Lucy Gray
  Upon the lonesome wild.

O'er rough and smooth she trips along,
  And never looks behind;
And sings a solitary song
  That whistles in the wind.

Mary's Little Lamb

Mary had a little lamb,
  It's fleece was white as snow;
And everywhere that Mary went
  The lamb was sure to go.

He followed her to school one day—
  That was against the rule;
It made the children laugh and play,

To see a lamb at school.

The teacher therefore turned him out;
  But still he lingered near,
And on the grass he played about
  Till Mary did appear.

At once he ran to her, and laid
  His head upon her arm,
As if to say, I'm not afraid—
  You'll keep me from all harm.

"What makes the lamb love Mary so?"
  The little children cry;
"Oh! Mary loves the lamb you know,"
  The teacher did reply.

We are Seven

I met a little cottage girl;
  She was eight years old, she said;
Her head was thick with many a curl
  That clustered round her head.

She had a rustic, woodland air,
  And she was wildly clad;
Her eyes were fair, and very fair,
  Her beauty made me glad.

"Sisters and brothers, little maid,
  How many may you be?"
"How many? Seven in all," she said,
  And wondering, looked at me.

"And where are they? I pray you tell."
  She answered, "Seven are we;
And two of us at Conway dwell,

And two are gone to sea.

"Two of us in the churchyard lie—
  My sister and my brother;
And in the churchyard cottage I
  Dwell near them with my mother."

"You say that two at Conway dwell,
  And two are gone to sea;
Yet ye are seven! I pray you tell,
  Sweet maid how this may be?"

Then did the little maid reply,
  Seven boys and girls are we;
Two of us in the churchyard lie,
  Beneath the churchyard tree."

"You run about, my little maid,
  Your limbs they are alive!
If two are in the churchyard laid,
  Then ye are only five."

"Their graves are green, they may be seen,"
  The little maid replied;
"Twelve steps or more, from my mother's door,
  And they are side by side.

"My stockings there I often knit,
  My kerchief there I hem;
And there upon the ground I sit,
  I sit and sing to them.

"And often after sunset, sir,
  When it is light and fair,
I take my little porringer,
  And eat my supper there.

"The first that died was little Jane;
  In bed she moaning lay,
Till God released her of her pain,

135

And then she went away.

"So in the churchyard she was laid;
　And, when the grass was dry,
Together round her grave we played,
　My brother John and I.

"And when the ground was white with snow,
　And I could run and slide,
My brother John was forced to go,
　And he lies by her side."

"How many are you then? said I,
　"If they two are in heaven!"
The little maiden did reply
　"O master! we are seven."

"But they are dead; those two are dead;
　Their spirits are in heaven!"
'Twas throwing words away; for still
The little maid would have her will,
　And say, "Nay, we are seven."

The Poor, but Kind Girl

Young Lucy Payne lives on the Village Green;
　Mary, you know the cottage, I am sure,
Under the hawthorn! 'Tis so neat and clean,
　Though Widow Payne, alas! is blind and poor.

She plies her needles, and she plies them well,
　And Lucy never spends an idle hour;
On market days their mits and socks they sell,
　And thus their balls of worsted turn to flour.

I pass'd one morning by their cottage door;
　Lucy was talking to a little child,
A ragged thing that lives upon the moor;

It's parents leave it to run rude and wild.

Hanger had tamed the little wilding thing,
  It's cheeks were hollow, but it's air was light;
Young Lucy did not know I saw her bring
  That porringer she kept so clean and bright.

  It was her breakfast—all the darling had;
  But oh! she gave it with a heart so glad.

Grace Darling

"Over the wave, the stormy wave,
  Hasten, dear father, with me,
The crew to save from a wat'ry grave,
  Deep in the merciless sea.
Hear ye the shriek, the piercing shriek,
  Hear ye the cry of despair?
With courage quick the wreck we'll seek;

Danger united we'll dare.

"Out with the boat, the gallant boat;
 Not a moment to be lost;
See! she's afloat, proudly afloat,
 And high on the waves we're tossed;
Mother, Adieu, a short adieu;
 Your prayers will rise to heaven;
Father to you—your child and you—
 Power to save is given.

"I have no fear, no maiden fear;
 My heart is firm to the deed,
I shed no tear, no coward tear;
 I've strength in time of need.
Hear ye the crash, the horrid crash?
 Their mast over the side is gone;
Yet on we dash, 'mid lightning flash,
 Safe through the pelting storm.

"The wreck we near, the wreck we near,
 Our bonny boat seems to fly,
List to the cheer, their welcome cheer,
 They know that succour is nigh."
And on that night, that dreadful night,
 The father and daughter brave,
With strengthened might they both unite,
 And many dear lives they save.

Hail to the maid, the fearless maid,
 The maid of matchless worth;
She'll e'er abide the cherished pride
 Of the land that gave her birth.
The send her gold, her name high uphold,
 Honour and praise to impart;
But, with true regard, the loved reward
 Is the joy of her own brave heart.

The Tidy Girl

Who is it each day in the week may be seen,
With her hair short and smooth, and her hands and face clean;
In a stout cotton gown, of dark and light blue,
Though old, so well mended, you'd take it for new;
Her handkerchief tidily pinned o'er her neck.
With a neat little cap, and an apron of check;
Her shoes and her stockings all sound and all clean?
She's never fine outside and dirty within.

Go visit her cottage, though humble and poor.
'Tis so neat and so clean you might eat off the floor;
No rubbish, no cobwebs, no dirt can be found,
Though you hunt every corner, and search all around.
Who sweeps it so nicely, who makes all the bread,
Who tends her sick mother, and works by her bed?
'Tis the neat, tidy girl—she needs no other name;
Abroad or at home, she is always the same.

I Will be Good To-Day

"I will be good, dear mother,"
I heard a sweet child say;
"I will be good; now watch me—
I will be good all day."

Oh, many, many, bitter tears
'Twould save us, did we say,
Like that dear child, with earnest heart,
"I will be good to-day."

My Own Dear Little Sister

I have a little sister,
She's only three years old;

139

I do most dearly love her,
  She's worth her weight in gold.
We often play together
  And I begin to find,
To make my sister happy,
  I must be very kind.

What Our Ruby Did

She danced like a Fairy,
She sung like a Frog,
She squeaked like a Pig,
She barked like a dog.

  Oh yes! Oh yes! She did! She Did!
  And Frog-gy played a tune.

She mooed like a Bullock,
She baaed like a Ram,
She leaped like a Goat,
She skipped like a Lamb—Oh yes!

She brayed like a Donkey,
She cried like a Hare,
She neighed like a Horse,
She growled like a Bear!—Oh yes!

She munched like a Rabbit,
She gnawed like a Rat,
She popped like a Mouse,
She flew like a Bat—Oh yes!

She talked like a Parrot,
She quacked like a Drake,
She mewed like a Cat,
She hissed like a Snake—Oh yes!

She climbed like a Squirrel,
She flopped like a Seal,
She ran like a Deer,
She slid like an Eel—Oh yes!

She crept like a Tortoise,
She soared like a Lark,
She drank like a Fish,
She ate like a Shark—Oh yes!

She roared like a Lion,
She dived like a Whale,
She swam like a Goose,
She crawled like a Snail—Oh yes!

She croaked like a Raven,
She screeched like an Owl,
She cawed like a Crow,
She crowed like a Fowl—Oh yes!

She grinned like a Monkey,
She hummed like a Bee,
She buzzed like a Fly,
She jumped like a Flea—Oh yes!

Our dear little daughter once went to a children's ball dressed as a fairy. She was proud of being a fairy, and looked so nice that I put together the above nursery dog- gerel to please her, and in honour of the event, little thinking that she would soon leave this world. It might be considered better by some to remove this page, but as children like it I venture to let it stand with this explana- tion.

E. W. C.

Sacred to the Memory of our dear LITTLE RUBY, who departed this life March 27th, 1890, aged 8 years. She was intelligent, industrious, affectionate and sociable, and is deeply regretted by all who knew her.

There is no flock, however watched and tended
  But one dead lamb is there!
There is no fireside, howsoever defended
  But has one vacant chair!

There is no death! what seems so is transition
  This life of mortal breath,
Is but a suburb of life Elysian
  Whose portal we call death.

She is not dead—the child of our affection—
  But gone unto that school
Where she no longer needs our poor protection
  And GOD himself doth rule.

143

Our Vally had a Clever Dog,
whose name was EBENEZER.
Sometimes this dog was very good,
At other times a TEASER.

One day they went to take a bath,
And both sat on a rail;
Our Vally hung his legs right down,
The dog hung down his tail.

This funny Dog one Christmas day,
Directly after dinner,
Just lean'd his sleepy head against
Old Tom, our snoozing sinner.

Tommy Trot, a man of law,
Sold his bed and lay upon straw;
Sold the straw and slept on grass,
To buy his wife a looking-glass.
——

Little Jack Jingle,
He used to live single;
But when he got tired of this kind of life,
He left off being single, and lived with his wife.

—

I'll tell you a story
  About Jack Nory,—
And now my story's begun:
  I'll tell you another
  About Jack his brother,—
And now my story's done.

—

  Poor old Robinson Crusoe!
  Poor old Robinson Crusoe!
They made him a coat
Of an old nanny-goat,
  I wonder how they could do so!
With a ring and a ting tang,
And a ring and a ting tang,
  Poor old Robinson Crusoe!

—

"John, come sell thy fiddle,
  And buy thy wife a gown."
"No; I'll not sell my fiddle
  For any wife in town."

—

Jacky, come give me thy fiddle
  If ever thou mean'st to thrive;
Nay, I'll not give my fiddle
  To any man alive.
If I should give my fiddle,
  They'll think that I'm gone mad,
For many a joyful day
  My fiddle and I have had.

—

Jack was a fisherman
  Who went out one day,
But couldn't catch a single fish,
  And so he came away.
And then he came home,
  This angler so bold,
And found he'd caught something—
  For he'd caught a cold.

—

  The Queen of Hearts,
  She made some tarts,
All on a summer day;
  The Knave of Hearts
  He stole those tarts
And took them clean away.

  The King of Hearts
  Called for the tarts,
And beat the knave full sore;
  The Knave of Hearts
  Brought back the tarts,
And vowed he'd steal no more.

—

Charley Wag
Ate the pudding and left the bag.

—

Tom, The Piper's Son

  Tom, Tom, the piper's son,
  Stole a pig and away did run!
  The pig he eat, and Tom they beat,

147

And Tom went roaring down the street.

Tom, he was a piper's son:
He learned to play when he was young:
But all the tunes that he could play
Was, "Over the hills and far away;
Over the hills and a great way off,
And the wind will blow my topknot off."

Now Tom with his pipe made such a noise,
That he pleased both the girls and the boys,
And they stopped to hear him play
"Over the hills and far away."

Tom with his pipe did play with such skill,
That those who heard him could never keep still:
Whenever they heard they began for to dance,
Even the pigs on their hind legs would after him prance.

As Dolly was milking her cow one day,

Tom took out his pipe and began for to play;
So Doll and the cow danced "the Cheshire round,"
Till the pail they broke and the milk ran on the ground.

He met old Dame Trot with a basket of eggs,
He used his pipe and she used her legs;
She danced about till all the eggs she broke,
She began for to fret, but he laughed at the joke.

He saw a cross fellow beating an ass,
Heavily laden with pots, pans, dishes and glass;
He took out his pipe and played them a tune,
And the jackass did kick off his load very soon.

Tom met the parson on his way,
Took out his pipe, began to play
A merry tune that led his grace
Into a very muddy place.

The mayor then said he would not fail
To send poor Tommy off to gaol.
Tom took his pipe, began to play,
And all the court soon danced away.

'Twas quite a treat to see the rout,
How clerks and judges hopped about;
While Tommy still kept playing the tune,
"I'll be free this afternoon."

The Policeman Grab, who held him fast,
Began to dance about at last;
Whilst Tom, delighted at the fun,
Slipped out of court and off did run.

—

Taffy was a Welshman, Taffy was a thief,
Taffy came to my house, and stole a piece of beef.
I went to Taffy's house, Taffy was not at home;
Taffy came to my house and stole a marrow-bone.

149

I went to Taffy's house, Taffy was not in.
Taffy came to my house, and stole a silver pin.
I went to Taffy's house, Taffy was in bed.
I took up a poker and flung it at his head.

—

Old King Cole
Was a merry old soul,
And a merry old soul was he;
He called for his pipe,
And he called for his bowl,
And he called for his fiddlers three.

—

Peter White will ne'er go right;
Would you know the reason why?
He follows his nose where'er he goes,
And that stands all awry.

The House That Jack Built

This is the house that Jack built.

This is the malt
That lay in the house that Jack built.

This is the rat,
That ate the malt,
That lay in the house that Jack built.

This is the cat,
That killed the rat,
That ate the malt,
That lay in the house that Jack built.

This is the dog,

That worried the cat,
That killed the rat,
That ate the malt,
That lay in the house that Jack built.

This is the cow with the crumpled horn,
That tossed the dog,
That worried the cat,
That killed the rat,
That ate the malt,
That lay in the house that Jack built.

This is the maiden all forlorn,
That milked the cow with the crumpled horn,
That tossed the dog,
That worried the cat,
That killed the rat,
That ate the malt,
That lay in the house that Jack built.

This is the man all tattered and torn,
That kissed the maiden all forlorn,
That milked the cow with the crumpled horn,
That tossed the dog,
That worried the cat,
That killed the rat,
That ate the malt,
That lay in the house that Jack built.

This is the priest all shaven and shorn,
That married the man all tattered and torn,
That kissed the maiden all forlorn,
That milked the cow with the crumpled horn,
That tossed the dog,
That worried the cat,
That killed the rat,
That ate the malt,
That lay in the house that Jack built.

This is the cock that crowed in the morn,

That awaked the priest all shaven and shorn,
That married the man all tattered and torn,
That kissed the maiden all forlorn,
That milked the cow with the crumpled horn,
That tossed the dog,
That worried the cat,
That killed the rat,
That ate the malt,
That lay in the house that Jack built.

This is the farmer sowing his corn,
That kept the cock that crowed in the morn,
That awaked the priest all shaven and shorn,
That married the man all tattered and torn,
That kissed the maiden all forlorn,
That milked the cow with the crumpled horn,
That tossed the dog,
That worried the cat,
That killed the rat,
That ate the malt,
That lay in the house that Jack built.

Simple Simon

Simple Simon met a pieman
  Going to the fair;
Says Simple Simon to the pieman:
  "Let me taste your ware."

Says the pieman to Simple Simon,
  "Show me first the penny."
Says Simple Simon to the pieman:
  "Indeed I have not any."

Simple Simon went a-fishing
  For to catch a whale—
All the water he had got
  Was in his mother's pail.

Simple Simon went to look
  If plums grew on a thistle;
He pricked his fingers very much,
  Which made poor Simon whistle.

He went to catch a dicky bird,
  And thought he could not fail
Because he'd got a little salt
  To put upon it's tail.

Then Simple Simon went-a-hunting,
  For to catch a hare.
He rode on a goat about the street,
  But could not find one there.

Simon made a great snowball,
  And brought it in to roast;
He laid it down before the fire,
  And soon the ball was lost.

Simple Simon went a-skating
  When the ice was thin,
And Simon was astonished quite

153

To find he tumbled in.

And Simon he would honey eat
Out of the mustard pot;
He bit his tongue until he cried:
"That was all the good he got."

Ten Little Indians

Ten little Indians going out to dine,
One choked his little self, and then there were Nine.

Nine little Indians crying at his fate,
One cried himself away, and then there were Eight.

Eight little Indians to travelling were given.
But one kicked the bucket, and then there were Seven.

Seven little Indians playing at their tricks,
One cut himself in halves, and then there were Six.

Six little Indians playing with a hive,
A bumble bee killed one, and then there were Five.

Five little Indians went in for law,
One got into Chancery, and then there were Four.

Four little Indians going out to sea,
A ref herring swallowed one, and then there were Three.

Three little Indians walking in the Zoo,
A big bear cuddled one, and then there were Two.

Two little Indians sitting in the sun,
One got frizzled up, and then there was One.

One little Indians living all alone,

He got married, and then there were None.

Jack the Giant Killer

Once upon a time there lived in Cornwall, England, a lad whose name was Jack, and who was very brave and knowing. At the same time there was a great Giant, twenty feet high and nine feet round, who lived in a cave, on an island near Jack's house. The Giant used to wade to the mainland and steal things to live upon, carrying five or six bullocks at once, and stringing sheep, pigs, and geese around his waist-band; and all the people ran away from him in fear, whenever they saw him coming.

Jack determined to destroy this Giant; so he got a pickaxe and shovel, and started in his boat on a dark evening; by the morning he had dug a pit deep and broad, then covering it with sticks and strewing a little mould over, to make it look like plain ground, he blew his horn so loudly that the Giant awoke, and came roaring towards Jack, calling him a villain for disturbing his rest, and declaring he would eat him for breakfast. He had scarcely said this when he fell into the pit. "Oh! Mr. Giant," says Jack, "where are you now? You shall have this for your breakfast." So saying, he struck him on the head so terrible blow with his pickaxe that the Giant fell dead to the bottom.

Just at this moment, the Giant's brother ran out roaring vengeance against Jack; but he jumped into his boat and pulled to the opposite shore, with the Giant after him, who caught poor Jack, just as he was landing, tied him down in his boat, and went in search of his provisions. During his absence, Jack contrived to cut a large hole in the bottom of the boat, and placed therein a piece of canvas. After having stolen some oxen, the Giant returned and pushed off the boat, when, having got fairly out to sea, Jack pulled the canvas from the hole, which caused the boat to fill and quickly capsize. The Giant roared and bellowed as he struggled in the water, but was very soon exhausted and drowned, while Jack dexterously swam ashore.

One day after this, Jack was sitting by a well fast asleep. A Giant named Blundebore, coming for water, at once saw and caught hold of him, and carried him to his castle. Jack was much frightened at seeing the heaps of bodies and bones strewed about. The Giant then confined him in an upper room over the entrance, and went for another Giant to breakfast off poor Jack. On viewing the room, he saw some strong ropes, and making a noose at one end, he put the other through a pulley which chanced to be over the window, and when the Giants were unfastening the gate he threw the noose over both their heads, and pulling it immediately, he contrived to choke them both. Then releasing three ladies who were confined in the castle, he departed well pleased.

About five or six months after, Jack was journeying through Wales, when, losing his way, he could find no place of entertainment, and was about giving up all hopes of obtaining shelter during the night when he came to a gate, and, on knocking, to his utter astonishment it was opened by a Giant, who did not seem so fierce as the others. Jack told him his distress, when the Giant invited him in, and, after giving him a hearty supper, showed him to bed. Jack had scarcely got into bed when he heard the Giant muttering to himself:

"Though you lodge with me this night,
You shall not see the morning light;
My club shall dash your brains out quite."

"Oh, Mr. Giant, is that your game?" said Jack to himself; "then I shall try and be even with you." So he jumped out of bed and put a large lump of wood there instead. In the middle of the night the Giant went into the room, and thinking it was Jack in the bed, he belaboured the wood most unmercifully; he then left the room, laughing to think how he had settled poor Jack. The following morning Jack went boldly into the Giant's room to thank him for the night's lodging. The Giant was startled at his appearance, and asked him how he slept, or if anything had disturbed him in the night? "Oh, no," says Jack, "nothing worth speaking about: I believe that a rat gave me a few slaps with his tail, but, being rather sleepy, I took no notice of it." The Giant wondered how Jack survived the terrific blows of his club, yet did not answer a word, but went and brought in two monstrous bowls of hasty pudding, placed one before Jack, and began eating the other himself. Determined to be revenged on the Giant somehow, Jack unbuttoned his leather provision bag inside his coat, and slyly filling it with hasty pudding, said, "I'll do what you can't." So saying, he took up a large knife, and ripping up the bag, let out the hasty pudding. The Giant, determined not to be outdone, seized hold of the knife, and saying, "I can do that," instantly ripped up his belly, and fell down dead on the spot.

After this Jack fought and conquered many giants, married the king's daughter and lived happily.

Jack and the Beanstalk

157

At some distance from London, in a small village, lived a widow and her son, whose name was Jack. He was a bold, daring fellow, ready for any adventure which promised fun or amusement. Jack's mother had a cow, of which she was very fond, and which, up to this time, had been their chief support. But as she had for some time past been growing poorer every year, she felt that now she must part with the cow. So she told Jack to take the cow to be sold, and he was to be sure to get a good round sum for her. On the road to market Jack met a butcher, who was carrying in his hat some things which Jack thought to be very pretty. The butcher saw how eagerly Jack eyed his beans, and said, "If you want to sell your cow, my fine fellow, I will give you this whole hatful of beans in exchange for her."

Jack was delighted; he seized the hat, and ran back home. Jack's mother was surprised to see him back so soon, and at once asked him for the money. But when Jack said he had sold the cow for a hatful of beans, she was so angry that she opened the window and threw them all out into the garden. When Jack rose up next morning he found that one of the beans had taken root, and had grown up, up, up, until its top was quite lost in the clouds. Jack resolved instantly to mount the Beanstalk. So up, up, up, he went till he had reached the very top. Looking round he saw at a distance a large house. Tired and weary, he crawled towards it and knocked on the door. The door was opened by a timid looking woman who started when she saw him, and besought him to run away as her husband was a cruel Giant who would eat him up if he found him there. But Jack begged so earnestly to be admitted that the woman, who was very kind-hearted, had pity on him, and so she brought him into the kitchen, and set before him on a table some bread, meat, and ale. Jack ate and drank, and soon felt quite refreshed. Presently the woman started and said, "My husband! quick, quick! he comes—he comes!" and opened the door to the oven and bid Jack jump in. The Giant was in a dreadful passion when he came in, and almost killed his wife by a blow which he aimed at her. He then began to sniff and smell—at last he roared out:

"Fee, fa, fi, fo, fum,
I smell the blood of an Englishman!
Be he alive, or be he dead,
I'll grind his bones to make me bread!"

His wife gave him an evasive answer, and proceeded to lay before him his supper. When the Giant could swallow no more, he called out to his wife to bring him his hen, which, after being brought, whenever the Giant said "Lay," the hen laid a golden egg. The Giant soon fell asleep, and Jack crept out softly and seized the hen, and made off without disturbing the Giant. Away ran Jack till he came to the Beanstalk; he was much sooner at the bottom of it now than at the top in the morning; and running to his mother he told all his adventure.

The hen laid as many golden eggs as Jack liked, and his mother before long had another cow and everything which she desired. A second time Jack climbed the Beanstalk, when he ran away with the Giant's bag of money. A third time Jack climbed the Beanstalk, and again gained admission to the Giant's house. He saw the Giant's wife, and asked her for a night's lodging. She at first said she could not let him into the house, but Jack begged so hard that at last she consented, and gave him some supper and put him to sleep in the copper boiler near the kitchen fireplace, where she thought the Giant would not find him.

When the Giant came in, his good nose served him in a moment: for he cried out "I smell fresh meat." Jack laughed at this, but it was no laughing matter; for the Giant looked all around the room, and even put his finger on the lid of the copper, till it seemed as if a stone of a hundredweight had fallen upon the lid. Just then his wife came in with a whole roasted bullock smoking hot, which the Giant sat down and ate for his supper, and then went down into the cellar, and drank about six gallons of Jamaica rum. The Giant now sat down and went to sleep, and Jack tried to run away with his golden harp, an instrument which, when the Giant said "play," played the most beautiful tunes. Now the harp was a fairy, and as soon as he touched it, it called out "Master!

Master!" so loud that the Giant awoke, but he was some time before he could understand what was the matter. He tried to run after Jack, but Jack got to the top of the beanstalk first. When he had descended a little way he looked up, and how great was his horror to see the huge hand of the Giant stretched down to seize him by the hair of the head! He slid and scrambled down the Beanstalk, hardly knowing how, and seeing the Giant just putting his feet over the top, he called out, "Quick, mother! A hatchet, a hatchet!" Jack seized it and chopped away at the beanstalk, when down it fell, bringing along with it the Giant. Jack instantly cut off his head. After this Jack and his mother lived very happily, and Jack was a great comfort to her in her old age.

Hop O' My Thumb

Once upon a time there was a woodman and his wife who had so many children that they did not know how to find food for them. So one night, when they were all in bed, the father told his wife that he thought they had better take them into the forest and lose them there. The youngest child, who was so very small that he was called Hop o' my Thumb, overheard his father, and as he was a very clever boy he made up his mind to find his way home again. So he went down to the brook very early the next morning, and filled his pocket with large smooth pebbles as white as snow. Bye-and-bye the woodman and his wife told the children that they might go with them into the wood to have a good game of play. They were all glad except Hop o' my Thumb who knew what his father intended. So they set out; the woodman and his wife first, then the boys, and last Hop o' my Thumb, who sprinkled pebbles all the way they went.

They spent a merry day; but bye-and-bye the parents stole away, and left the children all by themselves. They were very much frightened when they missed their father and mother, and called loudly for them; but when

Hop o' my Thumb told them what he had heard, and how they could find their way home by following the track of the pebbles, which marked the way they had come, they set out, and reached home safely, and their father and mother pretended to be very glad to see them back.

But soon after they again resolved to lose their children, if possible, in the forest. This time all the boys feared that they should be left behind, and the eldest brother said he would take some peas to sprinkle, to mark the pathway that led home. By-and-bye the cruel parents stole away, and left the little ones in the dark wood. At first they did not care, for they thought that they could easily find their way home; but, alas! when they looked for the line of peas which they had sprinkled, they found they were all gone—the wood-pigeons had eaten them up, and the children were lost in the wood. Holding each-others' hands and crying sadly they walked on to seek a place to sleep in. By-and-bye they came to a giant's castle, where they were taken in, and told that they might sleep in the nursery with the seven baby daughters of the giant, who were lying all in a row in one bed, with gold crowns on their heads. Hop o' my Thumb thought it was strange that the giant should be so kind, as he had been told that the ogres eat children. So in the night he got up softly and took off the little giant-esses' crowns and put them on his brothers' heads and his own, and lay down again. It was lucky for him that he did so, for in the night the giant came up in the dark to kill the boys, that they might be ready for the next day's breakfast. He felt the beds, and finding the crowns on the boy's heads took them for his own children, left them and went to the other bed and cut off the heads of his daughters instead. Then he went back to bed. Directly he was gone, Hop o' my Thumb and his brothers got up, stole down stairs, opened the door and fled away from the castle. But they did not go far. Hop o' my Thumb knew that the giant would come after them in his seven-league boots. So they got into a hole in the side of a hill and hid. Very soon after, they saw the giant coming at a great pace in his wonderful boots; but he took

161

such long steps that he passed right over their heads. They were afraid to move out till they had seen him go home again. So they remained quietly where they were.

By-and-bye the giant, who had been many miles in an hour, came back tired, and lay down on the hill-side and fell asleep. Then Hop o' my Thumb got out of the hole, and pulled off the giant's seven-league boots, and put them on his own feet. They fitted him exactly, for being fairy boots they would grow large or small just as one liked. He then got his brothers out of the hole, took them in his boots, marched for home, and although it was a great distance, got there in almost no time, but when he arrived at the house his father and mother were not there. He then hastened to make inquiries for them, and found they had been suspected of murdering their children,—who had all disappeared suddenly—that they had owned to leaving them in the wood, and that they were to be put to death for their crime. "We must go and save them," he said. So he took his brothers into the seven-league boots, and set out to the place where their parents were in prison. They arrived only just in time, for the guards were bringing out the woodsman and his wife to put them to death. Hop o' my Thumb took off the boors, and all the children called out, "We are alive! we are alive! Do not kill our mother and father."

Then there was great joy. The woodman and his wife were set free, and embraced their children. They had repented their wickedness, and were never unkind and cruel any more; and Hop o' my Thumb kept them all in comfort by going on errands for the king in his seven-league boots.

Tom Thumb

In the days of good King Arthur there lived a ploughman and his wife who wished very much to have a son; so the man went to Merlin, the enchanter, and asked him to let him have a child, even, if it were "*no bigger than his thumb.*" "Go home and you will find one," said Merlin; and when the man came back to his house he found his wife nursing a very, very, wee baby, who in four minutes grew to the size of the ploughman's thumb, and never grew any more. The fairy queen came to his christening and named him "Tom Thumb." She then dressed him nicely in a shirt of spider's web, and a doublet and hose of thistledown.

One day, while Tom's mother was making a plum-pudding, Tom stood on the edge of the bowl, with a lighted candle in his hand, that she might see to make it properly. Unfortunately, however, while her back was turned, Tom fell into the bowl, and his mother not missing him, stirred him up in the pudding, and put it and him into the pot. Tom no sooner felt the hot water than

163

he danced about like man; the woman was nearly frightened out of her wits to see the pudding come out of the pot and jump about, and she was glad to give it to a tinker who was passing that way.

The tinker was delighted with his present; but as he was getting over a style, he happened to sneeze very hard, and Tom called out from the middle of the pudding, "Hallo, Pickens!" which so terrified the tinker that he threw the pudding into the field, and scampered away as fast as he could. The pudding tumbled to pieces in the fall, and Tom, creeping out, went home to his mother, who was in great affliction because she could not find him. A few days afterwards Tom went with his mother into the fields to milk the cows, and for fear he should be blown away by the wind, she tied him to a thistle with a small piece of thread. Very soon after a cow ate up the thistle and swallowed Tom Thumb. His mother was in sad grief again; but Tom scratched and kicked in the cow's throat till she was glad to throw him out of her mouth again.

One day Tom Thumb went ploughing with his father, who gave him a whip made of barley straw, to drive the oxen with; but an eagle, flying by, caught him up in his beak, and carried him to the top of a great giant's castle. The giant would have eaten Tom up; but the fairy dwarf scratched and bit his tongue and held on by his teeth till the giant in a passion took him out again and threw him into the sea, when a very large fish swallowed him up directly. The fish was caught soon after and sent as a present to King Arthur, and when the cook opened it there was Tom Thumb inside. He was carried to the king, who was delighted with the little man.

The king ordered a little chair to be made, in order that Tom might sit on his table, and also a palace of gold a span high, with a door an inch wide, for little Tom to live in. He also gave him a coach drawn by six small mice.

This made the queen angry, because she had no a new coach too; therefore, resolving to ruin Tom, she complained to the king that he had spoken insolently to her. The king sent for him. Tom, to escape his fury, crept into an empty snail shell, and lay there till he was almost starved; when peeping out of the shell he saw a fine butterfly settled on the ground: he now ventured out, and getting on it, the butterfly took wing, and mounted into the air with little Tom on his back. Away he flew from field to field, from tree to tree, till at last he flew to the king's court. The king, queen, and nobles all strove to catch the butterfly but could not. At length poor Tom, having neither bridle or saddle, slipped from his seat and fell into a pool of water, where he was found nearly drowned. The queen vowed he should be beheaded, and while the scaffold was getting ready, he was secured in a mouse-trap; when the cat seeing something stir supposing it to be a mouse, patted the trap about till she broke it, and set Tom at liberty.

Sometimes Tom rode out on a mouse for a horse. One day a big black met him along the road, and wanted to kill the mouse. Tom jumped off the mouse's back, drew his sword, and fought the cat, and made her run away.

In order to show his courage and please the queen, the new knight undertook a terrible adventure.

In one corner of the palace garden there was found a great black spider, of which the lady was very much afraid.

Tom undertook to kill this insect; so he took a gold button for a shield, and his sharp needle-sword, and went out to attack the spider; the knights went also, to witness the combat.

Tom drew his sword and fought valiantly, but the spider's poisonous breath overcame him.

King Arthur and his whole Court went into mourning for little Tom Thumb. They buried him under a rose-bush, and raised a nice white marble monument over his grave.

Mr. Brown, the grocer, having nearly emptied a cask of sugar in front of his shop, a number of naughty boys, seeing his back turned, commenced to steal some. Mr. Brown, spying them through the window, came out, and the reader can see what happened—A bystander informs us that muttered howls of agony arose from the cask, and all the boys' interest in sugar was at an end.

Boy Who Stole Out Without Leave

I remember, I remember,
  When I was a little Boy,
One fine morning in September
  Uncle brought me home a toy.

I remember how he patted
  Both my cheeks in his kindliest mood;
"Then," said he, "you little Fat-head,
  There's a top because you're good."

Grandmamma—a shrewd observer—

I remember gazed upon
My new top, and said with fervour,
  "Oh! how kind of Uncle John."

While mamma, my form caressing—
  In her eyes the tear-drop stood,
Read me this fine moral lesson,
  "See what comes of being good."

I remember, I remember,
  On a wet and windy day,
One cold morning in December,
  I stole out and went to play.

I remember Billy Hawkins
  Came, and with his pewter squirt
Squibbed my pantaloons and stockings
  Till they were all over dirt.

To my mother for protection
  I ran, quaking every limb;
She exclaim'd, with fond affection,
  "Gracious goodness! look at him!"

Pa cried, when he saw my garment,
  'Twas a newly purchased dress—
"Oh! you nasty little varment,
  How came you in such a mess?"

Then he caught me by the collar,
  —Cruel only to be kind—
And to my exceeding dolour,
  Gave me—several slaps behind.

Grandmamma, while I yet smarted,
  As she saw my evil plight,
Said—'twas rather stony-hearted—
  "Little rascal! serve him right!"

I remember, I remember,

From that sad and solemn day,
Never more in dark December
  Did I venture out to play.

And the moral which they taught, I
  Well remember: thus they said—
"Little Boys, when they are naughty,
  Must be whipp'd and sent to bed!"

Dirty Jack

  There was one little Jack,
  Not very long back,
And 't is said to his lasting disgrace,
  That he never was seen
  With his hands at all clean,
Nor yet ever clean was his face.

  His friends were much hurt
  To see so much dirt
And often and well did they scour,
  But all was in vain,
  He was dirty again
Before they had done it an hour.

  When to wash he was sent,
  He reluctantly went
With water to splash himself o'er,
  But he left the black streaks
  Running down both his cheeks,
And made them look worse than before.

  The pigs in the dirt
  Could not be more expert
Than he was, in grubbing about;
  And people have thought
  This gentleman ought

To be made with four legs and a snout.

The idle and bad
 May, like to this lad,
Be dirty and black, to be sure.
 But good boys are seen
 To be decent and clean,
Although they be ever so poor.

Throwing Stones

Johnny Jones, why do you do it?
Those who throw stones
Surely will rue it;
Little of pleasure, evil may flow,
Mischief past measure comes of a blow.

Yes, yes! stone flinging.
Laugh as you may,
Woe may be bringing
Upon you some day.

Someone is watching,
Armed by the law,
Truncheon from pocket
Soon he will draw.
Off he will march you—
Dreadful to think!—to a dark prison:
Light through a chink,
Bread without butter, water for drink.

Dirty Dick

Dirty, noisy, mischievous Dick,
 Struggled and tore, and wanted to fight
Susan, the nurse, who in the bath

169

Began to wash him on Saturday night.

Her hair he tried to pull up by the roots,
  The water he splashed all over the floor,
Which ran downstairs, and one night made
  A terrible slop at the parlour door.

To give him advice was a waste of time,
  So his father resolved to try a stick,
And never since then has he been called
  Dirty, noisy, mischievous Dick.

Boy That Stole the Apples

A boy looked over a wall,
  And spied some lovely apples;
"But," says he "the tree is tall,
  And belongs to 'Grumpie Chapples!'
Still, I think some could be got
  By a climbing lad like me:
I'll try and steal a lot,
  So here goes up the tree."

The wall he then got over,
  And up the tree he went;
But Chapples, mowing clover,
  Espied the wicked gent.
He let him fill his school-bag—
  Get over the wall again;
Rushed up and played at touch-tag,
  Which surprised him much, and then:—

Look at the Picture!!!

Mischievous Fingers

Pretty little fingers,
  Wherefore were they made?
Like ten smart young soldiers,
  All in pink arrayed.

Apt and quick obedient
  To your lightest thought,
Doing in an instant
  Everything they're taught.

'T was for play or study,
  Pen to wield or ball;
Kite, top, needle, pencil,
  Prompt at parents' call.

Picking, poking, soiling
  Costly things and dear,
Wrecking, cracking, spoiling
  All that they come near.

Thus 't was with Robert Chivers,
  Brandishing a swish,
Broke a vase to shivers
  Filled with silver fish.

"Tick, tick" says the Dutch clock.
  Robert fain would know
How it's pendulum swinging
  Made it's wheels go.

Who not ask? No! foolish
  Robert takes a stick,
Pokes and breaks the clock, which
  Ceases soon to tick.

"Puff, puff," sighs the bellows.
  Robert wants to find,
Yet he will not ask, whence

Comes it's stock of wind.

With a knife upripping,
 Finds them void and flat.
Ah! be sure a whipping
 Robert caught for that.

The Boy who Played with Fire

Listen about a naughty boy
Who might have been a parent's joy,
But that he had a strong desire
To always meddle with fire.

One day when his mamma went out,
She said "Mind, dear, what you're about:
With your nice books and playthings stay,
And with the fire, oh! do not play."

But as soon as his mamma was gone,
And this bad boy left all alone,
Thought he, "In spite of all ma says,
Now we'll have a glorious blaze.

"No one is by, 't is quickly done,
And oh! 't will be such famous fun."
Quick then about the hearth he strewed
Some scraps of paper and of wood.

Then lighted them and drew them out,
And with them, laughing, ran about.
But soon he changed his merry note—
The flames, alas, had caught his coat,
And every moment, mounting higher,
His body soon was all on fire;
And though he screamed with shriek and shout,

No one came near to put it out:
So it happened, sad to say,
That boy was burned to death that day.

Wicked Willie

Willie was a wicked boy,
  Snubbed his poor old mother;
Willie was a dreadful boy,
  Quarrelled with his brother;
Willie was a spiteful boy,
  Often pinched his sister,
Once he gave her such a blow,
  Raised a great big blister!

Willy was a sulky boy,
  Sadly plagued his cousins,
Often broke folks' window panes,
  Throwing stones by dozens,
Often worried little girls,
  Bullied smaller boys,
Often broke their biggest dolls,
  Jumped upon their toys.

If he smelled a smoking tart,
  Willie longed to steal it;
If he saw a pulpy peach,
  Willie tried to peel it;
Could he reach a new plum-cake,
  Greedy Willie picked it,
If he spied a pot of jam,
  Dirty Willie licked it.

If he saw a poor old dog,
  Wicked Willie whacked it;
If it had a spot of white,
  Silly Willy blacked it,
If he saw a sleeping cat,

Horrid Willie kicked it;
If he caught a pretty moth,
　Cruel Willie pricked it.

If his pony would not trot,
　Angry Willie thrashed it;
If he saw a clinging snail,
　Thoughtless Willie smashed it;
If he found a sparrow's nest,
　Unkind Willie hit it.
All the mischief ever done,
　Folks knew Willie did it.

No one liked that horrid boy,
　Can you wonder at it?
None who saw his ugly head,
　Ever tried to pat it.
No one ever took him for a ride—
　Folks too gladly skipped him.
No one ever gave him bats or balls,
　No one ever "tipped" him.

No one taught him how to skate,
　Or to play at cricket;
No one helped him if he stuck
　In a prickly thicket.
Oh no! for the boys all said
　Willie loved to tease them,
And that if he had the chance,
　Willie would not please them.

And they shunned him every one,
　And they would not know him,
And their games and picture-books
　They would never show him,
And their tops they would not spin,
　If they saw him near them,
And they treated him with scorn
　Till he learned to fear them.

175

They all left him to himself,
  And he was so lonely,
But of course it was his fault,
  Willie's own fault only.
If a boy's a wicked boy,
  Shy of him folks fight then,
If it makes him dull and sad,
  Why, it serves him right then!

This is the Naughty Boy
who would go making Mud
Pies, and get his nice new
clothes all over mud.

He said he would be Good,
but he got into the mud,
and was a Naughty, Bad,
Bad Boy!!!

The Wicked, Rude, Bad, Naughty, Cross, Nasty, Bold, Dirty-faced Boy

Boys, stop your noise! Girls, stop your jumping and skipping!
While I tell you about a bad boy, who often deserves a whipping.
If this boy to you were named, to speak to him you'd feel ashamed,
So to-day I'll only say—He's a wicked, rude, bad, naughty, cross,
nasty, bold, dirty-faced boy!

I won't tell you his age, nor the colour of his hair,
Nor say anything about the clothes he sometimes does wear;
You never see them neat and clean, and seldom without a tear,
Because—He's a wicked, rude, bad, naughty, cross, nasty, bold,
dirty-faced boy!

If he's sent on a message, such a long time he stops,
To pelt stones at Chinamen, and stare in the shops;
Running behind drays, and wastes time so many ways,
That when he gets home his mother says—
Oh you wicked, rude, bad, naughty, cross, nasty, bold, dirty-faced
boy!

If his mother gives him lolly, cake, piece of beef or mutton,
In a corner he'll eat it by himself, he's such a nasty, greedy glutton.
And he'll smug from his playmates a marble, top or button,
That scarcely any one can with him have any fun,
Because—He's a wicked, rude, bad, naughty, cross, nasty, bold,
dirty-faced boy!

He's been going to school for years, I can't tell you how long,
If you ask him to spell three words, two are sure to be wrong;
If you saw the dirty books and broken slate which to him belong,
You'd easily guess from such a mess that—
He's a wicked, rude, bad, naughty, cross, nasty, bold, dirty-faced boy!

You can't believe a word he says, he tells so many lies.
He's such a coward, he'll only hit a girl or boy much less than his
size,
But if he gets a blow himself, he howls, bawls, yelps, and cries,
That anyone who sees him never tries to please him,

177

COLE

Because—He's a wicked, rude, bad, naughty, cross, nasty, bold, dirty-faced boy!

He won't play any game without being always cheating,
I often wonder how he so many times escapes a beating,
And he never says grace before or after eating.
He's scarcely better in the least than a brute beast,
Because—He's a wicked, rude, bad, naughty, cross, nasty, bold, dirty-faced boy!

What school he goes to at present I won't tell,
But I mean to watch him, and if he don't mind and behave well,
I'll go to every school and ring a little bell,
I'll make a great noise, and show all the girls and boys
This wicked, rude, bad, naughty, cross, nasty, bold, dirty-faced boy!

This is the Man who picked the Bad Boy out of the Mud.

Little Rascal Chow-Chow
(The Boy That Ran Away)

There was a little Chinese Boy,
  That ran away from home—
"Ha! ha!" he said, "I'll see the world
  And through the streets I'll roam.

"I won't go any more to school,
  Or go so soon to bed,
Nor yet be scolded if I choose
  To stand upon my head."

So little Rascal ran away,
  His tail flew in the wind;
He thought not of his good mamma
  Who was so very kind:

He knew she could not follow him
  Along the crowded street,
Because mammas in China have
  Such very tiny feet.

Now, as he went along he saw
  Such strange and lovely sights,
Such pretty painted houses—
  Such tops! and oh! such kites!

He saw so many gilded toys,
  and ivory things so white,
That he forgot about the time,
  Until he found it night.

Ah! then he saw such fireworks!
  They glistened in his eyes;
The crackers and the lanterns too
  Quite took him by surprise.

He listened to the music of
  The fiddle and the gong,

179

And felt that it was jolly, though
  He knew that it was wrong.

But after that he began to think
  Things were not so bright;
The men were going, and there came
  The watchman of the night;

And sleep was stealing over him,
  He scarce could lift his head,
So he lay on the cold, cold stones,
  Which served him for a bed.

Little Rascal Chow-Chow
  Woke up with early light,
And wandered far away from where
  He passed the dreary night;

He was so very worn and cold,
  And sadly wanted food,
So he sat upon a well
  In not a pleasant mood.

He saw the well was very deep,
  The water too was clear,
And soon he saw a golden fish
  That looked so very near.

He stretched his hand to catch the fish;
  But oh! how sad to tell,
He tumbled over and he sank
  To the bottom of the well.

Some other boys were playing there
  And saw him disappear,
And ran along the road to see
  If anyone was near.

A Great BIG Market Gardener,
  Was soon upon the ground,

And caught our little Rascal up,
  Who soon would have been drowned.

The boys began to jeer at him,
  For he was very wet;
They pulled his dripping tail, and called
  Him names that I forget.

One took his wooden shoes away,
  Another took his hat,
And someone said, "It serves him right,"
  Now only think of that!

When little Rascal ran away,
  His tail flew in the wind;
But when our Rascal turned again
  His tail hung down behind.

He wandered past the painted shops,
  Where they put up the tea,
And I am sure the boys at school
  Were happier than he.

Poor Rascal Chow was very tired,
  And very sore his feet,
When his mother saw him from
  The corner of a street.

She said he was a wicked boy,
  And ought to have a smack!
And yet I think she loved him more
  Because she'd got him back.

Now when I see a Chinaman,
  And that is every day,
I wonder if he is, grown up,
  The boy that ran away.

But what I still think most about
  When I this story tell,

Is the GREAT BIG Market Gardener
That raised him from the well

From Calvert's Australian Toy Books

That Nice Boy

"Nice child—very nice child," observed an old gentleman, crossing to the other side of the car and addressing the mother of the boy who had just hit him in the eye with a wad of paper. "How old are you, my son?"

"None of your business," replied the youngster, taking aim at another passenger.

"Fine boy," smiled the old man, as the parent regarded her offspring with pride. "A remarkably fine boy. What is your name, my son?"

"Puddin' Tame!" shouted the youngster, with a giggle at his own wit.

"I thought so," continued the old man, pleasantly. "If you had given me three guesses at it, that would have been the first one I would have struck on. Now, Puddin', you can blow those things pretty straight, can't you?"

"You bet!" squealed the boy, delighted at the compliment. "See me take that old fellow over there!"

"No, no!" exclaimed the old gentleman, hastily. "Try it on the old woman I was sitting with. She has boys of her own, and she won't mind."

"Can't you hit the lady for the gentleman, Johnny?" asked the fond parent.

Johnny cleverly landed the pellet on the end of the old woman's nose.

But she did mind it, and rising in her wrath soared down on the small boy like a hawk. She put him over the line, reversed him, ran him backwards, till he didn't know which end of him was front, and finally dropped him into the lap of the scared mother, with a benediction whereof the purport was that she'd be back in a moment to skin him alive.

"She didn't seem to like it, Puddin'," smiled the old gentleman, softly. "She's a perfect stranger to me; but I understand she is the matron of an Orphans' Home, and I thought she would like a little fun; but I was mistaken."

And the old man smiled sweetly as he went back to his seat. He was sorry for the poor little boy, but he couldn't help it.

A Wicked Boy

Of all the small boys in our town
  That Jones boy was the worst,
And if the "bad man" came around
  He'd take that Jones boy first.

One day he slipped away from home
  And went out for a skate
Down on a deep and dangerous pond
  Beyond the garden gate.

His mother missed him after a while,
  And thought he'd gone to skate;
And running to the fatal pond,
  She found she was too late.

For there, upon the cruel ice,
  Beyond an air-hole wide,
She saw his pretty little hat,
  And a mitten by it's side.

He was her boy, and all the love
  That fills a mother's heart
Came forth in tears and sobs and moans
  Beyond the strength of art.

She called the neighbours quick to come,
  They scraped along the ground;
Beneath the water and the ice—

The boy could no be found.

At last their search was given up
  Until a thaw should come;
The mother's sobs began afresh,
  Her sorrow was not dumb.

They turned to leave the fatal pool,
  A voice came clear and free—
"Hallo! If you want Frankie Jones,
  You'll find him up this tree."

And so it was—the mother's tears
  Were changed to smiles of joy;
But gracious heaven, how she spanked
  Her darling, fair-haired boy!

L'Envoi

Cooley's Boy

The boy not only preys on my melon-patch and fruit trees, and upon those of my neighbours, but he has an extraordinary aptitude for creating a disturbance in whatever spot he happens to be. Only last Sunday he caused such a terrible commotion in church that the services had to be suspended for several minutes until he could be removed. The interior of the edifice was painted and varnished recently, and I suppose one of the workers must have left a clot of varnish upon the back of Cooley's pew, which is directly across the aisle from mine. Cooley's boy was the only representative of the family at church upon that day, and he amused himself during the earlier portions of the service by kneeling upon the seat and communing with Dr. Jones' boy, who occupied the pew immediately in the rear. Sometimes, when young Cooley would resume a proper position, Jones's boy would stir him up afresh by slyly pulling his hair, whereupon Cooley would wheel about and menace Jones with his fist in a manner which betrayed utter indifference to the proprieties of the place and the occasion, as well as the presence of the congregation. When Cooley finally sank into a condition of repose, he placed his head, most unfortunately, directly against the lump of undried varnish, while he amused himself by reading the commandments and the other scriptural texts upon the wall behind the pulpit.

In a few moments he attempted to move, but the varnish had mingled with his hair, and it held him securely. After making one or two desperate but ineffectual efforts to release himself, he became very angry; and supposing that Jones's boy was holding him, he shouted:

"Leg go o' my hair! Leg go o' my hair, I tell you!"

The clergyman paused just as he was entering upon consideration of "secondly," and the congregation looked around in amazement, in time to perceive young Cooley, with his head against the back of the pew, aiming dreadful blows over his shoulder with his fist at some unseen person behind him. And with every thrust he exclaimed:

"I'll smash yer nose after church! I'll go for you, Bill Jones, when I ketch you alone! Leg go o' my hair, I tell you, or I'll knock the stuffin' out o' yer," etc, etc.

Meanwhile, Jones's boy sat up at the very end of his pew, far away from Cooley, and looked as solemn as if the sermon had made a deep impression upon him.

Max Adeler

185

Jack The Glutton

"Do look at those pigs, as they lay in the straw,"
  Little Richard said to his papa;
"They keep eating longer than ever I saw,
  What nasty fat gluttons they are!"

"I see they are feasting" his father replied,
  "They eat a great deal I allow;
But let us remember, before we deride,
  'Tis the nature, my dear, of a sow.

"But when a great boy, such as you, my dear Dick,
  Does nothing but eat all day
And keeps sucking things till he makes himself sick,
  What a glutton! indeed, we may say.

"When plumcake and sugar forever he picks,
  And sweetmeats, and comfits, and figs;
Pray let him get rid of his own nasty tricks,
  And then he may laugh at the pigs."

Tom the Dainty Boy

Never be dainty and throw food away;
'Tis sinful, as you must have heard many say;
Besides, you yourself may require food some day,
  Though well fed.

So don't smell your plate and turn over your food,
And doubt if it's wholesome, or pleasant, or good;
Such conduct is not only senseless,—but rude
  And ill-bred.

There was a young boy, who so dainty became,
That whether his dinner was fish, flesh or game,
He turned up his nose at them all, just the same,
  And would cry,

"I cannot eat this,"—and, "I do not like that;"—
"This chicken's too lean,"—and "That mutton's too fat;
The dog he may eat it up all, or the cat,
  But not I.

The consequence was that he soon became thin;
His bones they stuck out, and his cheeks they sunk in,
And his hands were not stronger nor thicker than tin,
  If so strong.

And his legs grew as slender as little hat-pegs,

187

And almost as small was his waist as his legs;
And he looked like the laths that are fastened round kegs,
   Thin and long.

And thinner, and thinner, and thinner he grew,
A shadow had been rather fat, of the two;
In fact, you might easily look him right through,
   If you tried.

And when he was quite the skeleton grown,
As weak as a reed, and as cold as a stone
He fell all to pieces, and with a faint groan,
   So he died.

Boy that robbed the Bird's nest

"To-whit! To-whit! To-whee!
Will you listen to me?
Who stole four eggs I laid,
And the nice nest I made?"

"Not I," said the cow. "Oh, no;
Such a thing I'd never do;
I gave you a wisp of hay,
But didn't take your nest away."

"Coo, coo! said the dove,
I'll speak a word my love;
Who stole that pretty nest
From a little red-breast?"

"Not I," said the sheep. "Oh, no.
I wouldn't treat a poor bird so;
I gave wool the nest to line,
But the nest was none of mine."

"Caw! Caw!" cried the crow,
"I should like to know
What thief took away
A bird's nest to-day."

"Cluck! Cluck!" said the hen,
Don't ask me again!
Why I hav'nt a chick
Would do such a trick.

We all gave her a feather,
And she wove them together;
I'd scorn to intrude
On her and her brood."

"Chirr-a-whirr! Chirr-a-whirr!
We will make a great stir;
Let us find out his name,
And all cry for shame!"

"I would not rob a bird,"
Said little Mary Green;

189

"I think I never heard
Of anything so mean."

"'Tis very cruel too,"
Said little Alice Neil:
"I wonder if he knew
How sad the bird would feel?"

A little boy hung down his head,
And hid his face, so crimson red;
For he stole that pretty nest
From little robin redbreast;
And he felt so full of shame,
I do not like to tell his name.

But during next week
Dressed in his Sunday best
This boy set out to seek
All for another nest.

He robbed a nest up high,
Suspended in a tree;
Two birds came through the sky,
What happened you can see.

Cruel Boy

What! go to see the kittens drowned
  On purpose in the yard!
I did not think there could be found
  A little heart so hard.

Poor kittens! No more pretty play
  With pussy's wagging tail:
Why! I'd go far enough away
  Before I'd see the pail.

Poor things! the little child that can

Be pleased to go and see,
Most likely, when he grows a man,
A cruel man will be.

And many a wicked thing he'll do
Because his heart is hard:
A great deal worse than killing you,
Poor kittens in the yard.

Tyrannical Pat

What became of tyrannical Pat,
Who pelted the dog, and beat the cat,
Why, puss scratched his face and tore his hat;
And Dash knocked him over as flat as a mat.
Mind that!

The little boy who bit his Nails

See here a naughty boy, John Thales,
Who had a shocking way
Of picking at his finger nails,
And biting them all day.
And though he had, like other boys,
Both soldiers, kites and drums,
He liked, much better than these toys,
His fingers and his thumbs.

Boy who tore his Hat

Above on a chair, a little boy sat,
For he had torn his nice new hat;
And so was punished for doing that.

191

Thief Charley

Charley, Charley, stole the barley
  Out of the baker's shop;
The baker came out, and gave him a clout,
  And made that Charley hop.

Snooks' Patent Whipping Machine for Flogging Naughty Boys in School.
"The Snooks' Whipping Machine has proved a total failure."—"Times."

Snook's Patent Whipping Machine for Flogging Naughty Boys in School

"The Snooks' Whipping Machine has proved a total failure."—"Times."

Declaration of a Distracted Schoolmaster.

A year ago I took charge of a school of 1000 boys. They were a very bad lot indeed, and I could do nothing

with them. Being of a mild disposition, I attempted to
reason with them; but I might as well have reasoned
with the pigs. I then thought of punishing them, but that
was a big task, and, besides, what mode of punishment
should I adopt? In my utmost perplexity I wrote to Professor Wilderspin—a great authority on the management
of boys—and he wrote as follows:

"Nearly all boys can be managed by an intelligent
schoolmaster
without punishment, but in a few cases it seems impossible to do
without it. In every large school in England, Ireland, and
Scotland
some corporal punishment is used, and some must continue to be used
as long as very vicious children continue to exist, or as
long as
parents spoil their children by over indulgence or by
wilful
criminal neglect before they send them to school.—
Yours truly,
Professor Wilderspin."

I then wrote to twenty-seven of the principal head-
masters in the world, and the following are the
replies:—

From the High School of Eton wrote head-master, Mr.
Squeers:
"If they don't behave as they should do, why, soundly
box their ears."
From the Grammar School of Harrow wrote head-
master, Mr. Phfool:
"If they do not behave themselves, expel them from the
school."
From the Training School of Rugby wrote head-master,
Mr Wist:
"Just take a handful of their hair, and give a sharp, short
twist."
From the College School of Oxford wrote Professor
Rarey Hook:
"Instead of nearly killing, overawe them with a look."

From the Bible School of Cambridge wrote Professor
William Brying:
"Well whip them with a birchen rod, and never mind
their crying."
From the Blue Coat School of London wrote Professor
Rupert Gower:
"At arm's length make them hold a book the space of
half-an-hour."
From the Naval School of Liverpool wrote head-master
Mr. Jointer:
"Just rap them on the knuckles with a common teacher's
pointer."
From the People's School of Manchester wrote head-
master Mr. Flowers:
"Make them kneel down as still as death for just about
two hours."
From the Infant School of Birmingham wrote Professor
Dory Heller:
"Just put on them a fool's cap, marked 'dunce,' 'thief,' or
'story-teller'."
From the Charity school of Sheffield wrote head-master,
Mr. Clay:
"If the boys are disobedient, do not let them out to play."
From the Gentleman's School at Brighton wrote Profes-
sor Robert Flask:
"If the boys will act unruly, why, just make them do a
task."
From the National School of Bristol wrote Professor
Mark Groom:
"If the boys are extra naughty, shut them in a dark
room."
From the District School of Edenburgh wrote head-
master, Mr. Glass
"The naughty boys should all be sent to the bottom of
the class."
From the Mixed School of Glasgow wrote Professor
Duncan Law:
"To keep a proper kind of school, just use the three-
tailed taw."
From the Latin School of Dublin wrote Professor Patrick
Clayrence:

"If the boys are very bad boys, write a letter to their parents."
From the Mission School, Calcutta, wrote the Rev. Mr. Mac Look:
"Try them by a boy jury, write the verdict in a blackbook."
From the Lyceum of New York wrote Professor Henry Bothing:
"Take your delinquent boys one hour and make them sit on nothing."
From the Public School, Chicago, wrote head-master, Mr. Norrids:
"If they will not behave themselves, why, just you slap their foreheads."
From, the Academy of San Francisco wrote head-master, Mr. Power:
"Make them stoop and hold their fingers on the floor for just an hour."
From the Mormon School of Utah wrote Professor Orson Pratt:
"First strip and make them fast, and then just use the little cat."
From the King's College, Lisbon, wrote Professor Don Cassiers:
"If you want to make them good boys, pull, pinch, and twist their ears."
From the Cadet's School of Paris wrote Professor Monsieur Sour:
"Just make them hold their hands above their heads for one full hour."
From the Royal School of Amsterdam wrote Professor Vander Tooler:
"If they will not behave themselves, just trounce them with a ruler."
From the Model School of Pekin wrote Professor Cha Han Coo:
"Just put their hands into the stocks and beat with a bamboo."
From the Normal School of Moscow wrote Professor Ivan Troute:
"To make your boys the best of boys, why, just use the

knout."

From the Muslim School of Cairo wrote the Mufti, Pasha Saido:

"Upon the bare soles of their feet give them the basti-
nado."

From the Common School of Berlin wrote Professor
Von de Rind:

"There's nothing like the old, old way that ever could I
find;

Just lay them right across your knee and cane them well
behind.

I've only just been speaking mit mine goot frien', Doctor
Whistim,

And he says that it does no harm, but is felt throughout
the system."

At last, as I was thinking deep how puzzling all this
looks,

I received a tempting offer from a certain Mr. Snooks.

His "great machine to whip with speed" I brought with
flusteration,

But to see just how it did succeed you view the illustra-
tion.

**And then look at "Professor Cole's Gentle Per-
suader." next page.**

Cole's Patent Whipping Machine for Flogging Naughty Boys in School.

Cole's Patent Whipping Machine for Flogging Naughty Boys in School

Testimonial from a Schoolmaster
(To Mr. Cole, Book Arcade, Melbourne)

SIR—Your Patent Flogger is a "keen"
Success as a labor-saving machine;
'Twill yet be held in great esteem,
Already 'tis the Poet's theme;
It's the greatest patent that's ever been
In or out of a schoolroom seen;
And as you have got it to go by steam,
School-life will now be all serene.

I have not had a bad boy remaining now, but before I used your machine they used to be a frightful lot of young scamps. For instance, in my school of 1000, the first day the machine was introduced, 741 were punished for various misdeeds, and 103 for single offences, were flogged as follows:—

John Hawking, for talking

197

William Winning, for grinning
George Highing, for crying
Edward Daring, for swearing
Henry Wheeling, for stealing
Peter Bitting, for spitting
Robert Hocking, for smoking
Frederick Mention, for inattention
Joseph Footing, for pea-shooting
Luke Jones, for throwing stones
Matthew Sauter, for squirting water
Nicholas Storms, for upsetting forms
Reuben Wrens, for spoiling pens
Samuel Jinks, for spilling ink
Simon McLeod, for laughing aloud
Timothy Stacies, for making faces
Victor Bloomers, for taking lunars
Vincent James, for calling names
Caleb Hales, for telling tales
Daniel Padley, for writing badly
David Jessons, for cribbing lessons
Edmond Gate, for coming late
Ezra Lopen, for leaving the door open
Edwin Druent, for playing the truant
Charles Case, for leaving his place
Ernest Jewell, for eating during school
Coo Ah Hi, for using a shanghai
Francis Berindo, for breaking a window
Harold Tate, for breaking his slate
Isaac Joys, for making noise
Jacob Crook, for tearing his book
Christopher Moyes, for teasing other boys
Elisha Sewell, for bolting from school
Conrad Draper, for throwing chewed paper
Ebenezer Good, for telling a falsehood
Felix Snooks, for coming without books
Cyril Froude, for speaking too loud
Elijah Rowe, for speaking too low
Gregory Meek, for refusing to speak
Hannibal Hartz, for throwing paper darts
Horace Poole, for whistling in school
Hubert Shore, for slamming the door

Jesse Blane, for hiding the cane
Jonah Platts, for hiding boys' hats
Aaron Esk, for cutting the desk
Abner Rule, for sleeping in school
Adam Street, for changing his seat
Albert Mayne, for splitting the teacher's cane
Alexander Tressons, for reading during other lessons
Alfred Hoole, for eating lollies in school
Ambrose Hooke, for blotting his copy-book
Amos Blair, for not combing his hair
Andrew Grace, for not washing his face
Anthony Sands, for not washing his hands
Arnold Cootz, for coming in with dirty boots
Benjamin Guess, for coming with untidy dress
Clarence Hyneman, for annoying a stray Chinaman
Michael McToole, for bringing stones to school
Cuthbert Flindow, for climbing through the window
Edgar Gasking, for going without asking
Eric Grout, for kicking boys' hats about
Enoch McKay, for pinching the next boy
Gabriel Cook, for tearing a boy's book
Hyram Pope, for pulling the bell rope
Humphrey Proof, for getting on the roof
Jonah Earls, for chasing school-girls
Jonathan Spence, for climbing over the fence
Phillip Cannister, for sliding down the bannister
Lambert Hesk, for sliding on a desk
Lawrence Storm, for standing on a form
Lazarus Beet, for stamping with his feet
Leopold Bate, for swinging on the gate
Lewis Lesks, for kicking legs of desks
Mark Vine, for overstepping the toe-line
Nathan Corder, for not marching in order
Norman Hall, for scribbling on the wall
James Mace, for hitting a boy in the face
Thomas Sayers, for pushing boys down the stairs
Oswald Hook, for losing a school-book
Ralph Chesson, for not knowing his lesson
Sampson Skinner, for eating another boy's dinner
Solomon Brook, for scribbling in his book
Stephen Platt, for chasing the master's cat

199

Neal M'Kimney, dropping a brick down the chimney
Theodore Le Soof, for throwing stones on the roof
Valentine Rapp, for turning on the water-tap
Walter Hope, for climbing up the bell-rope
Joshua Gail, for catching flies on the wall
Raymond Esk, for sticking pins in the desk
Julian State, for drawing pictures on his slate
Gerald Astor, for being impudent to the master
Augustus Roff, for not taking his hat off
Rupert Keats, for fixing pens in boys' seats
Maurice Took, for having a dirty copybook
Esau Klaster, for drawing caricatures of the master
Paul Bhool, for letting a bird loose in school
Jabez Breeding, for not knowing the place at reading
Levi Stout, for stopping too long when let out
Guy M'Gill, sharpening a knife on the window-sill
Duncan Heather, pinning two boys' coat-tails together
Ezekiel Black, pinning paper on another boy's back
Patrick O'Toole, for bursting a paper-bag in school
Eli Teet, for putting cobbler's wax on master's seat

My Lady Doll

My Lady-doll is pretty,
　My Lady-doll is sweet;
I like to show my Lady-doll
　To every one I meet

My Sweet Dolly Rose

O sweet, so sweet,
Is my Dolly Rose!
Just all that I know
My Dolly knows;
And when I am glad
The darling is glad
And when I am sad
The darling is sad.
How dear she is,
O, nobody knows,
No, no, not even
My precious Rose

Polly's Dolly

Shining eyes, very blue,
　Opened very wide;
Yellow curls, very stiff,
　Hanging side by side;
Chubby cheeks, very pink,
　Lips red as holly;
No ears, and only thumbs—
　That's Polly's Dolly.

Pretty Doll

201

Oh dear! what a beautiful doll
  My sister has bought at the fair
She says I must call it Miss Poll,
  And make it a bonnet to wear.

Oh pretty new doll, it looks fine!
  It's cheeks are all covered with red.
But pray will it always be mine?
  And please may I take it to bed?

How kind was my sister to buy
  This dolly with hair that will curl;
Perhaps, if you want to know why,
  It's because I've been a good girl.

POEMS FOR CHILDREN

Puss's Doll

Now Puss had a doll
  That Dame Trot bought to please her,
And gave it the beautiful

Name of Louisa
And when Kitty was lonesome
  Or wanted to play,
She'd cry for Loo! Loo!
  In a comical way.

The dolly was petted,
  Was kissed and caressed,
Though often quite roughly
  It must be confessed
And so pleased was Miss Puss
  With Louisa's fair charms,
She took her cat's meat,
  With the doll in her arms

Pussy and Doggy Fighting for Dolly

And once, I remember,
  Oh, sad was the day,
The cat answered back
  In an impudent way.
And tray was so jealous,
  The two had a fight,
And between them the doll
  Was a terrible fright

COLE

Dolly Tumbled out of Bed

'Tis very well to smile—now,
  But you gave me such a fright,
When I missed you, darling Dolly,
  In the middle of the night.

I thought we played together,
  And you fell into a stream;
Yet I said—just half awaking—
  "'Tis nothing but a dream.

"For safe upon my pillow
  Lies her curly golden hair,"
Then I reached my hand to touch you,
  But I couldn't find you there.

I felt so sad and lonely
  That I cried, but all in vain;
So to see if I could find you,
  I went off to sleep again.

Now, fancy! in the morning
  There you were, all safe and right;
And nurse said, "Here's poor Dolly,

Been upon the floor all night!"

Your pretty curls are tangled,
  They were so nice and smooth before;
So promise, Dolly darling,
  You will tumble out no more!

Dolly and I

I love my dear dolly;
  I'll tell you her name,
I called her "Sweet Polly"
  The day that she came.

My Uncle John brought her
  From over the sea;
And no one shall part us,
  My dolly and me.

She has cheeks like red roses,
  And eyes blue and bright,
That open with daylight,
  And close with the night.

She cries, and says, "Mam-ma,
  Mam-mam-ma," so well,
That it is not a baby
  You scarcely can tell.

You know, I'm her own ma;
  A small one, you'll say,
But just right for dolly,
  Who wants nought but play.

No teaching, no training,
  Few clothes and no food;
And I like being her ma,
  Because she's so good.

Dolly's Broken Arm

Mamma, do send for Doctor Man,
  And tell him to be quick,
My dolly fell and broke her arm,
  So she is very sick.

I thought that she was fast asleep,
  And laid her on her bed,
But down she dropped upon the floor;
  O dear! she's almost dead!

Poor dolly! she was just as brave,
  And did not cry at all;
Do you suppose she ever can
  Get over such a fall?

But when the doctor mends her arm,
  And wraps it up so tight,
Then I will be her little nurse,
  And watch her all the night.

And if she only will get well,
  And does not lose her arm,
I'll never let her fall again,
  Nor suffer any harm.

Little Polly

  Little Polly,
  Had a dolly,
    With a curly wig;
  And Miss Polly
  And her dolly,
    Often danced a jig.

Also Polly
had a collie,
  A fine dog was he;
Blithe and jolly,
Jumped round Polly,
  Barking loud with glee.

One day Polly
Knocked her dolly,
  Broke its pretty head.
"Oh, fie, Polly!
Don't hurt dolly,"
  Said her brother Ned.

Then did Polly
Take up Dolly,
  Throw it on the floor.
Said Miss Polly,
In her folly
  "I will play no more."

Up ran collie,
Seized poor dolly,
  Ran off to a friend.
Friend helped collie
To tear up dolly—
  That was poor dolly's end.

Reading Dolly Lane.

Two Dollies Getting Up.

A Little Girl's Song to Her Dolly

Lie down, little Dolly.
  Lie still on my lap,
It's time now to put on
  Your night dress and cap;
You have not been to sleep
  All through this long day
Oh, what a long time
  For a Dolly to play!

The bright sun went down
  More than two hours ago;
It is long past your bedtime,
  You very well know:
The stars are now peeping
  From out the blue skies;
Then go to sleep, Dolly!
  Come, shut your blue eyes.

Mamma says the flowers
  Were asleep long ago—

Sweet roses and lilies,
  Their heads bending low;
She says 'tis a lesson
  For me and for you—
That children and dollies
  Should be asleep too.

Hark! Susan is calling—
  Now out goes the light;
I will tug you up snugly,
  And kiss you good night.
It is time you were sleeping
  For do you not know
The dear little birds
  Went to sleep long ago?

Don't Cry My Dolly

Hushy, baby, my dolly,
  I pray you don't cry,
And I'll give you some bread
  And some milk by and by;
Or perhaps you like custard,
  Or maybe a tart,—
Then to either you're welcome,
  With all my whole heart.

The Little Girl and Her Doll

There, got to sleep, Dolly,
  In own mother's lap.
I've put on your nightgown
  And neat little cap.
So sleep, pretty baby,
  And shut up your eye.
Bye-bye, little Dolly,

Lie still, and bye-bye.
I'll lay my clean handkerchief
  Over your head,
And then make believe
  That my lap is your bed;
So hush, little dear,
  And be sure you don't cry.
Bye-bye, little Dolly,
  Lie still, and bye-bye.

There, now it is morning
  And time to get up,
And I'll give you some milk
  In my doll's china cup.
So wake up, little baby
  And open your eye,
For I think it high time
  To have done with bye-bye.

Jane Taylor

Sleep, Dolly Sleep

Sleep, Dolly, sleep.
You must not, must not weep.
Now close your eyes so brown,
And let me lay you down.
  Sleep, Dolly, sleep.
Wake, Dolly, wake,
Too long a nap you take;
It's time to make the tea,
And you must help, you see.
  Wake, Dolly, wake.
Run, Dolly, run,
Run out in golden sun;
Run up the hill with me,

And then to the apple-tree.
Run, Dolly, run.

Mrs Hibbert

My Dolly

Shut your eyes, my darling!
  When the shadows creep,
When the flowers are closing
  Little ones must sleep.

Don't be frightened, Dolly!
  In my arms you lie;
Nestle down and slumber
  To my lullaby

Dolly is so active,
  Always full of fun.
Wakeful still and smiling
  E'en when day is cone

Hush thee now, my dearest,
  To my slumber-song;
Children lose their roses,
  Sitting up too long.

My Dolly

I must go home to do ly,
  And put her to bed;
I know she's so tired,
  She can't raise her head.

Some dolls are so old,
  They can sit up till eight,

212

But mine gets quite ill
If she stays up so late!

Dolly's Asleep

Tell me a story
  Just one, mother dear.
Candles are coming
  Bedtime is near
There is my hand to hold
  Bend down your head,
Don't speak too loud, mother,
  Dolly's in bed

No! not the story
  Of old Jack and Jill
They were so stupid
  To tumble down the hill.
I'm tired of Jack Horner
  And Little Bo-peep.—
Stay! let me see
  If Dolly's asleep.

Hush, Dolly darling!
  I'm watching, you know
No one shall hurt you;
  I will not go.
You are so warm,—
  Like a bird in it's nest.
Go to sleep, darling,—
  Rest, Dolly, rest.

Ah! there is Mary
  Just come in with a light:
Now there is no time
  For a story to-night,
Please make the boys, mother,
  Mind how they tread.

Their boots are so heavy,
  And—Dolly's in bed.

Good night, dear mother!
  Ask papa, please,
When he comes home,
  Not to cough or to sneeze
Give me your hand, Mary
  Hush! softly creep;
We must not wake her,—
  Dolly's asleep.

If at all restless
  Or wakeful she seems,
Don't be to anxious;
  I fancy she dreams.
Say to her softly,
  Just shaking your head;
"Go to sleep, Dolly —
  Adie's in bed."

HUSH!

Lost Dolly

The sunflowers hang their heavy heads
  And wish the sun would shine;
The clouds are grey; the wind is cold.
  "Where is that doll of mine?
The dark is coming fast," said she.
  "I'm in a dreadful fright.
I don't know where I left my doll,
  And she'll be out all night

"Twice up and down the garden-walks
  I looked; but she's not there,
Oh! yes, I've hunted in the hay;
  I've hunted everywhere.
I must have left her out of doors,
  But she is not in sight.
No Dolly in the summer-house,
  And she'll be out all night.

"The dew will wet her through and through

And spoil her dear best dress;
And she will wonder where I am
  And be in such distress;
The dogs may find her in the grass,
  And bark or even bite;
And all the bats will frighten her
  That fly about at night.

"I've not been down into the woods
  Or by the brook to-day.
I'm sure I had her in my arms
  When I came out to play,
Just after dinner; then I know,
  I watched Tom make his kite.
Will anybody steal my doll
  If she stays out all night.

"I wonder where Papa has gone?
  Why, here he comes; and see
He's bringing something in his hand;
  That's Dolly certainly!
And so you found her in the chaise,
  And brought her home all right?
I'll take her to the baby-house.
  I'm glad she's home tonight."

Sarah O. Jewett

Talking To Dolly

Well, Dolly, what are you saying,
  When you blink and wink your eyes?
I'm sure your thoughts are straying,
  For you look so very wise.

I wonder what you think about,
  And why you never talk.
And how it is you never shout,

And never try to walk!

I wonder if you're ever sad,
  And if you ever weep;
I wonder if you're ever glad
  When I rock you off to sleep.

I wonder if you love me well—
  As well as I love you
I do so wish you'd try and tell;
  Come, Dolly, darling, do!

Darling Dolly

Darling Dolly's house shall be
High as lofty apple-tree;
It shall have a door inlaid,
Of the sweetest light and shade.

It shall have for pictures fair
Fancies that are rich and rare;
It shall have a golden roof,
And tapestry with stars for woof.

And it shall have a dome of blue
With the moonligh streaming through,
And stately pillars, straight as firs,
Bending to each wind that stirs.

Darling Dolly's house shall be
High as a lofty apple-tree;
It shall have a door inlaid,
Of the sweetest light and shade.

217

Sour Grapes

"Such a doll! I wouldn't have it,
  With its trailing baby dress!
Pooh! a dolly twice as handsome
  I could have for asking, Bess.
Needn't ask me if it's pretty,
  No, I do not care to wait,
I am in an awful hurry,
  If you keep me, I'll be late."

Off went Nannie, proud lip curling,
  Head uplifted in disdain,
Bessie hugged her dolly closely,
  Laughing over truth so plain.
"Nan was envious, Dolly darling,
  'Twasn't aught of wrong in you,
But the trouble lay in Nannie,
  She would like to own you too."

My Dolly House.

Oh, you Naughty Dog to Bite my Dolly.

Boo! Boo! Boo! He has Swallowed my Dolly.

Ten Little Dollies

Ten little dollies
  Standing in a line,
One tumbled down,
  And then there were nine.

Nine little dollies
  Sitting up so late,
One went to sleep
  Then there were eight.

Eight little dollies—
  All their ages even,
One grew up tall
  And then there were seven.

Seven little dollies,
  Full of funny tricks,
One snapt her head off

Then there were six.

Six little dollies—
  Looked almost alive,
One lost her "pin-back,"
  Then there were five.

Five little dollies,
  Walking by a door,
One got her nose pinched,
  Then there were four.

Four little dollies
  On their mamma's knee,
One cried her eyes out,
  Then there were three.

Three little dollies,
  Didn't know what to do,
One tore her bows off,
  Then there were two.

Two little dollies,
  Very fond of fun,
One melts her nose off,
  Then there was one.

One little dolly,
  Living all alone,
Died broken-hearted,
  Then there were none.

Teaching Dolly A B C.

Kissing after a Doll Quarrel.

My Week

On Monday I wash my dollies' clothes,
  On Tuesday smoothly press 'em,
On Wednesday mend their little hose,
  On Thursday neatly dress 'em.

On Friday I play they're taken ill,
  On Saturday something or other;
But when Sunday comes, I say, "Lie still,
  I'm going to church with mother."

223

Dirty Dolly

Naughty Miss Dolly played out in the mud,
  And got all her clothes quite black;
And now such a rubbing, and scrubbing and tubbing
  As we have to give them, good lack!

'Tis hard to be mothers and laundresses too,
  And nurses and cooks beside.
Grown people don't know all we chicks have to do,
  For how can they tell till they've tried?

Washing Day Troubles

I know a little girl who tried,
  To wash her dolly's clothes, one day,
In Bridget's great, big tub, and cried

Because mamma sent her away

To find her own small dolly-tub,
　More fit for little girls to use.
But naughty Sally shook her head
　And all suggestions did refuse.

And when she found herself alone,
　She went to Bridget's tub again,
But, as is sure to be the case,
　Her disobedience brought her pain.

For, what do you think? she tumbled in,
　And gave herself an awful fright,
And no one pitied her; in fact,
　They all laughed at her in her plight.

Washing Dolly

　Miss Mary standing at the tub
　Giving dolly a thorough scrub.
　Trying to make her nice and sweet
　Before she dresses for the street.
　If health an happiness you'd glean
　Remember always to keep clean.

Doll Rosy's Bath

'Tis time Doll Rosy had a bath,
　And she'll be good, I hope;
She likes the water well enough,
　But she doesn't like the soap.

Now soft I'll rub her with a sponge,
　Her eyes and nose and ears,
And splash her fingers in the bowl

225

And never mind the tears.

There now—oh, my! what have I done?
  I've washed the skin off—see!
Her pretty pink and white are gone
  Entirely! oh, dear me!

The New Tea-Things

Come, Dolly, come quick,
  For I want you to see
The present mamma
  Has just given to me;
A set of new tea-things
  That really hold tea.

A dear little teapot
  To keep the tea hot,
And tiny white cups
  With a pretty blue spot,
And a glass sugar-basin.
  How nice, is it not?

And I am to use them
  This same afternoon;
So Dolly I'll give you
  Some tea very soon
In a little white cup,
  With a saucer and spoon.

Doll Dress-making

Making Dolly's dresses,
  Don't you think it's fun?
Here is one already,

227

That I've just begun

Oh, how many stitches!
  And such a tangly thread!
When I pricked my finger
  I just guess it bled

There! the needle's broken—
  Bending all about—
That's a sign my dolly'll
  Wear the dresses out

Youth's Companion

Dolly Town

Have you ever been down to Dolly Town?
The sight would do you good
  There the dollies walk,
  And the dollies talk,
  And they ride about
  In a grand turn-out,
  With a coachman thin
  Who is made of tin,
And a footman made of wood

There are very fine houses in Dolly Town,
Red, and green and blue
  And a doctor, too,
  Who has much to do,
  Just to mend their toes
  And their arms and nose,
  When they tumble down
  And crack their crown
And the stuff they take is glue

But the finest sight in Dolly Town
That place to children dear—

228

Is no dolly at all,
Though so neat and small
If you've time to spare,
Go on tiptoe there,
See the pretty girl, the rose, the pearl,
Who is Queen of Dolly Town

My Little Doll Rose

I have a little doll,
I take care of her clothes
She has soft flaxen hair,
And her name is Rose

She has pretty blue eyes,
And a very small nose,
And a cunning little mouth,
And her name is Rose

I have a little sofa
Where my dolly may repose,
Or sit up like a lady;
And her name is Rose

My doll can move her arms,
And can stand upon her toes,
She can make a pretty curtsey
My dear little Rose

How old is your dolly?
Very young I suppose,
For she cannot go alone,
My pretty little Rose

Indeed I cannot tell
In poetry or prose

229

How beautiful she is,
My darling little Rose.

E. Follen

Sewing For Dolly

Such a busy little mother!
  Such a pretty little "child"!
Did you ever see a dolly
  With a face more sweet and mild?

Such a comfort to her mother,
  Who is busy all the day,
And who never finds a moment
  With her little girl to play

There are dresses to be altered,
  There are aprons to be made,
"For my child in wardrobe matters
  Must not be thrown in shade"

Says the busy little mother,
  As she clips and works away,
And a brand new dress for Dolly
  Will be made this very day

The Lost Doll

I once had a sweet little doll, dears,
  The prettiest doll in the world;
Her cheeks were so red and so white, dears,
  And her hair was so charmingly curled.

But I lost my poor little doll, dears,
  As I played in the heath one day;

I cried for her more than a week, dears,
  But I could never find where she lay.

Folks say she is terribly changed, dears,
  For her paint is all washed away,
And her arms trodden off by the cows, dears,
  And her hair is not the least bit curled;
Yet for old sake's sake she is still, dears,
  The prettiest doll in the world.

Charles Kingsley

Dolly's Patchwork Counterpane

Oh, Mary, see what the nurse has found,
  Such store of pieces in my box!
Some green, and some with lilac ground.
  They'll make such lovely blocks

She says she'll teach me how to make
  A counterpane for Dolly's bed,
This lovely piece first will take,
  With sprays of roses white and red

And thin this piece with purple spots
  Will look so pretty next to that!
I'll keep my cotton free from knots,
  And make my stitches neat and flat

And "when I've finished it," she says
  She'll line it with a square of white.
Oh, Dolly dear your little bed
  Will be a most enchanting sight!

231

The Wooden Doll

I'm but a wooden doll,
  Have neither wit nor grace;
And very clumsy in my joints
  And yet I know my place.

Most people laugh at a wooden doll,
  And wooden I may be,
But little children love me much
  And that's enough for me.

When I am dressed in fine long clothes,
  In fur, and silk, and lace,
I think myself I'm not so bad
  And yet I know my place.

Let people laugh—I know I'm wood:
  Wax I can never be
But little children think I'm grand—
  That's quite enough for me.

Buy My Dolls

Come buy my dolls, my pretty dolls:
  Come buy my dolls, I pray:
    I've such a heap,
    And I sell so cheap.
  I almost give them away.

I've waxen dolls, and china dolls,
  And dollies made of gum,
    Some are small,
    And some are tall,
  Some talk and some are dumb.

Bald head dolls, and dolls with hair,
  All beauties in their way—

So very nice,
So low in price,
Please buy my dolls to-day.

Laughing dolls, and crying dolls;
Dolls of various ages,
Infant dolls,
And lady dolls,
Dolls in all the stages.

Go where you may, you will not find
Such bargains as are these
Make my heart light,
Buy them to night,
To grace your Christmas trees.

Doctor Charlie and His Patient

Run for the doctor!
  Dolly's very sick!
Mary, you'll have to go,
  I cannot leave her,
Tell him to pack his bottles
  And come quick;
I think she has got
  A very dangerous fever."

In stalks a hat and cane;
  If you look close,
You'll see Doctor Charlie,
  Somewhere under;
He takes a pinch of snuff
  And blows his nose,
While poor sick Dolly
  Seems to stare in wonder.

He feels her pules, he
  Gravely shakes his head:
His hat dropped o'er his eyes
  With the shake he gave it;
He says poor dolly
  Must be put to bed
And have her head shaved—
  He, in fact, will shave it.

Poor mamma sober looks,
  But says at once
That "Dolly's head shall
  Not be shaved! I guess not!
Her hair would never grow
  Again, you dunce!"
"It shall!" "It shan't!"
  "She'll die then, if it's not!"

But Mary, ere the quarrel
  Gets too grave
(Already in her hand
  A bowl of gruel),
Says, "Don't you know
  That doctors do not shave?
And then besides,
  It really would be cruel!"

"I'll give her pills, then,
  When she's safe in bed,
Plenty and sweet—of sugar
  I will make them;
As dolly cannot eat,
  'Twill do instead
For you and me and
  Mary here to take them."

Dollies' Broken Noses

Two little babies
  In carriages two,
Two little nurses
  With duty to do.

Both little nurses
  Were careful at first,
Soon both grew careless—
  Which was the worst.

O what a pitiful
  Wail from the street!
One broken rail
  Trips four little feet.

Over went carriages,
  Babies and all,
And two china noses
  Were cracked in the fall.

The Soldier Dolly

There once was a sweet tiny maiden,
  A wee little woman of four,
Who scarce could reach up to the table,
  Or open the nursery door.

And this poor little maid, she was crying—
  Her dolly had such a fall!
Yes there on the ground he was lying—
  Her darling, the best of them all.

This dolly had been a brave soldier,
  With uniform, sabre, and all
And worshipp'd a doll in the doll's-house,

That stood by the side of the wall.

She was only a poor tiny maiden,
  A wee little woman of four,
And she sat with her heart nearly breaking,
  With the doll in her lap on the floor.

And the poor, tiny, sorrowful maiden,
  The wee little woman of four,
Now lies with her dead soldier dolly,
  Asleep on the nursery floor.

The Dead Doll

You needn't be trying to comfort me—
  I tell you my dolly is dead!
There's no use saying she isn't—
  With a crack like that on her head.
It's just like you said it wouldn't hurt
  Much to have my tooth out that day.
And then when they most pulled
  My head off, you hadn't a word to say.

And I guess you must think I'm a baby,
  When you say you can mend it with glue!
As if I didn't know better than that!
  Why, just suppose it was you?
You might make her look all mended—
  But what do I care for looks?
Why, glue's for chairs and tables,
  And toys, and the backs of books!

My dolly! my own little daughter!
  Oh, but it's the awfullest crack!
It just makes me sick to think of the sound
  When her poor head went whack
Against this horrible brass thing
  That holds up the little shelf.

237

Now, Nursey, what makes you remind me?
  I know that I did it myself?

I think you must be crazy—
  You'll get her another head!
What good would forty heads do her?
  I tell you my dolly is dead!
And to think that I hadn't quite finished
  Her elegant New Year's hat!
And I took a sweet ribbon of hers
  List night to tie on that horrid cat!

When my mamma gave me that ribbon—
  I was playing out in the yard—
She said to me most expressly:
  "Here's a ribbon for Hildegarde."
And I went and put it on Tabby,
  And Hildegarde saw me do it;
But I said to myself, "Oh, never mind,
  I don't believe she knew it!"

But I know that she knew it now,
  And I just believe, I do,
That her poor little heart was broken,
  And so her head broke too.
Oh, my baby! my little baby!
  I wish my head had been hit!
For I've hit it over and over,
  And it hasn't cracked a bit.

But since the darling is dead,
  She'll want to be buried of course;
We will take my little wagon, Nurse,
  And you shall be the horse;
And I'll walk behind and cry;
  And we'll put her in this—you see,
This dear little box—and we'll bury
  Them under the maple tree.

And papa will make a tombstone,

Like the one he made for my bird;
And he'll put what I tell him on it—
  Yes, every single word!
I shall say: "Here lies Hildegarde,
  A beautiful doll that is dead;
She died of a broken heart,
  And a dreadful crack in her head."

Margaret Vandegrift

Dolly's Doctor

Dolly, my darling, is dreadfully sick;
  Oh, dear! what shall I do?
Despatch to the doctor a telephone quick
  To bring her a remedy new.

Hush! that is the doctor's tap! tap! tap!
  Don't make such a terrible noise—
Don't you see how the darling lies still on my lap,
  And never looks up at you boys!

Come, doctor, and tell me now just what you think
  Would be best for my darling so sweet.
'Give dolly a bucket of water to drink,
  In a bowl of hot gruel put her feet.'

Dollies Courting.

Christening Dolly

See, this is my Christmas dolly.
  Two weeks ago she came;
And, oh! the trouble I have had
  To find a pretty name.

At first I thought of Marguerite—
  A French name, meaning "pearl"—
But Nellie said, "Oh! that's too stiff

For such a graceful girl."

And then I mentioned, one by one,
 Susanna, Ruth, and Poll,
"But they are too old-fashioned names
 Said Nell, "to suit your doll."

So the next day I got a great big book,
 And searched it through and through,
Then shook my head and sadly said:
 "There's not one name will do."

My brother Tom was sitting near,
 He raised his eyes and smiled;
"Why, Pussy dear," he kindly said,
 "Suppose I name your child."

"Oh! will you Brother Tom?" I cried,
 And then I hugged him, so; (hugging her doll.)
"We'll play you are the parson
 That christens folks, you know."

So then, he took her in his arms
 And solemnly and slow
He said: "This baby's name shall be
 Miss Josephine, or Jo."

And there, before I knew it,
 My baby had a name;
And what I like about it, is,
 That mine is just the same.

E.C. and J.T. Rook

The Dollies Visit

Three little girls brought each a doll,
 To pass an afternoon;

241

The dresses all were soon displayed,
　Their bangles made a tune;
And when they parted to go home,
　One young girl shrewdly said:
"Our dollies have behaved real nice—
　They have no scandal spread."
　　　　　W.

The Little Girl Over The Way

Whenever I'm tired of reading,
　Or lonely in my play,
I come to the window here, and watch
　The little girl over the way.

But she will not look nor listen,
　Nor stand for a moment still;
And though I watch her the livelong day,
　I'm afraid she never will.

For some day some one will buy her,
　And carry her quite away;—
She is only a doll in a great glass-case,
　The little girl over the way.

Maggie's Talk to Doll

　My dolly dear,
　　Come sit up here!
And say why you don't cry.
　I've struck your head
　Against the bed,
And cracked your pretty eye,

　My dolly dear,
　Do sit up here,

242

And let me see your face;
  And say, my pet,
  Why you don't fret
Now Pug has got your place.

  My pretty Poll
  My dear, dear doll,
Why don't you eat or talk?
  Like sister Jane
  And Sally Blanc,
And then go for a walk?

  You have an eye,
  But never cry,
And lips, but never prattle;
  You've fingers ten,
  Like brother Ben,
But never shake the rattle.

  You never eat,
  Nor drink, nor sleep,
Nor move unless you're carried:
  And when I pinch,
  You never flinch,
Nor say that you are worried.

Minnie to Dolly

Your hair is so pretty,
  Your eyes are so blue,
Your cheeks are so rosy,
  Your frock is so new,
You're the prettiest dolly
  I ever did see.
Though your hair is so pretty,
  And your eyes are so blue,
I'd rather be Minnie

Than I would be you,

For you can't see the flowers
　When they come up in spring;
You can't hear the birdies,
　How sweetly they sing;
Nor run out of doors
　To look in the sky,
And see the white clouds
　As they pass swiftly by.

You've no kind of papa
　Or mamma to be near,
To love you and teach you;
　So, dolly, my dear,
Though your cheeks are so rosy,
　And your dress is so new,
I'd rather be Minnie
　Than I would be you.

My Dolly

My Dolly, Polly Angelina Brown,
Has a pretty little bonnet,
　And a pretty little gown;
　A pretty little bonnet,
　With a lovely feather on it;
Oh, there's not another like it
　To be found in all the town!

My Dolly, Polly, is a precious little pet;
Her eyes are bright as jewels,
And her hair is black as jet;
　I hug her, and I kiss her!
　And oh, how I should miss her
If she were taken from me;
Oh how I should grieve and fret!

My little brother Charles,
  Says my Dolly is "a muff,"
And he calls her other horrid names
  Though that is bad enough;
  And though he's very clever,
  I never, no, I never
Let him handle her or dandle her,
  For boys, you know, are rough.

My Dolly's always smiling;
  She was never known to frown.
And she looks so very charming
  In her Sunday hat and gown.
  You really ought to see her
  To get a good idea
Of the beauty of my Dolly,
  Polly Angelina Brown.

Dolly's Wedding

  Come along; come along;
  The rain has gone away.
  Dingle-dong, dingle dong;
  It is Dolly's wedding-day!

Charley has got his night-gown on.
  Mary has put the chairs:
Charley is the clergyman
  Who'll marry them up-stairs.
  Come along; come along;
  The rain has gone away.
  Dingle-dong! dingle dong;
  It is Dolly's wedding-day!

Sambo has got an old white hat,
  And a coat with but one tail;
Sambo's face is very black,
  Dolly's is rather pale.

245

Come along; come along;
The rain has gone away.
Dingle-dong! dingle dong;
It is Dolly's wedding-day!

Sambo has got a woolly pate,
Dolly has golden hair.
When Sambo marries Dolly,
They'll be a funny pair!
Come along; come along;
The rain has gone away.
Dingle-dong! dingle dong;
It is Dolly's wedding-day!

Dollies in School.

My Doll

I found my old dolls
  In the attic to-day,
In a box where I long ago
  Laid them away.
It was silly, I know,
  But 'twas such a surprise,
The sight of their faces
  Brought tears to my eyes.

There was poor little Flossie,
  With azure eyes closed.
For many a month
  She had quietly dozed,
In the little silk gown
  In which I last dressed her—
That time was brought back
  So I stopped and caressed her;

And then, as I raised her,
  She opened her eyes,
And stared at her mother
  In such sad surprise
That I kissed her and laid
  Her again in her place
To keep her reproachful
  Blue eyes off my face.

And next I uncovered
  My little bisque Mabel,
To meet whose brown eyes
  I was still more unable.
There gaze was surprised,
  But exceedingly mild,
My poor little, dear little,
  Led-away child!

And I kissed her, her face
  Looked so childish and sweet,
And I held for a moment
  Her little kid feet,
For her stockings were scattered,
  And so were her shoes,
And then, when I found them,
  They gave me the blues.

I kissed her, and laid her
  Back in the box, but
She looked at me still
  (For her eyes would not shut)
And hastily covering
  Her face from my sight,
I searched till wax Elsie
  I brought to the light.

Now, that poor little doll
  Was only my niece,
Her eyes were dark blue
  And her curls white as fleece
But her nose was so flat,
  'Twas no longer a nose,
And her wax cheeks had faded
  And lost all their rose.

From losing her sawdust
  Her body was slender,
Yet for those very reasons
  My kiss was more tender,
And I laid the poor thing
  Away with a sigh,
And feeling, I must say,
  Like having a cry.

One big doll was missing,—
  My dear Rosabel,—
How much I did love her,
  I really can't tell.

It is painful, indeed,
  To be talking about,
But I loved her so much
  That I quite wore her out.

Well, well, I am older,
  But I'm sure I'm not glad.
The thought of those old times,
  In fact makes me sad.
And, although the feeling
  Is silly, I know,
I cannot help sighing:
  "Oh! why did I grow?"

Bertha Gerneaux Davis

Mistress Of Four Dollies

This little girl, I'm glad to say,
Is eight years old this very day.
She makes a hat for the little "Doll,"
And puts in it a feather tall.

One doll is large, and one is small,

249

Another short another tall.
She talks to them. They won't obey,
And then she says, "You cannot play."

Grandmamma's Visit

With grandma's cap upon her head,
  And spectacles on her nose,
And grandma's shawl upon her back,
  Grace to her sister goes.

"My dear grandchild, although I am
  Now getting very old,
I've toddled all this way to ask
  About your Dolly's cold."

"Dear Grandmamma, I thank you much,
  And I am glad to say
She had a good sound sleep last night,
  And is quite well to-day."

Lucy's Dolls

Five little dolls
  To claim my care
To fix their clothes
  And comb their hair;

Five little dolls
  To dress and keep
And put away
  Each night to sleep.

I don't think grown
  Folks ever know
What troubles small

Folks undergo;

I have to cook
  To please all five—
I wonder much
  That I'm alive!

Please Mend my Dolly

251

Dolly Is Dead

I can't help crying! Oh dear!
My doll is dead, I fear,
  Yes, she must be dead,
  For she's lost her head,
And she looks so horribly queer.
But they say our doctor's a clever man,
I'll get him to put on her head if he can.

The Doll Show

(For seven little girls—six with dolls. The seventh to be
the judge.)

First girl enters, with doll in her arms.

We're going to have a dolly show,
  This very afternoon—
The little girls will bring their dolls,
  (I think they'll be here soon),

And then we'll have such lots of fun,
  We'll place them in a row,
And the one the judge declares the best
  Will take the prize, you know.

My dolly is all ready,
  I've dressed her as a bride;
Don't she look sweet; She'll take the prize,
  Of that I'm satisfied.

Places her doll on a bench or chair, and takes a seat.

Second Girl

Oh, such a time as I have had,

252

I thought I would be late;
I took so very, very long
To dress my little Kate,

But here she is, my infant doll,
So white, and clean, and pure,
Oh, yes, my precious darling,
You'll take the prize, I'm sure.

Places doll next to doll No. 1 and takes a seat.

Third Girl—Carrying a handsome French Doll.

My dolly came from Sunny France,
Her name is Antoinette,
She's two years old on Christmas day,
And she's my dearest pet.

Her feet and hands are very small,
Her hair is soft and light,
Her eyes the deepest, darkest blue,
And very large and bright.

This handsome dress from Paris came,
Also this stylish hat,
Why, she of course will take the prize,
I'm positive of that.

Places her doll by doll No. 2, and takes a seat.

Fourth Girl

I hope they've saved a little space
For Jack, my sailor lad,
The bravest, best, and nicest son
A mother ever had.

He wears a suit of navy blue—
I've brought him to the show
Because he looks so very nice,

He'll take the prize, I know.

Places it by doll No. 3, and sits down.

*Fifth Girl—a very small girl holding by the arm a large
rag baby with a long dress.*

My mamma's writing letters,
And told me—"run away,"
And so I brought my dolly
To the baby show, to-day.

She isn't very pretty,
But she's very nice, I think,
Her eyes, and nose, and little mouth,
My mamma made with ink.

I love my Dolly, 'cause she's good—
She never never cries,
So don't you think she'll be the one
To carry off the prize?

Places her doll by doll No. 4, and takes a seat.

Sixth Girl

They mustn't crowd my baby out,
Although she's black as night.
I think she'll stand as good a chance
As babies that are white.

She's very neat, and nice, and clean,
Her lips are cherry red,
She wears a gay bandanna
Tied round her curly head.

She's a very handsome lady,
And if the judge be wise,
I do not have the slightest doubt

That she will take the prize.

Places her doll by doll No. 5, and sits down.

First Girl—to the girls

Do not open your mouths,
Nor shut your eyes!
For here comes the judge
To award the prize.

*Seventh Girl—Enters carrying a wand. She views each
doll in turn with critical eyes, then pointing to the first
doll, says—*

Number one is very pretty,
But I think she's rather tall.

Points to No. 2

And this cunning little baby,
Is a little bit too small.

No. 3

Number three—a fine French lady,
Too Frenchy is, I fear.

Points to No. 4

And Master Jack, I like your looks,
But I think you dress too queer.

No. 5

And this old-fashioned baby doll,
I guess lived in the ark;

No. 6

No, no, Miss Dinah, no prize for you,
  Your skin is much too dark.

Then turning to the little girls, she continues:

And now, dear anxious mothers,
  I find I can't decide
Which doll shall have the premium,
  But I' l be satisfied

If you'll cal another meeting
  To-morrow afternoon,
I need more t me to settle this—
  To-day is much too soon.

So, mothers, now I give these babies
  Back to your loving care;
And I thank you much for bringing them
  To our famous Baby Fair.

Hands each doll to it's owner.

Exit all.

Please, Puss, don't Hurt Me

A Doll's Adventures Round the World

All round the world and back again
 Dolly and I have been;
By sea and land we've travelled far,
 The strangest sights have seen.

To Greenland first we sailed away
 To see the snow and ice,
But Dolly's nose—it nearly froze—
 Oh, dear! that wasn't nice!

So off we tripp'd to Canada,
 There 'twas not quite so cold—
But there the Indians in the woods
 Rushed after us so bold.

We ran away to Montana,
 O'er Rocky Mountains high,
To picnic in wild Oregon,
 Famous for pumpkin pie.

Then down to California,
 Through many a field of gold,
And over ancient Mexico,
 Past temples manifold.

The Sandwich Isles we visited,

Where grew such radiant flowers,
And pretty girls danced all the day
  In fragrant, rosy bowers.

We crossed the Equatorial Seas,
 And, sailing round and round
The lovely islands of the main,
  Sweet coral groves we found.

New Zealand's shores we landed at,
  The country of strange things—
Cherries that carried the stones out-side,
  And flowers with butterflies' wings.

Oh, when we reach Australia—
  What heaps and heaps of gold!
And a million sheep and lambs we saw
  Straying from fold to fold.

To buy some tea-pots and some trays,
  We called at quaint Japan,
Where a very polite old Japanese
  Gave Dolly an ivory fan.

We took a trip to Chinese land
  To take a cup of tea,
But neither sugar nor cream was given,
  Which didn't suit Dolly and me.

Then travelling to Hindustan,
  We met a tiger there,
Who looked as though he would eat us up—
  So off we flew elsewhere.

And found ourselves in the Khyber Pass,
  In the midst of a Caravan,
With which we travelled night and day
  To reach Afghanistan.

Across the Red Sea next we sail'd

And through the Suez Canal,
To purchase a camel at old Cairo,
  With a trot most magical

Across the Desert we rode apace,
  No water was there to drink,
Ah, oh!—while climbing a Pyramid
  Dolly dropped down a chink.

An Arab kindly rescued her—
  (She did so ruffle her hair;
If ever she plays that trick again
  She'll have to be left down there.)

At last we left the Desert drear,
  To sail upon the Nile,
In the Pasha's beautiful dahabeheh
  Past many a crocodile.

We saw no end of wonders now
  In Africa's strange land—
Forests full of lions fierce,
  And many a savage band.

Our steamer on the Congo sank—
  We were in a dreadful plight
Until we met with Stanley true,
  And then we steered aright.

We said good-bye to Africa,
  And, though winds proved contrary,
Northward our wondrous way we took
  To the Isles of sweet Canary.

Thence favouring gales conveyed us far
  Beyond the Spanish shore;
Fast by the coast of France we sped
  To our own land once more.

And now we're safe at home again,

And wise as wise can be;
For seeing all the world's wonders
  Improves my Doll and me.

    Sabina

The Story of a Doll

I stood in the semi-darkness
  And watched a child at her play;
Her cares were of multiform nature,
  And the daylight was speeding away.

Her dolly demanded attention,
  To be petted and kissed and be fed;
To have on its little nightgown,
  And then to be put in its bed.

All this with a motherly yearning
  She had learned by the instinct of love;
And the dolly but faintly presented
  A gift from the heaven above.

The dear little creature had finished
  And was just about turning to go,
When the scene all changed in a moment
  And turned into weeping and woe.

A boy, almost reaching to manhood,
  Dashed wildly from the room,
And seizing the doll from the cradle
  Rushed out again into the gloom.

There was one wild scream from the maiden,
  A clasp of the hands and a chase;
But the boy thought the thing was funny
  And was in for a brotherly race.

But soon, when the screaming was louder
  And he saw all the pain he had caused.
He threw down the doll on the flooring,
  And sneering, he suddenly paused.

"I wouldn't be such a cry-baby," he said,
  With a half-mocking drawl;
"I can buy plenty more that's just like it,
  "It's only a plaster doll.

"Why don't you get one made of china,
  Instead of that plaster thing?
An then I would try to respect it,"
  And he took himself off with a fling.

"Oh, my dolly, my dolly is broken,"
  And quick in her bosom she hid
The maimed little bit of her sunshine,
  "I Loved it, I loved it, I did.

"I don't care if it was only plaster;
  'Twas my dolly, my dolly, my own."
And she knelt by the mangled plaything.
  "And now I am left all alone."

Ten years from that very evening,
  I stood by the couch of a child,
While a man knelt and wept beside it,
  With a face both haggard and wild.

'Twas the old scene of the dolly repeated,
  The boy had to manhood grown;
A hand crushed his plaster idol
  And left him to mourn all alone.

Ah me! how the world is repeated,
  The work of each day o'er and o'er.
We all have our broken dollies
  Away on the golden shore.
Did he think, I wonder, of that one

He threw, on the carpetless floor.

Watson

I am homesick, Dolly Dear

Dolly knows what's the matter—
  Dolly and I.
It isn't the mumps nor the measles—
  Oh! dear, I shall die!
It's the mothering we want, Dolly,
  The—what shall I call it?
And grandpa says he has sent—
  He put the 'spatch safe in his wallet.

I know well enough that he dropped
  That telegraph 'spatch in the fire,
If mother just knew, she'd come
  If 'twas on the telegraph wire!

262

She'd take my poor head,
  That is splitting this very minute,
And she'd sing "There's a Happy Land,"
  And the hymn that has "Darling" in it.

Course, I like grandpa's house;
  It's the splendidest place to stay,
When there's all the outdoors to live in,
  And nothing to do but to play;
Somehow you forget your mother—
  That is, just the littlest bit,
Though if she were here, I suppose
  That I shouldn't mention it.

But oh! there's a difference, Dolly,
  When your head is so full of pains
That ('cepting the ache that's in 'em)
  There's nothing left of your brains,
Remember how nice it feels, Dolly,
  To have your head petted and "poored."
Ache? Why I ache all over,
  And my bed is as hard as a board.

Nurse says "It's a sweet, lovely morning."
  It may be for all that I care;
There's just one spot in this great wide world
  That is pretty—I wish I was there!
I can see the white roses climbing
  All over the low porch door,
And the daisies and buttercups growing—
  I never half loved them before.

And mother—let's see! she's standing
  In that very same door, no doubt;
She loves to look out in the morning
  And see what the world is about,
In a pale-blue something-or-other—
  A loose sort of wrapper, I guess;
As if a few yards of sky

Had been taken to make a dress.

And up from the pine woods yonder
  Comes a beautiful woodsy smell,
And the breeze keeps a hinting of May flowers—
  The real-pink arbutus bell;
And I think most likely the robins
  Have built in the cherry tree;
And by and by there'll be birdies—
  And I shall not be there to see!

Did you hear any noise, Dolly!
  Speak, Dolly, you little witch!
As if someone was laughing—or crying!
  I couldn't tell which!
We've kept from crying, so far;
  We've choked but we wouldn't cry;
I've just talked it out to you, dear;
  I had to, or else I'd die.

But if that is you, mother—
  And I know by your lips that it is—
I'll just squeeze your head off!—
  You think that all I want is a kiss!
O mother! to papa and Tom
  You needn't got mention it,
But you know it was homesickness
  Almost killed your poor little Kit!

American Indian Dolls.

Japanese Dolls.

Dolls of Europe, Africa and Asia.

Every Dolly Should Have A Name

A Thousand Names For Dollies And Babies

Adam and Madam,
Hagar and Jagar,
Lottie and Tottie,
Dinah and Nina,
Hebe and Phoebe,
Claude and Maude,
Connell and Donnell,
Dove and Love,
   Are all good names for dolls.

Ruth and Truth,
Ducie and Lucy,
Casper and Jasper,
Mercy and Percy,
Angeletta and Vangeletta,

266

Gilliam and William,
Luby and Ruby,
Ada and Saida,
   Are all good names for dolls.

Abihu and Elihu,
Becky and Jacky,
Alf and Ralph,
Giles and Miles,
Colin and Rollin,
Lubin and Reuben,
Arthur and Marthur,
Marybella and Sarybella,
   Are all good names for dolls.

Hubert and Rupert,
Nice and Rice,
Bryan and Ryan,
Alpin and Galpin,
Duke and Luke,
Mulic and Ulic,
Bessy and Hessy,
Hildalene and Tildalene,
   Are all good names for dolls.

Mose and Rose,
Gordon and Jordan,
Donald and Ronald,
Ervin and Mervin,
Mirzah and Tirzah,
Alick and Gallic,
Handel and Randal,
Fredelena and Tedelena,
   Are all good names for dolls.

Bridget and Midget,
Louisa and Theresa,
Hillah and Zillah,
Milfred and Wilfred,
Larkin and Martyn,

Horam and Joram,
Jael and Shaul,
Fannyette and Nannyette,
    Are all good names for dolls.

Abisha and Elisha,
Abitub and Ahitub,
Crissylene and Sissylene,
Averil and Daveril,
Botolph, and Rodolph,
Lilian and Milian,
Maynard and Reynard,
Kizzylene and Lizzylene,
    Are all good names for dolls.

Prichard and Richard,
Darian and Marian,
Dowzabel and Rosabel,
Artemus and Bartemus,
Dathan and Nathan,
Germaine and Hermaine,
Abelard and Ermengarde,
Dovelene and Loyelene,
    Are all good names for dolls.

Nicodemus and Polyphemous,
Marianne and Sarianne,
Lucylena and Nucylena,
Edmond and Redmond,
Nebulon and Zebulon,
Jeanette and Mynette,
Apollyon and Napoleon,
Jinnylene and Winnylene,
    Are all good names for dolls.

Coralius and Doralius,
Horatius and Ignatius,
Agnes and Dagnes,
Eldred and Meldred,
Obijah and Orijah,

Adriel and Gabriel,
Ivan and Sivan,
Claudelius and Maudelius,
   Are all good names for dolls.

Brunius an Junius,
Simon and Timon,
Bobab and Hobab,
Darnell and Parnell,
Jirah and Sirah,
Marylena and Sarylena,
Faban and Laban,
Lilianette and Millianette,
   Are all good names for dolls.

Lubylene and Rubylene,
Manuel and Samuel,
Herodicus and Herodotus,
Ella and Zella,
Flavius and Zavius,
Grace and Mace,
Borgia and Georgia,
Dinalene and Minalene,
   Are all good names for dolls.

Ira and Myra,
Claudia and Maudia,
Laymond and Raymond,
Gisborn and Lisborn,
Fernando and Hernando,
Paul and Saul,
Hulia and Julia,
Lancylene and Nancylene,
   Are all good names for dolls.

Barret and Garret,
Diamond and Simund,
Bathilda and Matilda,
Charissa and Clarissa,
Minnielene and Tinnielene,

Abinoam and Ahinoam,
Clarice and Paris,
Bessielene and Jessielene,
   Are all good names for dolls.

Josiah and Sophia,
Bariah and Mariah,
Jeziah and Keziah,
Amariah and Amaziah,
Josibiah and Josiphia,
Uriah and Jeremiah,
Obadiah and Zachariah,
   Are all good names for dolls.

Florence and Laurence,
Athaliah and Jocaliah,
Abira and Sapphira,
Donetta and Johnetta,
Biddy and Liddy,
Janette and Nanette,
Dometta and Tometta,
Agrippa and Phillippa,
   Are all good names for dolls.

Lucretia and Venetia,
Criscilla and Priscilla,
Belinda and Selinda,
Dara and Hara,
Ambrose and Lambrose,
Frances and Nances,
Bertie and Gertie,
Ruthelene and Truthelene,
   Are all good names for dolls.

Dorna and Lorna,
German and Herman,
Josanna and Johanna,
Alfred and Talfred,
Hamar and Tamar,
Ashur and Jasher,

Baruch and Saruch,
Mollyetta and Pollyetta,
   Are all good names for dolls.

Angelena and Vangelena,
Cherubima and Seraphima,
Bede and Reid,
Josabad and Rosabad,
Lulia and Tulia,
Harold and Jarold,
Jeroboam and Rehoboam,
Paulina and Saulina,
   Are all good names for dolls.

Tunice and Unice,
Sambrose and Vambrose,
Meshach and Sheshach,
Bertram and Gertram,
Amon and Samon,
Claudius and Maudius,
Borelius and Horelius,
Bonalene and Monalene,
   Are all good names for dolls.

*The Reading over of these 1000 Names, all different,
will give splendid Exercise in Spelling and Pronuncia-
tion.*

   Gomer and Homer,
   Selah and Telah,
   Rasman and Tasman,
   Barak and Sarak,
   Janet and Nanet,
   Heavenbella and Sevenbella,
   Ahaz and Azaz,
   Antimeg and Antineg,
     Are all good names for dolls.

   Allon and Fallon,
   Abdiel and Zabdiel,
   Andronicus and Veronicus,
   Anthony and Vanthony

271

Amery and Zamery,
James and Kames,
Antonius and Santonius,
Mattylene and Pattylene,
  Are all good names for dolls.

Bedrodach and Nedrodach,
Festus and Vestus,
Geoffrey and Zeffrey,
Henry and Kenry,
Gilbert and Hilbert,
Anim and Banim,
Noah and Joah,
Mercylene and Percylene,
  Are all good names for dolls.

Dovetta and Lovetta,
Azel and Bazel,
Corinda and Dorinda,
Besar and Cesar,
Doram and Horam,
Ananiah and Apia,
Floralius and Horalius,
Marionette and Sarionette,
  Are all good names for dolls.

Coralene and Doralene,
Floralene and Noralene,
Dathan and Nathan,
Abiram and Ahiram,
Imon and Dimon,
Cornelius and Aurelius,
Ethelene and Bethelene,
Jera and Terah,
  Are all good names for dolls.

Ben and Glen,
Neziah and Tiziah,
Madoc and Zadoc,
Pauline and Sauline,

Abihud and Ahihud,
Kiza and Liza,
Dius and Pius,
Nucy and Sucy,
    Are all good names for dolls.

Alfric and Salfric,
Frank and Hank,
Kobina and Rosina,
Florinda and Laurinda,
Deborah and Ketorah,
Shebaniah and Shecaniah,
Sherariah and Shemariah,
    Are all good names for dolls.

Abia, Beriah and Neriah,
Alberic, Almeric & Alperic,
Volinda, Wolinda & Zolinda
Abijah, Ahijah and Elijah,
Dida, Ida and Fida,
Dias, Elias and Tobias,
Quick, Vic and Zic,
Hugh, Leu and Pugh,
    Are all good names for dolls.

Cora, Dora and Flora,
Lora, Nora and Zora,
Biram, Hiram and Miram,
Vessie, Wessie and Zessie,
Barrat, Jarrat and Garrat
Ham, Lam and Zam,
Adelia, Afelia and Amelia,
Dugo, Hugo and Nugo,
    Are all good names for dolls.

Ivy, Livy and Zivy,
Betty, Hetty and Letty,
Netty, Petty and Zetty,
Linny, Winny and Zinny,
Hester, Lester and Nestor,

Helena, Serena and Sabina,
Mab, Nab and Rab,
Dottielene, Lottielene & Tottielene
   Are all good names for dolls.

Bruno, Juno and Uno,
Eugene, Nugene and Sugene,
Dorman, Gorman and Norman,
Jean, Vean and Zean,
Hew, Seu and Zue,
Azur, Kazur and Nazur,
Davia, Flavia and Pavia,
Apulias, Julius and Tulias,
   Are all good names for dolls.

Biram, Hiram and Piram,
Katline, Matline and Patline,
Seba, Sheba, and Zebah,
Aubrey, Daubrey and Vaubrey,
Nebo, Nego and Necho,
Andrew, Mandrew and Vandrew,
Dalwin, Talwin and Zalwin,
Abi, Ahi and Ami,
   Are all good names for dolls.

Larissa, Narissa and Varrissa,
Di, Guy and Nie,
Dot, Lot and Tot,
Delicia, Felicia and Letitia,
Bona, Jonah and Mona,
Queenie, Teenie and Weenie,
Edward, Nedward, Tedward,
Dom, Pom and Tom,
   Are all good names for dolls.

Muric, Uric and Zurich,
Doddard, Goddard and Stoddard,
Heggie, Meggie and Peggie,
Darvey, Harvey and Jarvey,
Haddox, Maddox and Zaddox,

Joel, Loel and Noel,
Aaron, Saron and Zaron,
Bilhah, Hillah and Zillah,
   Are all good names for dolls.

Anneline, Fannylene & Nannylene,
Albina, Aldina and Alvina,
Annie, Fannie and Nanny,
Elim, Phelim and Selim,
Bobbie, Robbie & Zobbie,
Alma, Palma and Talma,
Gillis, Phillis and Willis,
Bettylene, Hettylene & Lettylene,
   Are all good names for dolls.

Bennet, Jennet and Kennet,
Dobe, Job and Robe,
Bruce, Druce and Pruce,
Lillybella, Millybella & Tillybella,
Baruch, Karuch and Saruch,
Kilbert, Wilbert and Zilbert,
Leo, Neo and Zeo,
Dosabel, Josabel and Rosabel,
   Are all good names for dolls.

Darion, Marion and Sarion,
Devalene, Evalene and Nevalene,
Josephine, Mosephine & Rosephine,
Ezra, Dezra and Kezra,
Dollybella, Mollybella & Pollybella,
Halena, Kalena and Salena,
Byra, Dyra and Lyra,
Iralene, Liralene and Miralene,
   Are all good names for dolls.

Lavinia, Savinia and Vavinia,
Duckylene, Luckylene and Zuckylene,
Tiglath-Pileser and Tilgath-Pilneser,
Abinadab, Ahinadab and Aminadab,
Abimelech, Ahimelech and Elimelech,

Felix, Kelix and Selix,
Alpheus, Dalpheus and Ralpheus,
Balak, Halak and Lamech,
    Are all good names for dolls.

Randal, Sandal and Vandal,
Arabella, Carrabella and Clarabella,
Harriet, Marriet and Variet,
Abilene, Mabilene and Fabilene,
Erwin, Kirwin and Mirwin,
Agar, Dagar and Zagar,
Alice, Dalice and Zalice,
Bab, Tab and Zab,
    Are all good names for dolls.

Emmeline, Femmeline and Jermeline,
Lemmeline, Pemmeline and Zemmeline,
Haggylene, Maggylene and Peggylene,
Hilda, Kilda and Lilda,
Milda, Tilda and Zilda,
B—etta, C—etta and D—etta,
E—etta, G—etta and V—etta,
Catalina, Matalina and Patalina,
    Are all good names for dolls.

Lerman, Merman and Zerman,
Ariel, Dariel and Zariel,
Gibeon, Tibeon and Zibeon,
Jessie, Kessie and Sessie,
Dias, Pius, Thias and Zius,
Doll, Moll, Poll and Noll,
A—etta, J—etta, K—etta and Mayetta,
Annabella, Fannybella and Nannybella,
    Are all good names for dolls.

Boy, Foy, Joy and Moy,
A—, J—, K—and May,
Eliza, Ebiza, Ediza, and Egisa,
Ehiza, Eniza, Eriza and Etiza,
Bell, Nell, Val and Zell,

Bem, Em, Sem and Zem,
Arc, Clark, Mark and Park,
Kat, Nat, Mat and Pat,
   Are all good names for dolls.

Celia, Delia, Melia and Zelia,
Phil, Till, Will and Zill,
Binny, Dinny, Finny and Jinny,
Birza, Girza, Mirza and Tirza,
Edwin, Fredwin, Nedwin, and Tedwin,
Jorah, Korah, Nora and Zorah,
Boswald, Goswald, Oswald and Roswald,
Carley, Charley, Harley and Varley,
   Are all good names for dolls.

Clara, Lara, Sara and Zara,
Florace, Horace, Morris and Norris,
Cary, Fairy, Mary and Sary,
Barry, Carrie, Harry and Larry,
Crissy, Kissy, Sissy and Melissy,
Harman, Darman, Jarman and Sharman,
Ubenia, Igenia, Ulenia and Uphemia,
Birene, Irene, Mirene and Sirene,
   Are all good names for dolls.

Acelius, Adelius, Afelius and Amelius,
Anelius, Apelius, Arelius and Avelius,
Dannah, Hannah, Jannah and Mannah,
Aram, Naram, Saram and Zaram,
Benny, Denny, Jenny and Kenny,
Albert, Dalbert, Falbert and Galbert,
Barlo, Carlo, Marlo and Varlo,
Jemuel, Kemuel, Lemuel and Shemuel,
   Are all good names for dolls.

Bon, Con, Don and John,
Cain, Jane, Mayne and Payne,
Jimmy, Mimmy, Simmy and Timmy,
Dick, Hick, Mick and Nick,
Ally, Lally, Sally and Vally,

Bill, Hill, Lill, Mill and Phil,
Bolo, Molo, Polo, Rollo and Solo,
Levi, Nevi, Sevi, Vevi and Zevi,
   Are all good names for dolls.

Hatty, Katty, Matty, Natty and Patty,
Billy, Lily, Milly, Tilly and Willy,
Dolly, Jolly, Molly, Nolly and Polly,
Dizzy, Kizzy, Lizzy, Sizzy and Tizzy,
Eddy, Freddy, Neddy, Ready and Teddy,
Beric, Deric, Eric, Leric and Zeric,
Eva, Deva, Neva, Seva and Zeva,
Addi, Daddi, Laddi, Vaddi and Zaddi,
   Are all good names for dolls.

Dina, Mina, Nina, Vina and Zina,
Adar, Badar, Kadar, Nadar and Zadar,
Bira, Ira, Kira, Lira, Mira and Sira,
Chloe, Floe, Joey, Loe, Moe and Zoe,
Agg, Dagg, Greig, Mag, Peg and Zag,
Bell, Hal, Lal, Mell, Nell and Sal,
Jim, Kim, Nim, Sim, Tim, Vim and Zim,
Ann, Dan, Fan, Jan, Nan, Pan and San,
   Are all good names for dolls.

E. W. Cole

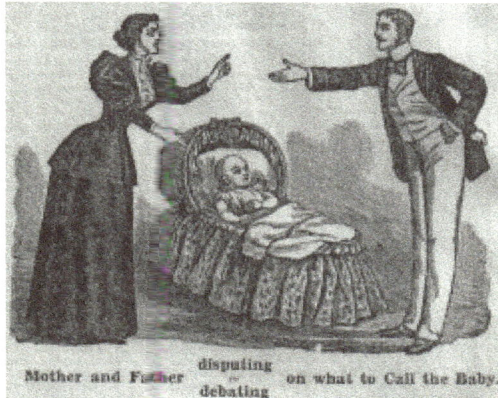

Mother and Father disputing ~ debating on what to Call the Baby.

278

All Old Dollies should be hunted up and Named.

Three Hundred more Names for Dollies, Doggies, Pussies, and Babies.

Abigail and Abihail,
Allamlech & Anammelech,
Azariah and Hezeliah,
Boyetta and Joyetta,
Hosea and Josea,
Baxter and Dexter,
Deleus and Peleus,
Borcas and Dorcas,
    Are all good names for dolls.

Dickylene and Mickylene,
Dicketta and Micketta,
Bennylene and Pennielene,
Billyetta and Willyetta,
Daddylene and Laddilene,
Dinahlene and Ninalene,
Claudelene and Maudelene,
Ruthetta and Truthetta,
    Are all good names for dolls.

Ducylene and Lucylene,
Jinnyetta and Winnyetta,
Fidalene and Icalene,
Adalene and Sadalene,
Beckylene and Jackylene,
Arthuretta & Marthuretta,
Claudelena and Maudelena,
Marianetta and Sarianetta,
    Are all good names for dolls.

Elizalene and Lrizalene,
Coraetta and Doraetta,
Millylene and Tillylene,
Simonetta and Timonetta,
Lucyetta and Mucyetta,

Marylene and Sarylene,
Lubyetta and Rubyetta,
Claralene and Sarahlene,
   Are all good names for dolls.

Bennyetta and Jennyetta,
Gladdilena and Paddylena,
Maryetta and Sarietta,
Borgialene and Georgialene,
Cyliene and Lyliene,
Maxalene and Rexaline,
Maxetta and Rexetta,
Maxabella and Rexabella,
   Are all good names for dolls.

Selina and Serena,
Sallyetta and Vallyetta,
Iralena and Myralena,
Bessielena and Jessielena,
Honeylene and Moneylene,
Bertielina and Gertielina,
Gilbertine and Wilbertine,
Julietta and Tulietta,
   Are all good names for dolls.

Biddylene and Liddylene,
Edwardetta & Tedwardetta,
Bertielene and Gertieline,
Henryetta and Benryetta,
Carrielene and Harrylene,
Bennylene and Glennylene,
Nellyetta and Sellyetta,
Bobbielene and Robbielene,
   Are all good names for dolls.

Cornelia and Cordelia,
Sundaylena & Mondaylena,
Hellen and Tellin,
Angelus and Vangelus,
Saletta and Valetta,

Irene and Ilene,
Kittylene and Myrilene,
Iralius and Myralius,
   Are all good names for dolls.

Pussies have Thrown Dolly out of the Cradle.

Southetta and Louthetta,
Melbalena and Selbalena,
Lidneylena & Sydneylena,
Adelena and Madelena,
Mirthelena and Perthalena,
Brisbanetta and Lisbonetta,
Rasmanetta & Tasmanetta,
Lowrylena and Maorilena,
   Are all good names for dolls.

Dollybel, Mollybel and Pollybel,
Catilius, Matilius, and Patilius,
Cinalene, Hinalene and Linalene,
Bess, Chess, Hess and Zess,
Didas, Fidas and Midas,
Linalene, Winalene and Zinalene,
Dillius, Millius and Fillius,
Hestor, Lestor and Nestor,

281

Are all good names for dolls.

Dollyus, Mollyus and Pollyus,
Lene, Mene, Tene and Vene,
Basalene, Masalene and Vasalene,
Lucia, Mucia and Nucia,
Danope, Fanope and Panope,
Hero, Nero, Pero and Thero,
Ida, Sida, Vida and Zida,
Hictor, Rictor and Victor,
    Are all good names for dolls.

Belus, Helus, Nelus and Zelus,
Eno, Leno and Zeno,
Daniel, Ananial and Nathanel,
Abel, Jabel, Mabal and Nabal,
Kish, Mish and Wish,
Dolletta, Molletta and Polletta,
Haletta, Naletta and Saletta,
Barryetta, Harryetta & Larryetta,
    Are all good names for dolls.

Abeletta, Mabeletta & Nabeletta,
Lilyetta, Millyetta and Tillyetta,
Bonalene, Jonahlene & Monalene,
Deolene, Neolene and Leolene,
Jimmylene, Simmylene, Timmylene,
Ino, Dino, Kino and Mino,
Dana, Hana, Jana and Nana,
    Are all good names for dolls.

Annetta, Fanetta and Nanetta,
Edicus, Tedicus and Fredicus,
Eddyetta, Teddyetta & Freddyetta,
Emilus, Remilus and Zemilus,
Faula, Paula and Saula,
Callio, Sallio and Vallio,
Delios, Helios and Melios,
Deo, Leo, Neo and Zeo,
    Are all good names for dolls.

Dollian, Mollian and Pollian,
Dorabella, Florabella, Norabella,
Lilo, Milo, Philo, Silo and Tilo,
Bella, Kella, Nella and Stella,
Dollyetta, Lollyetta & Nollyetta,
Sunnylena, Honeylena, Moneylena,
Moonelena, Noonelena, Doonelena,
Stellalena, Bellalena & Ellalena,
    Are all good names for dolls.

E.W.C.

283

P.S. Nebuchadnezzar and Nebuchadrezzar,
Wandiligong & Croajingoalong,
Are four good names for pussies.

A Bad-tempered Baby Boy.

Good Mamma

Love, come and sit upon my knee,
And give me kisses, one, two, three,
And tell me whether you love me.
    My baby.

For this I'm sure, that I love you,
And many, many things I do,
And many an hour I sit and sew
    For baby.

And then at night I lie awake,
Thinking of things that I can make,
And trouble that I mean to take
    For baby.

An when you're good and do not cry,
Nor into angry passions fly,
You can't think how papa and I
    Love baby.

But if my little child should grow
To be a naughty child, I know
'Twould grieve mamma to serve her so,
    My baby.

And when you saw me pale and thin,
By grieving for my baby's sin,
I think you'd wish that you had been
    A better baby.

How They Made Up

Two naughty little people
    Had a quarrel one sad day,
Each said that with the other,

She never more would play.

And so upon each other
  Their little backs they turned,
And all the old time fondness
  Alas! they coldly spurned.

But oh! their angry hearts grew weary,
  The anger died away,
Each hoped that soon the other
  Would have a word to say.

Each waited, oh how sadly!
  Each moved a little near,
And each "around the corner"
  Began, at last, to peer.

Then Nellie held her dolly
  To Annie with a smile:
"You may have it if you want to.
  An play with it awhile."

Then Annie quickly followed
  The rule she knew was right:
"I've got an apple Nellie,
  I'll give you a big bite."
And somehow the sweet faces
  Met fair and square at last,
And kisses sweet and loving
  Sent the quarrel flying fast.

Little Whimpy

Whimpy, little Whimpy,
  Cried so much one day;
His grandma couldn't stand it,
  And his mother ran away!
He was waiting by the window

When they all came home to tea.
And a gladder boy than Whimpy,
  You never need hope to see!

A Naughty, Naughty, Naughty Girl.

Master Cross Patch

Cross Patch, cross Patch,
  What's the matter now?
Why that wail of fretfulness,
  And a scowl upon your brow?

Milk upset and wasted!
  Water in your plate,
No one's sorry, old cross Patch,
  For your wretched fate.

You began the morning
  With a frown, my lad
And every word that you have said

287

Has made your mother sad.

And by your pettish temper,
  You've spoiled your breakfast, too.
Cross Patch, cross Patch,
  No one pities you.

Sulky Sarah

Why is Sarah standing there,
Leaning down upon a chair,
With such an angry lip and brow?
I wonder what's the matter now.

Come here my dear and tell me true,
It is because I spoke to you
About the work you'd done so slow,
That you are standing fretting so?

Why then, indeed, I'm grieved to see,
That you can so ill-tempered be:
You make your fault a great deal worse
By being angry and perverse.

Oh! how much better 'twould appear,
To see you shed a humble tear,
And then to hear you meekly say,
"I'll not do so another day."

Jane Taylor

A Naughty Bad-Tempered Boy who broke
his Sister's Playthings.

A New Year's Gift

A charming present comes from town,
  A baby-house quite neat;
With kitchen, parlours, dining-room,
  And chambers, all complete.

A gift to Emma and to Rose,
  From grandpa it came;

289

The little Rosa smil'd delight,
  And Emma did the same.

They eagerly exam'in'd all—
  The furniture was gay;
And in the rooms they plac'd their dolls,
  When dress'd in fine array.

At night, their little candles lit,
  And as they must be fed,
To supper down the dolls were plac'd,
  And then were put to bed.

Thus Rose and Emma pass'd each hour
  Devoted to their play;
And long were cheerful, happy, kind—
  No cross disputes had they.

Till Rose in baby-house would change
  The chairs which were below
"This carpet they would better suit;
  I think I'll have it so."

"No, no indeed," her sister said,
  "I'm older, Rose, than you;
And I'm the pet—the house is mine:
  Miss, what I say is true."

The quarrel grew to such a height,
  Mamma she heard the noise,
And coming in, beheld the floor
  All strew'd with broken toys.

"O fie, my Emma naughty Rose!
  Say, why this sulk and pout?
Remember this is New Year's Day,
  And both are going out."

Now Betty calls the little girls
  To come upstairs and dress:

They still revile, with threats
  And angry rage express

But just prepar'd to leave their room,
  Persisting yet in strife,
Rose sick'ning fell or Betty's lap.
  As void of sense or life

Mamma appear'd at Betty's call—
  John for the doctor goes;
The measles, he begins to think,
  Dread symptoms al disclose.

"But though I stay, my Emma, you
  May go and spend the day."
"O no, mamma," replied the child,
  "Do suffer me to stay.

"Beside my sister's bed I'll sit,
  And watch her with such care,
"No pleasure can I e'er enjoy,
  Till she my pleasure share.

"How silly now seems our dispute,
  Not one of us she knows;
How pale she looks how hard she breathes,
  Poor pretty little Rose "

Adelaide Taylor

Quarrelling

  Let dogs delight to bark and bite,
    For God hath made them so
  Let bears and lion growl and fight,
    For 'tis their nature too.

Dr Watts

Angry Words

Poison-drops of care and sorrow,
  Bitter poison-drops are they,
Weaving for the coming morrow,
  Saddest memories of to-day.

Angry words, oh! let them never
  From the tongue unbridled slip;
May the heart's best impulse ever
  Check them ere they soil the lip.

Love is much too pure and holy,
  Friendship is too sacred far,
For a moment's reckless folly
  Thus to desolate and mar.

Angry words are lightly spoken,
  Bitterest thoughts are rashly stirred,
Brightest links of life are broken,
  By a single angry word.

The Tear And The Smile

A little tear and a little smile
  Set out to run a race;
We watched them closely all the while—
  Their course was baby's face.

The little tear he got the start
  We really feared he'd win,
He ran so fast and made a dart
  Straight for her dimpled chin.

But somehow, it was very queer,
  We watched them all the while—

The little, shining, fretful tear
  Got beaten by the smile.

Love One Another

Silly little Mary,
  Sulking all the day,
While the other children
  Run about and play.

Silly little Mary,
  Wears a peevish look,
When she sees the others
  Laughing at the brook.

Silly little Mary,
  Will not skip or swing,
Won't at puss-in-corner play,
  Won't do anything.

Silly little Mary
  Hides behind the bank,
In among the rocks and weeds,
  All so thick and rank.

Mary hears a footstep
  O'er the velvet moss,
Sees a roguish little face
  It is Willie Ross.

I have found you, Mary.
  Won't you come play too?
And with cheeks all crimsoned,
  Whispers—I love you.

Ah! but love has conquered
  Fall the tears like rain,
Then our little Mary

Is herself again.

Where are sulks and tears now?
  All are fled away.
And our little Mary
  Will both laugh and play.

A Naughty Sulky Boy.

A Bad-Tempered Girl.

Anger

Oh! anger is an evil thing
  And spoils the fairest face;
It cometh like a rainy cloud
  Upon a sunny place.

One angry moment often does
  What we repent for years:
It works the wrong we ne'er make right
  By sorrow or tears.

It speaks the rude and cruel word
  That wounds a feeling breast:
It strikes the reckless sudden blow—
  It breaks the household rest.

We dread the dog that turns in play,
  All snapping, fierce and quick;
We shun the steed whose temper shows
  In strong and savage kick.

But how much more we find to blame,
  When passion wildly swells
In hearts where kindness has been taught,
  And brains where reason dwells!

The hand of peace is frank and warm
  And soft as a ring-dove's wing;
And he who quells an angry thought
  Is greater than a king.

Shame to the lips that ever seek
  To stir up jarring strife,
When gentleness would shed so much
  Of Christian joy through life!

Ever remember in thy youth,
  That he who firmly tries
To conquer an to rule himself,

Is noble, brave and wise.

Eliza Cook

The Little Girl That Beat Her Sister

Go, go, my naughty girl, and kiss
  Your little sister dear;
I must not have such things as this,
  Nor noisy quarrels here.

What! little children scold and fight,
  That ought to be so mild:
Oh! Mary, 'tis a shocking sight
  To see an angry child.

I can't imagine, for my part,
  The reason of your folly,
As if she did you any hurt
  By playing with your dolly.

See, see the little tears that run
  So quickly from her eye:
Come, my sweet innocent, have done,
  'Twill do no good to cry.

Go, Mary, wipe her tears away
  And make it up with kisses:
And never turn a pretty play
  To such a pet as this is.

Home Peace

"Whatever brawls disturb the street
  There should be peace at home;
Where sisters dwell and brothers meet

Quarrels should never come."

Dr. Watts

Little Dick Snappy

Little Dick Snappy
Was always unhappy
Because he did nothing but fret;
And when he once cried,
'Twas in vain that you tried
To make him his troubles forget.

His mother once brought him
A drum, which she bought him
Hard by at a neighbouring fair,
And gave such another
To Edward his brother,
And left them their pleasures to share.

Little Edward began
Like a nice little man,
To play with his little new drum;
But Dick, with a pout,
Only turned his about
In his hands, and looked sulky and glum.

"What's the matter, dear Dick?
You look sad; are you sick?
Come, march like a soldier with me:
The enemy comes
Let us beat on our drums,
And mamma will our merriment see."

"No! I don't like my new toy,"
Said my ill-humoured boy,
"And yours is the best and most new;
If you'll give me yours,

297

Then I'll go out of doors;
But if not, I'll kick mine in two."

"Oh no! brother, no—
Pray do not say so
Of a trifle, in anger and haste;
Though they are equally new,
Yet my drum I'll give you,
But I've tied it in knots round my waist."

Then quarrelsome Dick
Gave his brother a kick;
But he did not give him another,
But, saying no more,
Edward walked to the door,
Only giving one look at his brother.

Then, bursting with spite,
With his utmost of might
Master Dick trod his drum on the floor;
The parchment did crack,
When lo; Edward comes back,
And his drum in his hands then he bore.

"The string is untied,
Dearest brother," he cried—
"So now I with pleasure will change;"
But when Dick's drum he found
Lying broke on the ground,
Oh! how did his countenance change.

"I'm really ashamed,"
Dick, sobbing, exclaimed,
"At the difference between you and me;
But continue my friend,
And I'll try to amend,
And a good-tempered fellow to be."

Which Shall It Be, Dear?

If fretting pays you, fret,
And get into a pet,
And slam and bang
The doors with a whang,
And flame and flare,
And say "Don't care."
And slip round sly,
And make the baby cry,
And thus get sent to bed, to sob it out.

But if it does not pay
Why then, my dear, do pray
Just do the other thing,
And toot and sing,
And whistle like a bird.
Letting your voice be heard,
From morn till night,
In echoes bright,
Sending the best of cheer into the home.

I will be Good, Mamma.

Quarrelsome Boys.

Govern Your Temper

Oh, Govern your temper!
  For music, the sweetest,
Was never so sweet—
  Nor one-half so divine,
As a heart kept in tune,
  Which, the moment thou greetest,
Breathes harmony dearer
  Than notes can combine!

Never say it is nature.
  And may not be cured;
One tithe of the time,
  Which to music we yield
Would render the conquest
  Of temper insured,
And bring us more music

Than a song e'er revealed.

Oh, govern your temper!
  For roses, the fairest,
Were never so fair,
  Nor so rich in perfume,
As the flowers, which e'en thou,
  Chilly winter sparest—
The flowers of the heart,
  Which unchangingly bloom!

Never think it is nature—
  For oh! if it be,
The sooner the spirit
  Of nature is shown,
That the spirit of heaven
  Is higher than she,
The sooner, the longer,
  Will love be our own.

A Bad, Wicked Bully.

Where Do You Live

I knew a man, and his name was Horner,
He used to live at Grumble Corner,—
Grumble Corner, in Cross Patch Town,—
And he never was seen without a frown.
He grumbled at this, he grumbled at that;
He growled at the dog, he growled at the cat;
He grumbled at morning, he grumbled at night,
And to grumble and growl was his chief delight.

He grumbled so much at his wife, that she
Began to grumble as well as he;
And all the children wherever they went
Reflected their parents' discontent.
If the sky was dark and betokened rain,
Then Mr. Horner was sure to complain;
And if there was never a cloud about,
He'd grumble because of threatened drought.

One day, as I loitered along the street,
My old acquaintance I chanced to meet.
Whose face was without the look of care
And the ugly frown it used to wear.
"I may be mistaken, perhaps," I said.
As, after saluting, I turned my head;
"But it is, and it isn't, the Mr. Horner
Who lived so long at Grumble Corner."

I met him next day, and I met him again,
In melting weather, in pouring rain;
When stocks were up and when stocks were down;
But a smile, somehow, had replac'd the frown.
It puzzled me much, and so, one day,
I seized his hand in a friendly way,
And said "Mr. Horner, I'd like to know
What can have happened to change you so."

He laughed a laugh that was good to hear,
For it told of a conscience calm and clear,

And he said, with none of the old-time drawl,
"Why, I've changed my residence, that is all."
"Changed your residence?" "Yes," said Horner,
"It wasn't healthy at Grumble Corner,
And so I've moved: 'twas a change complete;
And you'll find me now at Thanksgiving Street."

And every day, as I move along
The streets, so filled with busy throng,
I watch each face, and can always tell
Where men, and women, and children dwell.
And many a discontented mourner
Is spending his days at Grumble Corner,
Sour and sad, whom I long to entreat
To take a house in Thanksgiving Street.

Temper

Bad temper, go,
You shall never stay with me;
Bad temper, go,
You and I shall never agree.

For I will always be kind, and mild,
And gentle pray to be,
And do to others as I wish
That they should do to me.

Temper bad
With me shall never stay;
Temper bad
Can never be happy and gay.

Naughty Boys Fighting.

A Vain old Fop.

A Fine Lady

Did ever you see such wondrous airs!
  Oh, oh! my Lady Jane!
Your airs will blow you quite away,
You'll go to Vanity-land to stay,
  And ne'er come back again.

Pray, what's the price of your hat my dear?
  And what'll you take for your gloves?
And how'll you sell each pink kid shoe?

And your wonderful dressed-up poodle, too?
  You're a precious pair of loves.

You're all too fine for us, you know,
  With your airs and stately tread,
From your pretty feet to your pretty dress,
And up to your ruffled neck, oh, yes,
  And on to your feathered head.

So go your way, my Lady Jane,
Till you come from Vanity-land again.

To A Little Girl Who Liked To Look In The Glass

Why is my silly girl so vain,
Looking in the glass again?
For the meekest flower of spring
Is a gayer little thing.

Is your merry eye so blue
As the violet, wet with dew?
Yet it loves the best to hide
By the hedge's shady side.

Is your bosom half so fair
As the modest lilies are?
Yet their little bells are hung
Bright and shady leaves among.

When your cheek the brightest glows,
Is it redder than the rose?
But its sweetest buds are seen
Almost hid with moss and green.

Little flowers that open gay,
Peeping forth at break of day,
In the garden, hedge, or plain,
Have more reason to be vain.

The Ragged Girl's Sunday

"Oh, dear Mamma, that little girl
  Forgets this is the day
When children should be clean and neat,
  And read and learn and pray!

Her face is dirty and her frock,
  Holes in her stockings, see;
Her hair is such a fright, oh, dear!
  How wicked she must be!

She's playing in the kennel dirt
  With ragged girls and boys;
But I would not on Sunday touch
  My clean and pretty toys.

I go to church, and sit so still,
  I in the garden walk,
Or take my stool beside the fire,
  And hear nice Sunday talk.

I read my bible, learn my hymns,
  My catechism say;
That wicked little girl does not—
  She only cares to play."

"Ah! hush that boasting tone, my love,
  Repress self-glorying pride;
You can do nothing of yourself—
  Friends all your actions guide."

Criminal Pride

Hark the rustle of a dress
Stiff with lavish costliness!
Here comes on whose cheek would flush
But to have her garment brush

'Gainst the girl whose fingers thin
Wove the weary 'broidery in,
Bending backward from her toil,
Lest her tears the silk might soil,
And in midnight's chill and murk,
Stitched her life into the work.
Little doth the wearer heed
Of the heart-break in the brede;
A hyena by her side
Skulks, down-looking—it is Pride.

J. R. Lowell

Foolish Fanny

Oh! Fanny was so vain a lass,
If she came near a looking-glass,
She'd stop right here for many a minute
To see how pretty she looked in it.

She'd stand and prink, and fix her hair
Around her forehead with great care;
And take some time to tie a bow
That must, to please her, lie just so.

Her mother's bonnet she'd put on,
And all her richest dresses don,
And up and down the room parade,
And much enjoy her promenade.

She always liked to wear the best
She had, and being so much dress'd
Could not enjoy the romps with those
Who wore much less expensive clothes.

Each day she grew so fond of dress
It gave her great unhappiness
If every day, and all the while,

307

COLE

She wasn't in the latest style.

If asked to turn the jumping-rope
Her pretty parasol she'd ope,
Lest she should freckle in the sun:
And that was her idea of fun!

She didn't dare to take the cat
Or poodle-dog from off the mat,
Lest they should catch their little toes
In laces, frills, or furbelows.

The very things that gave her joy,
Her peace and comfort would destroy,
For oft an ugly nail would tear
The costly dress she chose to wear.

The foolish girl turned up her nose
At those who dressed in plainer clothes,
And lived in quiet style, for she
With wealthy people chose to be

She never was the least inclined
With knowledge to enrich her mind;
And all the mental food she ate
Was served upon a fashion-plate.

As this was so, you'll see at once
That Fan grew up a silly dunce:
An there was nothing to admire
About her, but her fine attire.

Foolish Fanny.

Mr. Importance walking along the street.

Pride

Come, come, Mr. Peacock,
  You must not be so proud,
Although you can boast such a train,
  For there's many a bird
    Far more highly endowed,
And not half so conceited and vain.

Let me tell you, gay bird,
  That a suit of fine clothes
Is a sorry distinction at most,
  And seldom much valued

309

Excepting by those
Who only such graces can boast.

The nightingale certainly
  Wears a plain coat,
But she cheers and delights with her song;
  While you, though so vain,
  Cannot utter a note
To please by the use of your tongue.

The hawk cannot boast
  Of a plumage so gay,
But more piercing and clear is her eye;
  And while you are strutting
  About all the day,
She gallantly soars in the sky.

The dove may be clad
  In a plainer attire,
But she is not so selfish and cold;
  And her love and affection
  More pleasure inspire
Than all your fine purple and gold.

So, you see, Mr. Peacock,
  You must not be proud,
Although you can boast such a train,
  For many a bird
  Is more highly endowed,
And not half so conceited and vain.

Sinful Pride

How proud we are, how fond to shew
Our clothes, and call them rich and new,
When the poor sheep and silkworm wore
That very clothing long before!

The tulip and butterfly
Appear in gayer coats than I;
Let me be dress'd as fine as I will,
Flies, worms, and flowers exceed me.

Dr. Watts

Finery

In a frock richly trimm'd
  With a beautiful lace,
And hair nicely dress'd
  Hanging over her face,
Thus deck'd, Harriet went
  To the house of a friend,
With a large little party
  The ev'ning to spend.

"Ah! how they will all
  Be delighted, I guess,
And stare with surprise
  At my elegant dress!"
Thus said the vain girl,
  And her little heart beat,
Impatient the happy
  Young party to meet.

But, alas! they were all
  To intent on their fun,
To observe the gay clothes
  This fine lady had on;
And thus all her trouble
  Quite lost is design,
For they saw she was proud,
  But forgot she was fine.

'Twas Lucy, tho' only
  In simple white clad,

(Nor trimmings, nor laces,
  Nor jewels she had,)
Whose cheerful good nature
  Delighted them more,
Than all the fine garments
  That Harriet wore.

'Tis better to have
  A sweet smile on one's face,
Than to wear a rich frock
  With an elegant lace,
For the good-natur'd girl
  Is lov'd best in the main,
If her dress is but decent,
  Tho' ever so plain.

T I

A Fop

A little cane,
  A high-crowned hat,
A fixed impression,
  Rather flat.

A pointed shoe,
  A scanty coat,
A stand-up collar
  Round his throat

A gorgeous necktie
  Spreading wide,
A small moustache—
  Nine on a side.

Arms at right angles,
  Curved with ease,
A stilted walk

And shaky knees.

A languid drawl,
  The "English" swing,
An air of knowing
  Everything.

A vacant stare,
  Extremely rude,
And there you have
  The perfect dude.

Pride

Hark the rustle of a dress
Stiff with lavish costliness!
Here comes on whose cheek would flush
But to have her garment brush
'Gainst the girl whose fingers thin
Wove the weary 'broidery in,
Bending backward from her toil,
Lest her tears the silk might soil,
And in midnight's chill and murk,
Stitched her life into the work.
Shaping from her bitter thought,
Heart's-ease and forget-me-not,
Satirizing her despair
With the emblems woven there,
Little doth the wearer heed
Of the heart-break in the blede;
A hyena by her side
Skulks, down-looking—it is Pride.

    J. R. Lowell

Vain Lizzie

COLE

It surely is not good to see,
Lizzie so full of vanity,
  So fond of dress and show.
For when a fine new frock she wears,
She gives herself most silly airs,
  Wherever she may go.

She thinks herself a charming girl;
But when folks see her twist and twirl,
  They stop in every street,
They smile, or fairly laugh outright,
And say: "She's really quite a sight,
  Was ever such conceit?"

314

Greedy Ned

Mamma gave our Nelly an apple,
  So round, and big, and red;
It seemed, beside dainty wee Nelly,
  To be almost as large as her head.

Beside her young Neddie was standing—
  And Neddie loves apples, too,
"Ah! Nelly!" said Neddie, "give brother
  A bite of your apple—ah! do!"

Dear Nelly held out the big apple;
  Ned opened his mouth very wide—
So wide, that the startled red apple
  Could almost have gone inside!

And oh! what a bite he gave it!
  The apple looked small, I declare,
When Ned gave it back to his sister,
  Leaving that big bite there.

Poor Nelly looked frightened a moment,
  Then a thought made her face grow bright;
"Here, Ned, you can take the apple—

I'd rather have the bite!"

Eva L. Carson, In "St. Nicholas"

The Biggest Piece Of Pie

Once, when I was a little boy,
  I sat me down to cry,
Because my little brother had
  The biggest piece of pie.

They said I was a naughty boy,
  But I have since seen men
Behave themselves as foolishly
  As I behaved then.

For we are often thankless for
  Rich blessings when we sigh,
To think some lucky neighbour has
  A "bigger piece" of pie.

The Greedy, Impatient Girl

"Oh! I am so hungry,
  I'm sure I can't wait,
For my apple-pudding to cool,
  So, Mary, be quick now
  And bring me a plate,
For waiting for dinner
  I always did hate,
Tho' forced oft to do it at school.

"But at home, when mamma
  Is not in the way,
I surely will do as I choose;
  And I do not care for

What you please to say—
The pudding won't burn me—
No longer I'll stay.
What business have you to refuse?"

And now a large slice
Of the pudding she got,
And, fearful she should have no more,
She cramm'd her mouth full
Of the apple so hot,
Which had but a minute
Come out of the pot,
But quickly her triumph was o'er.

Her mouth and her tongue
Were so dreadfully sore,
And suffer'd such terrible pain,
Her pride and her consequence
Soon were all o'er,
And she said, now unable
To eat any more,
"Oh! I never will do so again!"

And thus, by not minding
What she had been told,
Young Ellinor lost all her treat;
Too greedy to wait
Till the pudding was cold,
By being impatient,
Conceited, and bold,
Not a mouthful at last could she eat.

C. Horwood.

A Story Of An Apple

Little Tommy, and Peter, and Archie, and Bob
Were walking, one day, when they found

317

An apple: 'twas mellow, and rosy, and red,
  And lying alone on the ground.

Said Tommy: "I'll have it." Said peter: "'Tis mine."
  Said Archie: "I've got it; so there!"
Said Bobby: "Now, let us divide it in four parts
  And each of us boys have a share."

"No, no!" shouted Tommy, "I'll have it myself."
  Said Peter: "I want it, I say."
Said Archie: "I've got it, and I'll have it all,
  I won't give a morsel away."

Then Tommy he snatched it, and Peter he fought,
  ('Tis sad and distressing to tell!)
And Archie held on with his might and his main,
  Till out from his fingers it fell.

Away from the quarrelsome urchins it flew
  And then, down a green little hill
That apple it roll'd, and it roll'd, and it roll'd
  As if it would never be still.

A lazy old brindle was nipping the grass,
  And switching her tail at the flies,
When all of a sudden the apple rolled down
  And stopped just in front of her eyes.

She gave but a bite and a swallow or two—
  That apple was seen nevermore!
"I wish," whimpered Archie, and Peter, and Tom,
  "We'd kept it and cut it in four."

      Sydney Dyer

Greedy Richard

"I think I want some pies this morning"

Said Dick, stretching himself and yawning;
So down he threw his slate and books,
And saunter'd to the pastry-cook's.

And there he cast his greedy eyes
Round on the jellies and the pies,
So to select, with anxious care,
The very nicest that was there.

At last the point was thus decided:
As his opinion was divided
'Twixt pie and jelly, he was loth
Either to leave, so took them both.

Now Richard never could be pleas'd
To stop when hunger was appeas'd,
But he'd go on to eat and stuff,
Long after he had had enough.

"I shan't take any more," said Dick,
"Dear me, I feel extremely sick:
I cannot eat this other bit;
I wish I had not tasted it."

Then slowly rising from his seat,
He threw the cheesecake in the street,
And left the tempting pastry-cook's
With very discontented looks.

Jane Taylor

The Plum Cake

"Oh! I've got a plum cake,
And a rare feast I'll make,
I'll eat, and I'll stuff, and I'll cram;
Morning, noontime, and night,
It shall be my delight;—

What a happy young fellow I am."

Thus said little George,
And, beginning to gorge,
With zeal to his cake he applied;
While fingers and thumbs,
For the sweetmeats and plums,
Were hunting and digging besides.

But, woeful to tell,
A misfortune befell,
Which ruin'd this capital fun!
After eating his fill,
He was taken so ill,
That he trembled for what he had done.

As he grew worse and worse,
The doctor and nurse,
To cure his disorder were sent;
And rightly, you'll think,
He had physic to drink,
Which made him his folly repent.

And while on his bed
He roll'd his hot head,
Impatient with sickness and pain;
He could not but take
This reproof from his cake,
"Don't be such a glutton again!"

Another Plum Cake

"Oh! I've got a plum cake,
And a feast let us make,
Come, school-fellows, come at my call;
I assure you 'tis nice,
And we'll each have a slice,

Here's more than enough for us all."

Thus said little Jack,
  As he gave it a smack,
And sharpen'd his knife for the job!
  While round him a troop,
  Formed a clamorous group,
And hail'd him the king of the mob.

With masterly strength
  He cut thro' it at length,
And gave to each playmate a share;
  Dick, William, and James,
  And many more names,
Partook of his benevolent care.

And when it was done,
  And they'd finish'd their fun,
To marbles or hoop they went back,
  And each little boy
  Felt it always a joy
To do a good turn for good Jack.

In his task and his book,
  His best pleasures he took,
And as he thus wisely began,
  Since he's been a man grown,
  He has constantly shown
That a good boy will make a good man.

Ann Taylor

The Great Glutton

'Twas the voice of the glutton,
  I heard him complain:
My waistcoat unbutton,
  I'll eat once again.

321

The Glutton

The voice of the glutton
 I heard with disdain—
"I've not eaten this hour,
 I must eat again;
Oh! give me a pudding,
 A pie, or a tart,
A duck or a fowl,
 Which I love from my heart.

"How sweet is the picking
 Of capon or chicken!
A turkey and chine
 Are most charming and fine;
To eat and to drink
 All my pleasure is still,
I care not who wants
 So that I have my fill."

Oh! let me not be,
 Like a glutton, inclined
In feasting my body
 And starving my mind,
With moderate viands
 Be thankful, and pray
That the Lord may supply me
 With food the next day.

Not always a-craving
With hunger still raving;
But little and sweet
Be the food that I eat.
To learning and wisdom
 Oh let me apply.
And leave to the glutton
 His pudding and pie.

J. Taylor

Selfish Edith

Selfish Edith, not to give
　Her sister one, when she has two!
I wouldn't and I couldn't love
　A selfish girl like her, could you?

Hear Bessie ask in plaintive tone,
　"Please, Edith, let me play with one!"
While naughty Edith shakes her head:
　I fear she'll have but little fun

With toys unshared so selfishly;
　But when she tires of lonely play,
Perhaps she'll secretly resolve
　To be more kind another day.

Hoggish Henry

Oh! Henry eats like any pig;
　He drives his mother mad.
She scolds. He does not care a fig,
　It's really very sad.

She says: "Your sister, little dear,
　Is always clean and neat;
And though she's younger by a year,
　How nicely she can eat."

It's all in vain. He does not care;
　He's shocking to behold.
The table-cloth and napkin there

323

Are smeared in every fold.

Upon the floor, crumbs thickly lie,
　As though for chickens laid,
Around his mouth and nose, oh fie!
　Is dirt of every shade.

He looks, bedaubed with smear and stain,
　Just like some savage wild,
His hands as forks are used, it's plain.
　For shame! You dirty child!

Selfishness

Look at the selfish man! see how he locks
Tight in his arms his mortgages and stocks!
While deeds and titles in his hand he grasps,
And gold and silver close around he clasps.
But not content with this, behind he drags
A cart well-laden with ponderous bags;
The orphan's wailings, and the widow's woe
From mercy's fountain cause no tears to flow;
He pours no cordial in the wounds of pain;
Unlocks no prison, and unclasps no chain;
His heart is like the rock where sun nor dew
Can rear one plant or flower of heavenly hue.
No thought of mercy there may have its birth,
For helpless misery or suffering worth;
The end of all his life is paltry pelf,
And all his thoughts are centred on—himself:
The wretch of both worlds; for so mean a sum,
First starved in this, then damn'd in that to come.

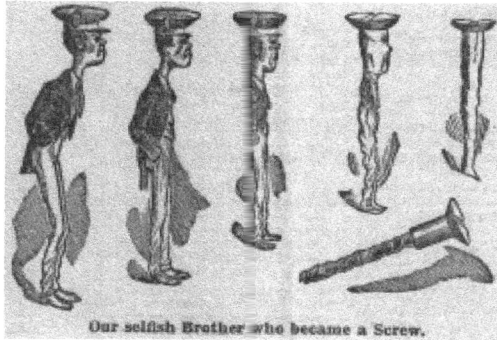

Our selfish Brother who became a Screw.

Bad Boy having broken a Vase told his Mother that the
Dog did it, but when his Mother was going to beat the
poor Innocent Dog he felt sorry, and told the truth.

Truthful Dottie; Or The Broken Vase

Nellie and Dottie
  Both here mamma say,
"Pray from the drawing-room

325

COLE

Keep away.

Don't take your toys there,
  Lest someone should call:
Run out in the garden
  With rope, bat and ball."

The garden is lovely,
  This bright summer day;
But Nellie and Dottie
  Too soon came away.

Into the drawing-room
  Dottie comes skipping,
With her new rope
  All the furniture flipping:

Down goes the tall vase,
  So golden and gay,
Smashed all to pieces,
  "What will mamma say?"

Cries Nell with her hands raised,
  "Oh Dottie, let's run;
They'll think it was pussy,
  Who did it in fun."

Dot answers, through big tears,
  "But, Nell, don't you see,
Though nobody watched us,
  God knows it was me.

Mamma always says,
  That, whatever we do,
The harm's not so great,
  If we dare to be true.

So I'll go up and tell her
  It caught in my rope;
Perhaps she won't scold much,

At least, so I'll hope."

"That's right!" cries her mother,
  Who stands by the door,
"I would rather have ten vases
  Were smashed on the floor

Than my children should once break
  The bright words of truth,
The dearest possession
  Of age or of youth.

The vase can be mended,
  And scarce show a crack,
But a falsehood once spoken
  Will never come back."

However much grieved for
  By young folks or old,
An untruth once uttered,
  Forever is told.

The Liar Reclaimed

O! 'tis a lovely thing for youth
  To walk betimes in wisdom's way;
To fear a lie, to speak the truth,
  That we may trust to all they say.

But liars we can never trust,
  Tho' they should speak the thing that's true,
And he that does one fault at first,
  And lies to hide it makes it two.

The Truth

327

Why should you fear the truth to tell?
Does falsehood ever do you so well?
Can you be satisfied to know
There's something wrong to hide below
No! let your fault be what it may,
To own it is the happy way.

So long as you your crime conceal,
You cannot light or gladsome feel;
Your heart will ever feel oppressed,
As if a weight were on your breast:
And e'en your mother's eye to meet
Will tinge your face with shame and heat.

False Alarms

Little Mary one day most loudly did call,
  "Mamma! oh, mamma, pray come here!
A fall I have had—oh! a very sad fall."
  Mamma ran in haste and in fear;
Then Mary jump'd up, and she laugh'd in great glee,
  And cried, "Why, how fast you can run!
No harm has befallen, I assure you, to me,
  My screaming was only in fun."

Her mother was busy at work the next day,
  She heard from without a loud cry,
"The big dog has got me! O help me! Oh! pray!
  He tears me—he bites me—I die!"
Mamma, all in terror, quick to the court
  And there little Mary she found;
Who, laughing, said, "Madam pray how do you do!"
  And curtsey'd quite down to the ground.

That night little Mary, when long gone to bed,
  Shrill cries and loud shriekings were heard;
"I'm on fire, O mamma, come up or I'm dead!"

Mamma she believ'd not a word.
"Sleep, sleep, naughty child " she call'd out from below,
　"How often have I been deceived?
You're telling a story, you very well know:
　Go to sleep, for you can't be believed."

Yet still the child scream'd—now the house fill'd with smoke.
　That fire is above Jane declares.
Alas! Mary's words they soon found were no joke,
　When ev'ryone hastened upstairs.
All burnt and all seam'd is her once pretty face,
　And how terribly mark'd are her arms,
Her features all scarr'd, leave a lasting disgrace,
　For giving Mamma false alarms.

　　　　Adelaide Taylor

To A Little Girl That Has Told A Lie

　　And has my darling told a lie?
　　Did she forget that God was by?
　　That God who saw the thing she did,
　　From whom no action can be hid;
　　Did she forget that God could see,
　　And hear, wherever she might be?

　　He made you eyes and can discern
　　Whichever way you think to turn;
　　He made your ears, and He can hear
　　When you think nobody is near;
　　In ev'ry place, by night or day,
　　He watches all you do and say.

　　You thought, because you were alone,
　　Your falsehood never could be known,
　　But liars always are found out,
　　Whatever ways they wind about;
　　And always be afraid, my dear,

To tell a lie,—for God can hear!

I wish, my dear, you'd always try
To act as shall not need a lie;
And when you wish a thing to do,
That has been once forbidden to you,
Remember that, and never dare
To disobey—For God is there!

Why should you fear to tell me true?
Confess, and then I'll pardon you:
Tell me you're sorry, and you'll try
To act the better by and bye,
And then whate'er your crime has been,
It won't be half so great a sin.

But cheerful, innocent, and gay,
As passes by the smiling day,
You'll never have to turn aside,
From any one your faults to hide;
Nor heave a sigh, nor have a fear,
That either God or I should hear.

Ann Taylor

The Blind Man reading to t¹e Deaf and Dumb Man after business hours, and their w¹cked Dog looking out.

Naughty lazy Boy who would not go to School.

Idle Mary

Oh, Mary, this will never do!
  This work is sadly done, my dear,
And such little of it too!
  You have not take¹ pains, I fear.

On no, your work h¹s been forgotten,
  Indeed you've harc ly thought of that;
I saw you roll your ¹all of cotton
  About the floor to ¹lease the cat.

See, here are stitche¹ straggling wide,
  And others reachir¹ down so far;
I'm very sure you h¹ve not tried

At all to-day to please mamma.

The little girl who will not sew
  Should never be allowed to play;
But then I hope, my love, that you
  Will take more pains another day.

Lazy Sal

A lazy, lazy, lazy girl!
Her hair forever out of curl,
Her feet unshod, her hands unclean,
Her dress in tatters always seen.

Lounging here and dawdling there,
Lying out 'most anywhere
About the barn-yard. Not a thought
Of studying lessons as she ought;

But happiest when in sunny weather
She and "the other pig" together
Are playing tricks. No wonder, then,
The farmer, jolliest of men,

Is apt to say, when tired out
With seeing her sprawling round about,
"Beats all what ails that lazy gal!
Why, piggy's twice as smart as Sal!"

The Work-bag

To Jane her aunt a work-bag gave,
  Of silk with flowers so gay,
That she a place might always have
  To put her work away.

And then 'twas furnished quite complete
  With cotton, silk and thread,
And needless in a case so neat,
  Of all the sizes made.

A little silver thimble, too,
  Was there among the rest;
And a large waxen doll, quite new,
  That waited to be dress'd.

But Jane was very fond of play,
  And loved to toss her ball;
An I am quite ashamed to say,
  She scarcely worked at all.

But if at any time she did,
  'Twas but a stitch or two;
And though she often has been bid,
  But little more would do.

The pretty little bag, indeed,
  Was hung upon her chair;
But cotton, needles, silk, and thread
  Were scattered here and there.

Her aunt, by chance, came in that day,
  And asked if the doll was dress'd;
Miss Jane has been engaged in play,
  And careless of the rest.

The silk, to make her little dress,
  Was on the table laid,
And, with an equal carelessness,
  The cap had also stayed.

With gauze and lace the floor was strewed,
  All in disorder lay,
When, bounding in with gesture rude,
  Came Jane, returned from play.

She little thought he aunt to find,
  And blushed to see her there;
It brought her carelessness to mind,
  And what her doll should wear.

"Well, Jane, and where's your doll, my dear?
  I hope you've dress'd her now;
But there is such a litter here,
  You best know when and how."

So spoke her aunt, and, looking round
  The empty bag she spied;
Poor Jane, who no excuse had found,
  Now hid her face and cried.

"Since," said her aunt, "no work, you do,
  But waste your time in play;
The work-bag, of no use to you,
  I now shall take away."

But now, with self-conviction, Jane
  Her idleness confessed,
And ere her aunt could come again,
  Her doll was neatly dressed.

The Two Gardens

When Harry and Dick
  Had been striving to please,
Their father (to whom it was known)
  Made two little gardens,
    And stocked them with trees,
And gave one to each for his own.

Harry thank'd his papa,
  And with rake hoe, and spade,
Directly began his employ;
  And soon such a neat

Little garden was made,
That he panted with labour and joy.

There was always some bed
Or some border to mend,
Or something to tie or stick:
And Harry rose early
His garden to tend,
While snoring lay indolent Dick.

The tulip, the rose,
And the lily so white,
United their beautiful bloom!
And often the honey-bee
Stoop'd from his flight,
To sip the delicious perfume.

A neat row of peas
In full blossom was seen,
French beans were beginning to shoot!
And his gooseb'ries and currents,
Tho' yet they were green,
Foretold of plenty of fruit.

But Richard loved better
In bed to repose,
And snug as he curl'd himself round,
Forgot that not tulip,
Nor lily, nor rose,
Nor plant in his garden was found.

Rank weeds and all nettles
Disfigur'd his beds,
Nor cabbage nor lettuce was seen,
The slug and the snail
Show'd their mischievous heads,
And eat ev'ry leaf that was green.

Thus Richard the idle,
Who shrank from the cold,

Beheld his trees naked and bare;
Whilst Harry the active
Was charmed to behold
The fruit of his patience and care.

Ann Taylor.

Doing Nothing

I asked a lad what he was doing;
  "Nothing, good sir," said he to me.
"By nothing well and long pursuing,
  Nothing," said I, "you'll surely be."

I asked a lad what he was thinking;
  "Nothing," said he. "I do declare."
"Many," said I, "in vile inns drinking,
  By idle minds were carried there."

There's nothing great, there's nothing wise,
  Which idle hands and minds supply;
Those who all thought and toil despise,
  Mere nothings live, and nothings die.

A thousand naughts are not a feather,
  When in a sum they all are brought;
A thousand idle lads together
  Are still but nothings joined to naught.

And yet of merit they will boast,
  And sometimes pompous seem, and haughty,
But still 'tis very plain to most,
  That "nothing" boys are mostly naughty.

Lazy Sam

There was a lazy boy named Sam,
  The laziest ever known,
Who spent his time in idleness,
  Like any other drone.
He loved to lie in bed till noon,
  With covers closely drawn,
And when he managed to get up
  He'd yawn, and yawn, and yawn.

If asked to do a simple task
  He always would refuse,
And say that he was lame or sick,
  His action to excuse.
And over pretty picture-books—
  Twas really very odd—
This lazy boy would soon begin
  To nod, and nod, and nod.

If on an errand forced to go,
  He'd slowly, slowly creep,
Just like a snail; you might suppose
  That he was half asleep.
And those who would despatch in haste
  A note, or telegram,
Would chose a swifter messenger
  Than such a lazy Sam.

If he was caught out in a storm
  'Twould drench him to the skin,
Because he was too incolent
  To hurry to get in.
Deep in his trouser's pockets he
  His idle hands would cram,
And children crowded to the doors
  To look at lazy Sam.

This lazy boy would lounge about
  The docks, and often wish
That he could carry home to cook

337

A string of nice fresh fish;
But though he was provided with
  A reel extremely fine,
Said Sam "I do not think 'twill pay
  To wet my fishing line!"

Oh, Sam was always late at meals,
  And always late at school,
And everybody said that he
  Would be a first-class fool.
For boys not half so old as he
  Above him swiftly pass,
While Sam, the great big dunce! remains
  The lowest in the class.

In every way, and every day
  This lazy boy would shirk,
And never lift his hand to do
  A bit of useful work.
His clothes were always on awry,
  His shoe-strings left untied,
His hair uncombed, his teeth uncleaned,
  Alas, he had no pride!

And so he went from bad to worse—
  The good-for-nothing scamp!—
Until he settled down to be
  A ragged, dirty tramp.
Through cities, towns, and villages,
  He begged his daily bread,
And slept at night wherever he
  Could chance to find a bed.

Men shuddered as they passed him by,
  And murmured sadly, "Oh!
How can a human being sink
  So very, very low?"
And e'en the jackass pricks his ears,
  And brays aloud "I am
Not such a donkey, I declare

As yonder lazy Sam!"

The Beggar Man

Abject, stooping, old, and wan,
See you wretched beggar-man;
Once a father's hopeful heir,
Once a mother's tender care.
When too young to understand,
He but scorched his little hand,
By the candle's flaming light
Attracted—dancing, spiral, bright.
Clasping fond her darling round,
A thousand kisses healed the wound,
Now abject, stooping, old and wan,
No mother tends the beggar-man.

Then nought too good for him to wear,
With cherub face and flaxen hair,
In fancy's choicest gauds arrayed,
Cap of lace with rose to aid,
Milk-white hat and feather blue,
Shoes of red, and coral too,
With silver bells to please his ear,
And charm the frequent ready tear.
Now abject, stooping, old, and wan,
Neglected is the beggar-man.

See the boy advance in age,
And learning spreads her useful page;
In vain! for giddy pleasure calls,
And shows the marbles, tops, and balls,
What's learning to the charms of play?
The indulgent tutor must give way.
A heedless, wilful dunce, and wild,
The parents' fondness spoil'd the child;
The youth in vagrant courses ran;
Now abject, stooping, old, and wan,

Their fondling is the beggar-man.

Lamb

Good-for-nothing Lazy Man

A good for nothing lazy lout,
Wicked within and ragged without.
Who can bear to have him about?
Turn him out! Turn him out!

The Old Beggar Man

I see an old man sitting there,
His withered limbs are almost bare,
And very hoary is his hair.

Old man, why are you sitting so?
For very cold the wind doth blow:
Why don't you to your cottage go?

Ah, master, in the world so wide,
I have no home wherein to hide,
No comfortable fire-side.

When I, like you, was young and gay,
I'll tell you what I used to say,
That I would nothing do but play.

And so, instead of being taught
Some useful business as I ought,
To play about was all I sought.

An now that I am old and grey,
I wander on my lonely way,

And beg my bread from day to day.

But oft I shake my hoary head,
And many a bitter tear I shed,
To think the useless life I've led.

J. T.

Lazyland

Three travellers wandered along the strand,
Each with a staff in his feeble hand;
  And they chanted low:
  "We are go-o-o-
  Ing slow-o-ow-
  Ly to Lazyland.

"They've left off eating and drinking there;
They never do any thinking there;
  They never walk,
  And they never talk,
And they fall asleep without winking there.

"Nobody's in a hurry there;
They are not permitted to worry there;
  'Tis a wide, still place
  And not a face
Shows any symptom of flurry there.

"No bells are rung in the morning there,
They care not at all for adorning there;
  All sounds are hushed,
  And a man who rushed
Would be treated with absolute scorning there.

"They do not take any papers there;
No politicians cut capers there;
  They have no 'views'

And they tell no news,
And they burn no midnight tapers there.

"No lovers are ever permitted there;
Reformers are not admitted there;
  They argue not
  In that peaceful spot,
And their clothes all come ready-fitted there.

"Electricity has not been heard of there;
And steam has been spoken no word of there;
  They stay where they are,
  And a coach or a car
They have not so much as a third of there.

"Oh, this world is a truly crazy land;
A worrying, hurrying, mazy land;
  We cannot stay,
  We must find the way—
If there is a way—to Lazyland."

Two Donkeys.

Lazy Willie

Oh! Willie is a lazy boy,
  A "Sleepy Head" is he,
"Wake up!" his little sister cries,
  "Wake up and talk to me."

The birds are singing in the trees,
  The sun is shining bright,
But sleepy Willie slumbers on
  As though it yet were night.

Oh! lazy boys will never grow
  To clever manhood, you must know,
So lift your eyelids, sleepy head,
  Wake up, and scramble out of bed.

The Lazy Boy

The lazy boy! and what's his name?

I should not like to tell;
But don't you think it is a shame,
  That he can't read or spell.

He'd rather swing upon a gate,
  Or paddle in a brook,
Than take his pencil and his slate,
  Or try to con a book.

There, see! he's lounging down the street,
  His hat without a brim,
He rather drags than lifts his feet—
  His face unwashed and grim.

He's lolling now against a post;
  But if you've seen him once,
You'll know the lad among a host
  For what he is—a dunce.

Don't ask me what's the urchin's name;
  I do not choose to tell;
But this you'll know—it is the same
  As his who does not blush for shame
That he don't read or spell.

The Sluggard

'Tis the voice of the sluggard;
  I heard him complain,
"You have waked me too soon,
  I must slumber again."
As the door on it's hinges,
  So he on his bed
Turns his sides, and his shoulders,
  And his heavy head.

"A little more sleep
  And a little more slumber;"

Thus he wastes half his days
  And his hours without number,
And when he gets up
  He sits folcing his hands,
Or walking about sauntering,
  Or trifling he stands.

I pass'd by his garden,
  And saw the wild brier,
The thorn and the thistle
  Grow broader and higher;
The clothes that hung on him
  Are turning to rags,
And his money still wastes
  Till he starves or he begs.

I made him a visit,
  Still hoping to find
That he took better care
  For improving his mind;
He told me his dreams,
  Talked of eating and drinking,
But he scarce reads his Bible,
  And never loves thinking.

Said I then to my heart,
  "Here's a lesson for me;
This man's but a picture
  Of what I might be;
But thanks to my friends
  For their care in my breeding,
Who taught me bedtimes
  To love working and reading."

Watts

Idle Dicky And The Goat

345

John Brown is a man
  Without houses or lands,
Himself he supports
  By the work of his hands.
He brings home his wages
  Each Saturday night,
To his wife and his children,
  A very good sight.

His eldest boy, Dicky,
  On errands when sent,
To loiter and chatter
  Was very much bent;
The neighbours all call'd him
  An odd little trout,
His shoes they were broke,
  And his toes they peep'd out.

To see such old shoes
  All their sorrows were rife;
John Brown he much grieved,
  And so did his wife,
He kiss'd his boy Dicky,
  And stroked his white head,
"You shall have a new pair,
  My dear boy," he then said.

"I've here twenty shillings,
  And money has wings;
Go first get this note changed,
  I want other things."
Now here comes the mischief—
  This Dicky would stop
At an ill-looking, mean-looking
  Greengrocer's shop.

For here lived a chattering
  Dunce of a boy;
To prate with this urchin

Gave Dicky great joy.
And now in his boasting,
  He shows him his note,
And now to the green-stall
  Up marches a goat.

The laughed, for it was
  This young nanny-goat's way
With those who pass'd by her
  To gambol and play.
All three they went on
  In their frolicsome bouts,
Till Dick dropt the note
  On a bunch of green sprouts.

Now what was Dick's wonder
  To see the vile goat,
In munching the green sprouts,
  Eat up his bank note!
He crying ran back
  To John Brown with the news,
And by stooping to idle
  He lost his new shoes.

Adelaide Taylor

Idleness and Mischief

How doth the little busy bee
  Improve each shining hour,
And gather honey all the day
  From every opening flower.

How skilfully she builds her cell;
  How neat she spreads the wax;
And labours hard to store it well;
  With the sweet food she makes.

347

In works of labour or of skill
  I would be busy too:
For Satan finds some mischief still
  For idle hands to do

In books, or work, or healthful play
  Let my first years be passed;
That I may give you every day
  Some good account at last.

Watts

Come and Go.

Dick Dawdle had land
  Worth two hundred a year,
Yet from debt and from dunning
  He never was free,
His intellect was not
  Surprisingly clear,
But he never felt satisfied
  How it could be.

The raps at his door,
  And the rings at his gate.
And the threats of a gaol
  He no longer could bear:
So he made up his mind
  To sell half his estate,
Which would pay all his debts,
  And leave something to spare.

He leased to a farmer
  The rest of his land
For twenty-one years;
  And on each quarter-day
The honest man went
  With his rent in his hand,

348

His liberal landlord
  Delighted to pay.

Before half the term
  Of the lease had expired,
The farmer, one day
  With a bagful of gold,
Said, "Pardon me, sir,
  But I long have desired
To purchase my farm,
  If the land can be sold.

"Ten years I've been blest
  With success and with health,
With trials a few—
  I thank God, not severe—
I am grateful. I hope,
  Though not proud of my wealth,
But I've managed to lay
  By a hundred a year."

"Why how," exclaimed Dick,
  "Can this possibly be?"
(With a stare of surprise,
  And a mortified laugh,)
"The whole of my farm
  Proved too little for me,
And you it appears,
  Have grown rich upon half."

"I hope you'll excuse me,"
  The farmer replies,
"But I'll tell you the cause,
  If your honor would know;
In two little words
  All the difference lies,
I always say Come,
  And you used to say Go."

"Well, and what does that mean,

My good fellow?" he said.
"Why this, sir, that I
Always rise with the sun;
You said 'Go' to your man,
As you lay in your bed,
I say 'Come, Jack, with me,'
And I see the work done."

R. S. Sharpe

The Tables turned—Instead of the Bad
Boys setting the poor Dogs fighting, the
bad Dogs are setting the poor Boys fighting.

The Cruel Boy

Tom sat at the kitchen window
  Watching the folks go by,
But what he was really doing
  Was pulling the legs from a fly.

Yes, there he sat in the twilight,
  Tormenting the tiny things;
First pulling their legs from their sockets,

And afterwards pulling their wings.

He knew not that his father
  Was standing behind his back;
And very much wished to be giving
  His cruel young fingers a crack.

But he waited till after dinner,
  When Tommy was having a game;
Then he thought he would give him a lesson,
  And treat him a little the same.

So catching his son of a sudden,
  And giving his elbow a twist;
He pulled his two ears till he shouted,
  Then hit him quite hard with his fist.

And did he not roll on the carpet?
  And did he not cry out in pain?
But, when he cried out "Oh, you hurt me!"
  His father would hit him again.

"Why, Tom, all this is quite jolly,
  You don't seem to like it, my boy;
And yet, when you try it on others,
  You always are singing with joy;

"It seems very strange," said his father,
  And this time his nose had a pull;
But Tommy could stand it no longer;
  He bellowed and roared like a bull.

"Hush! hush! while I pull your right leg off,
  And scrape off the flesh from your shin;
What you often yourself do to others,
  Sure you do not think harm or a sin.

"Now, Tommy, my boy," said his father,
  "You'll leave these poor things alone,
If not, I go on with my lesson."

351

"I will," cried poor Tom, with a groan.

But hark! from the woodlands the sound of a gun,
  The wounded bird flutters and dies;
Where can be the pleasure for nothing but fun,
  To shoot the poor thing as it flies?

Or you, Mr. Butcher, and Fisherman, you
  May follow your trades, I must own:
So chimneys are swept when they want it—but who
  Would sweep them for pleasure alone?

If men would but think of the torture they give
  To creatures that cannot complain,
They surely would let the poor animals live,
  And not make a sport of their pain.

The Worm

Turn, turn thy hasty foot aside,
  Nor crush that helpless worm
The frame thy wayward looks decide
  Required a God to form.

The common Lord of all that move,
  From whom thy being flow'd,
A portion of His boundless love
  On that poor worm bestow'd.

The sun, the moon, the stars He made
  To all the creatures free;
And spreads o'er earth the grassy blade
  For worms as well as thee.

Let them enjoy their little day,
  Their lowly bliss receive;
Oh, do not lightly take away

The life thou canst not give.

Gisborne

Story Of Cruel Frederick

Here is cruel Frederick, see!
A horrid wicked boy was he:
He caught the flies, poor little things,
And tore off their tiny wings;

He kill'd the birds, and broke the chairs,
And threw the kitten down the stairs;
And Oh! far worse than all beside,
He whipp'd his Mary till she cried.

The trough was full, and faithful Tray
Came out to drink one sultry day;
He wagg'd his tail, and wet his lip,
When cruel Fred snatch'd up a whip,
And whipp'd poor Tray till he was sore,
And kick'd and whipp'd him more and more.

At this, good Tray grew very red,
And growl'd and bit him till he bled;
Then you should only have been by,
To see how Fred did scream and cry!

So Frederick had to go to bed,
His leg was very sore and red!
The doctor came and shook his head
And made a very great to-do,
And gave him nasty physic too.

Don't Throw Stones

Boys, don't throw stones!
That kitten on the wall,
Sporting with leaves that fall,
Now jumping to and fro,
Now crouching soft and low,
Then grasps them with a spring,
As if some living thing.
As happy as can be,
Why cause her misery
It is foolish stones to fling
Boys, do as you'd be done by.

Boys, don't throw stones
That squirrel in the tree,
Frisking in fun and glee,
Is busy in his way,
Although it looks all play,
Picking up nuts—a store
Against the winter hour
Frisking from tree to tree,
So blithe and merrily,
It is cruel stones to fling,
Boys, do as you'd be done by.

Boys, don't throw stones!
That bird upon the wing,
How sweet its song this Spring,
Perchance it seeks the food,
To feed its infant brood,
Whose beaks are open wide,
Until they are supplied;
To and fro to and fro,
The parent bird must go.
It is sinful stones to throw
Boys, do as you'd be done by.

Boys, don't throw stones!
That stray dog in the street,
Should with your pity meet,

And not with shout and cry,
And brick-bat whirling by:
The dog's a friend to man,
Outvie him if you can:
So faithful, trusty, true,
A pattern unto you;
It is wicked stones to throw,
Boys, do as you'd be done by.

Boys, don't throw stones!
It can no pleasure give
To injure things that live;
That beauteous butterfly,
The bird that soars on high,
The creatures every day
That round our pathway play;
If you thought of your cruelty;
You wouldn't wish even one to die.
Only cowards stones will throw
Boys, do as you'd be done by.

Instead of the Bad Boys Beating the Poor
Dog, the Bad Dogs are beating the poor
Boy.

Boys caught stealing Apples.

No One Will See Me

"No one will see me,"
  Said little John Day,
For his father and mother
  Were out of the way,
And he was at home
  All alone;

"No one will see me,"
  So he climbed on a chair,
And peeped in the cupboard
  To see what was there,
Which of course he ought
  Not to have done.

There stood in the cupboard,
  So sweet and so nice,
A plate of plum-cake
  In full many a slice,
And apples so ripe,
  And so fine;

"Now no one will see me,"
  Said John to himself,

356

As he stretched out his arm
  To reach up to the shelf;
"This apple, at least,
  Shall be mine."

John paused and put back
  The nice apple so red,
For he thought of the words
  His kind mother had said,
When she left all these
  Things in his care;

"And no one will see me,"
  Though he, "'tis not true;
For I've read that God sees us
  In all that we do,
And is with us
  Everywhere."

Well done, John;
  Your father and mother obey,
Try ever to please them;
  And mind what they say,
Even when they
  Are absent from you;

And never forget that,
  Though no one is nigh,
You cannot be hid from
  The Glance of God's eye,
Who notices all
  That you do.

Principle Put To The Test

A youngster at school,
  More sedate than the rest,
Had once his integrity

Put to the test:—
His comrades had plotted
  The orchard to rob
And asked him to go
  And assist in the job.

He was very much shocked,
  And answered, "Oh no!
What! rob our poor neighbour!
  I pray you don't go;
Besides, the man's poor,
  His orchard's his bread;
Then think of his children,
  For they must be fed."

"You speak very fine,
  And you look very grave,
But apples we want,
  And apples we'll have;
If you will go with us,
  We'll give you a share,
If not, you shall have
  Neither apple nor pear."

They spoke, and Tom pondered—
  "I see they will go;
Poor man! What a pity
  To injure him so!
Poor man! I would save him
  His fruit if I could,
But staying behind
  Will do him no good.

"If this matter depended
  Alone upon me,
His apples might hang
  Till they dropped from the tree;
But since they *will* take them,
  I think I'll go too,
He will lose none by me,

Though get a few."

His scruples this silenced,
  Tom felt more at ease,
And went with his comrades
  The apples to seize;
He blamed and protested
  But joined in the plan,
He shared in the plunder,
  But pitied the man.

Cowper

Advice

Who steals a pin
Commits a sin
Who tells a lie
Has cause to sigh.

When ask'd to go
And sin, say, No!
The guilty breast
Is ne'er at rest.

You must not sin
A world to win
Why should you go
The way to woe.

The Boy And His Mother

In Aesop, we are told, a boy,
Who was his mother's pride and joy,
At school a primer stole one day,

359

And homeward then did wend his way.

He told his mother of the theft,
While she, of principle bereft,
Patted him on the head and smil'd.
And said, "You are my own dear child."

She praised him for the cunning feat,
And gave him a nice apple sweet.
In course of years the boy grew fast,
Till he became a man at last

But all the time he slyly stole—
Sometimes a piece—sometimes the whole,
Till, finally, he grew so bold,
He kill'd a man and took his gold.

The day on which he had to swing
Did a large crowd together bring.
Among the rest his mother came,
And called him fondly by his name.

The sheriff gave him leave to tell
The broken-hearted dame farewell!
About his neck her arms she flung,
And cried, "Why must my child be hung?"

He answered, "Call me not your dear."
And by one stroke bit off her ear;
While all the crowd cried, "Oh! for shame!
Not satisfied to blast her name.

You add this violence to one
Whose happiness you have undone"
"Good people," he replied, "I'll vow
I would not be a felon now.

If my mother had only tried
To win me to the better side.
But when in infancy I took

What was not mine, a small torn book,

Instead of punishing the feat
She gave to me an apple sweet;
She prais'd me too, and softly smil'd,
And said, 'You are my own dear child!'

I tell you here, both foe and friend,
This is the cause of my sad end."

Australian Blacks Stealing.

Naughty Boys Stealing

The Boys And The Apple Tree

As Billy and Tommy
  Were walking one day,
They came by a fine orchard side;
  They'd rather eat apples
    Than spell, read, or play,
And Tommy to Billy then cried,

  "O brother, look! see
    What fine clusters hang there,
I'll jump and climb over the wall;
  I will have an apple,
    I will have a pear,
Or else it shall cost me a fall."

  Said Billy to Tommy,
    "To steal is a sin,
Mamma has oft told this to thee;
  O never yet stole,
    Nor now will begin,
So red apples hang on the tree."

  "You are a good boy,
    As you ever have been,"
Said Tommy; let's walk on, my lad;
  We'll call on our school-fellow
    Little Bob Green,
And to see us know he'll be glad."

  They came to a house,
    And they rang at the gate,
And asked, "Pray, is Bobby at home?"
  But Bobby's good manners
    Did not let them wait;
He out of the parlour did come.

  Bob smil'd and he laughed,
    And he caper'd with joy,
His little companions to view.
  "We call'd in to see you,"

Said each little boy.
Said Bobby. "I'm glad to see you.

"Come walk in our garden,
So large and so fine;
You shall, for my father gives leave;
And more, he insists
That you'l stay here to dine:
A rare jolly day we shall have!"

But when in the garden,
They found 'twas the same
They saw as they walk'd in the road;
And near the high wall,
When these little boys came,
They started as if from a toad.

"That large ring of iron,
Which lies on the ground,
With terrible teeth like a saw,"
Said Bobby, "the guard
Of our garden is found;
It keeps wicked robbers in awe.

"The warning without,
If they should set an nought,
This trap tears their legs—O! so sad!"
Said Billy to Tommy,
"So you'd have been caught,
A narrow escape you have had."

Cried Tommy, I'll mind
What my good mamma says,
And take the advice of a friend;
I never will steal
To the end of my days,
I've been a bad boy, but I'll mend."

Adelaide

Honest

With honest heart go on your way,
  Down to your burial sod,
And never for a moment stray
  Beyond the path of God;
And everything along your way
  In colours bright shall shine;
The water from the jug of clay
Shall taste like costly wine!

Holte

Thou Shalt Not Steal

On the goods that are not thine,
  Little child, lay not a finger;
Round thy neighbour's better things
  Let no wistful glances linger.

Pilfer not the smallest thing;
  Touch it not, howe'er thou need it,
Though the owner have enough,
  Though he know it not, nor need it.

Taste not the forbidden fruit,
  Though resistance be a trial;
Grasping hand and roving eye,
  Early teach them self-denial.

Upright heart and honest name
  To the poorest are a treasure;
Better than ill-gotten wealth,
  Better far than pomp and pleasure.

Poor and needy though thou art,

Gladly take what God has given;
With clean hands and humble heart,
  Passing through this world to heaven.

The Thief

Why should I deprive my neighbour
  Of his goods against his will?
Hands were meant for honest labour,
  Not to plunder, nor to steal.

'Tis a foolish self-deceiving
  By such tricks to hope for gain:
All that's ever got by thieving
  Turns to sorrow, shame, and pain.

Oft we see the young beginner
  Practice little pilfering ways,
Till grown up a hardened sinner,
  Then the gallows ends his days.

Theft will not be always hidden,
  Though we fancy none can spy;
When we take a thing forbidden,
  God holds it with His eye.

Guard my heart, O God of heaven,
  Lest is covet what's not mine;
Lest I take what is not given,
  Guard my heart and hands from sin.

Watts

Highway Robbery

The Thieves' Ladder

The girls were helping in the house
  With bustle and with show,
And told the boys to go away,
  And not disturb them so.
And the boys went whistling down the streets,
  And looking in the shops
At tempting heaps of oranges,
  And piles of sugar-drops.

"Here, Willie, to the grocer's run;
  Be sharp, now—there's a man,
And bring me home a pound of plums
  As quickly as you can!
"Don't touch a plum—be sure you don't;
  To-morrow you shall eat."
"I won't." he said, and, like a top,
  Went spinning down the street.

The grocer weigh'd them in his scales,
  And there was one too much;
He took it out, and all was right,
  The scale was to a touch.

He wrapp'd them up in whitey-brown,
  And tied them with a string,
And put the money in the till,
  As 'twere a common thing.

Young Willie watched, with greedy eyes,
  As this affair went on.
The plums—they look'd so very nice!
  He wouldn't take but *one*.
So going quick behind a post,
  He tore the paper so
That he could take out two or three,
  And nobody would know.

There was a little voice that said,
  Close by, in Willie's heart,
"Don't tear the hole—don't take the plum—
  Don't play a thievish part!"
The little voice—it spoke in vain!
  He reach'd his mother's door;
She did not see the hole he'd made,
  His trouble then was o'er.

And what a trifling thing it seem'd,
  To take one single plum!
A little thing we hold between
  Our finger and out thumb.
And yet upon that Christmas eve,
  That period so brief,
Young Willie set his foot upon
  "The ladder of the thief!"

And as he lay awake that night,
  He heard his parents speak;
He heard distinctly what they said,
  The blood rush'd to his cheek.
He lay and listn'd earnestly;
  They might have found him out,
And he might get a flogging too,

'Twas that he thought about.

A guilty person cannot rest,
  He always is in fear;
Not knowing what may happen next
  To make his guilt appear.
So, when he heard his mother speak,
  He rose up in his bed
And did not lose a syllable
  Of every word she said:—

"We have not any turnips, John,
  I could not spare the pence;
But you can go and get us some
  Through Farmer Turner's fence.
"There's nobody to see you now,
  The folks are off the road;
The night looks dark and blustering,
  And no one is abroad.

"It is not far—you'll soon be back—
  I'll stand outside to hear;
The watchman now is off his track,
  And won't be coming near."
The father he went softly out,
  And down the lane he crept,
And stole some turnips from the field
  Whilst honest people slept!

'Tis not the words that parents say,
  It is their very deed;
Their children know the difference,
  And follow where they lead.
How often if their lives are good,
  Their children's are the same;
Whilst, if they're thievish, drunken,
  Their children come to shame!

Now, Willie laid him down in bed,
  His conscience found relief;

"I'm not the only one," he said—
  "My father is a thief!
"How foolish 'twas to be afraid
  About a little plum!"
He pull'd the bed-clothes o'er his head,
  And dream'd of feasts to come.

On Christmas-day they had the pies.
  The turnips, and the beef;
And Willie's foot was firm upon
  The ladder of the thief.
And ere the snow was on the plain,
  And Christmas-day came round,
And boys were sliding, once again,
  Upon the frozen ground,

He, step by step, had further gone
  Upon that dreadful road
That brings a man to misery,
  And takes him far from God.
He cheated with his marbles first,
  And then at other play;
He pilfered any little thing
  That came within his way.

His parents did not punish him;
  He went from bad to worse,
Until he grew so confident,
  He stole a lady's purse.
Then he was seized, and brought before
  The city magistrate;
And the police and lady came
  The robbery to state.

And Willie he was proved a thief,
  And nothing had to say;
So to the dreadful prison-house
  He soon was led away.
In vain he cried, and pleaded hard
  They would not take him there;

369

He would not do such things again
  If they would hear his prayer.

It was too late! The prison door,
  With bolt, and bar, and chain,
Was opened to take Willie in,
  And then was shut again.
He saw the handcuffs on the wall,
  The fetters on the floor;
And heavy keys with iron rings
  To lock the dungeon door.

He saw the little, lonely cells
  Where prisoners were kept,
And all the dreary passages,
  And bitterly he wept.
And through the strong-barred iron grate,
  High up and far away,
He saw a piece of clear blue sky
  Out in the blessed day.

And "Oh!" he said, "my brothers now
  Are out of school again,
And playing marbles on the path,
  Or cricket on the plain.
"And here am I, shut up so close
  Within this iron door;
If ever I get out again
  I'll give this business o'er "

And Willie went to sleep that night
  In his dark cell alone;
But often in his troubled dreams
  He turned with heavy moan.
What sound is that at early morn
  That breaks upon his ear?
A funeral bell is tolling slow,
  It tolls so very near.

And in the court he sees a crowd,

So haggard and so pale,
And they are whispering fearfully
  A sad and awful tale.
And all seem looking at a man
  Who stands with fetters bound,
And guards and executioner
  Are gathered close around.

And he beheld that wretched man,
  Who trembled like a leaf:
His foot no more would stand upon
  The ladder of the thief.
For he had climbed it step by step,
  Till murder closed the whole;
The hangman came to take his life,
  But where would be his soul?

And still the bell went tolling on;
  It tolled so heavily
As that young man went up the stairs,
  Out to the gallows-tree.
It tolled—it tolled—Oh! heavy sound!
  It stopped—the deed is o'er;
And that young man upon the earth
  Will now be seen no more:

Oh! parents watch your little ones,
  Lest you have such a grief;
Help not their tender feet to climb
  The ladder of the thief.
I have not heard young Willie's end,
  I hope he learned that day;
But 'tis a thing most difficult
  To leave a wicked way.

Sewell

371

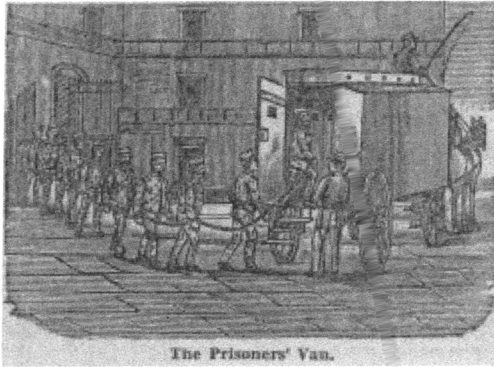

The Prisoners' Van.

I have given no Fairy Tales in this Childland. For in this *matter-of-fact* age belief in Fairy Tales and all kinds of wonderful fictions is fast vanishing. Santa Claus, the "bestest" "goodest" fairy of all alone remains: and even he is gradually being doubted by all but the most innocent children, but as he as a personality is still largely amongst us, I give his popular history culled from many sources.

Santa Claus Land

At the top of the earth, which they call the North Pole,
Is where Santa Claus lives, a right jolly old soul!
And the ice and the snow lie so thick on the ground
The sun cannot melt them the whole summer round.

All wrapped up in furs from his head to his toes,
No feeling of coldness dear Santa Claus knows,
But travels about with a heart full of joy,
As happy as if he were only a boy.

His cheeks are like roses; his eyes are as bright
As stars that shine out overhead in the night,

And they twinkle as merrily too all the while,
And broad as a sunbeam is Santa Claus' smile.

He never is idle except when asleep,
And even in dreams at his labours will keep,
And all thro' the day and the night, it is true,
He is working and planning, dear children, for you.

On top of his tower with spy-glass in hand,
He goes every morning to look o'er the land,
And though there are hills all around, I suppose,
He sees, oh, much further than any one knows.

He peeps into houses whose doors are tight shut;
He looks through the palace, and likewise the hut;
He gazes on cities, and villages small,
And nothing, no, nothing is hidden at all.

He knows where the good children live beyond doubt,
He knows where the bad boys and girls are about,
And writes down their names on a page by themselves;
In a book that he keeps on his library shelves.

For good little children, the gentle and kind,
The prettiest presents of toys are designed,
And when Christmas comes round, as it does once a year,
'Tis certain that Santa Claus then will appear.

His work-shop is, oh! such a wonderful place,
With heaps of gay satins, and ribbons, and lace;
With houses and furniture, dishes and pans,
And bracelets and bangles, and all sorts of fans.

There are horses that gallop, and dollies that walk,
And some of the pretty doll-babies can talk.
There are pop-guns, and marbles, and tops for the boys,
And big drums and trumpets that make a big noise.

There are games for all seasons, the base-ball and kite,
And books which the children will seize with delight,

373

And the skates and the sleds, far too many to count,
And the bicycles ready for wheelmen to mount.

There are farm-yards in plenty, with fences and trees,
And cows, sheep, and oxen, all taking their ease,
And turkeys and ducks, and fine chickens and hens,
And dear little piggies to put in their pens.

There are gay Noah's Arks, just as full as can be
Of animals, really a wonder to see;
There are lions and tigers, and camels and bears,
And two of each kind, for they travel in pairs.

There are elephants stretching their noses quite long;
And reindeer and elks with their antlers so strong,
And queer kangaroos all the others amid,
With their dear little babies in pockets well hid.

Is Santa Claus happy? There's no need to ask,
For he finds such enjoyment indeed in his task,
That he bubbles with laughter, and whistles and sings,
While making and planning the beautiful things.

He's a jolly good fellow, but ever so shy,
And likes to do all his good deeds on the sly,
So there's no use spoiling a good winter's nap
For you'll not catch a glimpse of the jolly old chap.

When Christmas Eve comes, into bed you must creep,
And late in the night when you are asleep,
He is certain to come; so your stockings prepare,
And hang them up close by the chimney with care.

The baby's wee stockings you must not forget,
For Santa will have something nice for the pet,
And those who are thoughtful for others will find
The good saint at Christmas time has them in mind.

There is Tommy, who tended the baby with care,
A nice train of cars he shall have for his share,

And how happy will Eliza be when she looks
For her presents, and finds such a budget of books.

For dear little Mary, a doll there will be;
And for Alice and Jenny a gay Christmas tree;
And wee little Georgie the baby, will find
A big stick of candy, just suiting his mind.

Oh, a jolly good sight is this funny old chap
When he's dressed in his bear-skin and fur-bordered cap,
All ready to start on his way through the cold,
In a sleigh covered over with jewels and gold.

While his deer from the mountains all harnessed with care,
Like race-horses prance through the clear frosty air;
'Tis fun just to watch them, and hear the bells ring,
And the stars seem to think it a comical thing.

For old Santa is bundled so close to the chin,
That there is not a chance for the cold to get in,
His cheeks are so rosy, his eyes how they flash!
No horses nor driver e'er cut such a dash!

He cracks his long whip, and he whistles a tune,
While he winks at the stars, and he bows to the moon,
And over the tree-tops he drives like the wind,
And leaves all the night-birds a long way behind.

His steeds speed away on a journey so fleet,
That they seem to have wings to their swift-flying feet,
For there's work to be done by a cheery old man,
And his coursers will help him as well as they can.

His sleigh is with toys and trinkets well packed,
You never beheld one with pleasures so stacked;
And though of good children he has such a list,
Not one is forgotten, not one will be missed.

An army he gives to the boy who is neat,
And never is rude in the house or the street;

375

And a farm to the lad who goes smiling to school,
Who knows all his lessons and minds every rule.

And if you would please him—dear Bertie and Jack—;
And win a nice prize from the old fellow's pack,
Be good little children, your parents obey,
And strive to be happy at work or at play.

At Christmas old Santa Claus toils like a Turk,
For the cheery old fellow is fond of his work.
With his queer looking team through the air he will go,
And alight on the house-tops all covered in snow.

Then down through the chimneys he'll dart without noise
And fill up the stockings with candy and toys.
There'll be presents for Julia, and Nellie, and Jack,
And plenty more left in the old fellow's pack.

And if Frank behaves well, and minds what is said,
Quits teasing the cat and goes early to bed;
He'll find for his present a sled or a gun,
A ready companion in frolic and fun.

On Santa Claus hurries, and works with a will,
For many tall Christmas trees he has to fill,
And loads them with treasures from out his rich store,
Till they blossom as trees never blossomed before.

Though round as a dumpling, and ever so fat,
In running and climbing he's spry as a cat,
And if the long ladder should happen to break,
And he should fall down, what a crash it would make!

I told you his home was up North by the Pole,
In a palace of hives lives this worthy old soul,
And though out of doors it may furiously storm,
Indoors as we know, it is sunny and warm.

When Christmas is over old Santa Claus goes
To his home in the North, and his well-earned repose,

And when he is rested and feeling tip-top,
The good-natured workman goes back to his shop.

And there he will labor from morning till night,
To make others happy his aim and delight,
And if his good-will the dear children would earn,
They must strive to be happy and good in return.

He comes like an angel of light from above,
To do on the earth sweetest errands of love;
And our hearts and our homes to so fill with good cheer
That we cannot help knowing when Christmas is near.

Then let us be glad, so that Christmas may be
A real Merry Christmas to you and to me!
And now that the story is ended we'll give
Three cheers for old Santa Claus! Long may he live!

Children Praying for Christmas Presents.

A Visit From St. Nicholas

'Twas the night before Christmas, when all through the house
Not a creature was stirring, not even a mouse;
The stockings were hung by the chimney with care,
In hopes that St. Nicholas soon would be there.

The children were nestled all snug in there beds,
While visions of sugar-plums danced through their heads;
And mamma in her kerchief and I in my cap
Had just settled our brains for a long winter's nap,
When out in the lawn there arose such a clatter,
I sprang from my bed to see what was the matter.

Away to the window I flew like a flash,
Tore open the shutters and threw up the sash;
The moon, on the breast of the new-fallen snow,
Gave a lustre of midday to objects below;

When what to my wondering eyes should appear
But a miniature sleigh and eight tiny reindeer,
With a little old driver so lively and quick
I knew in a moment it must be St. Nick.

More rapid than eagles his coursers they came,
And he whistled and shouted and called them by name;
"Now Dasher! now, Dancer! now, Prancer and Vixen!
On Comet! on, Cupid! on, Donder and Blitzen!
To the top of the porch, to the top of the wall,
Now, dash away, dash away, dash away all!"

As dry leaves that before the wild hurricane fly,
When they meet with an obstacle, mount to the sky,
So up to the housetop the coursers they flew,
With a sleigh full of toys, and St. Nicholas too;
And then in a twinkling I heard on the roof
The prancing and pawing of each little hoof.

As I drew in my head and was turning around,
Down the chimney St. Nicholas came with a bound,
He was dressed all in fur from his head to his foot,

And his clothes were all tarnished with ashes and soot;
A bundle of toys he had flung on his back,
And he looked like a peddler just opening his pack,
His eyes, how they twinkled! his dimples, how merry!
His cheeks were like roses, his nose like a cherry.
His droll little mouth was drawn up like a bow,
And the beard on his chin was as white as the snow.

He was chubby and plump—a right jolly old elf—
And I laughed when I saw him, in spite of myself;
A wink of his eye and a twist of his head
Soon gave me to know I had nothing to dread.

He spoke not a word, but went straight to his work,
And filled all the stockings, then turned with a jerk,
And laying his finger aside of his nose,
And giving a nod, up the chimney he rose.

He sprang to his sleigh, to his team gave a whistle,
And away they all flew like the down of a thistle;
But I heard him exclaim ere he drove out sight;
"Happy Christmas to all, and to all a good night."

Clement C. Moore

What Santa Claus Brings

Lovely little girls and boys,
Santa brings all sorts of toys.
Boxes filled with wooden bricks,
Monkeys climbing yellow sticks.

Dollies' houses painted red,
Tiny soldiers made of lead,
Noah's Arks, and Ninepins too,
Jack in boxes, painted blue.

Cups and Saucers, Pots and Pans,

379

China figures, Chinese fans,
Railway trains, with Tops and Tables,
Fairy Tales and Aesops Fables,

Clockwork Mice, and Coloured Marbles
Painted Bird that sweetly warbles,
Dolls of every age and size,
With flaxen hair and moving eyes.

Cows and horses, Chickens, Cats,
Rattles, Windmills, Boats and Bats,
Ducks and Geese, and golden Fishes,
Skipping ropes and copper Dishes.

Books and coloured pictures, too,
And a thousand other things for you;
Dainty maidens, merry boys,
Santa brings all sorts of toys.

Little Mary

Dear little Mary,
  With eyes so blue,
What has Santa Claus
  Brought for you?

He has brought me a cup,
  And a curly sheep,
And a cradle where dolly
  May go to sleep.

The best of all
  Is this funny box
That winds with a key
  Just like the clocks.

And when you've wound
  The spring up tight,

The monkey dances
  With all his might,

And Fido barks
  And the puppies play:
We're all very happy
  This Christmas day.

Christmas

Dainty little stockings
  Hanging in a row,
Blue, and grey, and scarlet,
  In the firelight's glow.

Curly-pated sleepers
  Safely tucked in bed;
Dreams of wondrous toy-shops
  Dancing through each head.

Funny little stockings
  Hanging in a row
Stuffed with sweet surprises,
  Down from top to toe.

Skates, and balls, and trumpets,
  Dishes, tops, and drums,
Books and dolls and candles,
  Nuts and sugar-plums.

Little sleepers waking:
  Bless me, what a noise!
Wish you merry Christmas,
  Happy girls and boys!

The Nursery

Santa Claus making Toys for Good Girls and Good Boys.

Santa Claus looking in his Big Diary for the
Names of Boys and Girls who have been Good
since last Christmas.

Christmas

When the children have been good,
That is, be it understood,
Good at meal-times, good at play,
Good all night and good all day,—
They shall have the pretty things
Merry Christmas always brings.

382

Santa Claus starting to distribute Toys.

A Christmas Eve Adventure

Once on a time in a queer little town,
  On the shore of the Zuyder Zee,
When all the good people were fast asleep,
  A strange thing happened to me.

Alone, the night before Christmas,
  I sat by the glowing fire,
Watching the flame as it rose and fell,
  While the sparks shot high and higher.

Suddenly one of these sparks began
  To flicker and glimmer and wink
Like a big bright eye, till I hardly knew
  What to do or to say or to think.

Quick as a flash, it changed to a face,
  And what in the world did I see
But dear old Santa Claus nodding his head,

383

And waving his hand to me

"Oh! follow me, follow me!" soft he cried,—
  And up through the chimney with him
I mounted, not daring to utter a word
  Till we stood on the chimney's rim.

"Now tell me, I beg you, dear Santa Claus,
  Where am I going with you?"
He laughingly answered, "Why, don't you know?
  To travel the whole world through!

"From my crystal palace, far in the North,
  I have come since dark,—and see
These curious things for the little folk
  Who live on the Zuyder Zee.'

Then seating himself in his reindeer sledge,
  And drawing me down by his side,
He whistled, and off on the wings of the wind
  We flew for our midnight ride.

But first, such comical presents he left
  For the little Dutch girls and boys,—
Onions and sausages, wooden-faced dolls,
  Cheeses and gingerbread toys

Away we hurried far to the South,
  To the beautiful land of France;
And there we showered the loveliest gifts,—
  Flaxen-haired dolls that could dance.

Soldiers that marched at the word of command,
  Necklaces, bracelets and rings
Tiny gold watches, all studded with gems,
  And hundreds of exquisite things.

Crossing the Channel, we made a short call
  In Scotland and Ireland, too;
Left a warm greeting for England and Wales,

Then over the ocean we flew

Straight to America, where by myself,
  Perched on a chimney high,
I watched him scramble and bustle about
  Between the earth and the sky.

Many a stocking he filled to the brim,
  And numberless Christmas trees
Burst into bloom at his magical touch!
  Then all of a sudden a breeze

Caught us and bore us away to the South,
  And afterwards blew us "out West;"
And never till dawn peeped over the hills
  Did we stop for a moment's rest.

"Christmas is coming!" he whispered to me,
  "You can see his smile in the sky,—
I wish Merry Christmas to all the world!
  My work is over,—good-bye!"

Like a flash he was gone, and I was alone,—
  For all of this happened to me
Once on a time, in a queer little town
  On the shore of the Zuyder Zee!

M. M.

Little Bennie

I had told him, Christmas morning,
  As he sat upon my knee,
Holding fast his little stockings,
  Stuffed as full as can be,
And attentive listening to me,
  With a face demure and mild,
That old Santa Claus, who filled them,

385

Did not love a naughty child.

"But we'll be good, won't we, moder?"
  And from off my lap he slid,
Digging deep among the goodies
  In his crimson stockings hid.
While I turned me to my table,
  Where a tempting goblet stood,
Brimming high with a dainty custard,
  Sent me by a neighbour good.

But the kitten, there before me,
  With his white paw, nothing loth,
Sat, by way of entertainment,
  Lapping off the shining froth;
And, in not the gentlest humour
  At the loss of such a treat,
I confess I rather rudely
  Thrust him out into the street.

Then how Bennie's blue eyes kindled;
  Gathering up the precious store
He had busily been pouring
  In his tiny pinafore,
With a generous look that shamed me
  Sprang he from the carpet bright,
Showing, by his mien indignant,
  All a baby's sense of right.

"Come back Harney," called he loudly,
  As he held his apron white,
"You shall have my candy wabbit;"
  But the door was fastened tight.
So he stood, abashed and silent,
  In the centre of the floor,
With defeated look, alternate
  Bent on me and on the door.

Then, as by some sudden impulse,
  Quickly ran he to the fire,

And while eagerly his bright eyes
  Watched the flames grow high and higher,
In a brave, clear key he shouted,
  Like some lordly little elf,
"Santa Kaus, come down the chimney,
  Make my mother 'have herself."

"I'll be a good girl, Bennie,"
  Said I, feeling the reproof;
And straightway recalled poor Harney,
  Mewing on the galley roof.
Soon the anger was forgotten,
  Laughter chased away the frown,
And they gambolled 'neath the live oaks,
  Till the dusky night came down.

In my dim, fire-lighted chamber
  Harney purred beneath my chair,
And my play-worn boy beside me
  Knelt to say his evening prayer:
"God bess fader, God bess moder,
  God bess sister," then a pause,
And the sweet young lips devoutly
  Murmured "God bess Santa Kaus."

He is sleeping: brown and silken
  Lie the lashes, long and meek,
Like caressing, clinging shadows,
  On his plump and peachy cheek;
And I bend above him, weeping,
  Thankful tears: O undefiled;
For a woman's crown of glory,
  For the blessing of a child.

Annie C. Ketchum

Santa Claus filling the Stockings.

Old Santa Claus

Old Santa Claus sat alone in his den,
  With his leg crossed over his knee;
While a comical look peeped out at his eyes,
  For a funny old fellow was he.

His queer little cap was tumbled and torn,
  And his wig it was all awry,
But he sat and mused the whole day long,
  While the hours went flying by.

He had been busy as busy can be,
  In filling his pack with toys;
He had gathered his nuts and baked his pies,
  To give to the girls and boys.

There were dolls for the girls, and whips for the boys,
  With wheelbarrows, horses and drays,
And bureaus and trunks for Dolly's new clothes;

All these in his pack he displays.

Of candy too, both twisted and striped,
  He had furnished a plentiful store,
While raisins and figs, and prunes and grapes,
  Hung up on a peg by the door.

"I am almost ready," quoth he, quoth he,
  "And Christmas is almost here;
But one thing more—I must write a book,
  And give to each one this year."

So he clapped his specs on his little round nose,
  And seizing the stump of a pen,
He wrote more lines in one little hour
  Than you ever could write in ten.

He told them stories all pretty and new,
  And wrote them all out in rhyme;
Then packed them away with his box of toys
  To distribute one at a time.

And Christmas Eve, when all were in bed,
  Right down the chimney he flew;
And stretching the stocking-leg out at the top,
  He clapped in a book for you.

Santa Claus and the Mouse

One Christmas Eve, when Santa Claus
  Came to a certain house,
To fill the children's stockings there,
  He found a little mouse.

"A merry Christmas, little friend,"
  Said Santa, good and kind.
"The same to you, sir!" said the mouse,

389

"I thought you wouldn't mind

If I should stay awake tonight,
  And watch you for a while."
"You're very welcome, little mouse,"
  Said Santa, with a smile.

And then he filled the stockings up,
  Before the mouse could wink,—
From toe to top, from top to toe,
  There wasn't left a chink.

"Now, they won't hold another thing,"
  Said Santa Claus with pride.
A twinkle came in mousie's eyes,
  But humbly he replied:

"It's not nice to contradict—
  Your pardon I implore,—
But in the fullest stocking here,
  I could put one thing more."

"Oh, ho!" laughed Santa, "silly mouse!
  Don't I know how to pack?
By filling stockings all these years,
  I should have learned the knack."

And then he took the stocking down
  From where it hung so high,
And said: "Now put in one thing more;
  I give you leave to try."

The mousie chuckled to himself,
  And then he softly stole
Right to the stocking's crowded toe,
  And gnawed a little hole!

"Now, if you please, good Santa Claus,
  I've put in one thing more;
For you will own, that little hole

Was not in there before."

How Santa Claus did laugh and laugh;
 And then he gaily spoke;
"Well, you shall have a Christmas cheese,
 For that nice little joke."

A Nice Little Present

"Our Santa Claus" cried Bettie,
 "Is nice as any other;
He brought the nicest present
 To me and to my mother.

"It was—oh, you can't guess it—
 A darling little brother.
He kicks and cries and shuts his eyes,
 And he's sweet enough to eat.

"I'd rather have my baby brother
Than dolls or candy—so would my mother."

The Night Before Christmas

Curly heads, so softly pillowed;
 Chubby arms outspread;
Thousand fancies swiftly flying
 Through each little head.

Clasping treasures newly garnered,
 Dolly, book, and ball,
Still they dream of coming pleasures
 Greater than them all.

Christmas-trees of gorgeous beauty,
 Filled with presents rare;

Toys unheard of, joys unnumbered,
  All delights are there.

Angel forms, with smiling faces,
  Hover round the bed;
Angel feet make echoing music
  As they lightly tread.

Angel voices, softly thrilling,
  Chant a lullaby:
"Darlings, dream, and sweetly slumber,
  We are watching by."

Who from dreams like these would waken
  To a world of pain?
"Hush, then, dear ones! Have we roused you?
  Turn and dream again"

Baby waking up nearly caught Santa Claus.

Annie And Willie's Prayer

'Twas the eve before Christmas; good night had been said,
And Annie and Willie had crept into bed.
There were tears on their pillows, and tears in their eyes,
And each little bosom was heaving with sighs;

For to-night their stern Father's command had been given,
That they should retire precisely at seven
Instead of at eight; for they had troubled him more
With questions unheard of than ever before.

He had told them he thought this delusion a sin;
No such creature as "Santa Claus" ever had been;
And he hoped, after this, he should never more hear
How he scrambled down chimneys with presents each year.

And this was the reason that two little heads
So restlessly tosses on their soft, downy beds.
Eight, nine, and the clock on the steeple tolled ten;
Not a word had been spoken by either till then;

When Willie's sad face from the blanket did peep,
And he whispered: "Dear Annie, is 'ou fast asleep?"
"Why, no, Brother Willie," a sweet voice replies;
"I've long tried in vain, but I can't shut my eyes;

"For somehow it makes me so sorry because
Dear Papa has said there is no Santa Claus.
Now we know there is, and it can't be denied
For he came every year before dear mamma died;

"But then, I've been thinking, that she used to pray,—
And God would hear everything dear mamma would say,—
And, maybe, she asked him to send Santa Claus here
With the sack full of presents he brought every year."

"Well, why tannot we p'ay, dust as mamma did, den,

393

And ask Dod to send him with p esents aden?"
"I've been thinking so, too;" and without a word more
Four little bare feet bounded out on the floor,

And four little knees on the soft carpet pressed,
And two tiny hands were clasped close to each breast,
"Now, Willie, you know, we must firmly believe
That the presents we ask for we're sure to receive;

"You must wait just as still till I say the 'Amen,'
And by that you will know that your turn has come then.—
"Dear Jesus, look down on my brother and me,
And grant us the favours we're asking of Thee.

"I want a wax dolly, a tea-set and a ring,
And an ebony work-box that shuts with a spring.
Bless papa, dear Jesus, and cause him to see
That Santa Claus loves us as much as does he.

"Don't let hem get fretful and angry again,
At dear brother Willie and Annie Amen."
  "Dear Desus, 'et Santa Taus turn down to night
And bring us some p'esents before it is 'ight;

"I want he sood div' me a nice little sled,
Wid bight shinin' 'unners, and all painted 'ed
A box full of tandy, a book, and a toy,
Amen. And den, Desus, I'll be a food boy."

Their prayers being ended, they raised up their heads,
And with hearts light and cheerful again sought their beds;
They were soon lost in slumber both peaceful and deep,
And with fairies in dreamland were roaming in sleep.

Eight, nine, and the little French clock had struck ten
Ere the father had thought of his children again;
He seems now to hear Annie's self-suppressed sighs,
And to see the big tears stand in Willie's blue eyes.

"I was harsh with my darlings," he mentally said,

"And should not have sent them so early to bed:
But then I was troubled: My feelings found vent;
For the bank-stock to-day has gone down two percent.;

"But of course they've forgotten their troubles ere this,
And that I denied them the thrice-asked-for kiss;
But just to make sure I'll steal up to their door—
To my darlings I have never spoke harshly before."

So saying, he softly ascended the stairs,
And arrived at the door to hear both of their prayers;
His Annie's "Bless papa" drew forth the big tears,
And Willie's grave promise fell sweet on his ears.

"Strange, strange! I'd forgotten," he said with a sigh,
"How I longed when a child to have Christmas draw nigh
I'll atone for my harshness," he inwardly said,
"By answering their prayers ere I sleep in my bed."

Then he turned to the stairs, and softly went down,
Threw off velvet slippers and silk dressing gown.
Donned hat, coat and boots, and was out in the street,
A millionaire facing the cold, driving sleet!

Nor stopped he until he had bought everything,
From the box full of candy to the tiny gold ring:
Indeed, he kept adding so much to his store,
That the various presents outnumbered a score.

Then homeward he turned, when his holiday load,
With Aunt Mary's help, in the nursery was stow'd.
Miss Dolly was seated beneath a pine tree,
And the side of a table spread out for her tea;

A work-box, well- filled, in the centre was laid,
And on it the ring for which Annie had pray'd.
A soldier in uniform stood by a sled,
With bright shining runners, and all painted red.

There were balls, dogs, horses; books pleasing to see;

COLE

And birds of all colours were perched in the tree;
While Santa Claus, laughing, stood up in the top,
As if getting ready more presents to drop.

Now, as the fond father the picture surveyed,
He thought for his trouble he'd amply been paid;
As he said to himself, as he brushed off a tear,
"I'm happier to night than I have been for a year;

"I've enjoyed more true pleasure than ever before;
What care I if bank-stock fell two per cent. more!
Henceforward I'll make it a rule, I believe,
To have Santa Clause visit us each Christmas-eve."

So thinking, he gently extinguished the light,
And, slipping downstairs, retired for the night.
As soon as the beams of the bright morning sun
Put the darkness to flight, and the stars one by one,

Four little blue eyes out of sleep opened wide,
And at the same moment the presents espied.
Then out of their beds they sprang with a bound,
And the very gifts prayed for were all of them found.

And they laughed and they cried in their innocent glee,
And shouted for papa to come quick and see
What presents old Santa Claus brought in the night
(Just the things they wanted!), and left before light.

"And now," added Annie, in a voice soft and low,
"You'll believe there's a Santa Claus, papa, I know;"
While dear little Willie climbed up on his knee,
Determined no secret between them should be;

And told, in soft whispers, how Annie had said
That their blessed mamma, so long ago dead,
Used to kneel down and pray by the side of her chair,
And that God up in heaven had answered her prayer.

"Den we dot up and p'ayed just as well as we tood,

And Dod answered our 'ayer, now wasn't He dood?"
"I should say that He was, if He sent you all these,
And knew just what presents my children would please."

("Well, well, let them think so, dear little elf!
'Twould be cruel to tell 1im I did it myself.")

Blind father! who caused your stern heart to relent,
And the hasty words sp>ken so soon to repent?
'Twas the Being who bade you steal softly upstairs
And made you His agent to answer their prayers.

Mrs. Sophia F. Snow

Boy Nailing up his Father's Trousers.

Budds' Christmas Stocking

It was Christmas-time, as all the world knew;
It stormed without, and the cold wind blew,
But within all was cheerful, snug, and bright,
With glowing fires and many a light.

Budd B. was sent quite early to bed,
His stocking was hung up close to his head,
And he said to himself "When all grows still

397

I will find a big stocking for Santy to fill."

Now, good, honest Hans, who worked at the house,
Had gone to his bed as still as a mouse;
The room where he slept was one story higher
Than Budd's little room, with gaslight and fire.

Now, Hans loved "the poy," and petted him too,
And often at night, when his task was all through,
He would tell him strange stories of over the sea,
While Budd listened gravely or laughed out in glee.

This night Hans had promised to wake Budd at four;
He would softly come down and open his door;
But suddenly Budd bounded out of his bed,
And stole softly up to the room overhead.

On his hands and his knees he crept softly in,
"I'll borrow Han's stocking," he said, with a grin;
Old Santy will fill it up to the top,
And Hans—oh, such fun! will be mad as a hop."

He moved very slowly, and felt near the bed;
No stocking was there, but down on his head
Came a deluge of water, well sprinkled with ice,
While honest Hans held him as if in a vice.

"Vat is dat?" he cried out; "von robber I find,
Den I pound him, and shake him, so much as I mind"
"It's me," called out Budd; "Stop, Hans! oh, please do;
I'm only a boy; I could not rob you."

But Hans did not pause—his temper was hot—
And he dragged the young robber at once from the spot,
When he reached the hall light great was his surprise
To find his young master with tears in his eyes.

"I wanted your stocking," muttered Budd B.;
It is bigger than mine; boo hoo! I can't see,
And I'm all wet and cold." thus cried Budd aloud,

398

Until guests and his parents ran up in a crowd.

He was wrapped up with care and taken to bed,
But, strangest of all, not a harsh word was said.
He flattered himself as he fell asleep
That Hans and his friends the secret would keep.

Next morning, when Christmas songs filled all the air,
Budd found, to his grief and boyish despair,
That his neck was so stiff that he could not turn his head,
And must spend the whole day alone in his bed.

What was worse, his own stocking hung limp on a chair,
And on it these words were written most fair:
"To him who is greedy I leave less than all;
The world is so large and my reindeer so small.

"My pack is elastic when children are kind,
But it shuts with a snap and leaves nothing behind,
When a boy or girl is selfish or mean.
Good-bye, little Budd, I am off with my team.
    (Signed) Santa Claus."

Christmas

Again the Christmas holidays have come,
We soon will hear the trumpet and the drum;
We'll hear the merry shout of the girls and boys
Rejoicing o'er their gifts of books and toys.

Old Santa Claus comes by at dead of night,
And down the chimney creeps—a funny sight;
He fills the stockings full of books and toys,
But puts in whips for naughty girls and boys.

One Christmas-eve the moon shone clear and bright;
I thought I'd keep awake and watch all night,
But it was silent all around and stilled,

399

Yet in the morn I found my stockings filled.

Christmas Morning

They put me in a square bed, and there they bade me sleep;
I must not stir; I must not wake; I must not even peep;
Right opposite that lonely bed, my Christmas stocking hung;
While near it, waiting for the morn, my Sunday clothes were flung.

I counted softly, to myself, to ten and ten times ten,
And went through all the alphabet, and then began again;
I repeated that Fifth-Reader piece—a poem called "Repose,"
And tried a dozen various ways to fal into a dose—

When suddenly the room grew light. I heard a soft, strong bound,
'Twas Santa Claus, I felt quite sure, but dared not look around.
'Twas nice to know that he was there, and things were going rightly,
And so I took a little nap, and tried to smile politely.

"Ho! Merry Christmas!" cried a voice I felt the bed a-rocking;
Twas daylight—brother Bob was up! and oh, that splendid stocking!

St. Nicholas

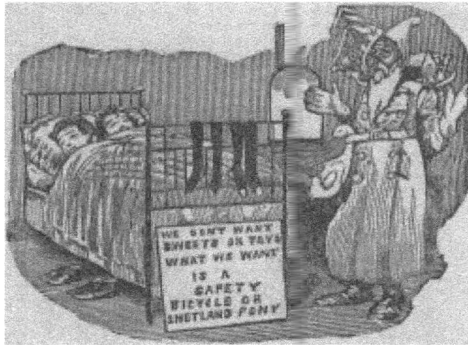

What the Rich Man's Child got.

Little Nellie's Visit From Santa Claus

Santa Claus is coming to-night, papa;
Please let me sit up and see him, mamma;
Loaded with presents, I'm sure he'll be.
He'll have something nice for you and for me.

"Mamma, do find something fresh and quite new,
For dear old Santa Claus, when he comes through,
I'll give it myself; I'll keep wide awake;
I know he'll be glad my present to take.

"Now all go to bed as quick as you please,
I'll wait for him," said the bright little tease,
"He surely will ring, no doubt about that,
I'll bid him come in and then have a chat."

Soon came a quick step on the piazza floor,
Just then a loud ring was heard at the door.
The little miss rose with dignified air,

401

Quick ushered him in, and set him a chair.

All covered o'er with little bells tinkling,
Shaking and laughing, twisting and wriggling,
A funny old man, with little eyes blinking,
Looking at Nellie, what was he thinking?

Not a word did he say—tired of waiting,
Nellie arose, her little heart quaking,
Held out her present, courage most failing,
"Santa Claus, take this"—now she is smiling.

"His furry old hand, twisting and trembling,
Took the sweet gift—"You dear little darling,"
Uttered quite softly, tenderly kissing,
The bright little face, ne'er a bit shrinking.

Lots of presents quickly bestowing,
Thanking her kindly—he must be going,
Shaking and laughing, his little bells jingling,
Down the steps, hastening off in a twinkling.

Brave little lady! all are now saying,
Santa Claus truly! bright eyes are asking;
See her dear papa, secretly laughing
At her true faith in Santa Claus' coming.

Yes! she believes it, ever so truly,
Dear precious darling! rob her not surely,
Of childhood's sweet faith, now in its glory,
While she's relating her own simple story.

Mrs. C. E. Wilbur

Christmas Stockings

'Tis Christmas day,
And little May

Peeps from her bed in the morning grey.

She looks around,
But not a sound
Breaks on the quietness profound.

So, heaving sighs,
She shuts her eyes,
And hard to go to sleep she tries.

But sleep has fled
That little bed.
And weary moves the curly head,

Until the light
(Oh, welcome sight!)
Has banished every trace of night.

Then out of bed,
With hurried tread,
She runs to waken brother Fred;

For oh, what joys,
In the shape of toys,
Does Christmas bring to girls and boys!

Fred gives a groan,
Or a sleepy moan,
And mutters, "Do let me alone!"

But bonnie May
Will not have nay;
She whispers, 'It is Christmas day!"

Oh, magic sound!
For Fred turns round,
And in a trice is on the ground.

"Our stockings, where?"
"They're on that chair."

"Oh, what has Santa Claus put there?"

May laughs with glee,
The sight to see,
Of stockings filled from toe to knee

With parcels queer,
That stick out here,
Before, behind, in front and rear.

"Oh, Fred! a dolly!
I'll call her Molly."
"Why, may, a penknife here; how jolly!"

"A necktie blue!
A paintbox too!"
"Oh, Fred, a pair of kid gloves new!"

"May, here's a gun!
Won't we have fun,
Playing at soldiers!—You'll be one."

"Now that is all.
No; here's a ball;
Just hold it, or these things will fall."

"What's in the toe,
May, do you know?
Biscuits and figs!—I told you so."

"I think," said May,
That Christmas day,
Should come at least every second day."

And so say we;
But then you see
That Santa Claus would tired be.

And all his toys
And Christmas joys

Would vanish then from girls and boys.

From "The Prize"

Hang Up Baby's Stocking

Hang up the baby's stocking:
  Be sure you don't forget:
The dear little dimpled darling
  Has never seen Christmas yet.

But I told him all about it,
  And he opened his big blue eyes;
I'm sure he understood it,
  He looked so funny and wise.

Ah, what a tiny stocking;
  It doesn't take so much to hold
Such little toes as baby's
  Safe from the frost and cold.

But then, for the baby's Christmas
  It never will do at all;
For Santa Claus wouldn't be looking
  For anything half so small.

I know what will do for baby;
  I've thought of a first-rate plan;
I'll borrow a stocking of grandma—
  The longest that I ever can.

And you shall hang it by mine, mother,
  Right here in the corner—so;
And write a letter for baby.
  And fasten it on the toe.

"Old Santa Claus, this is a stocking
  Hung up for our baby dear;

You never have seen our darling,
  He has not been with us a year,

"But he is a beautiful baby;
  And now, before you go,
Please cram this stocking with presents,
  From the top of it down to the toe.

"Put in a baby's rattle,
  Also a coral ring,
A bright new ribbon for his waist;
  Some beads hung on a string

"And mind a coloured ball please,
  And a tiny pair of shoes;
You'll see from this little stocking,
  The size you have to choose."

Santa Claus

A health to good old Santa Claus,
  And to his reindeer bold,
Whose hoofs are shod with elder-down,
  Whose horns are tipped with gold.

Ho comes from utmost fairyland
  Across the wintry snows;
He makes the fir-tree and the spruce
  To blossom like the rose.

Over the quaint old gables,
  Over the windy ridge,
By turret wall and chimney tall,
  He guided his fairy sledge;

He steals upon the slumbers
  Of little rose-lipped girls,
And lays his waxen dollies down

Beside their golden curls.

He scatters blessings on his way,
  And sugar-coated plums;
He robs the sluggard from his rest
  With trumpets, guns, and drums.

Small feet, before the dawn of day,
  Are marching to and fro,
Drums beat to arms through all the house,
  And penny trumpets blow.

A health to brave old Santa Claus,
  And to his reindeer bold,
Whose hoofs are shod with elder-down,
  Whose horns are tipped with gold.

S. H. Whitman

The Rabbit on the Wall

The children shout with laughter,
  The uproar louder grows;
Even grandma chuckles faintly,

407

And Johnny chirps and crows.
There ne'er was gilded painting,
  Hung up in lordly hall,
Gave half the simple pleasure
  As this rabbit on the wall.

The cottage work is over,
  The evening meal is done;
Hark! thro' the starlight stillness
  You hear the river run.
The little children whisper,
  Then speak out one and all;
"Come, father, make for Johnny,
  The rabbit on the wall."

He—smilingly assenting,
  They gather round his chair;
"Now, grandma, you hold Johnny;
  Don't let the candle flare."
So speaking, from his fingers
  He throws a shadow all,
That seems, a moment after,
  A rabbit on the wall.

Holiday Time

With these three little girls and two little boys
There is sure to be plenty of laughter and noise;
But nobody minds it, because don't you see,
At school they are quiet with lessons to say—
But when the holidays come they can play the whole day.

The Fairy Queen

Let us laugh and let us sing,
Dancing in a merry ring

We'll be fairies on the green,
Sporting round the Fairy Queen.

Like the seasons of the year,
Round we circle in a sphere;
I'll be Summer, you'll be Spring,
Dancing in a fairy ring.

Harry will be Winter wild;
Little Annie, Autumn mild;
Summer, Autumn, Winter, Spring,
Dancing in a fairy ring.

Spring and Summer glide away,
Autumn comes with tresses grey;
Winter, hand in hand with Spring,
Dancing in a fairy ring.

Faster! faster! round we go
While our cheeks like roses glow;
Free as birds upon the wing,
Dancing in a fairy ring.

Come and Play in the Garden

Little sister, come away,
And let us in the garden play,
For it is a pleasant day.

On the grassplot let us sit,
Or, if you please, we'll play a bit,
And run about all over it.

But the fruit we will not pick,
For that would be a naughty trick,
And, very likely, make us sick.

Nor will we pluck the pretty flowers

That grow about the beds and bowers,
Because, you know, they are not ours.

We'll pluck the daisies, white and red,
Because mamma has often said,
That we may gather them instead.

And much I hope we always may
Out very dear mamma obey,
And mind whatever she may say.

Little Romp

I am tired to death of keeping still
  And being good all day.
I guess my mamma's company
  Forgot to go away,
I've wished and wished they'd think of it,
  And that they would get through;
But they must talk for ever first,
  They almost always do.

I heard Tom calling to me once,
  He's launched his boat, I know;
I wanted to get out and help,
  But mamma's eyes said no.
The ladies talk such stuff to me,
  It makes me sick to hear—
"How beautiful your hair curls!" or,
  "How red your cheeks are, dear!"

I'd ten times rather run a race,
  Then play my tunes and things;
I wouldn't swop my dogs and balls
  For forty diamond rings.
I've got no 'finement, aunty says,
  I 'spect she knows the best;
I don't need much to climb a tree,

Or hunt a squrrel's nest.

"Girls are like berries," papa says,
  "Sweeter for running wild,"
But Aunt Melissa shakes her head,
  And calls me "Horrid child!"
I'll always be a romp she knows—
  But sure's my name is Sadie,
I'll fool 'em all some dreadful day,
  By growing up a lady.

Hide and Seek

"We will have a game of hide and seek,
  Now mind you do not look."
And Willie went and hid himself
  In a dark and lonely nook.

Then the children went to find him;
  They hunted all about.
It was a funny way in which
  At last they found him out.

Just as they got where he was hid,
  In his nose he felt a tickling
That made him sneeze, and so you see
  They found him in a twinkling.

Our Tea Party.

Tired of Play

Tired of play! tired of play!
What hast thou done this livelong day?
The birds are silent, and so is the bee;
The sun is creeping up temple and tree;

The doves have flown to the sheltering eves
And the nests are dark with the drooping leaves.
Twilight gathers and day is done,

412

How hast thou spent it, restless one?

Playing? But wha_ has thou done beside,
To tell thy mother at eventide?
What promise of norn is left unbroken?
What kind word to thy playmate spoken?

Whom hast thou pitied and whom forgiven,
How with thy faults has duty striven,
What hast thou learned by field and hill?
By greenwood path, and singing rill?

Well for thee if thou couldst tell,
A tale like this of a day spent well,
If thy kind hand has aided distress,
And thou pity hast felt for wretchedness;

If thou hast forgiven a brother's offence,
And grieved for thine own with penitence;
If every creature has won thy love
From the creeping worm to the brooding dove,
Then with joy and peace on the bed of rest,
Thou wilt sleep as on thy mother's breast.

Sea-side Play

Two little boys, all neat and clean,
  Came down upon the shore:
They did not know old Ocean's ways—
  They'd ne'er seen him before.

So quietly they sat them down,
  To build a fort of sand;
Their backs were turned to the sea,
  Their faces toward the land.

They had just built a famous fort—
  The handkerchief flag was spread—

When up there came a stealthy wave,
And turned them heels over head.

After School Hours

School is closed and tasks are done,
Flowers are laughing in the sun;
Like the songsters in the air,
Happy children, banish care!

Riding on a Gate

Sing, sing,
What shall we sing,
  A gate is a capital
  Sort of thing.

If you have not a horse,
Or haven't a swing,
  A gate is a capital
  Sort of thing.

Cry, cry,
Finger in eye,
  Go home to mother
  And tell her why;

You've been riding,
  And why not I?
Each in turn, isn't that the rule
For work or play, at home or school.

Walking Song

Come, my children, come away,
For the sun shines bright to-day;
Little children, come with me,
Birds, and brooks, and posies see;
Get your hats and come away,
For it is a pleasant day.

Bring the hoop and bring the ball,
Come with happy faces all,
Let us make a merry ring,
Talk, and laugh, and dance, and sing
Quickly, quickly come away,
For it is a pleasant day.

The Lost Playmate

The old school-house is still to day,
  The rooms have no gay throng;
No ringing laugh is on the air,
  There is no snatch of song.
The white-haired master sits upon
  The seat beneath the tree,
And thinks upon the vanished face,
  With all its boyish glee.

But a few short days ago, the lad
  Was gayest of the gay,
Quick at the page of knowledge, and
  The heartiest in play.
The pride of the home beside the stream,
  With his pigeons in their cots,
And finding life a very dream,
  In pleasant homely spots.

His school companions loving him,
  And old folks speaking praise,

415

Of the well-loved boy, with frankest eyes,
  And cheery, happy ways.
All in the village knew the boy,
  From parson down to clerk,
And his whistle in the village street
  Was clear as the song of lark.

But like a dream he's passed away,
  And from the chamber dim,
In the fair light of summer day,
  The peasants carry him.
And playmates gather at the grave,
  The old schoolmaster there,
While blossomed boughs wave over-head,
  And all around is fair.

True is the grief that brings the tear,
  There is no empty show;
The simple neighbours see their loss,
  And there is heart-felt woe.
They talk of the bright and lively lad,
  Cut down in boyish prime,
And old folks think how strange is life,
  More strange with passing time!

Oh! simple sight on green hill-side,
  Away from pomp and power;
Here are the truths so oft denied
  To the imperial hour.
Dear child, how precious are the tears,
  Suffusing friendly eyes!
Sublimity is in their gleam,
  A light from God's own skies.

Naughty Mice Teasing the Poor Kitten.

Chinese Toy Merchant.

In the Toy Shop

Cups and saucers, pots and pans,
China figures, Chinese fans,
Railway trains, with tops and tables,
Fairy tales, and Aesop's fables.

Clockwork mice, and colored marbles,
Painted bird that sweetly warbles,
Dolls of every age and size,

417

With flaxen curls and moving eyes.

Cows and horses, chickens, cats,
Rattles, windmills, boats and bats,
Ducks and geese, and golden fishes,
Skipping ropes, and copper dishes.

Books with coloured pictures, too,
And a thousand other things for you;
Dainty maidens, merry boys,
Here you are, all sorts of toys.

Neat Little Clara

"Little Clara, come away,
Little Clara, come and play;
Leave your work, Maria's here,
So come and play with me, my dear."

"I will come, and very soon,
For I always play at noon;
But must put my work away,
Ere with you I come and play.

First my bodkin I must place
With my needles in their case;
I like to put them by with care,
And then I always find them there.

There's my cotton, there's my thread
Thimble in its little bed;
All is safe—my box I lock,
Now I come—'tis twelve o'clock."

Playing Store

"Ting-a-ling!" Now they
  Have opened the store,
Never was such
  An assortment before;
Mud pies in plenty,
  And parcels of sand,
Pebbles for sugar plums,
  Always on hand.

Plenty of customers
  Coming to buy,
"Brown sugar, white sugar
  Which will you try?
Paper for money;
  Their wealth, too, is vast;
In spite of the plenty,
  They scatter it fast.

Quick little hands
  Tie bundles with care,
Summer's glad music
  Is filling the air;
Birdies fly over,
  And wonder, no doubt,
What all these gay
  little folks are about.

Our Shop.

Fishing

He took a stick, he took a cord,
 He took a crooked pin,
And went a-fishing in the sand
 And almost tumbled in.
But just before he tumbled in,
 By chance it came about,
He hooked a whiting and a sole,
 And made them tumble out.

Hide and Seek

When the clean white cloth is laid,
 And the cups are on the table,
When the tea and toast are made,
 That's a happy time for Mabel.

Stealing to her mother's side,
 In her ear she whispers low,

420

"When papa comes I'll hide;
  Don't tell him where I go,"

On her knees upon the floor,
  In below the sofa creeping;
When she hears him at the door,
  She pretends that she is sleeping.

"Where is Mabel?" father cries,
  Looking round and round about.
Then he murmurs in surprise,
  "Surely Mabel can't be out."

First he looks behind his chair,
  Then he peers beneath the table,
Seeking, searching everywhere
  All in vain for little Mabel;

But at last he thinks he knows,
  And he laughs and shakes his head,
Says to mother "I suppose
  Mabel has been put to bed."

But when he sits down to tea,
  From beneath the sofa creeping,
Mabel climbs upon his knee,
  Clasps her hands: "I was not sleeping."

When he asks, 'Where is my girl's
  Very secret hiding-place?"
Mabel only shakes her curls,
  Laughing, smiling, in his face.

Johnny Giving his Sister a Ride.

Our Playhouse Coach.

Little Sailors

Now, Harry, pull the chairs up,
 And, Fanny, get the shawl;
We'll play that we are sailors,
 And that we're in a squall.

The fire will be a lighthouse,
 To warn us off the shore;
And we will place the footstools

For rocks, out on the floor.

Now this chair is the stern
  And that one is the bow;
But there, you must be careful,
  And not lean hard, you know.

Now, sailors, pull that sail up,
  And tuck the corners in—
Well if you want it tighter,
  Ask mother for a pin.

Now couldn't we sing something
  About the "Ocean Blue"?
Well, never mind, "By-baby"
  Or anything will do.

Take care, you careless sailors,
  And mind what you are about,
You know the sea will drown you,
  If you should tumble out.

Brother Playing

Up and down the play-room,
  Then behind the door,
Now upon the sofa,
  Now upon the floor.

In below the table,
  Round the big arm-chair,
Goes my little brother,
  Crying "Are you there?"

And when brother sees me,
  Then away I run;
And he follows after,

423

Merry with the fun.

So at hide and seek we play.
And pass the happy hours away.

Girls and Boys, Come Out to Play

Girls and boys,
  Come out to play,
The sun is shining
  Away, away.

Into the meadow
  Over the way,
Tumbling and tossing
  The new-mown hay.

Into the hedgerow
  Picking the May;
Over the hills
  And far away.

Down by the brook
  Where the ripples play,
Whirling and winding
  Their silvery way,

Then home again
  By a different way,
Picking an armful
  Of wildflowers gay.

For mother dear
  To gladden her way,
And wake in her heart
  A cheerful lay.

For every leaf

Has its sunny ray;
All nature is happy
And seems to say:

Girls and boys,
  Come out to play.
The sun is shining
  Away, away.

Two Merry Men

Two merry men,
  One summer day,
Forsook their toys,
  And forgot their play.

Two little faces,
  Full of fun,
Two little hearts
  That beat as one.

Four little hands,
  At work with a will,
Four little legs
  That can't keep still.

For labour is sweet,
  And toil is fun,
When mother wants
  Any work to be done.

Mud Pies

Tell me little ladies,
  Playing in the sun,
How many minutes

Till the baking's done?

Susy gets the flour,
　All of golden dust;
Harry builds the oven,
　Lily rolls the crust.

Pat it here, and pat it there;
　What a dainty size!
Bake it on a shelf of stone,
　Nice mud pies!

Now we want a shower—
　For we need it so—
It would make a roadside,
　Such a heap of dough.

Turn them in, and turn them out,
　How the morning flies!
Ring the bell for dinner—
　Hot mud pies!

The Playful Girl

I know a little girl,
　Who is very fond of play:
And if her ma would let her,
　Would do nothing else all day.

She has a little doll,
　And another one quite large.
She plays she has a little home,
　And house cares to discharge.

But when her mamma calls her,
　Some real work to do,
She does not like to leave her play,
　And pouts till she is through.

Hay Making

In the hay, in the hay,
  Toss we and tumble;
No one to say us nay,
All through this Summer's day!
  No one to grumble.

In the hat, in the hay,
  Arthur we'll smother;
Bring armfuls, heap them high,
Pile them up—now good-bye,
  Poor little brother!

In the hay, in the hay,
  Snugly reclining,
Shaded from the noontide heat,
Smelling the clover sweet,
  See us all dining;

While the haymakers sit
  Under the willows,
Each with his bread and cheese
Spread out upon his knees,
  Hay for their pillows.

Hark! how the laugh and chat,
  Happy, light hearted!
Now to their work they go,
Raking up one long row,
  Fit to be carted.

Now comes the wagon near,
  Quickly they're loading;
Rake away! rake away!
While it's fine make the hay—
  Rain is foreboding.

Now that the sunset ray
  Says the day's over,
Homeward we make our way,
In the cart strewn with hay,
  Smelling of clover.

Mrs. Hawtrey

American Indian Boys at Play

Thomas Mending his Bat.

My Dog and I Dancing.

Johnny the Stout

"Ho! for a frolic!"
　Said Johnny the stout;
"There's coasting and sledding;
　I'm going out."

Scarcely had Johnny
　Plunged in the snow,
When there came a complaint
　Up from his toe:

"We're cold" said the toe,
　"I and the rest;
There's ten of us freezing,
　Standing abreast."

Then up spoke an ear;
　"My, but it's labor—
Playing in winter. Eh!
　Opposite neighbour!"

"Pooh!" said his nose,

429

Angry and red;
"Who wants to tingle?
  Go home to bed!"

Eight little fingers,
  Four to a thumb
All cried together—
  "Johnny, we're numb!"

But Johnny the stout
  Wouldn't listen a minute;
Never a snow-bank
  But Johnny was in it.

Tumbling and jumping,
  Shouting with glee,
Wading the snow-drifts
  Up to his knee.

Soon he forgot them,
  Fingers and toes,
Never once thought of
  The ear and the nose.

Ah! What a frolic!
  All in a glow,
Johnny grew warmer
  Out in the snow.

Often his breathing
  Came with a joke;
"Blaze away, Johnny!
  I'll do the smoke."

"And I'll do the fire,"
  Said Johnny the bold.
"Fun is the fuel
  For driving off cold."

Going to dig Sand.

Sorry He Played.

Our Lamb Playing Tennis.

COLE

Our Pass Blowing Bubbles.

Training Time

Supper is over,
  Now for fun,
This is the season
  Children must run;

Papa is reading;
  Says, of these boys;
"Pray did you ever
  Hear such a noise?"

Riding on "camels"
  Over the floor,
See, one's a squirrel
  Climbing the door;

There goes the baby
  Flat on his nose,
Brother was trying
  To tickle his toes.

Little he minds it,
  Though he would cry,
Changed it to laughter

As Lyn galloped by;

Order is nowhere,
  Fun is the rule;
Think, they are children
  Just out of school.

Home is their palace;
  They are the kings
Let them be masters,
  Of just a few things;

Only one short hour
  Out of all day,
Give them full freedom;
  Join in their play.

Do not be angry
  Do not forget
You liked to make noise
  Sometimes do yet;

Home will be sweeter
  Till Life is done
If you will give them
  An hour of fun.

Our Puss Playing Cricket.

433

Our Frogs Playing Cricket.

Playtime

Play-time, play-time hurrah!
  Out in the fields together!
Don't let us lose a moment's time,
  This fine, bright, glorious weather.

Run, boys! Run, boys! faster!
  Ball and the bats for cricket;
Jack, you're the fastest runner here,
  Be off, and pitch the wicket.

Football for those who choose—
  The goal stick—go, Jim, fix it;
Give us the ball; who's won the toss?
  Now, for the first who kicks it.

No lazy ones today;
  Off, stretch your legs running!
Now for the hip, hip, hip, hurrah!
  And let the noise be stunning.

Hear how it echoes round!
  Another and another!
No fear of noise, it won't disturb

434

Old granny and poor mother.

Hullo there! no foul play!
  Dick, what is that you're saying?
No bad words and no cruel sport;
  We're come for fun and playing.

Romping

Why now, my dear boys, this is always the way,
You can't be contented with innocent play;
But this sort of romping, so noisy and high,
Is never left off till it ends in a cry.

What! are there no games you can take a delight in,
But kicking and knocking, and tearing, and fighting?
It is a sad thing to be forced to conclude
That boys can't be merry, without being rude.

Now what is the reason you never can play
Without snatching each other's playthings away?
Would it be any hardship to let them alone,
When every one of you has toys of his own?

I often have told you before, my dear boys,
That I do not object to your making a noise;
Or running and jumping about, anyhow,
But fighting and mischief I cannot allow.

So, if any more of these quarrels are heard,
I tell you this once, and I'll keep to my word,
I'll take every marble, and spintop and ball,
And not let you play with each other at all.

Nurse's Song

When the voices of children are heard on the green,
  And laughing is heard on the hill,
My heart is at rest within my breast,
  And everything else is still

"Then come home my children, the sun is gone down
  And the dews of the night arise;
Come, come, leave off play, and let us away,
Till the morning appears in the skies."

"No, no, let us play, for it is yet day,
  And we cannot go to sleep;
Besides in the sky the little birds fly,
  And the hills are covered with sheep."

"Well, well, go and play till the light fades away,
  And then go home to bed."
The little ones leaped, and shouted and laughed,
  And all the hills echoed.

W. Blake

Our See-Saw

Our Owls See-Sawing

Our Pigs See-Sawing

Swinging

Here we go on the garden swing,
  Under the chestnut tree.
Up in the branches birdies sing
  Songs to Baby and me,
  Baby and Kitty and me.
Then up, high up, for the ropes are long,
And down, low down, for the branch is strong.

And there's room on the seat for three,
  Just Baby and Kitty and me
    Merrily swinging,
    Merrily singing,
  Under the chestnut tree.

437

Up to the clustering leaves we go,
  Down we sweep to the grass,
Touching the daisies there below,
  Bowing to let us pass,
  Smiling to us as we pass.
Then up, high up, for the ropes are long,
And down, low down, for the branch is strong.

And there's room on the seat for three,
Just Baby and Kitty and me
  Merrily swinging,
  Merrily singing,
Under the chestnut tree.

Skating

One day it chanced that Miss Maud did meet
  The poet's little son,
"I'm going skating, Sir," she said;
  "And so am I," said John.

"If you can skate and I can skate,
  Why let me skate with you,
We'll go the whole world round and round,
  And skate the whole year through."

They skated left, and skated right,
  Miss Maud and little John,
That is—as long as there was ice
  For them to skate upon.

And then they did unstrap their skates
  Like other girls and men,
And never used them once—until
  They put them on again!

The Skipping Rope

Lessons now at last are over,
　Books and slates are put away;
　Hymns attentively repeated,
　Copy without a blot completed,
Now's the time for fun and play.

Lessons done with cheerful spirit
Bring the sure reward of merit,
Smiling face and heart so gay;
　In this bright and smiling weather,
　Merrily they all together,
With the skipping rope will play;

And if only Tom and Polly
Will come too, it will be jolly!
Here they are now, foot it lightly,
Hand in hand they skip so sprightly,
　Bees are humming,
　Summer's coming.

Birds are singing as they're bringing
Twigs from many a distant tree;
　Lined with down, and moss, and feather,
　Where they'll sit and chirp together,
Oh! how snug those homes will be!

O'er the ropes so lightly skipping,
O'er the grass so lightly tripping,
　The children are as glads as they.
Lessons are done with cheerful spirit,
Bring the sure reward of merit;

And remember, too, that they
Who work hardest day by day,
Always most enjoy their play.

Our Piggy Swinging.

Our Kangaroo Jumping.

Our Kangaroos Skipping.

The Baby's Debut

My brother Jack was nine in May,
And I was eight on New Year's day;
  So in Kate Wilson's shop
Papa (he's my papa and Jack's)
Bought me, last week, a doll of wax,
  And brother Jack a top.

Jack's in the pouts and this it is,
He thinks mine came to more than his;
  So to my drawer he goes,
Takes out the doll, and, O, my stars!
He pokes her head between the bars,
  And melts off half her nose!

Quite cross, a bit of string I beg,
And tie it to his peg-top's peg,
  And bang with might and main,
It's head against the parlor door:
Off flies the head, and hits the floor,
  And breaks a window-pane.

This made him cry with rage and spite:
Well, let him cry, it serves him right.
  A pretty thing, forsooth!
If he's to melt, all scalding hot.
Half my doll's nose, and I am not
  To draw his peg-top's tooth!

Aunt Hannah heard the window break,
And cried "O naughty Nancy Lake,
  Thus to distress your aunt:
No Drury-lane for you to-day!"
And while papa said "Pooh, she may!"
  Mamma said "No she sha'n't!"

Well, after many a sad reproach,
They got into a hackney coach,
  And trotted down the street.

I saw them go: one horse was blind,
The tails of both hung down behind,
  Their shoes were on their feet.

The chaise in which poor brother Bill
Used to be drawn to Pentonville,
  Stood in the lumber-room:
I wiped the dust from off the top,
While molly mopp'd it with a mop,
  And brush'd it with a broom.

My uncle's porter, Samuel Hughes,
Came in at six to black the shoes,
  (I always talk to Sam:)
So what does he, but takes, and drags
Me in the chaise among the flags,
  And leaves me where I am.

My father's walls are made of brick,
But not so tall and not so thick
  As these; and, goodness me!
My father's beams are made of wood,
But never, never half so good
  As those that now I see.

What a large floor! 'tis like a town!
The carpet, when they lay it down,
  Won't hide it, I'll be bound;
And there's a row of lamps!—my eye!
How they do blaze I wonder why
  They keep them on the ground.

Let the Child Play

He who checks a child with terror,
  Stops its play and stills its song,
Not alone commits an error

But a great and grievous wrong.

Give it play, and never fear it;
 Active life s no defect.
Never, never break its spirit;
 Curb it only to direct.

Would you stop the flowing river,
 Thinking it would cease to flow?
Onward in must flow forever;
 Better teach it where to go.

Our Lassies' Fan Dance.

Our Dog Dance.

Our Round Dance.

Our Pussies Reading Childland.

Our Monkey Learning from Childland.

Reading

"And so you do not like to spell,
Mary, my dear oh, very well:
'Tis dull and troublesome,' you say,
And you had rather be at play.

"Then bring me al your books again;
Nay, Mary, why do you complain?
For as you do not choose to read,
You shall not have your books, indeed.

"So, as you wish to be a dunce,
Pray go and fetch me them at once;
For if you will not learn to spell,
'Tis vain to think of reading well.

"Do you not think you'll blush to own
When you become a woman grown,
Without one good excuse to plead,
That you have never learnt to read?"

"Oh, dear mamma,' said Mary then,
"Do let me have my books again;
I'll not fret any more indeed,
If you will let me learn to read."

Jane Taylor

Mrs Grammar's Ball

Mrs Grammar once gave a fine ball
To the nine differen parts of our speech;
 To the short and the tall,
 To the stout and the small,
There were pies, plums and puddings for each.

And first little Articles came,

In a hurry to make themselves known—
  Fat *A*, *An*, and *The*;
  But none of the three
Could stand for a minute alone.

The Adjectives came to announce
That their dear friends the Nouns were at hand,
  Rough, *rougher* and *roughest*,
  Tough, *tougher* and *toughest*,
Fat, *merry*, *good-natured* and *grand*.

The Nouns were indeed on their way,
Tens of thousands, and more, I should think;
  For each name we could utter,
  Shop, *shoulder*, or *shutter*,
Is a noun: *lady*, *lion* or *Fink*.

The Pronouns were hastening fast
To push the Nouns out of their places:
  I, *thou*, *he*, and *she*,
  You, *it*, *they*, and *we*,
With their sprightly intelligent faces.

Some cried out, "Make way for the Verbs!
A great crowd is coming in view!"
  To *light* and to *smile*,
  To *fight* and to *bite*,
To *be*, and to *have*, and to *do*.

The Adverbs attended on the Verbs,
Behind as their footmen they ran;
  As this, "to fight *badly* "
  And "run *away gladly* "
Shows how fighting and running were done.

Prepositions came *in*, *by*, and *near*;
With Conjunctions, a wee little band,
  As *either* you *or* he,
  But *neither* I *nor* she;

They held their great friends by the hand.

Then, too, with a *hip, hip, hurrah!*
Rushed in Interjections uproarious;
  Dear me! well-a-day!
  When they saw the display,
"*Ha! Ha!*" they all shouted out, "glorious!"

But, alas! what misfortunes were nigh!
While the fun and the feasting pleased each,
  Pounced on them at once
  A monster—a Dunce!
And confounded the nine parts of speech!

Help! friends! to the rescue! on you
For aid Verb and Article call;
  Oh! give your protection
  To poor Interjection,
Noun, Pronoun, Conjunction, and all!

Grammar In Rhyme

Three little words we often see,
And Article, *a, an, the.*

Noun's the name of anything,
As *school* or *garden, hoop* or *string.*

Adjective tells the kind of noun,
As *great, small, pretty, white* or *brown.*

Instead of nouns, the Pronoun stand
John's head, *his* face, *my* arm, *your* hand.

Verbs tell us of something being done,
To *read, write, count, sing, jump,* or *run.*

How things are done, the Adverbs tell,

447

As *slowly, quickly, ill,* or *well.*

A Preposition stands before
A noun, as *in* or *through* a door.

Conjunctions join the nouns together
as men *and* children, wind *and* weather.

The Interjection shows surprise,
As *Oh,* how pretty! *Ah* how wise!

The whole are called nine parts of speech,
Which reading, writing, speaking teach.

Value of Reading

The poor wretch who digs the mine for bread,
Or ploughs so that others may be fed,—
Feels less fatigue, than that decreed
To him that cannot think or read!

Hannah More

Our Dogs Reading Childland.

Our Rook Reading Childland.

Our Rabbit Reading Childland.

Our Storks Reading Childland.

Little Flo's Letter

A sweet little baby brother
  Had come to live with Flo,
And she wanted it brought to the table,
  That it might eat and grow.
"It must wait a while," said grandma,
  In answer to her plea,
"For a little thing that hasn't teeth
  Can't eat like you and me."

450

"Why hasn't it got teeth, grandma?"
  Asked Flo in great surprise,
"O my, but isn't it funny?—
  No teeth, but nose and eyes.
"I guess," after thinking gravely,
  They must have been forgot.
Can't we buy him some like grandpa's?
  I'd like to know why not."

That afternoon, to the corner,
  With paper, and pen, and ink,
Went Flo, saying, "Don't talk to me;
  If you do, it'll sturb my think.
I'm writing a letter, grandma,
  To send away to-night,
An' 'cause it's very 'portant,
  I want to get it right."

At last the letter was finished,
  A wonderful thing to see,
And directed to "God, in Heaven."
  Please read it over to me,"
Said little Flo to her grandma,
  "To see if it's right, you know."
And here is the letter written
  To God by little Flo:—

"Dear God: The baby you brought us
  Is awful nice and sweet,
But 'cause you forgot his tooffies
  The poor little thing can't eat.
That's why I'm writing this letter,
  A purpose to let you know.
Please come and finish the baby,
  That's all—From Little Flo."

Eben. E. Rexford

451

Exercise Makes Perfect

True ease in writing
  Comes from art, not chance,
As those move easiest
  Who have learned to dance.

Pope

Hurrah for the Postman

Hurrah for the postman
  Who brings us the news!
What a lot it must take
  To pay for his shoes.

For he walks many miles
  Each day of the week,
And though he would like to,
  Must not stay to speak.

Red stripes round his blue cap,
  With clothing to match it;
If he lost any letters,
  Oh, wouldn't he catch it!

Two Letters

FIRST

Dear Grandmamma—I write to say
  (And you'll be glad I know,)
That I am coming, Saturday,
  To spend a week or so.

I'm coming, too, without mamma,

You know I'm eight years old!
And you shall see how good I'll be,
  To do as I am told.

I'll help you lots about your word—
  There's so much I can do—
I'll weed the garden, hunt for eggs,
  And feed the chickens, too.

And maybe I will be so good
  You'll keep me there till fall;
Or, better still, perhaps you'll say
  I can't go home at all!

Now grandmamma, please don't forget
  To meet me at the train,
For I'll be sure to come—unless
  It should cloud up and rain!

SECOND

Dear Mamma—Please put on your things,
  And take the next express;
I want to go back home again—
  I'm very sick, I guess!

My grandma's very good to me,
  But grandma isn't you;
And I forgot, when I came here,
  I'd got to sleep here, too!

Last night I cried myself to sleep,
  I wanted you so bad!
To day, I cannot play or eat,
  I feel so very sad.

Please, mamma, come, for I don't see
  How I can bear to wait!
You'll find me, with my hat and sack

453

Out by the garden gate.

And grandma will not care a bit
  If you should come, I know;
Because I am your own little girl,
  And I do love you so.

Nell's Letter

Dear Grandmamma, I will try to write
  A very little letter;
If I don't spell the words all right,
  Why next time I'll do better.

My little rabbit is alive
  And likes his milk and clover,
He likes to se me very much,
  But is afraid of Rover.

I have a dove as white as snow,
  I hall her "Polly Feather";
She flies and hops about the yard,
  In every kind of weather.

The hens are picking off the grass,
  And singing very loudly;
While our old peacock struts about,
  And shows his feathers proudly.

I think I'll close my letter now,
  I've nothing more to tell
Please answer soon, and come to see
  Your loving, little Nell.

Baby's Letter to Uncle

Dear Old Uncle—I dot oor letter;
My dear mamma, she ditten better;
She every day a little bit stronger,
Don't mean to be sick very much longer.

Dear little baby had a bad colic;
Had to take three drops of nassy palagolic.
Toot a dose o' tatnip—felt worse as ever;
Shan't tate no mors tytnip, never!

Wind on tomut, felt pooty bad;
Worse fit of sickness ever I had!
Ever had stomit ate, ole uncle Bill?
Ain't no fun, now, say what oo will.

I used to sleep all day, and cry all night;
Don't do it now, 'cause it ain't yite.
Got a head of hair jess as black as night
And big boo eyes, yat look very bright.

My mamma say, never did see
Any ozzer baby half as sweet as me.
Grandma come often, aunt Sarah, too;
Baby loves zem, baby loves oo.

Baby sends a pooty kiss to his uncles all,
Aunties and cousins, big folks and small.
Can't say any more, so dood by—
Bully olc uncle wiz a glass eye!

The First Letter

"Did you ever get a letter?
 I did the other day.
 It was in a real envelope,

And it came a long, long way.

A stamp was in the corner
    And some printing when it came,
And the one that wrote the letter
    Had put 'Miss' before my name.

Then there came a lot more written,
    I forget now what it read,
But it told the office people
    Where I lived, mamma said.

Don't you s'pose those letter-persons,
    If they hadn't just been told,
Would have thought 'twas for a lady
    Who was awful, awful old?

For it looked real big and heavy,
    The outside was stuck with glue,
So they couldn't know I'm little,
    I don't think they could. Do you?"

Youth's Companion

I'm Going to Write to Papa

I'm going to write to papa,
    I guess he'd like to hear
What his little girl is doing,
    The same as when he is near;

I'll tell him how I miss him,
    And how I'd wish he'd come,
And never, never, leave us,
    But always stay at home.

I'll tell him 'bout my dolly,
    She's sleeping on the floor,

I fear that noise will wake her,
  Oh! please don't slam the door.

For I must not be bothered,
  That's just what ma would say,
When she begins a letter,
  And sends me off to play.

I'll send him lots of kisses,
  And one bright shining curl,
I'll ask him to remember
  His lonely little girl;

I want so much to see him,
  But I won't cry a wink,
Cause when I write my letter,
  The tears would blot my ink.

I'm going to write to papa,
  And oh! how glad he'll be.
To get a little letter
  That was written all by me.

Old Letters

I gaze upon ye, once again,
  Old records of the past,
And o'er the dim and faded lines
  My tears are falling fast;

I deem'd not there was a power yet,
  In these few simple words,
To stir within my quiet heart
  Such old familiar chords.

Ye bring me back mine early dreams—
  Oh, but to dream them now,
With childhood's fresh, unwearied heart,

And pure unsadden'd brow!

The loved—the lost—the changed—
    The dead—all these we conjure up,
And mingled in the draught
    That lies in memory's magic cup.

Old letters—sad mementoes ye,
    Of friendship's shatter'd chain,
Oh! that the hand these pages traced,
    My own might clasp again.

They tell me yet of early love,
    Of feelings glad and gay,
Of childhood's April hopes and fears—
    The writers, where are they?

Time's changes are for deeper things
    Than folly's vain pursuit,
Spring blossoms fade, to leave a place
    For autumn's ripen'd fruit.

Look back upon the buried past,
    But not with vain regret,
Be grateful for the many joys
    That bloom around thee yet.

Bend heavenward thine onward course,
    That years of coming age
May leave an impress in life's book,
    Pure as its opening page!

Papa's Letter

I was sitting in my study,
    Writing letters, when I heard:
"Please, dear mamma, Mary told me

That you mustn't be disturbed.

But I'se tired of the kitty,
  Want some ozzer thing to do.
Writing letters is 'ou mamma?
  Tan't I write a letter, too?"

"Not now, darling, mamma's busy;
  Run and play with kitty now."
"No—no mamma; me wite letter,
  Ten you will show me how."

I would paint my darling's portrait,
  As his sweet eyes searched my face—
Hair of gold and eyes of azure,
  Form of childish witching grace.

But the eager face was clouded,
  As I slowly shook my head,
Till I said: "I'll make a letter,
  Of you, darling boy, instead."

So I parted back the tresses
  From his forehead high and white,
And a stamp in sport I pasted,
  'Mid its waves of golden light.

Then I said: "Now, little letter,
  Go away and bear good news,"
And I smiled as down the staircase
  Clattered loud the little shoes.

Leaving me, the darling hurried
  Down to Mary in his glee:
"Mamma's witting lots of letters;
  I'se a letter, Mary, see."

No one heard the little prattler,
  As once more he climbed the stair.
Reached his little cap and tippet,

459

Standing on the table there.

No one heard the front door open,
  No one saw the golden hair,
As it floated o'er his shoulders
  On the crisp October air.

Down the street the baby hastened,
  Till he reached the office door:
"I'se a letter, Mr. Postman,
  Is there room for any more?

'Cause this letter's going to papa;
  Papa lives with God, 'ou know:
Mamma sent me for a letter;
  Does 'ou fink at I tan do?"

But the clerk in wonder answered,
  "Not to-day, my little man;"
"Den I'll find anozzer office,
  'Cause I must go if I tan."

Fain the clerk would have detained him,
  But the pleading face was gone,
And the little feet were hastening,
  By the busy crowd swept on.

Suddenly the crowd was parted,
  People fled to left and right,
As a pair of maddened horses
  At that moment dashed in sight.

No one saw the baby figure,
  No one saw the golden hair,
Till a voice of frightened sweetness
  Rang out on the autumn air.

'Twas too late: a moment only
  Stood the beauteous vision there:
Then the little face lay lifeless

Covered o'er with golden hair.

Rev'rently they raised my darling,
  Brushed away the curls of gold,
Saw the stamp upon the forehead
  Growing now so icy cold.

Not a mark left the face disfigured,
  Showing where a hoof had trod;
But the little life was ended—
  "Papa's letter" was with God.

Bessie's Letter

I have got a letter,
  A letter of my own,
It has my name upon it,
  Miss Bessie L. Stone.

My papa sent it to me,
  He's away from home—you see
I guess the postman wondered
  Who Bessie Stone could be.

I'd like to send an answer,
  But I don't know how to spell;
I'll get mamma to do it,
  And that will do as well.

A Little Boy's Valentine

Little girl across the way,
  You are so very sweet,
I shouldn't be a bit surprised
  If you were good to eat.

Now what I'd like if you would too,
  Would be to go and play—
Well, all the time, and all my life,
  On your side of the way.

I don't know anybody yet
  On your side of the street,
But often I look over there
  And watch you—you're so sweet.

When I am big, I tell you what,
  I don't care what they say,
I'll go across—and stay there, too,
  On your side of the way.

Letter Writing

Heaven first taught letters
  For some wretch's aid,
Some banish'd lover,
  Or some captive maid.

They live, they speak,
  They breathe what love inspires,
Warm from the soul
  And faithful to its fires;

The virgin's wish
  Without her fears impart,
Excuse the blush,
  And pour out all the heart—

Speed the soft intercourse
  From soul to soul,
And waft a sigh
  From Indus to the pole.

Boil it Down

Whatever you have to say my friend,
  Whether witty, grave, or gay,
Condense as much as ever you can,
  And that is the readiest way;
And whether you write of rural affairs,
  Or particular things in town,
Just take a word of friendly advice—
  "Boil it down."

Letters from Home

Letters from home! How musical to the ear
  Of the sailor-boy on the far-off main,
When, from the friendly vessel drawing near,
  Across the billow floats the gentle strain,
The words the tear-drops of his memory move;
  They tell a mother's or a sister's love;
And playmates, friends, and sweetheart to him come
  Out to him on the sea, in letters from his home.
How warmly there the tender home-light shines!
  What household music lives in those dear tender lines.

Polly's Letter to Brother Ben

  Dear Brother Ben,
  I take my pen
To tell you where,
  And how, and when,
I found the nest
  Of our speckled hen.
  She would never lay,
  In a sensible way,
Like other hens,

463

In the barn or the hay;

But here and there
And everywhere,
On the stable floor,
  And the wood-house stair,
  And once on the ground
  Her eggs I found.
  But yesterday
  I ran away,
With mother's leave,
  In the barn to play.

  The sun shone bright
On the seedy floor,
  And the doves so white
  Were a pretty sight
As they walked in and out
  Of the open door,
  With their little red feet
  And their features neat,
Cooing and cooing
  More and more.

  Well, I went out
  To look about
  On the platform wide,
  Where side by side
I could see the pig-pens
  In their pride;
And beyond them both,
  On a narrow shelf,
I saw the speckled hen
  Hide herself

Behind a pile
  Of hoes and rakes
And pieces of boards
  And broken stakes.
"Ah! ha! old hen,

I have found you now,
But to reach your nest
  I don't know how,
Unless I could creep
  Or climb or crawl
Along the edge
  Of the pig-pen wall."

  And while I stood
  In a thoughtful meed,
The speckled hen cackled
  As loud as she could,
  And flew away,
  As much as to say,
"For once my treasure
  Is out of your way."
I did not wait
  A moment then:
I couldn't be conquered
  By that old hen!

  But along the edge
  Of the slippery ledge
  I carefully crept,
  For the great pigs slept,
And I dared not
  even look to see
If they were thinking
  Of eating me
  But all at once,
  Oh, what a dunce!

I dropped my basket
  Into the pen,
The one you gave me,
  Brother Ben;
There were two eggs in it,
  By the way,
That I found in the manger
  Under the hay.
Then the pigs got up

And ran about
With a noise between
  A grunt and a shout.

And when I saw them,
  Rooting, rooting,
Of course I slipped
  And lost my footing,
  And tripped,
  And jumped,
  And finally fell
Right down among
  The pigs pell-mell.
For once in my life
  I was afraid;
  For the door that led
  Out to the shed

Was fastened tight
  With and iron hook,
And father was down
  In the fields by the brook,
Hoeing and weeding
  His rows of corn,
And here was his Polly
  So scared and forlorn,
But I called him, and called him,
  As loud as I could.
I knew he would hear me—
  He must and he should.

"O father! O father!
  (Get out, you old pig).
O father! oh! oh!"
  For their mouths are so big.
Then I waited a minute
  And called him again,
"O father! O father!
  I am in the pig pen!"
And father did hear,
  And he threw down his hoe,

466

And scampered as fast
  As a father could go.

The pigs had pushed me
  Close to the wall,
And munched my basket,
  Eggs and all,
And chewed my sun-bonnet
  Into a ball.
And one had rubbed
  His muddy nose
All over my apron,
  Clean and white;

And they sniffed at me,
  And stepped on my toes,
But hadn't taken
  The smallest bite,
When father opened
  The door at last,
And oh! in his arms
  He held me fast.

E. W. Denison

Writing

Little pens of metal,
  Little drops of ink,
Make the wicked tremble,
  And the people think.

Value of Writing

Blest be that gracious power
  Who taught mankind

To stamp a lasting image
On the mind:

Beasts may convey,
  And tuneful birds may sing
Their mutual feelings
  In the opening spring;

But man alone has skill
  And power to send
The heart's warm dictates
  To the distant friend:

Tis his also to please,
  Instruct, advise,
Ages remote,
  And nations yet to rise.

Crabbe

Use the Pen

Use the pen! there's magic in it,
  Never let it lag behind;
Write thy thought, the pen can win it
  From the chaos of the mind.

Many a gem is lost forever
  By the careless passer-by,
But the gems of thought should never
  On the mental pathway lie.

Use the pen! reck not that others
  Take a higher flight than thine.
Many an ocean cave still smothers
  Pearls of price beneath the brine.

So thy words and thoughts securing

Honest praise from wisdom's tongue,
May, in time, be as enduring
  As the strains which Homer sung.

J. E. Carpenter

Power of the Pen

Beneath the rule of men entirely great,
The pen is mightier than the sword.

Lord Lytton

Letters

Such a little thing—a letter,
  Yet so much it may contain:
Written thoughts and mute expressions
  Full of pleasure, fraught with pain.

When our hearts are sad at parting,
  Comes a gleam of comfort bright,
In the mutual promise given:
  "We will not forget to write."

Plans and doings of the absent;
  Scraps of news we like to hear,
All remind us, een though distant,
  Kind remembrance keeps us near.

Yet sometimes a single letter
  Turns the sunshine into shade;
Chills our efforts, clouds our prospects,
  Blights our hopes and makes them fade.

Messengers of joy or sorrow,

469

Life or death, success, despair,
Bearers of affection's wishes,
  Greetings kind or loving prayer.

Prayer or greeting, were we present,
  Would be felt, but half unsaid;
We can write—because our letters—
  Not our faces—will be read?

Who has not some treasured letters,
  Fragments choice of other's lives;
Relics, some, of friends departed,
  Friends whose mem'ry still survives?

Touched by neither time nor distance,
  Will their words unspoken last?
Voiceless whispers of the present,
  Silent echoes of the past!

The Right Method of Composition

Never be in haste in writing:
Let that thou utterest be of nature's flow,
Not art's, a fountain's, not a pump's. But once
Begun, work thou all things into thy work:
And set thyself about it, as the sea
About the earth, lashing it day and night:
And leave the stamp of thine own soul in it
As thorough as the fossil flower in clay:
The theme shall start and struggle in thy breast,
Like to a spirit in its tomb at rising,
Rending the stones, and crying—Resurrection.

P. J. Bailey

Our Lady Artist.

Our Gentleman Artist.

471

COLE

The Sunday Fisherman.

A fisherman, on angling bent,
One Sabbath morning left his tent.

The Tent,

He took his can, and very quick,
He dug his fish-worms with a pick.

The Pick,   The Worms,

He thought he'd try for bass and smelt,
And fix'd his fish-bag to his belt.

The Belt,   The Bag.

In case some fish of size he'd get,
He took along his landing net.

The Landing-Net

As fishermen get very dry,
They always have a flask hard by.

The Flask,

As fishermen get hungry, too,
Of pretzels he procured a few.

The Pretzels,

Some lines he took along on spools,
To teach them to the finny schools.

The Spools,

He had some entertaining books
Of highly-tempered Limerick hooks.

The Hooks,

And thus prepared, he got his boat,
And out upon the stream did float.

The Boat,

Whene'er the wind began to fail,
He used the paddle with the sail.

The Paddle,

He stopped to fish among the sedge,
A mile or so below the bridge.

The Bridge,

Some bites he straight began to get,
It was the gallinipper's bite.

The Gallinippers,

One of his lines spun off the reel,
He landed in the boat an eel.

The Eel,

Then quickly it began to rain,
But his umbrella was in vain.

The Umbrella,

Above his head the thunder crashed,
And all around the lightning flashed.

The Lightning,

The storm blew, and the boat upset,
The man went down into the wet.

The Upturned Boat,

And as he sank, his bubbles rose,
Smaller and smaller towards the close.

The Bubbles,

Oh, Sunday fishers, old and young,
You'll get drowned, or you'll get hung!

The Gallows,

Drawing Pussy's Likeness.

Working for a Prize.

Just cast your beautiful, your sparkling,
your penetrating, your discriminating

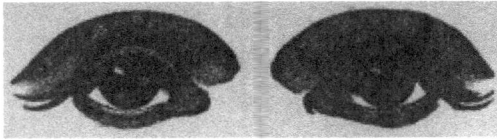

Over this page, and read, mark, learn,
and inwardly digest its Contents.

THE two greatest educating powers in the ancient world were Pictures and Poetry—the two greatest educating powers are pictures and poetry still, and pictures and poetry blended in an interesting manner is the intended educating feature of this PLEASANT-LEARNING-LAND, but my object in this place is to speak of pictures only, as perhaps the greatest of all educating powers, and to demonstrate that they are not sufficiently used for educational purposes. Firstly: pictures are in a universal language—when they are true to nature every person on the earth can understand them. Show a picture of a person or a bird, a horse or a house, a ship, a tree, or a landscape, and everyone knows what is meant, and this is why most of the peoples of the ancient world conveyed their ideas in picture language. FLETCHER, in his *Cyclopedia of Education*, says:— "It has long been accepted as an axiom that the best explanation of a thing is the sight and study of the thing itself, and the next best a true picture of the thing." DRYDEN, speaking of poetry and painting says:—

"The poets are confined to narrow space,
To speak the language of their native place;
The painter widely stretches his command,
His pencil speaks the tongue of every land."

Many writers, ancient and modern, have taught the great educational power of pictures. HORACE says:—A picture is a poem without words". SYDNEY SMITH says:—"Every good picture is the best of sermons and lectures." O. S. FOWLER says:—"A single picture often conveys more than volumes." W. M. HUNT says:— "From any picture we can learn something." HENRY WARD BEECHER says:—"A picture that teaches any affection or moral sentiment will speak in the language which men understand, without any other education than that of being born and of living." GARRICK, speaking of Hogarth, says:—

"His pictured morals mend the mind,
And through the eye improve the heart."

But pictures are not only a means of education, for they bring pleasure, comfort, and education combined. STEELE says:—"Beautiful pictures are the entertainment of pure minds." G. P. PUTMAN says:— "How many an eye and heart have been fascinated by an enchanting picture." CICERO says:—"The eyes are charmed by pictures, and the ears by music." JOHN GILBERT says:—"Pictures are consolers of loneliness; they are a sweet flatterer to the soul, they are a relief to the jaded mind; they are windows to the imprisoned thought; they are books, they are histories and sermons, which we can read without the trouble of turning over the leaves." UGO FOSCOLIO says:— "Pictures are the chickweed to the gilded cage, and make up for the want of many other enjoyments to those whose life is mostly passed amid the smoke and din, the bustle and noise of an overcrowded city." PANDOLFINI says:—Many an eye has been surprised into moisture by pictured woe and heroism; and we are mistaken if the glow of pleasure has not lighted in some hearts the flame of high resolve, or warmed into life the seeds of honorable ambition."

Many pictures, particularly portraits, by bringing up reminiscences, are a great source of consolation. In millions of houses the most-loved and treasured possession is the photographic album containing the likenesses of dear absent or departed friends. SHEE, writing of the soothing influences of the portrait, says:—

"Mirror divine! which gives the soul to view,
Reflects the image, and retains it too!
Recalls to friendship's eye the fading face,
Revives each look, and rivals every grace:
In thee the banished lover finds relief,
His bliss in absence, and his balm in grief:
Affection, grateful, owns thy sacred power,
The father feels thee in affliction's hour;
When catching life ere some lov'd cherub flies.
To take its angel station in the skies,
The portrait soothes the loss it can't repair,
And sheds a comfort, even in despair."
Or—
"The widow'd husband sees his sainted wife
In pictures warm, and smiling as in life,—
And—
    While he gazes with convulsive thrill,
And weeps, and wonders at the semblance still,
He breathes a blessing on the pencil's aid,
That half restores the substance in the shade."

But it is more particularly with pictures as a direct means of education that I have to speak. MR. STEAD holds that in the coming education of the world the magic lantern will play a very great part, for through its aid you can portray any object you wish—pictures of scenery, of buildings, of distant countries, of the microscopic world, and in fact any kind of pictures you choose, in a most beautiful life-like, interesting, and educational manner. I think and earnestly hope that MR. STEAD'S prediction will be fulfilled.

There are two other ways which I think that pictures should be used for educational purposes. Firstly, in books, as in this one, and secondly, on the walls of buildings—outside and inside if you like —but I will speak only of the inside in this paper. Why should not every room of every house be covered with pictures where it is not covered with furniture? In millions of rooms there is a great waste of opportunity. Many times I have thought why do they not have varying patterns of different scenery, etc, in the different rooms of the houses instead of the wall paper, with its uninteresting pattern perpetually repeated. There is no reason why a house of twelve rooms should not represent on its walls twelve different countries, or twelve histories of striking events, etc. Possibly this may take place later on. With respect to hanging pictures everywhere on the walls, it may be objected that it would be too expensive—so it would if they were costly pictures—but really good pictures are produced by the million now so cheaply, that the objection of expense vanishes. The walls can be covered now almost as cheaply with intellectual pictures as with unintellectual wall paper. SIR JOSHUA REYNOLDS says:—"A room hung with pictures, is a room hung with thoughts.' JOHN GILBERT says:—"A room with pictures in it, and a room without pictures, differ by nearly as much as a room with windows and a room without windows; for pictures are loopholes of escape to the soul, leading it to other scenes and to other spheres, as it were, through the frame of an exquisite picture, where the fancy for a moment may revel, refreshed and delighted."

I was convinced many years ago of the almost criminal waste of wall space, and issued the following doggerel lines, partly from trade and partly from sentimental motives:—

> Every cottage,
> Two-roomed cottage,
> Should contain full
> Twenty PICTURES.

Every cottage.
Four-roomed cottage,
Should contain full
Forty PICTURES.

Every cottage.
Six-roomed cottage,
Should contain full
Sixty PICTURES.

Every villa,
Eight-roomed villa,
Should contain full
Eighty PICTURES.

Every mansion,
Ten-roomed mansion,
Should contain a
Hundred PICTURES.

Every large school
For instruction
Should contain a
THOUSAND PICTURES.

Walls are made to
Keep out weather
And also to
Display PICTURES.

Count your PICTURES
All your walls on.
See if you have
Quite the number,
You will want more
You will wish more,
You will get more
Shouldn't wonder.

PICTURES they are
Made to please you—
First to please you
When you buy them,
Next to please your
Own dear children,
Pictures please and
Teach them too.
Next to please your
Friends and neighbours
When they kindly
Call on you.

They'll admire them
Then they'll praise them.
Then that pleases
You again.
PICTURES please and
Teach for ever,
All the Children,
Women, Men.

Even in the poorest houses pictures must always be a blessing. Many a poor man's cheerless home would be made much more comfortable and endurable if a few shilling's worth of good pictures were posted or hung round its bare walls. If houses were universally decorated with true speaking pictures what an immense influence for good it would bring them. What intellectual and refined tastes it would create and nurture. One most important thing in selecting pictures to cover the walls it to always choose good subjects. A poor picture takes up as much room as a good one, and generally costs as much. Always choose live speaking pictures that will interest and instruct. There is an immense multitude of poor, tame, an uninteresting pictures produced in the world, and which in millions of instances keep out the good ones. If these poor ones could be kept back or destroyed, and the best ones only take their place, the world would be better for it. In choosing materials to build up a bright, happy home, always select the best— the best books—the best music—the best pictures. In conclusion, there is one more suggestion I would make on the picture question, and I think it is the most important of all; it is that a good clear map of the world should be hung in every house in the world, to give every person an idea of the world they live in. For it is a most deplorable fact that ninety-nine out of every hundred of the inhabitants, even of the civilized world, have a very poor conception of the geography and ethnology of the world. And this should not be, for every person ought to have a clear idea of their world-fatherland, and of their fellow creatures, and a knowledge of the map of the world is the first esson to be learned in that most desirable direction.

E W COLE, Book Arcade, Melbourne.

Drawing Doggy's Likeness.

The New Slate

See my slate. I dot it new
  Cos I b'oke the other,
Put my 'ittle foot righ' froo,
  Runnin' after modder.

I tan make you lots of sings,
  Fass as you tan tell 'em,
T's and B's and O rings,
  Only I tan't spell 'em

I tan make an elephant,
  Wid his trunk a hang'n';
An' a boy—who says I tan't?
  Wid his dun a bangin'

An' the smoke a tummin' out;
  (Wid my t'umb I do it,
Rubbin' all the white about,)
  Sparks a flying froo it.

I tan make a pretty house,
  Wid a tree behind it,
And a 'ittle mousey-mouse
  Runnin' round to find it.

I tan put my hand out fat
  On the slate and draw it;
(Ticklin' is the worst of that!)
  Did you ever saw it?

Now, then, s'all I make a tree
  Wid a birdie on it?
All my pictures you s'all see
  If you'll wait a minute.

No, I dess I'll make a man

481

Jus≡ like Uncle Rolly,
See ≡ tummin', fass it tan!
Be≡ my slate is jolly!

Do Not Stare.

Doggy Drawing Pussy's Likeness.

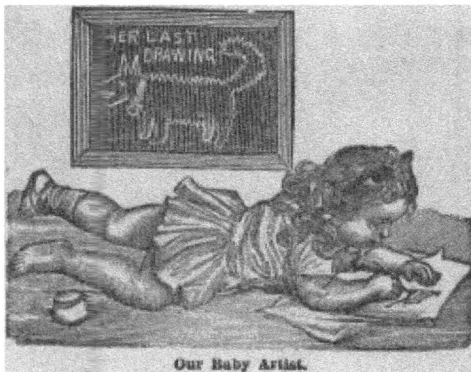
Our Baby Artist.

Doggies Sitting to have Their Portraits
Taken.

Learning to Draw

Come, here is a slate,
  And a pencil, and string.
And now sit you down dear,
  And draw pretty thing;
A man and a cow,
  And a horse and a tree,
And when you have finished
  Pray show them to me.

What! cannot you do it
  Shall I show you how
Come, give me your pencil;
  I'll draw you a cow.
You've made the poor creature
  Look very forlorn!
She has but three legs, dear,
  And only one horn.

Now look, I have drawn you

A beautiful cow;
And see, here's a dicky-bird,
   Perched on a bough,
And there are some more
   Flying down from above;
There now, is not that
   Very pretty, my love?

Oh, yes, very pretty!
   Now make me some more—
A house with a gate,
   And a window, and a door,
And a little boy flying
   His kite with a string;
Oh, thank you, mamma,
   Now I'll draw pretty thing.

Young Artist Touching Up.

A Fairy in Great Danger.

Our Picture Gallery.

A Lesson in Drawing

I.
Ta-e a pencil, black or red.
Dr=w a little loaf of bread
Or a piece of paper white—
Ma-e the bread extremely light.

II.
Th=n, before your work you stop,
Dr=w a little loop on top,
Ar-d a satchel will be found
Su-h as ladies carry round.

III.
Th=n you may, my pretty dears,
Ac-d a pair of little ears;
Ar-d, if Art is not in fault,
Th=re's a bag of extra salt.

IV.
Pa-se, and in rapture fine,
Co-template the great design—
Ac-d a flowing tail, and that
Ma-es a perfect pussy cat.

Wounded.

Drawing Lesson on the Slate.

Drawing Lesson on the Slate.

Drawing Lesson on the Slate.

Old Man and His Wife

There was an old man who lived in a wood,
  As you may plainly see,
He said he could do as much work in a day
  As his wife could do in three.

"With all my heart," the old woman said,
  "If that you will allow;
To-morrow you'll stay at home in my stead,
  And I'll go drive the plough.

"But you must milk the Tidy cow,
  For fear she may go dry.
And you must feed the little pigs
  That are within the sty;

"And you must mind the speckled hen,
  For fear she lay away;
And you must reel the spool of yarn
  That I spun yesterday."

The old woman took a whip in her hand,
  And went to drive the plough;
The old man took a pail in his hand,
  And went to milk the cow.

But Tidy hinched and Tidy flinched,
  And Tidy broke his nose,
And Tidy gave him such a blow
  That the blood ran down to his toes.

"Hi! Tidy! Ho! Tidy! Hi!
  Tidy! do stand still!
If ever I milk you, Tidy, again,
  'Twill be sore against my will."

He went to feed the little pigs,

That were within the sty;
He hit his head against the beam
And he made the blood to fly.

He went to mind the speckled hen,
  For fear she'd lay away;
And he forgot the spool of yarn
  His wife spun yesterday.

So he swore by the sun, the moon, the stars,
  And the green leaves on the tree,
If his wife didn't do a day's work in her life,
  She should never be ruled by he.

John Ball Shot Them All

John Ball shot them all.
John Scott made the shot,
  But John Ball shot them all.

John Wyming made the priming,
And John Bramme made the rammer,
And John Scott made the shot,
  But John Ball shot them all.

John Block made the stock,
And John Wyming made the priming,
And John Brammer made the rammer,
And John Scott made the shot,
  But John Ball shot them all.

John Crowder made the powder,
And John Block made the stock,
And John Wyming made the priming,
And John Brammer made the rammer,
And John Scott made the shot,

489

But John Ball shot them all.

John Puzzle made the muzzle,
And John Crowder made the powder,
And John Block made the stock,
And John Wyming made the priming,
And John Brammer made the rammer,
And John Scott made the shot,
  But John Ball shot them all.

John Clint made the flint,
And John Puzzle made the muzzle,
And John Crowder made the powder,
And John Block made the stock,
And John Wyming made the priming,
And John Brammer made the rammer,
And John Scott made the shot,
  But John Ball shot them all.

John Patch made the match,
John Clint made the flint,
John Puzzle made the muzzle,
John Crowder made the powder,
John Block made the stock,
John Wyming made the priming,
John Brammer made the rammer,
John Scott made the shot,
  But John Ball shot them all.

The Funny Old Man

There was an old man, and though 'tis not common,
Yet if he said true, his mother was a woman;
And though it's incredible, yet I've been told
He was a mere infant, but age made him old.
Whene'er he was hungry he wanted some meat,
And if he could get it, 'twas said he could eat;
When thirsty he'd drink, if you gave him a pot,

And his liquor most commonly ran down his throat.
He seldom or never could see without light,
And yet I've been told he could hear in the night.
He has oft been awake in the daytime 'tis said,
And has fall'n fast asleep as he lay in his bed.
'Tis reported his tongue always moved when he talked,
And he stirred both his arms and his legs when he walk'd,
And his gait was so odd, had you seen him you'd burst,
For one leg or t'other would always be first.
His face was the saddest that ever was seen,
For if 'twere not washed it was seldom quite clean;
He showed most his teeth when he happened to grin,
His mouth stood across 'twixt his nose and his chin.
At last he fell sick, as old chronicles tell,
And then, as folk said, he was not very well!
And what is more strange, in so weak a condition,
As he could not give fees, he could get no physician.
What a pity he died; yet 'tis said that his death
Was occasioned at last by the want of his breath.
But peace to his bones, which in ashes now moulder,
Had he lived a day longer he'd been a day older.

Piper and His Cow

There was and old piper who had a cow,

491

But he had no hay to give her,
So he took his pipes and played her a tune
"Consider, old cow, consider."

Old John Brown

Poor old John Brown is dead and gone,
  We ne'er shall see him more;
He used to wear an old brown coat,
  All button'd down before.

Three Wise Men

Three wise men of Gotham,
  Went to sea in a bowl;
If the bowl it had been stronger,
  My song would have been longer.

Frightened Old Man

There was a man and he had nought,
  And robbers came to rob him;
He crept up the chimney pot,
  And then they thought they had him;
But he got down on t'other side
  And so they could not find him;
He ran fourteen miles in fifteen days,
  And never look'd behind him.

A Man with a Wife

I had a little wife, the prettiest ever seen,

She washed up the dishes, and kept the house clean;
She went to the mill to fetch me some flour,
She brought it home in less than an hour;
She baked me my bread, she brewed me my ale,
She sat by the fire and told me many a fine tale.

Crooked Old Man

There was a crooked man,
And he went a crooked mile,
He found a crooked sixpence,
Against a crooked stile.
He bought a crooked cat,
Which caught a crooked mouse,
And they all lived together
In a little crooked house.

King Arthur

When good King Arthur ruled this land,
He was a goodly King;
He stole three pecks of barley meal,
To make a bag pudding.
A bag pudding the King did make,
And stuffed it well with plums;
And in it put great lumps of fat,
As big as my two thumbs.
The King and Queen did eat thereof,
And noblemen beside;
And what they could not eat that night
The Queen next morning fried.

Barney Bodkin

Barney Bodkin broke his nose,
Without feet we can't have toes,
Crazy folks are always mad,
Want of money makes us sad.

Funny Man

A man of words and not of deeds,
Is like a garden fill of weeds;
And when the weeds begin to grow,
It's like a garden full of snow;
And when the snow begins to fall,
It's like a bird upon the wall;
And when the bird away does fly,
It's like an eagle in the sky;
And when the sky begins to roar,
It's like a lion at the door;
And when the door begins to crack,
It's like a stick across your back;
And when your back begins to smart,
It's like a penknife in your heart;
And when your heart begins to bleed,
You're dead, and dead, and dead indeed.

Strange Man

There was a man and he was mad,
  And he jumped into a pea-pod;
The pea-pod was over-full,
  So he jumped into a roaring bull;
The roaring bull was over-fat,
  So he jumped into a gentleman's hat;
The gentleman's hat was over-fine,
  So he jumped into a bottle of wine;

The bottle of wine was over-dear,
  So he jumped into a bottle of beer;
The bottle of beer was over-thick,
  So he jumped into a club-stick;
The club-stick was over-narrow,
  So he jumped into a wheel-barrow;
The wheel-barrow began to crack,
  So he jumped into a hay-stack;
The hay-stack began to blaze,
  So he did nothing but cough and sneeze.

Jack Sprat

Jack Sprat could eat no fat,
  His wife could ea no lean,
And so between them both
  They licked the platter clean.
Jack ate all the lean,
  Joan ate all the fat,
The bone they both picked clean,
  Then gave it to the cat.

When Jack Sprat was young,
  He dressed very smart,
He courted Joan Cole,
  And soon gained her heart;
In his fine leather doublet
  And old greasy hat,
Oh! what a smart fellow
  Was little Jack Sprat.

Joan Cole had a hole
  In her petticoat,
Jack Sprat, to get a patch,
  Gave her a groat.
The groat bought a patch
  Which stopped the hole,
"I thank you, Jack Sprat,"

COLE

Says little Joan Cole.

Jack Sprat was the bridegroom,
  Joan Cole was the bride,
Jack said from the church
  His Joan home should ride.
But no coach could take her,
  The road was so narrow;
Said Jack, "Then I'll take her
  Home in a wheelbarrow."

Jack Sprat was wheeling
  His wife by a ditch,
Then the barrow turned over,
  And in she did pitch.
Says Jack, "She'll be drown'd!"
  But Joan did reply,
"I don't think I shall,
  For the ditch is quite dry."

Jack brought home his Joan,
  And she sat in a chair,
When in came his cat,
  That had got but one ear.
Says Joan "I've come home, Puss,
  Pray how do you do?"
The cat wagg'd her tail
  And said nothing but "mew."

Jack Sprat took his gun,
  And went to the brook;
He shot at the drake,
  But he killed the duck.
He bought it home to Joan,
  Who a fire did make,
To roast the fat duck
  While Jack went for the drake.

The drake was swimming
  With his curly tail,

Jack Sprat came to soot him,
  But happened to fail.
He let off his gun
  But missing the mark,
The drake flew away
  Crying "Quack, quack, quack."

Jack Sprat to live pretty
  Now bought him a pig,
It was not very little,
  It was not very big;
It was not very lean,
  It was not very fat,
"It will serve for a grunter,"
  Said little Jack Sprat.

Then Joan went to market
  To buy her some fowls,
She bought a jackdaw
  And a couple of owls;
The owls were white,
  The jackdaw was black,
"They'll make a rare breed,"
  Says little Joan Sprat.

Jack Sprat bought a cow,
  His Joan to please,
For Joan could make
  Both butter and cheese;
Or pancakes or puddings
  Without any fat;
A notable housewife
  Was little Joan Sprat.

Joan Sprat went to brewing
  A barrel of ale,
She put in some hops
  That it might not turn stale;
But as for the malt—
  She forgot to put that;

"This is a brave sober liquor."
  Said little Jack Sprat.

Jack Sprat went to market
  And bought him a mare,
She was lame of three legs,
  An as blind as she could stare.
Her ribs they were bare,
  For the mare had no fat;
"She looks like a racer,"
  Said little Jack Sprat.

Jack and Joan went abroad,
  Puss looked after the house;
She caught a large rat,
  And a very small mouse,
She caught a small mouse,
  And a very large rat,
"You're an excellent hunter,"
  Said little Jack Sprat.

Now I've told you the story
  Of little Jack Sprat,
Of sweet Joan Cole
  And the poor one-ear'd cat;
Now Jack he loved Joan,
  And good things he taught her,
Then she gave him a son,
  Then after a daughter.

Now Jack has got rich,
  And has plenty of pelf;
If you know any more
  you may tell it yourself.

Cross Old Man

There was a cross old man and what do you think,
He lived on nothing but victuals and drink;
Victuals and drink were his principal diet,
Yet this crabbed old man would never be quiet.

He teased a poor monkey who lived in a cage,
Till the animal got in a terrible rage,
And seized on his nose with finger so strong,
That it stretched it until it was quite a yard long.

Old Man in the Moon

The man in the moon came tumbling down,
  And asked his way to Norwich,
He went by the south, and burnt his mouth,
  With supping cold pease-porridge.

A Funny Man

There was a man of Newington,
 And he was wondrous wise,
He jump'd into a quickset hedge
 And scratch'd out both his eyes.
But when he saw his eyes were out
 With all his might and main
He jump'd into another hedge.
 And scratched them in again.

Dr. Faustus

Doctor Faustus was a good man,
He whipt his scholars now and then.
When he did he made them dance
Out of Scotland into France;
Out of France into Spain,
And then he whipped them back again.

If! If! If!

If all the would was apple pie,
 And all the sea were ink,
And all the trees were bread and cheese,
 What would we have to drink?
It's enough to make an old man
 Scratch his head and think.

Funny Men

Alderman Absolute Always Adjudicated with Astonishing Ability

After he had read some books from Cole's Book Arcade.

Benjamin Bouncer Banged a Brown Bear with a Blunderbuss,
In a lane at the back of Cole's Book Arcade.

Christopher Crabstick was Cross, Capticus, Cutting, and Caustic,
Whenever he could not get a book brought from Cole's Book Arcade.

Francis Fizgig Ferociously Fought and Frightened a Fiddler,
At midday, right in front of Cole's Book Arcade.

Gregory Gimcrack Grinned and Gaped at the Geese and Ganders
Exposed for sale in the Eastern Market, just above Cole's Book Arcade.

Horatio Headstrong Hurled a Hatchet at the Head of a Hawk
Which sat on top of Cole's Book Arcade.

Isaac Ichabod Inhabited an Isolated and Inhospitable Indian Island,
At an enormous and disheartening distance from Cole's Book Arcade.

Lugubrious Longface Loved Learning and Literary Lore,
Which he always got out of the books he bought at Cole's Book Arcade.

Marmaduke Meddlesome Munificently Meted out Mercy to a Miserable Man
Who stole a book at Cole's Book Arcade.

Obadiah Orpheus Opened an Original Overture Outrageously Oddly,
With a small whistle and a big drum, in front of Cole's Book Arcade.

Quinton Querulous Queerly Questioned a Quibbling and Querulous Quidnunc,
And asked Quizzingly if he had ever seen the inside of Cole's Book Arcade.

Reuben Ramble Ran a Ridiculous Rattling Race on a Railway,
And beat the train in hasting to get a book at Cole's Book Arcade.

Theodore Thunderbolt Told Terrible and Tremendous Tales of Travelling,
Which were afterwards printed in books and sold at Cole's Book Arcade.

Valentine Valiana Valorously Vanquished a Vapouring Villager,
Who spoke ignorantly and slightingly of Cole's Book Arcade.

Xenophon Xenocles eXhibited eXtraordinary and eXcessive eXcitability
Whenever he was not calmed down by books from Cole's Book Arcade.

Young Yokel, a Youthful Yorkshire Yeoman Yawned at York,
For want of a few interesting and entertaining books from Cole's Book Arcade.

Zachariah Zany Zealously studied Zoology
Out of the works which he bought at Cole's Book Arcade.

Utter Nonsense

There was an Old Person of Prague,
Who was suddenly seized with the plague,
But they gave him some butter, which caused him to mutter,
And cured that Old Person of Prague.

There was an Old Man with a gong,
Who bumped at it all the day long,
But they called out, "O, law! you're a horrid old bore!"
So they smashed that Old Man with a gong.

There was an Old Man of the Isles,
Whose face was pervaded with smiles,
He sang "Hi dum diddle," played on the fiddle,
That amiable Old Man of the Isles.

There was an Old Person of Dover,

Who rushed through a field of blue clover;
But some very large Bees stung His nose and his knees,
 So he very soon went back to Dover.

There was an Old Man of Quebec,—
 A beetle ran over his neck:
But he cried, "With a needle I'll slay you, O beetle!"
 That angry Old Man of Quebec

There was an Old Man of Vesuvius,
 Who studied the works of Vitruvius;
When the flames burned his book, to drinking he took,
 That morbid Old Man of Vesuvius.

There was an Old Person of Buda,
 Whose conduct grew ruder and ruder,
Till at last with a hammer they silenced his clamour,
 By smashing that Old Person of Buda.

There was an Old Man of Marseilles,
 Whose daughters wore bottle-green veils,
They caught several fish which they put in a dish,
 And sent to their Pa at Marseilles

There was an Old Man of Coblenz,
 The length of whose legs was immense,
He went with one prance from Turkey to France,
 That surprising Old Man of Coblenz.

There was an Old Person of Gretna,
 Who rushed down the crater of Etna;
When they said, "Is it hot?" he replied, "No, it's not!"
 That mendacious Old Person of Gretna.

There was an Old Person of Bangor,
 Whose face was distorted with anger;
He tore off his boots and subsisted on roots,
 That borascible Person of Bangor.

There was an Old Person of Spain,

503

Who hated all trouble and pain;
So he sat on a chair, with his feet in the air,
    That umbrageous Old Person of Spain.

There was an Old Man of the West,
    Who never could get any rest;
So they set him to spin on his nose and his chin,
    Which cured that Old Man of the West.

There was an Old Man in a tree,
    Who was horribly bored by a bee;
When they said, "Does it buzz?" he replied, "Yes it does!
    It's a regular brute of a bee!"

There was an Old Man who said, "How,
    Shall I flee from this horrible Cow?
I will sit on this stile and continue to smile,
    Which may soften the heart of this Cow."

There was an Old Man of Calcutta,
    Who perpetually ate bread and butter,
Till a great bit of muffin, on which he was stuffing,
    Choked that horrid Old Man of Calcutta.

There was an Old Man of the South,
    Who had an immoderate mouth;
But in swallowing a dish that was quite full of fish,
    He was choked, that Old Man of the South.

There was an Old Person of Dutton,
    Whose head was as small as a button;
So to make it look big, he purchased a wig,
    And rapidly rushed about Dutton.

There was an Old Man of some rocks,
    Who shut his wife up in a box;
When she said, "Let me out," he exclaimed, "Without doubt
    You will pass all your life in that box,"

There was an Old Person of Rheims,

Who was troubled with horrible dreams;
So to keep him awake they fed him with cake,
Which amused that Old Person of Rheims.

There was an Old Man with a flute,
A "sarpent" ran into his boot;
But he played day and night, till the "sarpent" took flight,
And avoided that Man with a flute.

There was an Old Man of Berlin,
Whose form was uncommonly thin;
Till he once, by mistake, was mixed up in a cake,
So they baked that Old Man of Berlin.

There was an Old Man of the Hague,
Whose ideas were excessively vague;
He built a balloon to examine the moon,
That deluded Old Man of the Hague.

A horrid Old Gentleman from Monaghan,
Sat down and refused to go on again,
Till they gave him a crown for leaving the town,
That wretched old humbug of Monaghan.

There was an Old Man if Nepaul,
From his horse had a terrible fall;
But, though split quite in two, with some very strong glue
They mended that Man of Nepaul.

There was an Old Man of Aoster,
Who possessed a large cow, but he lost her;
But they said, "Don't you see she has rushed up a tree?
You invidious Old Man of Aosta!"

There was an Old Man of the Nile,
Who sharpened his nails with a file,
Till he cuts of his thumbs, and said calmly, "This comes
Of sharpening one's nails with a file!"

There was an Old Person of Rhodes,
Who strongly objected to toads;
He paid several cousins to catch them by dozens,
That futile Old Person of Rhodes.

There was an Old Man of Cape Horn,
Who wished he had never been born;
So he sat on a chair until he died of despair,
That dolorous Man of Cape Horn.

There was an Old Person whose habits
Induced him to feed upon rabbits;
When he'd eaten eighteen, he turned perfectly green,
Upon which he relinquished those habits.

There was an Old Man with a nose,
Who said, "If you choose to suppose
That my nose is too long, you are certainly wrong!"
That remarkable Man with a nose.

There was an Old Man of Apulia,
Whose conduct was very peculiar;
He fed twenty sons upon nothing but buns,

That whimsical Man of Apulia.

There was an Old Man of Madras,
Who rode on a cream-coloured ass;
But the length of its ears so promoted his fears
That it killed that Old Man of Madras.

There was an Old Person of Sparta,
Whose had twenty-five sons and one daughter;
He fed them snails, and weighed them on scales,
That wonderful Person of Sparta.

There was an Old Person of Chilli,
Whose conduct was painful and silly;
He sat on the stairs, eating apples and pears,
That imprudent Old Person of Chilli.

There was an Old Man of the East,
Who gave all his children a feast;
But they all ate so much, and their conduct was such
That it killed that Old Man of the East.

There was an Old Man of Peru,
Who never knew what he should do;
So he tore off his hair, and behaved like a bear,
That intrinsic Old Man of Peru.

There was an Old Man in a boat,
Who said, "I'm afloat! I'm afloat!"
When they said, "No you a'int!" he was ready to faint,
That unhappy Old Man in a boat.

There was an Old Man of Bohemia,
Whose daughter was christened Euphemia,
But one day, to his grief, she married a thief,
Which grieved that Old Man of Bohemia.

There was an Old Person of Basing,
Whose presence of mind was amazing;
He purchased a steed, which he rode at full speed

507

And escaped from the people of Basing.

There was an Old Man on a hill,
Who seldom if ever stood still;
He ran up and down in his Grandmother's gown,
Which adorned that Old Man on a hill.

There was an Old Man of Kilkenny,
Who never had more than a penny,
He spent all that money on onions and honey,
That wayward Old Man of Kilkenny.

There was an Old Person of Perth,
The stingiest fellow on earth;
He fed—oh! 'twas cruel—on seaweed and gruel,
This stingy Old Person of Perth.

A dogmatic Old Fellow of Shoreham,
Would snub his companions and bore 'em,
By flat contradiction, which was an affliction
To the friends of this party of Shoreham.

There was an Old Person of Ischia,
Whose conduct grew friskier and friskier;
He danced hornpipes and jigs, and ate thousands of figs,
That lively Old Person of Ischia.

There was an Old Person of Hurst,
Who drank when he was not athirst;
When they said, "You'll grow fatter!" he answered, "What matter?"
That globular Person of Hurst.

The Diverting History Of John Gilpin

John Gilpin was a citizen
Of credit and renown,
A train-bound Captain eke was he
Of famous London town.

John Gilpin's spouse said to her dear,
  Though we have wedded been,
These twice ten tedious years, yet we
  No holiday have seen.

To-morrow is our wedding-day,
  And we then will repair
Unto the "Bell" at Edmonton,
  All in a chaise and pair,
My sister and my sister's child,
  Myself and children three,
Will fill the chaise, so you must ride
  On horse-back after we.

He soon replied—I do admire
  Of womankind but one,
And you are she, my dearest dear,
  Therefore it shall be done,
I am a linen-draper bold,
  As all the world doth know,
And my good friend the Calender,
  Will lend his horse to go.

Quoth Mrs Gilpin—That's well said;
  And for that wind is dear,
We will be furnished with our own,
  Which is both bright and clear;
John Gilpin kiss'd his loving wife,
  O'erjoyed was he to find
That, though on pleasure she was bent,
  She had a frugal mind.

The morning came, the chaise was brought,
  And yet was not allow'd
To drive up to the door, lest all
  Should say that she was proud;
So three doors off the post was stayed,
  Where they did all get in,
Six precious souls, and all agog

To dash through thick and thin.

Smack went the whip, round went the wheels,
  Were never folks so glad,
The stones did rattle underneath
  As if Cheapside were mad;
John Gilpin at his horse's side
  Seized fast the flowing mane,
And up he got in haste to ride,
  But soon came down again.

For saddle-tree scarce reached had he,
  His journey to begin,
When turning round his head, he saw
  Three customers come in.
So down he came—for loss of time,
  Although it grieved him sore,
Yet loss of pence, full well he knew,
  Would trouble him much more.

'Twas long before the customers
  Were suited to their mind,
When Betty, screaming, came down the stairs,
  "The wine is left behind."
Good lack! quoth he, yet bring it me,
  My leathern belt likewise,
In which I bear my trusty sword
  When I do exercise.

Now, Mistress Gilpin, careful soul,
  Had two stone bottles found,
To hold the liquor that she loved,
  And keep it safe and sound,
Each bottle had a curling ear,
  Through which the belt he drew,
And hung a bottle on each side,
  To make his balance true.

Then over all, that he might be
  Equipp'd from top to toe,

His long red cloak, well brush'd and neat,
  He manfully did throw,
Now see him mounted once again
  Upon his nimble steed,
Full slowly pacing o'er the stones
  With caution and good heed.

But, finding soon a smoother road
  Beneath his well-shod feet,
The snorting beast began to trot,
  Which gall'd him in his seat,
So, "Fair and softly," John, he cried,
  But John, he cried in vain;
That trot became a gallop soon,
  In spite of curb and rein.

So, stooping down, as needs he must,
  Who cannot sit upright,
He grasp'd the mane with both his hands,
  And eke with all his might,
His horse, who never in that sort,
  Had handled been before,
What thing upon his back had got
  Did wonder more and more.

Away went Gilpin, neck or nought,
  Away went hat and wig,
He little dreamt when he set out
  Of running such a rig;
The wind did blow, the cloak did fly,
  Like streamer long and gay,
Till, loop and button failing both,
  At last it flew away.

Then might people well discern
  The bottles he had slung,
A bottle swinging at each side,
  As had been said or sung,
The dogs did bark, the children scream'd,
  Up flew the windows all

And ev'ry soul cried out, Well done!
  As loud as he could bawl.

Away went Gilpin—who but he,
  His fame soon spread around—
He carries weight, he rides a race!
  'Tis for a thousand pound!
And still as fast as he drew near,
  'Twas wonderful to view
How in a trice the turnpike men
  Their gates wide open flew.

And now as he went bowing down
  His reeking head full low,
The bottles twain behind his back
  Were shatter'd at a blow;
Down ran the wine into the road,
  Most piteous to be seen,
Which made his horses flanks to smoke,
  As they had basted been.

But still he seem'd to carry weight,
  With leathern girdle braced,
For all might see the bottle-necks
  Still dangling at his waist;
Thus all through merry Islington
  These gambols did he play,
And till he came into the Wash
  Of Edmonton so gay.

And there he threw the wash about
  On both sides of the way,
Just like unto a trundling mop,
  Or a wild goose at play.
At Edmonton his loving wife
  From the balcony spied
Her tender husband, wond'ring much
  To see how he did ride.

Stop, stop, John Gilpin!—Here's the house—

They all at once did cry,
The dinner waits, and we are tired—
　Said Gilpin—So am I;
But yet this horse was not a whit
　Inclined to tarry there—
For why? His owner had a house
　Full ten miles off, at Ware.

So, like an arrow, swift he flew,
　Shot by an archer strong;
So did he fly—which brings me to
　The middle of my song.
Away went Gilpin, out of breath,
　And sore against his will,
Till at his friend the Calender's
　His horse at last stood still.

The Calender, amazed to see
　His neighbour in such trim,
Laid down his pipe, flew to the gate,
　And thus accosted him:—
What news? what news? your tidings tell!
　Tell me you must and shall—
Say why bare-headed you are come,
　Or why you come at all?

Now, Gilpin had a pleasant wit,
　And loved a timely joke,
And thus unto the Calender
　In merry guise he spoke—
I came because your horse would come,
　And if I well forbode,
My hat and wig will soon be here,
　They are upon the road.

The Calender, right glad to find
　His friend in merry pin,
Return'd him not a single word,
　But to the house went in.
When straight he came with hat and wig—

COLE

A wig that flow'd behind;
A hat not much the worse of wear—
    Each comely in its kind.

He held them up, and in its turn
    Thus showed his ready wit—
My head is twice as big as yours,
    They therefore needs must fit.
But let me scrape the dirt away
    That hangs upon your face,
And stop and eat, for well you may
    Be in a hungry case.

Said John, It is my wedding-day,
    And all the world would stare,
If wife should dine at Edmonton,
    And I should dine at Ware.
So, turning to his horse, he said—
    I am in haste to dine,
'Twas for your pleasure you came here,
    You shall go back for mine.

Ah, luckless speech, and bootless boast,
    For which he paid full dear;
For while he spake, a braying ass
    Did sing most loud and clear,
Whereat his horse did snort as he
    Had heard a lion's roar,
And gallop'd off with all his might,
    As he had done before.

Away went Gilpin, and away
    Went Gilpin's hat and wig;
He lost them sooner than the first,
    For why? they were too big.
Now, Mistress Gilpin when she saw
    Her husband posting down
Into the country far away,
    She pulled out half-a-crown.

And thus unto the youth she said
  That drove them to the "Bell"—
This shall be yours when you bring back
  My husband safe and well;
The youth did ride, and soon did meet
  John coming back again,
Whom in a trice, he tried to stop
  By catching at his rein.

But, not performing what he meant,
  And gladly would have done,
The frightened steed he frightened more,
  And made him faster run;
Away went Gilpin, and away
  Went post-boy at his heels—
The post-boy's horse right glad to miss
  The lumbering of the wheels.

Six gentlemen upon the road,
  Thus seeing Gilpin fly,
With post-boy scamp'ring in the rear,
  They raised the hue and cry:—
Stop thief! stop thief!—a highwayman!
An all and each that pass'd the way
  Did join in the pursuit.

And now the turnpike gates again
  Flew open in short space—
The toll-men thinking as before,
  That Gilpin rode a race;
And so he did, and won it, too,
  For he got first to town:
Nor stopp'd till, where he had got up,
  He did again get down,

Now let us sing: Long live the king,
  And Gilpin, long live he;
And when he next doth ride abroad,
  May I be there to see.

Books teach the children of men in many million schools;
Books make the difference between earth's learned and its fools.

Song Of The Book Arcade

Cole's Book Arcade, Cole's Book Arcade
  It is in Melbourne town,
Of all the book stores in the land
  It has the most renown,

It was the first, first Book Arcade
  That in the world was found;
It's still the finest Book Arcade
  In all the world around.

A lovely rainbow sign appears
  Above the Book Arcade
And 'tis the very grandest sign

Was ever yet displayed.

Full forty thousand sorts of books
    Are stored within its walls,
Which can be seen, looked at or bought,
    By anyone that calls.

The book you wish, the book you want,
    Is almost sure to be
Found somewhere in the Book Arcade,
    If you will call and see.
(Our Australian Choir has Cockatoos, Laughing Jack-
asses, Native Bears, Platypusses, Black Swans, Emus,
Magpies, Opossums, and Lyre Birds, also a BUNYIP to
sing deep bass, all the other Animals in the World sing
the chorus, each in his natural voice. The tune is
"MARY HAD A LITTLE LAMB.")

Value Of Books

BOOKS should be found in every house
    To form and feed the mind;
They are the best of luxuries
    'Tis possible to find.

For all the books in all the world
    Are man's greatest treasure;
They make him wish, and bring to him
    His best, his choicest pleasure.

BOOKS make his time pass happily
    Through many weary hours.
Amuse, compose, instruct his mind,
    Enlarge his mental powers.

BOOKS give to him the history
    Of each and every land;
BOOKS show him human action's past—

The bad, the good, the grand.

BOOKS show him arts, laws, learnings, faiths
  Of every time and place;
BOOKS show him how each thing is made
  Used by the human race.

BOOKS give to him descriptions of
  The world in which we live,
Of the universe around us,
  And better still they give.

BOOKS give to him the greatest thoughts
  Of all the good and wise;
BOOKS treasure human knowledge up,
  And so it never dies.

BOOKS show him all that men have done,
  What they have thought and said;

BOOKS show the deeds and wisdom of
The living and the dead.

BOOKS show him all the hopes and fears
Of every race and clan;
BOOKS clearly prove beyond a doubt
The brotherhood of man.

BOOKS give him hopes beyond the grave
Of an immortal life;
BOOKS teach that right and truth and love
Shall banish every strife.

BOOKS teach and please him when a child
In youth and in his prime;
BOOKS give him soothing pleasure when
His health and strength decline.

BOOKS please him in his lonely hours,
Wherever he may roam:
BOOKS please when read aloud among
His loving friends at home.

BOOKS like *strong drink* will drown his cares,
But do not waste his wealth;
BOOKS leave him *better*, drink the *worse*,
In character and health.

BOOKS therefore, are, of all man buys,
The choicest thing on earth,
BOOKS have, of all his household goods,
The most intrinsic worth.

BOOKS are the greatest blessing out,
The grandest thing we sell,
BOOKS bring more joy, BOOKS do more good
Than mortal tongue can tell.

E. W. Cole

THE OLD WOMAN WHO LIVED IN A SHOE

The Old Woman Who Lived In A Shoe

There was an old woman who lived in a shoe,
She had so many children—such naughty ones too!
She cried, "Oh, dear me, I don't know what to do,
Who would be an old woman and live in a shoe?"

Once ninety little fellows sat down on the floor
And lustily screamed, "We won't cry any more!"
"Then stop crying now," the old woman said,
"The noise you are making goes right through my head."

"Then she gave the boys broth without any bread,
And whipped them all soundly and sent them to bed.
She scolded the girls, and said, "Don't make a noise,
Or you shall be served just the same as the boys."

Mother Goose

Old Mother Goose, when
　She wanted to wander,
Would ride through the air
　On a very fine gander.

Mother Goose had a house,
　'Twas built of wood,
Where an owl at the door
　For sentinel stood.

She had a son Jack,
　A plain-looking lad,
He was not very good
　Nor yet very bad.

She sent him to market;
　A live goose he bought;
Here, mother, says he
　It will not go for nought.

Jack's goose and her gander
　They grew very fond;
They'd both eat together,
　Or swim in one pond.

Jack found one morning,
　As I have been told,
His goose had laid him
　An egg of pure gold

Jack rode to his mother,
　The news for to tell.
She call'd him a good boy,
　And said it was well.

Hack sold his gold egg
　To a rogue of a Jew
Who cheated him out of

521

The half of his due.

Then Jack went a-courting
  A lady so gay,
As fair as the lily,
  And sweet as the May.

The Jew and the Squire
  Came behind his back,
And began to belabour
  The sides of poor Jack.

Then old Mother Goose
  That instant came in,
And turned her son Jack
  Into fam'd Harlequin.

She then with her wand
  Touch'd the lady so fine,
And turn'd her at once
  Into sweet Columbine.

The gold egg in the sea
  Was quickly thrown, when
Jack gave a quick dive,
  And soon got it again.

The Jew got the goose,
  Which he vow'd he would kill,
Resolving at once
  His pockets to fill.

Jack's mother came in,
  And caught the goose soon,
And mounting its back,
  Flew up to the moon.

Old Woman under a Hill

There was an old woman liv·d under a hill,
Put a mouse in a bag, and se·t it to mill;
The Miller declar'd by the pc·int of his knife,
He ne'er saw such a big mouse in his life.

Old Woman under a Hill

There was an old woman lived under a hill;
And if she's not gone, she li·es there still.

Old Woman and Three Sons

There was an old woman had three sons;
Jerry, and James, and John.
Jerry was hung, James was drowned;
John was lost, and never was found;
And there was an end of the three sons,
Jerry, and James, and John.

Old Woman who Lived in a Shell

A little old woman, as I've heard tell,
Lived near the sea, in a nice little shell;
She was well off, if she wanted her tea—
She'd plenty of water from out of the sea.

Then if for her dinner she had the least wish,
Of course she had nothing to do but to fish;
So, really, this little old woman did well,
As she didn't pay any rent for the use of the shell.

Old Woman Swallowed

There was an old woman called Nothing-at-all,
Who rejoiced in a dwelling exceedingly small;
A man stretched his mouth to its utmost extent,
And down at one gulp house and old woman went.

Old Woman's Calf

There was an old woman sat spinning,
And that's the first beginning;
She had a calf, and that's half;
She took it by the tail,
And threw it over the wall and that's all.

Old Woman Drowned

There was an old woman, her name it was Peg;
Her head was of wood, and she wore a cork-leg.
The neighbours all pitched her into the water,
Her leg was drown'd first, and her head followed a'ter.

Old Woman of Stepney

At Stepney there lived,
As every one knows,
An old woman who had
A plum tree on her nose!

The boys, while she slept,
Would cautiously take
The plums from her tree
Before she could wake.

This old woman went
One day to the lawn
Of my Lord Cockagee,
And there saw a fawn.

Having shot him, she tied
His hind legs to her tree,

And so quitted the lawn
  Of my Lord Cockagee.

She'd nearly reached home,
  When the constable came,
And put her in prison
  For killing the game.

While locked in her cell,
  She thought again and again
Of how to escape,
  But kept thinking in vain.

She considered each plan,
  Till she found out a way
Of escaping the prison
  In the course of the day.

She cut the plum tree
  close off from her nose,
And made a scarecrow,
  Dress'd up in her clothes;

This she set on a stool,
  With it's back to the wall,
And watch'd near the door
  For fear it would fall.

Soon the jailor came in
  With her water and bread;
He stared at the figure,
  While from prison she fled.

The old woman reached home,
  Singing diddle-dee-dee;
And again on her nose
  There grew a plum tree.

Funny Old Women

There was an old person of Smyrna,
Whose Granny once threatened to burn her;
  But she seized on the cat,
  And said "Granny, burn that!
You incongruous old woman of Smyrna!"

There was an old lady of Bute,
Who played on a silver-gilt flute;
  She played several jigs
  To her Uncle's white pigs,
That amusing old lady of Bute.

There was an old lady of Ryde,
Whose shoe-strings were seldom untied,
  She purchased some clogs,
  And some small spotted dogs,
And frequently walked about Ryde.

There was an old lady of Parma,
Whose conduct grew calmer and calmer,
  When they said "Are you dumb?"
  She merely said "Hum!"
That provoking old lady of Parma.

There was an old lady of Troy,
Whom several large flies did annoy;
  Some she killed with a thump,
  Some she drowned at the pump,
And some she took with her to Troy.

There was an old person of Crete,
Whose toilet was far from complete,
  She dressed in a sack
  Spickle-speckled with black,
That ombliferous old person of Crete.

There was an old lady of Wales,
Who caught a large fish without scales;

When she rested her hook,
She exclaimed "Only look!"
That ecstatic old lady of Wales.

There was an old lady of Clare,
Who was sadly pursued by a bear;
  When she found she was tired,
  She abruptly expired,
That unfortunate lady of Clare.

There was an old lady of Dorking,
Who bought a large bonnet for walking;
  But it's colour and size,
  So bedazzled her eyes,
That she very soon went back to Dorking.

There was an old lady of Russia,
Who screamed so that no one could hush her;
  Her screams were extreme,
  No one heard such a scream,
As was screamed by that lady of Russia.

There was an old lady of Norway,
Who casually sat in a doorway;
  When the door squeezed her flat,
  She exclaimed, "What of that?"
That courageous old lady of Norway.

There was an old lady of Chertsey,
Who made a remarkable curtsey;
  She twirled round and round,
  Till she sank underground,
Which distressed all the people of Chertsey.

There was an old woman of Anerley,
Whose conduct was strange and unmannerly.
  She rushed down the Strand,
  With a pig in each hand,
But returning in the evening to Anerley.

There was an old lady of We ling,
Whose praise all the world was a-telling;
  She played on the harp,
  And caught several carp,
That accomplished old lady of Welling.

There was an old lady of Turkey,
Who wept when the weather was murky;
  When the day turned out fine,
  She ceased to repine,
That capricious old lady of Turkey.

Old Woman who went up in a Basket

There was an old woman went up in a basket,
  Ninety-nine times as high as the moon;
What she did there I could not but ask it,
  For in her hand she carried a broom.

"Old woman, old woman, old woman," quoth I,
"O whither, O whither, O whither, so high?"
"To sweep the cobwebs off the sky,—
And I shall be back again by and by!"

There was an old woman of Prague,
Whose ideas were horribly vague,
  She built a balloon,
  To examine the moon,
That deluded old woman of Prague.

There was an old woman of Hull,
Who was chased by a virulent bull;
  But she seized on a spade,
  And called out "Who's afraid?"
Which distracted that virulent bull.

There was an old lady of Poole,
Whose soup was excessively cool;
  So she put it to boil,
  By the aid of some oil,
That ingenious old lady of Poole.

There was an old lady of Burton,
Whose answers were rather uncertain;
  When they said "How d'ye do?"
  She replied "Who are you?"
That distressing old person of Burton.

There was an old lady of Lucca,
Whose lovers completely forsook her;
  She ran up a tree,
  And said "Fiddle-de-dee!"
Which embarrassed the people of Lucca.

There was an old woman of Norwich,
Who lived on nothing but porridge;
  Parading the town,
  She turned cloak into gown,
That thrifty old woman of Norwich.

There was an old woman of Leeds,
Who spent all her time in good deeds;
  She worked for the poor,
  Till her fingers were sore,

That pious old woman of Leeds.

There was an old woman in Surrey,
Who was morn, noon, and night in a hurry;
  Called her husband a fool,
  Drove the children to school,
That worrying old woman in Surrey.

There was an old lady whose bonnet
Came untied when the birds sat upon it;
  But she said "I don't care!
  All the birds in the air
Are welcome to sit on my bonnet!"

There was an old lady whose nose
Was so long that it reached to her toes;
  So she hired an old lady,
  Whose conduct was steady,
To carry that wonderful nose.

There was an old lady whose chin
Resembled the point of a pin;
  So she had it made sharp,
  And purchased a harp,
On which to play tunes with her chin.

There was an old lady whose eyes,
Were unique as to colour and size;
  When she opened them wide,
  People all turned aside,
And started away in surprise.

There was a young lady of Hexham,
Contradicted her friends jus to vex 'em;
  She talked about horses,
  And rode on racecourses,
This forward young lady of Hexham.

Strange History of Twenty-Six Funny Women

Angelina Armstrong Abruptly Asked an Adver-
tising Agent About an Alliterating Advertisement
Appearing, Announcing An Astonishing, Admi-
rable, Attractive, Agreeable, Artistic, And
Advanced Australian Arcade.
  Meaning **Cole's Book Arcade**.

Bridget Bradshaw Bamboozled the Barber's
Beautiful Baby By Bouncing it into Believing a
Bandbox to Be a Big Book.
  From **Cole's Book Arcade**.

Clarissa Cox Cautiously Crept & Caught with a
Candle extinguisher a Congregation of Catter-
wauling Cats Conducting a Confounded
Corroboree.
  On the roof of **Cole's Book Arcade**.

Dorothy Dwight in the Dark Drew a Decidedly
Delightful Drawing, Depicting a Dictating,
Domineering Despot; a Desperate Despoiling
Demogogue; a Disdainful Duchess Dowager; a
Dainty, Dressy Dandy, and a Downright Double-
Dealing Dodger.
  Which drawing can be inspected at **Cole's Book
Arcade** by anyone who can see clearly in the
Dark.

Eudocia Emul, the Eccentric Epicurian Empress
of Ethiopia, Electrified the East End of Egypt by
Eagerly and Easily Eating, as an Experiment, an
Egg, an Eagle, an Emu, and Electrical Eel, and an
Enormous Elephant, larger than the one Exhib-
ited next to **Cole's Book Arcade**.

Fanny Fagan's Fine, Flossy, Fashionable Feathers
Frequently Flopped, Flirted, and Flounced Forci-
bly From Fun.

When she read some of the lively books from
Cole's Book Arcade.

Georgina Gubbins Gently, Gracefully, Gravely,
Grammatically, Graphically, and Grandilo-
quently Grumbled at her Great-Grandmother.
  Because she so seldom went to **Cole's Book
Arcade**.

Harriet Hopkins Had an Habitual, Haughty,
Harsh, Hasty, Huffy, Hateful, Hideous, Horrid,
Headstrong, Heedless, Hysterical, Habit of Hen-
pecking Her Husband at Home.
  When he would not take her to **Cole's Book
Arcade**, to get a book on Saturday night.

Isabella Ingram Ironically Inquired of the Illustrious Imperial Indian If Idleness, Ignorance,
Impudence, Intemperance, Intolerance, Inhuman-
ity, and Infamy.
  Were the seven cardinal virtues. She was referred for an answer to the Instructive books in
Cole's Book Arcade.

Jemima Jenkins, the Jerusalem Jewess, Judi-
ciously Jotted Jokes in her Journal in June on her
Journey through Judea to Jericho, beyond Jordan.
  [N.B.—Jericho, beyond Jordan, is about 10,000
miles from **Cole's Book Arcade**.]

Kate Kearney Kidnapped a Knave, a Knight, a
Khan, a Kaiser and a King, and Kindly Kept
them upon Ketchup, Kale, Kidneys, Kingfishes,
Kittens and Kangaroos.
  She did not buy her cookery book at **Cole's
Book Arcade**: he doesn't sell books showing
how to cook Kittens.

Lucy Larkins Lately Let a Lovely, Lonely Lady
Look Leisurely at a Large Live Lobster by the

533

aid of a Lucid Little Lime-Light, Borrowed from
Cole's Book Arcade.

Mary Muggin's Mother Made a Mighty, Monstrous, Mammoth, Monument of Marmalade jars;
Mounted up, and Minutely Minced the Moon
into a Multitude of Magnificent stars.
 [N.B.—About 300 bushels of said stars fell on
top of **Cole's Book Arcade** and may be seen on
application.]

Old Woman Cutting the Moon into Stars.

Nancy Nuttall was a Nonsensical, Noodlesome,
Nincompoopish, Namby-pamby, Numskulled,
Needle-woman; Nevertheless, at Ninety-Nine she
Neatly and Nimbly Nabbed in the Nuptial Noose
a Notable Noble Nabob of Nagpoor.
 And directly after the marriage Nagged him into
sending for books to **Cole's Book Arcade.**

Olivia Oliphant, of Omeo, ordered an Obstinate
Old Organ-grinding Ostrich to Overwhelm with
Oil an Olive, an Onion, an Orange, an Onion, an
Orange, an Ocean, and an Oat.

And then go to **Cole's Book Arcade** and get a
book.

Papline Potts, a Poor, Penniless Peasant, Prettily,
Pleasantly, Pathetically and Perfectly Played a
Piece of music in a Parlour at a Pleasure-Palace
to a Picked, Packed Party of Particular Person-
ages, consisting of Peers, Peeresses, Princes and
Princesses.

The piece of music was bought Quarter-Price at
Cole's Book Arcade.

Quintina Quirk Quarrelled with the Queer,
Quaint, Quadroon Queen of Quito, and
Quizzingly Questioned her Quivering, Quaking
Quartermaster.

If he was Quite sure he bought all his pens and
pencils at **Cole's Book Arcade**.

Ruth Robertson's Rich Rival, Regardless of
Right, Rhyme, or Reason, Recently Ran a Rapid,
Rattling Race Round a Regiment of Royal Rus-
sian Red Republicans,

Instead of Running into **Cole's Book Arcade**.

Seraphina Susanna Selina Sally Snooks, a Sober,
Serious, Staid, Seraphic, and Sentimental
Sailoress, Solicited a Situation as Superior Sa-
loon Stewardess on the Splendid Spanish
Steamship *Salamanca*, and Straightway Stipu-
lated with the Sprightly Supercargo to Slyly and
Suddenly Sail Southward at Sunrise for Six
Shillingsworth of Select Stationery to **Cole's
Book Arcade**.

Theresa Toodles Thatched a Trumpery Tipperary
Theatre Three Thousand and Thirty-Three
Times, and Then Took To Table-Turning and
Table-Talking

But never Turned into nor Talked about **Cole's
Book Arcade** until afterwards.

Urania Upton was Uncouth, Ungraceful, Unfash-
ionable, Unladylike, Uninteresting,
Unpresentable, and Ugly. She was Unpoetical,
Unmusical, Unlearned, Uncultured, Unimproved,
Uninformed, Unknowing, Unthinking, Unwitty
and Unwise. She was Unlively, Undersized, Un-
wholesome and Unhealthy. She was Unlovely,
Ungentle, Uncivil, Unsociable, Untameable, and
altogether Unendurable. She was Unkind, Un-
feeling, Unloving, Unthankful, Ungrateful,
Unwilling, Unruly, Unreasonable, Unwomanly,
Unworthy, Unmotherly, Undutious, Unmerciful,
Untruthful, Unfair, Unjust and Unprincipled. She
was Unpunctual, Unthrifty, Unskilful, Unready,
Unsafe, Unfit, and totally Unprofitable. She was
Unknown, Unnoticed, Unheeded, Unobeyed,
Unloved, Unfriended, Unemployed, Unvalued,
Unpopular, and actually Unpitied. She was Un-
successful, Unfortunate, Unlucky, Unpaid,
Unshod, Unfed, Unquiet, Unsettled, Uncertain,
Undecided, Unhinged, Uneasy, Upset, Unhappy,
and Utterly Useless.

Until, by chance, she went to **Cole's Book Arcade**, and got some good instructive books, and
now she is the very best person in Australia, and
the best but two in the world.

Victoria Vincent Valiantly Vaccinated a Vapour-
ing, Verbose Varmit of a Vulgar Villainous
Vagabond, who Very Verdantly Ventured on a
Versatile, Veteran, Valueless Velocipede to Visit
the Viceroy of Venice, instead of Visiting **Cole's
Book Arcade**

Wilhelmina Wilkins Was a Worthy, Witty,
Widow Washerwoman, Who Washed Woollen
Waistcoats, Worsted Waistbands, and Water-
proof Wrappers With a Washing-Machine, and
lived Well upon Water-gruel; Whereupon Wil-
liam Watson, a Wide-awake Widowed
Waterman, Wisely Walked With her—
Whispered, Winked, Wooed, Won, Wedded, and
Wafted her across the Wide Waste of Water
Waves, and got her a Weird Waltz.
    Quarter-Price at **Cole's Book Arcade**.

Xantippe Xman, the eXiled eXqueen of the eX-
quimaux, eXceedingly eXcelled in eXerting an
eXquisite eXactness in eXpense in general; but
eXhibited the most eXceptional, eXtensive, eX-
traordinary, eXcessive, eXtravagant, but
eXcusable eXuberance.
    When she visited **Cole's Book Arcade**, to buy
books.

Yellena Yellat, the Yellow Yahoo of Yokohama,
Yawned Yesterday at Yon Yelping Yokel of the
Yankee Yeomanry.
    And told him that he, being ignorant, should go
at once and get educated at **Cole's Book Arcade**.

Zenobian Zoziman, the Zouave Zemindaress of
Zululand, was no Zany, but rode on a Zanzibar
Zebra, resided in a Zing-Zag Zenana, Zealously
studied Zanyism, Zealotism, Zoology, Zoonomy,
Zoophytology, Zoolatry, Zymology, Zincography
    And many other 'isms, 'ologies, 'olatries,
'ographies, etc., out of the works she bought at
Cole's Book Arcade.

Transportation

A Wonderful Search Journey by the 40 principal modes of travelling
in The World, and a Prize of £1000 offered for a Flying Machine.

I have always been a man of one idea at a time, and that one idea I have followed with unwavering determination until success has rewarded my efforts. Now listen to my story:—A short time ago, much desiring to obtain a particular article, I determined to get it if it was possible to do so in this world and so started on my search journey. I ran into Melbourne and asked

His Excellency the GOVERNOR of Victoria if he knew where I could get it he said he did not but I might ask the RAJAH of Sarawak. I took ship to Sarawak, asked

the Rajah, he said he did not know, but referred me to the MIKADO of Japan. I jumped into a boat, pulled

to Jedo, asked His Dual Majesty, Lord Paramount of Japan, and head of the Sintoo Faith, he said he did not know, but perhaps the TYCOON of Japan did. I got into a jimriksha and was trotted

away to the house of the unfortunate Tycoon, he said he could not help me, but referred me to the GREAT CHAM of Tartary. I jumped into a Chinese junk,

539

bore away to Pekin and saw the Great Cham of the Ce-
lestials, "Son of Heaven," "Brother to the Sun, Moon
and Stars," "Father of Mankind," "Governor of the
World" and head of the Confucian Faith. He conde-
scendingly said he did not know, but maybe the TIANG
of Nankin could inform me; I took a sailing wheelbarrow to the Centre of Wise Learning, saw the head

of the Taoist Faith, he could not tell me where to get it

540

but perhaps the GRAND LAMA of Thibet could, I jumped on the back of a Yak, rode to Lassa,

interviewed the head of the Buddhist Faith he said he wanted one himself, but did not know where to get it, go, says he, to the CZAR of Russia, present my compliments and ask him for one for yourself and one for me. I took passage in a reindeer sleigh to St.

Petersburg, saw the CZAR, he referred me to his brother monarch the KEIZAR of Austria. I jumped on a horse, galloped away to Vienna, saw the Keizar,

541

he did not know, b_t I could try the QUEEN of England, I jumped into an el ctric train, made for the metropolis

of the world, saw Her Royal, Imperial, and Republican Majesty the "Quee- of England," "Empress of India," Sovereign of Canada, Australia, and forty other countries, the most powerful and beloved ruler of the finest race of men, and the largest, mightiest, and grandest Empire the world ever saw. I now said to myself I surely shall get the article I want from the vast resources of Her Majesty, but in answer to my query she politely remarked that she did not think I should get in her dominions, but was almost certain that I could get it from the CHIEF of the Greenland Esquimeaux, I rose up in

a balloon, flew through the air across the Atlantic, saw the Chief, he could not say, but referred me to the VICEROY of the Dominion, I jumped on the back of a reindeer, trotted away to Ottawa, saw

the Viceroy, he was positively ignorant on the subject and referred me to the Mormon PROPHET. Got into an ice ship,

slid away over the snow to Utah, saw the Prophet, he had heard of it but did not know where I should get it, but I might at least ask the SACHAM of the Flat-Head Indians, I jumped into a dog-sleigh, scampered away, hailed the

Sachem, but he did not know, but perhaps the PRESIDENT of Peru did, rode on a one-man sedan to the City of Earthquakes,

saw the President, he did not know, but would I be so
good as ask the EMPEROR of Brazil, I sprang on to the
back of a llama, flopped away to Rio;

the American Emperor said he did not know himself, but
surely the SHEIKH of Timbuctoo ought to tell. I jumped
into a canoe, crossed the Atlantic,

545

reached the Negro city, asked the Sheikh, he said it was like my impudence asking him, how should he know such a thing? none of the traditions of the negro continent mentioned it, but if I thought such a thing existed I had better ask his Sublime Mightiness the SULTAN of Zanzibar, I jumped on the back of an ostrich, strode away to the

Isle of Beauty, saw the Sultan, he shook his head and referred me to the NEGUS of Abyssinia, I was carried rapidly in a head palenkeen on the heads of four

negroes to Magdala, spoke to the Negus, he referred me
to the KHEDIVE

of Egypt, I got into a water-velocipede, trod away up the
Red Sea to the city of the Pyramids, saw the Khedive, he
referred me to the SHERIF of Mecca, I at once bestrode
a donkey, cantered

away to the Sacre: City, asked the custodian of the Precious Tomb of the Great Prophet, the query nonplussed him, and he desired me to wait on the IMAUN of Muscat, I mounted a camel,

ambled across to the hot city of the Imaun, he could not say but referred me to the RAO of Cutch, I made for Bhooj on a raft, spoke to the Rao, he

had not got one, but referred me to the GUICOWAR of Gujerat and considerately lent me a pair of ten-feet stilts for the

journey. I waded from the City of Dismal Swamps and finally reached Baroda on my stilts, saw the Guicowar, he had never heard of the article, but referred me to the HIGH PRIEST of the Parsees. I got into a sedan, was borne

to Bombay, saw the head of the Parsee Faith, he had not
the article, did not believe that it existed, as it was not
mentioned in any of the sacred books of the Parsees, but
finally referred me ⊃ the BIBY of Canonore, I mounted
an Elephant

stamped down the coast, addressed the Biby, she said it
was the first time she had heard of the article, but the
MAHARAJAH of Mysore might have one. I stepped
into a palenkeen

and four men trotted away to Mysore, the Great Rajah said he had not got one, perhaps the NIZAM of Hyderabad could assist me. I got into a horse-sedan, went

to Hyderabad, saw the Nizam, he did not know and suggested the GRAND MAHUNT of Benares. I got into a horse-palenkeen, made straight for the

City of the Sacred Shrines, saw the head of the Hindoo Faith, he did not know where it could be got, but had I asked the THACKOOR of Bhrownnuggar? No!—or the Swat of Ackoond, or the Mudor of Cassala, or the Hospodar of Wallachia, or the Aboona of Gondar or the Patriarch of Constantinople, or the Archbishop of Canterbury? I said most decidedly not—that I would not waste my time consulting such insignificant magnates, then, says he, just you ask the GURO of the Sikhs. I jumped astride of a Bramah Bull, and

trotted away to Amritsar; saw the head of the Sikh Faith, he had not got the article, had not heard of it, but advised me to apply to the AMEER of Afghanistan. I got into an ox dooly and at

length reached Cabul, saw the Ameer, he had not got it, had not seen it, nor heard of it, did not believe the article existed, but the KHAN of Bokhara could speak more positively about it. I got into a Tocan or Hamockeen and was

carried by two men to Bokhara, interviewed the Khan, he said it was absurd for the Ameer to send to him, he knew nothing about it, but the SHAH of Persia probably did. I got into a mule sleigh,

glided away to Teheran, enquired of the Shah, could get no satisfaction, he never heard of it, was I sure there was such an article in existence? I told him that I wanted to find out, but I thought there must be somewhere. Oh, then, said he, try the CHIEF RABBI of Jerusalem. I got into a coach, tore away to

the Holy City of the Jews, asked the head of the Jewish Faith, he had not one, I had better ask the PASHA of Damascus. I jumped astride of a bicycle,

trundled away to the oldest city in the world; asked the Pasha, he could not say, I had better ask the EMIR of the Druses. I creeped up the Lebanon in a bullock-waggon, saw and asked the

head of the Druse Faith, he referred me to the BEY of Tunis. I got on to a tricycle, rode to Tunis, saw the Bey,

he could not tell, perhaps the POPE of Rome could. I
jumped into a ship

made for the Eternal City, asked the head of the Christian Church, His Holiness could not tell, perhaps the
GRAND SEIGNEUR of Turkey might. I stepped into a
railway steam carriage, swept

around to the Golden Horn; saw His Sublime Mightiness the PADISHAW, he

said that he had not got one and never heard of it; but when I described to him, in clear, concise and glowing terms, the real value of the article to the whole human race, he said that every person black or white, or brown, or yellow, or red, or any other colour whatever, in the world, should have one and that it was the duty of all Kings and Queens and Emperors, and Sultans, and Czars, and Keizars, and Khedives and Khans, and Shahs, and Ameers, and Deys, and Beys, and Great Chams, and Grand Lamas, to see that every one of their subjects obtained one without delay. I said those were exactly my sentiments; but where was it to be got. He again graciously assured me that he did not know, bit I might ask the GRAND MUFTI of Turkey, the fountain of all human knowledge, and custodian of the sacred Koran. I tore along in a goat-carriage, interviewed the head of

the Mahometan Faith; but in answer to my query this
Mighty Spiritual Magnate seemed taken aback; he affirmed that the Koran did not mention the article, and,
therefore, he believed that it could not exist, but had I
made a thorough search for it; had I tried the Dey of Al-
giers. I answered no! Had I tried the Doge of Venice—
the Elector of Saxony—the Begum of Oude—the Stad-
holder of Holland— the Peishwa of Poona—the Nabob
of Bengal—the Caliph of Bagdad— the Inca of Peru, or
the great Mogul. I looked at the Grand Mufti in speech-
less astonishment; he might as well have asked me if I
had enquired of Pharaoh or Nebuchadnezzer. I shook
my head and rushed from his presence, completely nonplussed, bewildered, frantic. Where on earth was I to get
the article? I had asked, and asked, and asked again, and
was tired of asking. I had travelled fifty thousand miles
by forty different modes of conveyance, consulted in
their own capitals with thirty secular monarchs, govern-
ing three-fourths of the world; and I had with earnest,
respectful enquiry approached the sacerdotal thrones of
the spiritual monarchs of the eleven principal religions
of mankind, and yet I could get no tidings of it. What
was I to do? I was now standing in front of the great
Mosque at Constantinople almost frantic with perplexity; some one approached and handed me a printed
announcement. I read it! It sent an inexpressible thrill
through me. I immediately took a steamer

for Melbourne, landed there, jumped into a cab, went straight to Cole's Book

Arcade, and saw a drawing of the very article I had ransacked the world over to obtain, and what do you think it was? It was a FLYING MACHINE! I wanted a flying machine, Mr. Cole informed me that he had not got his machine to fly yet, and that in all the world a machine was not yet invented that would fly, but that, through the active and progressive ingenuity of the human intellect, such a machine was certain to be invented in the future, and as an earnest of his strong conviction he handed me a document, which ran as follows:—

559

October 31st. 188?

  I, the undersigned, firmly believe that as man has already made
machines to run over the land and float over the water faster than
the swiftest animal, so shortly he will make machines to fly
through the air as fast, and finally faster, than the swiftest
birds do now. And I hereby offer a bonus of £1,000 to any person
who shall (in consequence of said bonus) within the next two years
invent a flying machine, to go by Electrical, Chemical, Mechanical,
or any other means, except by gas, a distance of 100 miles, and
shall come and stop in front of the Book Arcade, Bourke Street,
Melbourne, Australia, as easily and as safely as a carriage stops
there now.

  —E. W. Cole

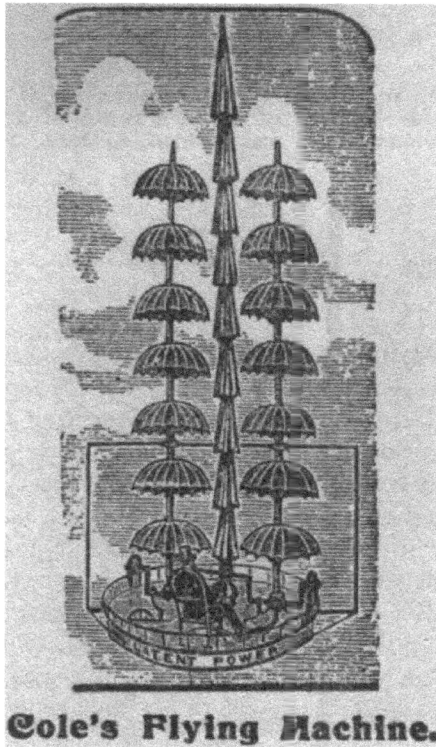

Cole's Flying Machine.

Cole's Flying Machine

A workable flying machine would be the grandest invention of the age. My offer may not bring it about, but suppose a shilling subscription was made throughout the civilised world; say twenty million people gave 1/- each. That would be one million pounds, and offer that as a bonus for a useful flying machine, that bonus, I am sure, would produce the article. The shillings would be well spent, and it would immortalise the twenty million people who put their names down.

My prophecy with regard to flying machines, as may well be seen by the original statement herewith, was made twenty-eight years before the French aviator brought his machine to Australia which was on 2nd November, 1910, or two weeks before his successful flight.

Subsequently Mr. Hammond flew over the city. He remarked: "I was to early for breakfast, and just thirty years too late to claim E. W. Cole's prize of £1,000."

I believe that the advance of flying machines will be so rapid that within the next decade they will be used with as much ease and safety as any other means of present locomotion.

I will further state that their utility will be so great as to enable China, with her three hundred millions, to succeed in taking correct statistics.

And eventually the velocity with which they will fly may materially assist in establishing the peace of the world and the Parliament of Man.

My prophecy with regard to flying machines was made in 1868, and the bonus of £1,000 (see previous page) was offered in 1882.

—E. W. Cole

The above are facsimiles of 16 of 50 of E. W. Cole's World Federation Motto-Medals.

Mr. H. Hawker,
The Man Who Flew.

Mr. Hawker was born at Brighton, Victoria, on 22nd January, 1889. He went to England in 1911, returning to Victoria in 1914, after three years experience of aviation in England. He just missed the £5000 prize given by the "Daily Mail" for a flight around the British Isles, meeting with an accident off the coast of Ireland.

Miss Linda Cole
Whose Flight with Mr. Hawker attained 4000 ft.

Mr. E. W. Cole
Prophesied Flying Machines and lived to see one of his daughters fly, and thus fulfilled his prophecy.

Miss Cole Entering The Sopwith Biplane Preparatory To Flying

Miss Cole And Mr. Harry Hawker

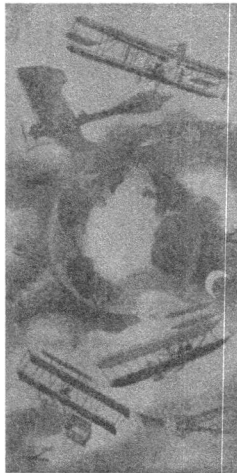

Companions In Space
Our World surrounded by one of the latest Inventions of man—"The Flying Machine."

Aviation In Melbourne
Passengers Accompany Harry Hawker To The Clouds.

It was Mr. E. W. Cole's enthusiasm and belief in the ultimate success of aerial navigation that induced Miss Linda Cole to fly with Mr. Hawker, the daring young aviator, at Elsternwick recently. Miss Cole was perfectly calm and collected when entering the biplane, and showed no signs of "nerviness." During the flight around St. Kilda, Brighton and Sandringham, and across the waters of Hobson's Bay, she conversed freely with Mr. Hawker, and commented on the panoramic views which unfolded themselves below. Miss Cole, having heard that Mr. Hawker had some intention of flying on a non-stop journey from Sydney to Melbourne—a distance of 500 miles—was most anxious to accompany him, provided the Sopwith biplane would carry two persons in addition to the tank of petrol which would, of course, be indispensable. Mr. Hawker, however, says he would not take a passenger should he undertake the journey. Miss Cole is most anxious for another sea flight, as she is of opinion that the power to see through the water to the bottom of the ocean is one of the utmost importance, as it would, in warfare, enable aviators to locate with accuracy mines in harbours and any other submerged dangers. Her most ardent wish is to become a lady aviator, and she is contemplating a trip to Europe to obtain up-to-date instruction in the aerial art.

The reason Miss Cole went up was because her father has always taken a great interest in aviation, and many years ago offered substantial prizes to constructors of airships. He has ever evinced great faith in the ultimate triumph of aerial navigation, and she is glad that his dreams are being realised. Miss Cole went up on Friday, on the thirteenth of the month. Friday and the number 13 are considered unlucky; but all big events in her life have been associated with the number 13.

Miss Cole Leaves The Aeroplane
After Having Experienced Her First Trip in the Art of Flying, at Elsternwick, on Friday, 13th February, 1914.

Minister Of Defence (Mr. Millen) Soars Aloft.

"Farman" Biplane

"Gastamabide and Mengin" Monoplane

Wright Bros.' Biplane

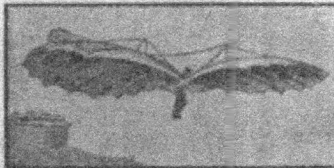

Lilienthal Gliding Machine

"Piquerez" Biplane

The R.E.P. Monoplane

COLE

Coventry Ordnance Military Biplane

"Avro" Aerial Taxicab

"Avro" Hydro-Aeroplane

"Short" Biplane

Santos Dumont's Monoplane, No. XIX

Paulman's New Aeroplane

"Ponche and Primard" Monoplane

"Short" Hydro-Aeroplane

"Curtiss" Hydro-Aeroplane

"Bleriot XI" Monoplane

The "Antoinette" Monoplane

French Military Aeroplane

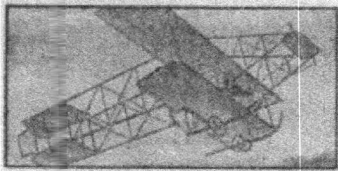

'Bristol' Military Biplane

"Vedovelli" Multiplane

Howard-Wright Biplane

"Givaudin II" Triplane

"Voisin" Type Biplane

"Farman" Hydro-Aeroplane

"Maxim" Biplane, 19 0

"Roe II" Biplane

"Vanniman" Triplane

"Tellier" Monoplane

"Goupy III" Biplane

"Herring-Curtiss" Biplane

"Rickman" Helicopter

"Jerme" Biplane

"Silver Dart" Biplane

New "Voisin" Biplane, 1911

"Cody" Biplane

"Dunne V" Biplane

Puzzles & Language

This is perhaps the Choicest Collection of Girls' Names in the English Language

To the Reader.—I beg to make one very important remark upon this immense variety of girl's names, and that
is:—Be sure and preserve the list carefully, as it will
serve from which to choose names for your daughters up
to the number of 555, without using the same name over
again. P.S.—If you should be very, very lucky, and have
more than 555 daughters, and want more names, call on
Professor Cole, at the Book Arcade, Melbourne, Australia, and he will give you an extra list.

555 NAMES

Abigail, my father's joy
Ada, happiness, rich gift
Adah, ornament
Adamana, red earth
Adela, noble cheer
Adelaide, noble cheer
Adeleve noble gift
Adelia, of noble birth
Adelina, noble manner
Adeline, noble snake
Agatha, good or honest
Agnes, pure, holy, chaste
Agneta, pure
Alberta, female Albert
Albina, white
Aldgitha, noble gift
Alethea, truth
Alexandra, helper
Alexandrina, helper
Alice, a princess
Alicia, noble cheer
Alison, holy fame
Almira, lofty
Althea, wholesome
Amabel, lovable
Amalia, work, industry
Amanda, worthy of love
Amata, she that is loved
Amelia, busy, energetic
Amice, beloved
Amicia, beloved
Amy, beloved
Anastasia, shall rise again
Andromache, heroic fight
Angel, angel
Angela, angel
Angelica, lovely, angelic
Angelina, angel
Angelletta, a messenger

Angelot, angel
Anisia, complete
Ann, grace
Anna, grace
Annabel, grace
Annabella, grace
Annaple, grace
Anne, grace
Annette, grace
Annice, grace
Annor, grace
Annora, eagle of Thor
Annie, grace
Anstace, resurrection
Antoinette, small Antonia
Antonia, inestimable
Antonina, inestimable
Arabella, eagle heroine
Arbella, God hath avenged
Athaliah, time for God
Auda, rich
Augusta, female Augustus
Aurelia, golden
Aureola, little, pretty
Aurora, fresh, brilliant
Averil, battle-maid
Avice, war refuge
Avis, war refuge
Barbara, stranger
Basilia, kingly
Bathilda, battle-maid
Bathsheba, 7th daughter
Beata, blessed
Beatrix, making happy
Becky, noosed cord
Bega, life
Belinda (uncertain)
Belle, oath of Baal
Bellona, warlike
Bernice, bringing victory
Bertalda, bright warrior

Bertha, bright, beautiful
Bessie, God's oath
Bessy, God's oath
Bethia, life
Beatrice, making happy
Benedicta, making happy
Betsy, oath of God
Bidulph, ruling wolf
Biddy, strength
Blanche, white
Bona, good
Brenda, sword
Bride, strength
Bridget, shining bright
Camilla, sacrificer
Caroline, noble-spirited
Carrie, noble-spirited
Cassandra, love-inflaming
Catharina, pure
Catherine, pure
Cecil, blind
Cecilia, blind
Cecily (or Cicily), blind
Celia, female Coelius
Celestine, heavenly
Charissa, love
Charley, man-girl
Charlotte, noble-spirited
Cherry, love
Chloe, blooming
Christabel, fair Christian
Christiana, Christian
Christina, Christian
Clare, she that is fair
Claribel, brightly fair
Clarissa, rendering famous
Clara, bright, fair
Clarice, light Clara
Clarinda, brightly fair
Claudia, female Claude
Clemeney, merciful, gentle

Clementina, merciful
Clementine, merciful
Cleopatra, father's fame
Colinette,
Columba, dove
Columbine, dove
Constancia, firm, constant
Constancia, firm
Cora, maiden
Cordelia, warm-hearted
Cornelia, born
Corinda, fair-maiden
Custance, firm
Cynthia, of Cynthus
Cyrilla, lordly
Damaria, little wife
Deborah, bee
Delia, of Delos
Delicia, delightful
Delilah, poor, small
Di, goddess
Diana, goddess
Dinah, judgement
Dionetta, of Dionysos
Dolly, gift of God
Dora, gift of God
Doralice, gift
Dorothea, divine gift
Dorothy, divine gift
Dowsabel, sweet, fair
Drusilla, dew-sprinkled
Dicia, sweet
Dulce, sweet
Duleibella, sweet, fair
Dye, goddess
Edeva, rich, gift
Edith, happiness
Edna, pleasure
Effie, fair speech
Ela, holy
Elaine, light

Elayne, light
Eleanor, light
Eleanora, light
Elfreda, hail increase
Elfrida, elf threatener
Elinor, light
Elisa, God's oath
Elizabeth, God's oath
Elle, elf friend
Ellen, light
Ellinor, light
Ellis, God the Lord
Else, noble cheer
Elspeth, God's oath
Emmelin, work ruler
Emily, work, industry
Emlyn, work, serpent
Emm, grandmother
Emma, diligent nurse
Emmeline, industrious
Emmott, grandmother
Enaid, the soul
Enid, soul
Eppie, soul
Ermengarde, public guard
Ernestine, earnest, serious
Essa, nurse
Essie, star
Esther, good fortune
Estienne, crown
Ethel, noble, noble lady
Ethelburga, protector
Etheired, threatener
Ethelind, noble snake
Ethelinde, noble snake
Etta, home rule
Eucaria, happy hand
Eucharis, happy grace
Eudora, happy gift
Eugenia, well-born
Eugenie, well-born

Eulalia, fair speed
Eunice, happy victory
Euphemia, fair fame
Euphrasia, mirth
Eva, life
Evangeline, happy herald
Eve, life-giving
Eveleen, pleasant
Evelina, little Eve
Eveline, pleasant
Eveline, little Eve
Everhilda, battle-maid
Fanny, free, liberal
Faith, faith
Faustina, lucky
Felicia, happy
Fenella, white-shouldered
Fidelia, faithful
Flora, flowers
Florence, flourishing
Florinda, pretty flower
Frances, free, liberal
Frederica, peace ruler
Frediswid, peace, strength
Frewissa, strong peace
Gabrielle, God's hero
Ganore, white wave
Gatty, spear maid
Genevieve, white wave
Georgina, thrifty wife
Georgiana, thrifty wife
Geraldine, spear power
Gerca, enclosure
Gertrude, spear maiden
Gil (or Gillet), downy
Gillespie, bishop's servant
Gillian, downy
Gladuse, lame
Godiva, divine gift
Grace, grace, favour
Griselda, stone heroine

Guoe, divine
Gunerada, war council
Guncred, war council
Gunhlda, war heroine
Gunnda, war battle-maid
Gunnoa, war protection
Gwendolen, white-browed
Gytha, happy
Hagar, a stranger
Hannah, grace, gracious
Harriet, a rich lady
Hatty, home rule
Havisia, war refuge
Helaine, light
Helen, light
Helewise, famous holiness
Henrietta, little Henry
Henny, home rule
Hepsy, my delight in her
Hermione, of Hermes
Hester, good fortune
Hetty, little Henry
Hilaria, cheerful, merry
Hilda, battle-maid
Honor, honour
Honora, honourable
Honoria, honourable
Hope, hope
Hortensia, gardener
Huldah, a weasel
Ida, happy, godlike
Inez, chaste, pure
Irene, peaceful
Isa, iron
Isabel, fair Eliza
Isabella, fair Eliza
Isadora, strong gift
Isbel, God's oath
Isobel, oath if God
Isolde, fair
Isolt, fair

Izod, fair
Jacintha, purple
Jacobina, supplanter
Jaquetta, supplanter
Jacqueline, beguiling
Jamesina, supplanter
Jane, grace of God
Janet, little Jane
Jeanette, beguiling
Jean, grace of God
Jemima, a dove
Jenny, grace of God
Jessica, grace of God
Jessie, grace of God
Jezebel, oath of Baal
Joan, the Lord's grace
Jodoca, sportive
Johanna, the Lord's grace
Joletta, violet
Joscelind, just
Josephine, addition
Josepha, addition
Joy, joy
Joyce, sportive, merry
Judith (or Judy), praise
Julia, soft-hearted
Juliana, downy-bearded
Juliet, downy-bearded
Justina, just
Kate, pure
Katharine, pure
Katherine, pure
Kathleen, pure
Katrina, pure
Katie, pure
Katrina
Kester, Christ bearer
Keturah, sweet perfume
Kezia, Cassia
Kissy, Cassia
Kitty, Pure

Laurinda, a laurel
Laura, laurel
Laurentia, laurel
Lavinia, of Latium
Leah, weary
Leonora, light
Letitia, gladness or mirth
Letiee, gladness
Levy, truth
Lilian, lily
Lilly, lily
Lizzie, oath of God
Lola, laurel
Lolinda, a laurel
Lottie, noble-spirited
Lotty, man
Louisa, famous holiness
Louise, an Amazon
Love, love
Loys, famous holiness
Lucia, shining
Lucilla, light
Lucinda, light
Lucrece, gain
Lucretia, gain
Lucy, light-shining
Lydia, born in Lydia
Mab, mirth
Mabel, beloved
Mabella, my fair maiden
Madeline, magnificent
Madge, pearl
Margaret, pearl
Maria, bitter
Marian, bitter grace
Marianne, bitter grace
Marion, bitter
Marjorie or Marjory, pearl
Martha, becoming bitter
Martina, of Mars, warlike
Mary, bitter

Matilda, battle-maid
Matty, becoming bitter
Maud (or Maud), noble
May, pearl
Melania, black
Melicent, work, strength
Melissa, bee
Melony, dark
Melva, chief
Menie, bitter
Mercy, compassion
Mercia, work rule
Meriel, nymph
Milcah, queen
Mildred, mild threatener
Millicent, work, strength
Milly, work, strength
Minella, resolute
Mingala, soft and fair
Minna, memory
Minnie, little
Miranda, to be admired
Miriam, bitter
Moina, soft
Mencha, adviser
Monica, adviser
Moore, great
Morgana, sea dweller
Morna, beloved
Moroli, sea protection
Mynette, resolute
Myra, a weeper
Mysie, pearl
Nancy (or Nanny), grace
Naomi, pleasant
Nelly, light
Nellie, light
Ninon (or Ninette), grace
Nora, honourable
Norah, honourable
Octavia, eighth-born

Olive, olive
Olympis, heavenly
Ophelia, serpent
Osberga, divine pledge
Osberta, divinely bright
Osyt, divine strength
Parne, a little stone
Patience, bearing up
Patricia, noble
Patty, becoming batter
Paulina, little Paul
Pauline, little Paul
Paula, little
Peace, peace
Peggy, pearl
Penelope, weaver
Pernel, stone
Petrina, stone
Petronela, stone
Phebe, light of life
Phemie, fair fame
Philadephia, fraternal
Philippa, lover of horses
Phillis, a little leaf
Phoebe, shining
Piety, piety
Polly, bitter
Portia, of the pigs
Priscilla, ancient
Prudence, prudent
Quenburga, queen of pledge
Rachel, ewe
Rebecca, full fed
Rebekah, enchanting
Rhoda, rose
Robina, bright fame
Rose, a rose
Rosabel, fair rose
Rosabella, fair rose
Rosalia, blooming rose
Rosalie, blooming rose

Rosalind, like a rose
Rosaline, famed serpent
Rosamond, protection
Rosamuad, rose of peace
Rosanne, rose
Rose, rose
Rosecleer, fair rose
Rosina, rose
Rowena, white skirt
Roxana, dawn of day
Ruth, watered or filtered
Sabina, religious
Sabrina, the Severn
Sally, princess
Sarah, princess
Sarai, lady or princess
Selina, moon or parsley
Selma, fair
Serena, serene
Sibella, wise old woman
Sidonia, of Sidon
Sigismunda, conquering
Sissie, little sister
Soloma, peace
Sophia, wisdom
Sophronia, of sound mind
Stella, star
Stephana, crown
Stratonice, army victory
Susie, a lily
Susan, a rose or lily
Susannah, lily
Sylvia, living in a weed
Tabitha, gazelle
Tamar, palm
Tamasine, twin
Temperance, moderation
Thalia, bloom
Thecla, divine fame
Theobalda, people's prince
Theodora, divine gift

587

Theophila, divinity-loved
Theresa, carrying corn
Thomasine, twin
Thyrza, pleasantness
Tibelda, people's prince
Tilda, mighty battle-maid
Timothea, fear God
Tirzah pleasantness
Tracy, carrying corn
Trix, blessed
Tryphena, dainty
Tryphosa, dainty
Ulrica, noble ruler
Una, famine
Urania, heavenly
Ursula, she bear
Valeria, female Valerius
Vanora, white wave
Vashti, one that drinks
Venetia, blessed
Venice, blessed
Veronica, a true image
Verosa, true
Vevina, melodious woman
Victoria, conqueror
Vida, life
Violet, violet
Viola, a violet
Virginia, flourishing
Walburg, gracious
Wenefride, white wave
Werburgha, protection
Wilfred, white stream
Wilhelmina, defendress
Williamina, defendress
Wilmett, cap of resolution
Winefride, lover of peace
Winifrid, white stream
Zenobia, sire's ornament
Zerah, rising of light
Zillah, shadow

Zoe, life
Zora, dawn

Be Sure And Pick A Nice Name For The Baby

**This is perhaps the Choicest Collection of
Boys' Names in the English Language**

To the Reader.—I beg to make one very important remark upon this immense variety of boy's names, and
that is:—Be sure and preserve the list carefully, as it will
serve from which to choose names for your sons up to
the number of 555, without using the same name over
again. P.S.—If you should be very, very lucky, and have
more than 555 sons, and want more names, call on Professor Cole, at the Book Arcade, Melbourne, Australia,
and he will give you an extra list.

555 NAMES

Aaron, lofty, inspired
Abel, vanity
Abelard, noble

Abiathar, sire of plenty
Abijah, child of God
Abijam, father of the sea
Abimelech, king's father
Abner, father of light
Abraham, sire of many
Abram, elevated father
Absalom, father of peace
Achiles, without lips
Adam, red earth
Adin, tender, delicate
Adolphus, noble wolf
Adrian, rich or wealthy
Aeneas, praise
Ahaz, visionary
Alan, cheerful
Alaric, noble ruler
Alban, white
Alberic, elf king, or all rich
Albert, nobly, bright
Aleuin, hall friend
Aldebert, nobly bright
Aldhelm, noble helmet
Alexander, helper of men
Alexis, helper
Alfred, good counseller
Algernon, with whiskers
Alick, helper of men
Allan (or Allen), cheerful
Almeric, work ruler
Alphonso, eager, willing
Alphin, e ?
Amadas, husbandman
Amasa, a burden
Ambrose, immortal, divine
Amos, a burden
Andrew, manly, valiant
Angus, excellent virtue
Anselm, divine helmet
Anstice, resurrection
Anthony, inestimable

Antony, inestimable
Appolos, of Apollo
Aquila, eagle
Archibald, powerful, bold
Aristides, son of the best
Arkles, noble fame
Arnold, strong as an eagle
Artemus, gift of Diana
Arth, high
Arthur, high, noble
Asa, physician or healer
Ascelin, servant
Asher, blessed, fortunate
Ashur, black or blackness
Athanasius, undying
Athelstan, noble stone
Athelwold, noble power
Aubrey, ruler of spirits
Audrey, noble threatener
Augustin, venerable
Augustus, majestic
Aureilus, golden
Austin, venerable
Aymar, work ruler
Bab, stranger
Baldie, sacred prince
Baldred, prince council
Baldric, prince ruler
Baldwin, bold friend
Banquo, white
Baptist, baptiser
Barak, lightning
Bardolf, bright helper
Barnabas, son of consolation
Barnard, bold as a bear
Barry, looking bright
Bartholomew, warlike son
Barthram, bright raven
Bartley, son of furrows
Bartram, bright raven
Barzillai, son of iron

Basi, kingly
Bat, son of furrows
Beavis, beautiful
Ben, son of the right hand
Benedict, blessed
Benjamin, same as Ben
Bennet, blessed
Benoni, son of sorrow
Berenger, bear spear
Berial, son of evil
Bernard, bold as a bear
Bertran, bright raven
Bertram, fair and pure
Blase (or Blaze), babbler
Bohemond, God's love
Boniface, well-doer
Botolph, ruling wolf
Boyd, yellow
Brithric, bright king
Brockwell, champion
Bruno, brown
Brush, immortal
Bryan, strong
Cadoe, war
Cadogar, war
Cadwallader, a general
Caesar, hairy
Cain, possession
Caleb, dog
Calvin, bald
Canute, hill
Caradoc, beloved
Carmichael, Michael's friend
Caswallon, hating lord
Cecil, blind
Charinas, grace
Charles, noble spirited
Christian, of Christ
Christopher, Christ bearer
Chrysostom, gold mouth
Clarence, illustrious

Claude, lame
Clement, merciful gentle
Colbert, cool, bright
Colborn, black bear
Colin, dove
Colomb, dove
Conachar, strong help
Coniah, appointed
Conmor, strength great
Connal, chief's courage
Connor, slaughter hound
Conrad, able speed
Constant, firm, faithful
Constantine, firm
Cornelius, horn
Cradock, beloved
Crispin, curly-haired
Cuthbert, noted splendour
Cymbeline, lord of the sun
Cyprian, of Cyprus
Cyril, lordly
Cyrus, the sun
Dan, a judge
Daniel, the judging God
Darcy, dark
Darius, king, preserver
David, beloved, the darling
Dennis, of Dionysos
Derrick, people's wealth
Dick, firm ruler
Didymus, twin
Diggory, the almost lost
Dionysius, of Dionysos
Dodd, of the people
Dominic, Sunday child
Donald, proud chief
Dougal, black stranger
Douglas, dark grey
Dudley, people's ruler
Duff, black
Dugold, black stranger

Duncan, brown chief
Ebenezer, stone of help
Edgar, protector of wealth
Edmund, rich protection
Edward, happy keeper
Edwin, rich friend
Egbert, formidably bright
Eldred, fierce in battle
Eli, a foster son
Elias, God the Lord
Elihu, He is my God
Elijah, God the Lord
Elisha, God the Saviour
Elizur, God my rock
Ellis, God the Lord
Emanuel, God with us
Emilius, work
Enoch, dedicated
Enos, mortal man
Ephriam, very fruitful
Erasmus, amiable, lovely
Erastus, lovely, amiable
Eric, era king, rich
Ernest, serious
Esaias, salvation of God
Esau, covered with hair
Esbert, bright for ever
Esdras, rising of light
Etheired, noble council
Eugene, well-born
Eusebius, pious
Eustace, healthy, strong
Evan, young warrior
Everard, strong as a boar
Ezekiel, strength of God
Ezra, rising of light
Farquhar, manly
Feargus, man of strength
Felim, ever good
Felix, happy, prosperous
Ferdinand, brave

Fergus, man's strength
Fernando, brave
Festus, joyful
Fingal, white stranger
Flavian, yellow
Francis, free, liberal
Frank, free
Franklin, free
Frederic, peaceful ruler
Frewen, free friend
Fulbert, bright resolution
Faulk, people's guard
Gabriel, hero of God
Gaius, rejoiced
Gamaliel, gift of God
Garratt, spear firm
Gavin, hawk of battle
Geoffrey, God's peace
George, husbandman
Gerald, spear power
Germaine, German
Gervas, war eagerness
Gibbon, bright pledge
Gideon, destroyer
Gilbert, bright as gold
Gilchrist, servant of Christ
Giles, a kid
Gillespie, bishop's servant
Gillies, servant of Jesus
Gisborn, pledge bearer
Goddard, pious, virtuous
Gedfrey, God's peace
Godric, divine king
Godwin, divine friend
Greg, fierce
Gregory, watchful
Griffith, strong-faithed
Grimbald, self-controlled
Gustavus, a warrior
Guy, a leader
Hadassah, myrt e

Halbert, bright stone
Hamyn, home
Hanan, grace
Hannibal, grace of Baal
Harold, a champion
Harry, home rule
Harvey, bitter
Hayron, home
Heber, a companion
Hector, a defender
Henry, a rich lord
Herbert, bright warrior
Hercules, lordly fame
Hereward, sword guardian
Herman, a warrior
Herodias, of a hero
Herodotus, noble gift
Hezekiah, strength of God
Hilary cheerful
Hildebert, a nobleman
Hildebrand, a warbrand
Hiram, most noble
Hodge, spear of fame
Homer a pledge
Horace worthy of love
Horatio worthy of love
Hoshea salvation
Hubbard, mind bright
Hubert, mind bright
Hugh, mind
Hugo, mind
Humphrey, home peace
Ian, grace of God
Ignatius, fiery
Immanuel, God with us
Increase, more faith
Ingram, ng's raven
Inigo, fiery
Innocent, harmless
Ira, watchful
Isaac, laughter

Issiah, salvation of God
Israel, soldier of God
Ivan, gift of God
Ives, archer
Izaak, laughter
Jabez, sorrow
Jacob, supplanter
James, superior
Japhet, extender
Jarratt, spear firm
Jason, healer
Jasper, treasure master
Jeffrey, good peace
Jehu, the Lord is he
Jenkin, Grace of God
Jeremiah, exalted of God
Jerome, holy name
Jervis, spear war
Jesse, wealth
Joachim, God will judge
Joab, son of God
Job, persecuted
Joel, strong-willed
John, the Lord's grace
Jonah (or Jonas), dove
Jonathan, gift of God
Jordan, descender
Joscelin, just
Joseph, addition
Joshua, a Saviour
Josiah, fire of God
Judah, praised
Julian, downy bearded
Julius, downy bearded
Justin, just
Justus, just
Kay, rejoicing
Kenelm, a defender
Kenneth, a leader
Laban, white
Lachlan, warlike

597

Lambert, illustrious
Lancelot, servant
Laurence, laurel crowned
Lawrence, laurel crowned
Lazarus, God will help
Leancer, lion-hearted
Lear, sea
Leonard, lion-strong
Leopold, bold for men
Levi, adhesion
Lewis, people's refuge
Lionel, lion
Llawelyn, lightning
Lloyd, grey
Lodowic, famed piety
Lorenzo, laurel crowned
Lot, lion
Lothar, glorious warrior
Lothario, great warrior
Louis, famous holiness
Lubin, love friend
Lucian, light
Ludovic, cold warrior
Luke, light
Luther, glorious warrior
Maddox, beneficent
Madoc, beneficent
Magnus, great
Malachi, angel of God
Malcom, of Colbumia
Manfred, mighty peace
Manual, God with us
Marcus, of Mars, a hammer
Mark, warlike
Marmaduke, sea leader
Martin, great martial
Martyn, great martial
Matthew, gift of God
Matthias, gift of God
Maurice, dark coloured
Maynard, great firmness

Meredith, sea protector
Merlin, sea hill
Michael, who is like God
Miles, crusher
Moore, great
Morgan, seaman
Morris, sea warrior
Moses, drawn from water
Napoleon, forest king
Narcissus, daffodil
Nathan, a gift
Nathanael, gift of God
Nero, strength, fortitude
Nicodemus, conqueror
Nicholas, conquered
Nicol, conquered
Niel, brave, dark
Niell, brave
Nigel, black
Noah, rest, comfort
Noel, Christmas-born
Norman, a Northman
Obadiah, servant of God
Octavius, the eighth-born
Odo, rich
Olave, ancestor's relic
Oliver, olive tree
Orlando, fame of the land
Orson, dear
Osbert, divinely bright
Osborn, divine bear
Oscar, bounding warrior
Osfred, divine peace
Oslaf, divine legacy
Osmond, divine perfection
Osric, divine rule
Oswald, divine power
Osyth, young warrior
Palmerin, sign of victory
Pancras, all-ruler
Pascoe, Easter child

599

Passion, suffering
Patrick, noble
Paul, little
Payne, countryman
Percival, holy cup-bearer
Peregrine, stranger
Peter, stone
Phelim, good.
Philadephius, brotherly
Phillip, lover of horses
Phineas, mouth of brass
Pius, pious
Pierce (or Piers), stone
Pilgrim, traveller
Polycarp, much fruit
Pompey, of Pompeii
Quentin, fifth-born
Ralph, help, counsel
Ranald, judging power
Randal, house wolf
Raphael, healing of God
Ravelin, council wolf
Raymond, wise protector
Raymund, quiet peace
Rayner, judge warrior
Redmond, counsel
Redwald, council, power
Reginald, judging power
Renfred, peace, judgement
Restyn, restored to
Reuben, behold a son
Reynard, firm judge
Reynold, judging power
Richard, stern king
Robert, bright in fame
Roderick, famous king
Rodolph, wolf of fame
Rodolphus, famous wolf
Roger, spear of fame
Roland, fame of the land
Rollo, wolf of fame

Rolph, wolf of fame
Ronan, seal
Ronald, judge power
Roswald, horse power
Rowland, fame of the land
Roy, red
Rufus, red-haired
Rupert, bright fame
Sampson, splendid sun
Samuel, asked of God
Saul, longed for
Saunders, helper of men
Sayer, conquering army
Seabert, bright victory
Seaforth, peace victory
Seaward, defender
Sebastian, venerable
Seth, appointed
Shawn, grace of God
Sholto, sower
Sibbald, conquering
Sigismund, conquering
Silas, living in a wood
Sim, obedient
Simeon, obedient
Simon, obedient
Solomon, peaceable
Stephen, crown
Swain, youth
Swithun, strong friend
Sylvanus, god of the wood
Sylvester, a rustic
Tancard, grateful guard
Tancred, grateful speech
Teague, poet
Terence, tender
Thaddaeus, praise
Theobald, people's prince
Theodore, divine gift
Theodosius, genius of God
Theodric, people's ruler

Theodoric, people's ruler
Theophilus, friend of God
Thias, gift of God
Thomas, a twin
Thorold, Thor's power
Thurstan, Thor's jewel
Tibal, people's prince
Tiernan, kingly
Timothy, God-fearing
Titus, safe
Tobias, goodness of God
Tom, a twin
Tristran, grave, sad
Tudor, divine gift
Turgar, Thor's spear
Tybalt, people's prince
Ulfric, wolf ruler
Ulick, mind, reward
Ulysses a hater
Urban, of the town
Uriah, light of God
Uric, noble ruler
Valentine, healthy, strong
Victor, conqueror
Vincent, conquering
Virgil, flourishing
Vivian, lively
Vortigern, great king
Vyvyan, living
Waldemar, powerful fame
Walstan, slaughter stone
Walter, powerful warrior
Warner, protector
Warren, protecting friend
Water, powerful warrior
Wattles, powerful warrior
Wawyn, hawk of battle
Wayland, artful
Wenceslaus, crown, glory
Wilfred, resolute peace
Wilfrith, resolute peace

Willfroy, resolute peace
William, protector
Willibald, much power
Wilmot, resolute mood
Winifred, friend of peace
Wulstan, comely
Yestin, just
Zachariah, man of God
Zaccheus, pure, clean
Zebulon, dwelling
Zechariah, man of God
Zedekiah, justice of God
Zephaniah, secret of God
Zerah, rising of light
Zoroaster, gold star

Look And See The Meaning Of Your Own Name

Cole's Game Of Hats And Bonnets
Or Husbands And Wives

One Hundred Little Ladies
Showing the 24 various modes by which they came into Cole's Book Arcade

One hundred *Little* ladies,
  All clever, learned and trained,
Half *WALKED* in-to Cole's Book Arcade,
  And fifty then remained.

Fifty *Thoughtful* little ladies,
  All lovers of book-lore,
Ten *RAN* in-to Cole's Book Arcade,

And there remained two-score.

Forty *Pretty* ladies,
  Racing but not flirty,
Ten *RACED* in-to Cole's Book Arcade,
  An then there were but thirty.

Thirty *Famous* ladies,
  Swimming in the Plenty.
Ten *SWAM* in-to Cole's Book Arcade,
  And then there were but twenty.

Twenty *Wealthy* ladies,
  Jumping in velveteen,
One *JUMPED* in-to Cole's Book Arcade,
  And then there were nineteen.

Nineteen *Noble* ladies,
  Going out a-skating,
One *SKATED* in-to Cole's Book Arcade,
  And then there were but eighteen.

Eighteen *Royal* ladies,
  All dancing with the Queen,
On *Danced* in-to Cole's Book Arcade,
  And there were seventeen.

Seventeen *Grand* ladies,
  Driving a bullock team,
One *DROVE* in-to Cole's Book Arcade,
  And then there were sixteen.

Sixteen *Gentle* ladies,
  All hopping on the green,
One *HOPPED* in-to Cole's Book Arcade,
  And then there were fifteen.

Fifteen *Modest* ladies,
  All creeping out unseen,
One *CREPT* in-to Cole's Book Arcade,

605

And then there were fourteen.

Fourteen *Handsome* ladies,
 All floating down a stream,
One *FLOATED* in-to Cole's Book Arcade,
 And then there were thirteen.

Thirteen *Lovely* ladies,
 All leaping out to delve,
One *LEAPED* in-to Cole's Book Arcade,
 And then there were but twelve.

Cole's Game Of Hats And Bonnets
Or Husbands And Wives

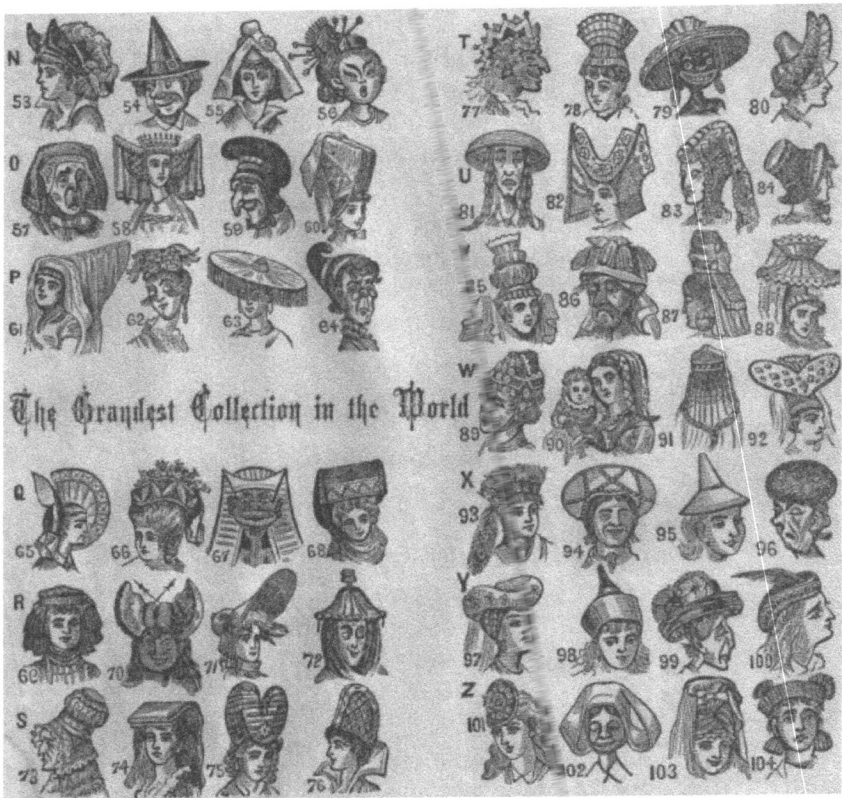

Twelve fine *Blooming* ladies,
 Flitting out for leaven,
One *FLITTED* in-to Cole's Book Arcade,
 And then there were eleven.

Eleven *Frightened* ladies,
 Dodging a lion when—
One *DODGED* in-to Cole's Book Arcade,
 And then there were but ten.

Ten most *Charming* ladies,
 All skipping in a line,
One *SKIPPED* in-to Cole's Book Arcade,
 And then there were but nine.

Nine most *Splendid* ladies,
 All swinging on a gate,
One *SWUNG* in-to Cole's Book Arcade,
 And then there were but eight.

Eight most *Superb* ladies,
 Flying under heaven,
One *FLEW* in-to Cole's Book Arcade,
 And then there were but seven.

Seven *English* ladies,
 All tripping out for sticks,
One *TRIPPED* in-to Cole's Book Arcade,
 And then there were but six.

Six fine *Irish* ladies,
 All going for a dive,
One *DIVED* in-to Cole's Book Arcade,
 And then there were but five.

Five fine *Scottish* ladies,
 All sailing to explore,
One *SAILED* in-to Cole's Book Arcade,
 And then there were but four.

Four fine *Yellow* ladies,
  All steaming on the sea,
One *STEAMED* in-to Cole's Book Arcade,
  And then there were but three.

Three fine *Jet-black* ladies,
  All riding on a moo,
One *RODE* in-to Cole's Book Arcade,
  And then there were but two.

Two most *Comic* ladies,
  Sliding about for fun,
One *SLID* in-to Cole's Book Arcade,
  And then there was but one.

One most *Frisky* lady,
  The nicest, last, and best,
She *BOUNCED* in-to Cole's Book Arcade,
  And read books with the rest.

Cole's Game Of Hats And Bonnets
Or Husbands And Wives

One Hundred Sorts of Hats

PROCLAMATION BY AUTHORITY.

Be it known unto all of you that to find your own portrait and the fashion of your hat or bonnet, your Christian name and the Alphabet are used.

The Alphabet is divided into four parts for the second letter of each person's name as follows:—The letters A B C D E F belong to No. 1 portrait in each row, and in the case of the first of the letter A include such names as Abigail, Ada, Aaron, Abraham, Adolphus. The letters G

H I J K L belong to the second portrait in each row, and in the case of the second portrait, of the letter A include such name as Agnes, Alice, Ahaz, Alfred. The letters M N O P Q R belong to the third portrait of each row, and in the case of the letter A include such names as Amy, Anna, Arabella, Amos, Andrew, Arthur. The letters S T U V W X Y Z belong to the fourth portrait in each row, and in the case of the letter A include such names as Athalia, Augusta, Asa, Augusta. The same rule is followed with each letter of the Alphabet: for instance, the first portrait in the row B belongs to such names as Barbara, Bessie, Bartholomew, Benjamin, and so on throughout the whole collection of portraits.

If a woman is looking for her future husband, she must find the number of her own portrait and then the corresponding number amongst the men's, and THAT IS TO BE HER HUSBAND: for instance, if her own portrait is No. 27, No. 27 amongst the men's is the portrait of her future darling. The same rule is to be followed by the men. If a man's portrait is No. 93, No. 93 amongst the ladies' IS TO BE HIS WIFE, his own future angel.

Cole's Game Of Hats And Bonnets
Or Husbands And Wives

If the persons who consult this oracle are single, the sweetheart that falls to their lot will be their first husband or wife, and if they are married it will be their second husband or wife, and if they have been married twice, it will be their third one, and so on up to 144 times of being married; and after that no one will be allowed to consult this oracle, look at it, speak of it, or even think about it, such objectionable persons being entirely excluded from its benefits.

Persons who consult this oracle must accept the husband or wife that falls to their lot just the same as if

611

they married them in the usual way, but if dissatisfied on account of ugliness, dress, or any other cause the consulter, by doing penance in the shape of a pilgrimage to a certain place in the exact centre of the world and paying a small sum, can obtain a DIVORCE.

The place to which the pilgrimage is to be made is Cole's Book Arcade, Bourke Street, Melbourne, Australia, where they must buy a book of some kind, and that act DIVORCES them at once.

Bashful persons need not mention their pilgrimage to the Book Arcade, when they purchase the book, unless they choose.

Anyone having obtained a DIVORCE will be allowed to choose out of 9 other portraits. If the number of the portrait that fell to their lot was 8, they can choose any other number ending with 8, as 18, 28, 38, 48, 58, 68, 78, 88 and 98, or if their first number was 65 they can choose from 5, 15, 25, 35, 45, 55, 75, 85, 95 and so on; whatever their number was, they may choose from the corresponding figures throughout the table.

If, after making a choice out of the 9 portraits, anyone is still dissatisfied, by making 10 pilgrimages to the Book Arcade, or by buying and giving away 10 copies of this Funny Picture Book, they can claim the indulgence of a GRAND DIVORCE and choose which they like out of the whole 104 portraits.

Given under our Royal hand and Seal at the Palace of the Book Arcade, this 21st day of November, 1890.— COLE, REX.

Riddles And Catches

Why are cowardly soldiers like butter?
Because they run when exposed to fire.

Why is hot bread like a caterpillar?
Because it's the grub that makes the butter

fly.

Why are ripe potatoes in the ground like
thieves?
Because they ought to be taken up.

Why is an acquitted prisoner like a gun?
Because he is taken up, charged, and then
let off.

Why is a beggar like a barrister?
Because he pleads for his daily bread.

Why are lawyers like scissors?
Because they never cut each other, but
only what is placed between them.

Why is a newspaper like an army?
Because it has leaders, columns, and re-
views.

Why is a prosy story-teller like a railway
tunnel?
Because he is a great bore.

Why is a dun like a woodcock?
Because he bores with his bill.

Why is grass like a mouse?
Because the cat'll (cattle) eat it.

Why is the sun like a good loaf?
Because it's light when it rises.

Why is a plum-cake like the ocean?
Because it contains many curra(e)nts.

Why are tears like potatoes?
Because they spring from the eyes.

Why is Queen Victoria like a hat?
Because they both have crowns.

What is the difference between a steep hill
and a large pill?
One is hard to get up, the other is hard to
get down.

What is the difference between a pastry-
cook and a billsticker?
One puffs up paste, the other pastes up
puffs.

What is the difference between an auction
and seasickness?
One is the sale of effects and the other is
the effects of a sail.

Why is a photographic album like a
drainer on a bar counter?
Because it is often a receptacle for empty
mugs.

Why is an interesting book like a toper's
nose?
Because it is read (red) to the end.

What relation is your uncle's brother to
you, if he is not your uncle?
Your father.

What is the best throw of the dice?
To throw them away.

What tree clothes half the world?—
Cotton.
What tree gives milk? The cow tree.
What tree is a city in Ireland?—Cork.
What plant is a letter of the alphabet?—
The Tea (T).

What kind of bat flies without wings?—A brickbat.

Why is a dog biting his own tail like a good manager?
Because he makes both ends meet.

Why is a dog's tail like the pith of a tree?
Because it's the farthest from the bark.

Why does a dog's tail resemble happiness?
Because, run after it as he will, he cannot catch it.

If the Devil lost his tail, where should he go to find a new one?
To a gin palace, for bad spirits are retailed there.

What key is hardest to turn?—A donkey.

Why is a whirlpool like a donkey?
Because it is an eddy.

What is it that smells most when you go
into a chemist's shop?
Your nose.

Why does a donkey prefer thistles to
corn?
Because he's an ass.

Why is a lollypop like a horse?
Because the more you lick it, the faster it
goes.

Why is a well-trained horse like a benevolent man?
Because it stops at the sound of woe.

I went to a wood and got it, I sat down to
look for it, and brought it home because I
could not find it—
A thorn in my foot.

Why is a naughty boy like a postage
stamp?
Because he is licked and put in the corner
to make him stick to his letters.

What is the difference between twice
twenty-eight and twice eight and twenty.
Twenty; because twice twenty eight is
fifty-six, and twice eight and twenty is
thirty-six.

What grows less tired the more it works?
A carriage wheel.

What is that which increases the more you
take from it?
A hole.

Why is a tight boot like an oak-tree?

Because it produces a-corn.

Who killed one-fourth of the people in the world?
Cain, when he killed Abel, there being then only four people in it.

Why is a retired milkman like the whale that swallowed Jonah?
Because he took the profit out of the water.

Where was Moses when the candle went out?
In the dark.

Why is your ear like a band of music?
Because it has a drum in it.

Why are book-keepers like chickens?
Because they have to scratch for a living.

Why is coffee like an axe with a dull edge?
Because it must be ground before it is used.

Why is a red herring like a mackintosh?
Because it keeps one dry all day.

Where are balls and routs supplied gratis?
On the field of battle.

Why is an omnibus like a medical student?
Because it is crammed and allowed to pass.

When has a person got as many heads as there are days in the year?

COLE

On the 31st of December.

What word is shorter for having a syllable
added to it?
Short.

If I shoot at three birds on a tree, and kill
one, how many will remain?
None; they will all fly away.

What should you keep after you have
given it to another?
Your word.

Which would travel fastest—a man with
one sack of flour on his back, or a man
with two sacks?
The man with two sacks, as they would be
lighter than one sack of flour.

Did you ever see a bun dance on a table?
I often see abundance on the table.

What does your ship weigh before she sets
sail?
She weighs anchor.

What is an old woman like who is in the
midst of a river?
Like to be drowned.

What is the difference between a schoolmaster and an engine driver?
One trains the mind, and the other minds
the train.

Who was the first man who went round
the world?
The man in the moon.

Important Notice

Wanted known to all of the name of
Crooks, that Cole's Book Arcade contains
80,000 sorts of books.
Wanted known to all not of the name of
Crooks, that Cole's Book Arcade contains
80,000 sorts of books.
Wanted known to all of the name of Blair
that they can get almost any book they
want there.
Wanted known to all not of the name of
Blair that they can get almost any book
they want there.
Wanted known to all of the name of Fitz-
gerald, Cole's was the first Book Arcade
opened in the World.
Wanted known to all not of the name of
Fitzgerald, Cole's is still the only Book
Arcade in the World.
Wanted all intelligent persons of the name
of Hall, to give Cole's Unique Book Ar-
cade an early call.
Wanted all intelligent persons not of the
name of Hall, to give Cole's Unique Book
Arcade a very early call.

Riddles About Babies And Ladies

Why is a new-born baby like a gale of
wind?
Because it begins with a squall.

When is a baby not a baby?
When it is a little duck.

Why is an infant like a diamond?

Because it is a dear little thing.

When is a soldier like a baby?
When he is in arms.

When is butter like Irish children?
When it is made into little Pats.

Why is a church-clock like a little boy
often receiving a beating?
Because it's hands move over it's face.

Why is a boy like a potato?
Because they both wear jackets.

Why is the earth like a school black-
board?
Because the children of men multiply
upon the face of it.

Why does a lad es' school, out for a walk,
resemble the notes of a flute?
Because it goes two, two, two, two (toot-
oot-oot-oot).

What tree is a lady's name?—Olive.

When do young ladies eat a musical instrument?
When they have a Piano-for-tea.

Why is a four-quart jug like a lady's side-
saddle?
Because it holds a gall-on.

Why is a vain young lady like a confirmed
drunkard?
Because neither of them is satisfied with a
moderate use of the glass.

Why is a flirt like a hollow India-rubber
ball?
Because she is very empty and has a deal
of bounce.

What is the difference between a soldier
and a fashionable young lady?
One faces the powder and the other powders the face.

Why does an engine resemble a young
lady?
Because it has a train behind, and puffs in
the air (hair).

If a bear were to go into a linen-draper's
shop, what would he want?
He would want muzzlin'.

What is the difference between a bantam
cock, and a dirty housemaid?
One is a domestic foul and the other a foul
domestic.

What were the first words Adam said to
Eve?
Nobody knows.

How is it proved that woman was created
before man?
Because Eve was the first maid (made).

What Christian name is spelt the same
way backwards and forwards?
Hannah.

What is the difference between a person
late for the train and a school-mistress?
One misses the train and the other trains

the misses.

What Miss is always making blunders?
Mistake.

What Miss plays more tricks than a
schoolboy?
Mischief.

What miss occasions a great many quarrels?
Mismanagement.

What is that which ladies look for, and
never wish to find?
A hole in their stocking.

What is that which a man nearly always
wears in his sleep, frequently takes off
and never puts on again?
His beard.

This nice looking man with a beard,
Remarked, "It's just as I feared;
Four larks and a hen, two owls and a

wren,
Have all built their nests in my beard."

What is that which has neither flesh nor
bone, and yet has four fingers and a
thumb?
A glove.

Why are ladies' dresses about the waist
like a meeting?
Because there is a gathering there, and
sometimes a good deal of bustle.

How does a well-fitting bonnet lose its
identity?
Because it 'becomes" the lady who wears
it.

What is the sweetest thing in bonnets this
season'
The ladies' faces.

Why is a kiss like a rumour?
Because it goes from mouth to mouth.

What is the difference between an accepted and rejected lover?
The one kisses his misses, and the other
misses his kisses.

Why are pretty girls like fire-works?
Because they soon go off.

Why are good resolutions like fainting
ladies?
Because they want carrying out.

Why are lovers like apples?
Because they are often paired (pared).

Why is first love like a potato?
Because it shoots from the eyes and becomes all the less by pairing (paring).

Which age do most girls wish to attain?
Marri-age.

What kind of men do women like best?
Husband-men.

What ties two people together, yet touches
one?
A wedding ring.

Why should a man never marry a woman
named Ellen?
Because by doing so he rings his own Nell
(knell).

Why is the bridegroom more expensive
than the bride?
Because the bride is given away, while the
bridegroom is usually sold.

Why are ladies like bells?
Because you seldom know what metal
they are made of till you ring them.

What money lasts longest when you get
it?
Matrimony.

Why is matrimony like a besieged city?
Because those who are in it wish to be
out, and those who are out wish to be in.

Why are some women like facts?
Because they are stubborn things.

Why are rough seats like domineering

wives?
Because they wear the breeches.

Why are husband and wife ten, instead of
one?
Because the wife is number one and the
husband goes for nought.

Why was the Archbishop of Canterbury
like the late Prince Consort?
Because he married the Queen.

Why is a nugget of gold found at Bendigo
like the Prince of Wales?
Because it is the produce of Victoria and
like to become a sovereign.

Why are ladies great thieves?
Because they steel their petticoats, bone
their stays, and crib their babies.

In what month do ladies talk the least?
In February; because it's the shortest.

What is the difference between ladies and
clocks?
One makes us remember time, and the
other makes us forget it.

Why is an empty room like another full of
married people?
Because there is not a single person in it.

Popular Errors

The commonly received notion that a man may
marry his first cousin, but must not marry his second is
not true; but it is quite true that Cole's Book Arcade is in

Bourke Street, Melbourne, about half-way between Swanston and Elizabeth Sts.

The rumour that a Yankee Gentleman had invented a machine to take the noise out of thunder has turned out not to be true; but it is quite true that Cole's Book Arcade is open from nine in the morning to ten at night, every working day in the year.

The fact that Cole's Book Arcade contains 80,000 sorts of books is not the cause of the sea being salt—of coca-nuts containing milk— of the growth of big gooseberries, nor of the multitude of great big fibs told annually about a sea-serpent.

It is not true that cats will suck the breath of children when they are asleep, but it is quite true that Cole's Book Arcade contains one interesting cat and 80,000 sorts of interesting books.

N.B.—The likeness of Cole's Cat can be seen on page 153.

Riddles And Catches

Which is the greatest peer that England
ever produced?
Shakespeare

What is the grandest verse in existence?
The universe.

What is the greatest stand ever made for
civilisation?
The inkstand.

What is that which, although black itself,
enlightens the world?
Ink.

What is that which is full of knowledge,
and yet knows nothing?

A book-case.

What is that which you and every living
man have seen, but can never see again?
Yesterday.

What is that which no man ever did see,
which never was, but always is to be?
To-morrow.

What thing is that that is lower with a
head than without one?
A pillow.

What volume is sure to bring tears to your
eyes?
A volume of smoke.

What is that which has form without substance, and size without weight?
A shadow.

Name me and you break me.
Silence.

What is that which renders life inert, and
yet restores it?
Sleep.

Formed long ago, yet made today,
  Employed while others sleep,
What few would like to give away,
  Nor any wish to keep.
A bed.

What is that which flies high, flies low,
wears shoes, and has no feet?
Dust.

What is that of which the common sort is

best?
Sense.

What is that which we often return yet
never borrow?
Thanks.

Name that bird which, if you do not, you
must die?
Swallow.

What is that which you cannot hold for
ten minutes although it is "as light as a
feather?"
Your breath.

What is that which never was seen, felt,
nor heard, never was and never will be,
and yet has a name?
Nothing.

What is that which Adam never saw,
never possessed, and yet gave two to each
of his children?
Parents.

What is that we wish for, and when we
have obtained we never know we have it?
Sleep.

When is it that a person ought not to keep
his temper?
When it is a bad one.

What is yours, and is used by others more
than yourself?
Your name.

Can a man's pocket be empty when he's
got something in it?

Yes: when he's got a big hole in it.

What is better than presence of mind in a
railway accident?
Absence of body.

Melbourne, Hotham, Collingwood, Prah-
ran, Richmond, Emerald Hill, and Cole's
Book Arcade, all begins with an A.

Why is a penny like a black cat at Cole's
Book Arcade?
Because it has a head and a tail.

Why is Cole's Book Arcade like a Crocodile?
Because it can't jump over the moon.

Why is Cole's Book Arcade like a learned
man?
Because it is well stocked with literature.

What is that which goes every morning at

eight o'clock from the Post Office to
Cole's Book Arcade, and every evening at
six o'clock fom the Parliament House to
Cole's Book Arcade, without moving?
Bourke Street.

How many s des are there to Cole's Book
Arcade?
Four. 1st, the right side; 2nd, the left side;
3rd, the outside; and 4th, the inside, where
the 80,000 sorts of books are.

What are the oldest tops in the world?
Mountain tops.

Which is the oldest table in the world?
The multiplication table.

What kind of ship has two mates and no
captain?
A courtship

What is that which is lengthened by being
cut at both ends?
A ditch.

What is that which one can divide, but
cannot see where it has been divided?
Water.

What is that which gives a cold, cures a
cold, and pays the doctor?
A draft.

What is the worst kind of fare for a man to
live on?
Warfare.

What vice is it that the greatest criminals
shun?

Ad-vice.

What is that which is often found where it
is not?
Fault.

What is that which we often catch hold of,
and yet never see?
A passing remark.

What is that which is often brought to the
table, often cut, but never eaten?
A pack of cards.

What is that which is full of holes and yet
holds water?
A sponge.

What window in your house is like the
sun?
The skylight.

What word is it of five letters, of which
two being removed one only one will remain?
St-one.

What is that from which if the whole be
taken some will remain?
The word "wholesome".

What word contains all the vowels in their
proper order?
Facetious.

How would you express in one word having met a doctor of medicine?
Metaphysician.

Why is a nobleman like a book?

Because he has a title.

Why is the alphabet like the mail?
Because it consists of letters.

Why is a book like a tree?
Because it has many leaves.

Mechanical Advertisement

The idea of a machine to go by perpetual motion is perpetual nonsense. Multitudes of boys and men have
wasted much valuable time in trying to find it, but they
never can, as it is contrary to natural laws, and therefore
impossible; but one certainty of the future is, that a million useful flying machines will flit hither and thither;
and one certainty of the present is, that while Cole's
Book Arcade contains 80,000 sorts of books, not a single person has yet been able to come to it for a supply in
a flying machine.—Laggard inventors, think of this!

N.B.—Cole once invented a flying machine, but it
wouldn't work!

Riddles And Catches

If a man has twenty sick (six) sheep and
one of them dies, how many will remain?
Nineteen.

Can a leopard change his spots?
Yes: when he is tired of one spot he can
go to another.

Why does a piebald pony never pay a toll?

Because his master pays it for him.

Where are you sure to find pity in the worst of misfortunes?
In the dictionary.

Where did the witch of Endor live?
At Endor.

What is most like a cat's tail?
A kitten's tail.

What is that which no other animal but a cat possesses?
Kittens.

What is the colour of a green-plot covered with snow?
Green.

When is a man not a man?
When he is a muff.

If a stone were thrown at you and fell into the water, what would it become?
Wet.

What is the oldest tree in Australia?
The Elder.

What trees bear the most fruit for the Market?
The axle-trees.

Why is a clock not wound up, like a mile-stone?
Because it stands still.

How can you make a currant cake without currants?

Put only one currant into it.

Which letters are never out of fashion?
F A S H I O N.

Why is your nose like St. Paul's?
Because it is flesh and blood.

Why do white sheep furnish more wool
than the black ones?
Because there are more of them.

What makes a pair of boots?
Two.

What did Adam first plant in his garden?
His foot.

How can a boy make his jacket last?
By making his coat and waistcoat first.

She was plump and beautiful, and he was
wildly fond of her; she hated him, yet
woman-like, she strove to catch him.
What was he?
He was a flea.

What is the difference between six dozen
dozen and half a dozen dozen?
One is six gross and the other is six dozen.

What is that which a man can put into his
right hand but never into his left?
His left elbow.

What is that which a man with two eyes
cannot see with one?
T'other eye.

Spell and pronounce the word Pot, without saying Teapot?

Cautiously start a conversation about
coins, and the ask, "Did you ever see any
of those coins two of which make eighteen pence?"
Of course they will say "no"; then show
them a shilling and a sixpence, and you
"have" them.

Would you rather an elephant killed you
or a gorilla?
Rather the elephant killed the gorilla.

WHEN SHALL WE THREE MEET AGAIN?

When Shall We Three Meet Again?

One donkey has met another donkey
and now there are two donkeys, as you see
and you have to guess where the third
donkey is: if you cannot guess it, some
kind friend will tell you.

There was a donkey on one side of a
river and some hay on the other side. The

donkey wanted the hay, but he couldn't swim over the river, jump over it, nor cross the bridge. How could he manage it? Do you give up? Yes. Answer—That is what the other donkey did.

Repeat This With A Friend
1. I went up one pair of stairs; 2. Just like me.
1. I went up two pair of stairs; 2. Just like me.
1. I went into a room; 2. Just like me.
1. I looked out of a window; 2. Just like me.
1. And there I saw a donkey; 2. Just like me.

"Around the rugged rocks the ragged rascals ran a truly rural race." Repeat this five times quickly without a mistake and see what it will come to?

A room with eight corners had a cat in each corner seven cats before each cat and a cat on every cat's tail. What was the total number of cats?
Eight cats.

Speaking of persons who have educated themselves, I once knew a person who educated himself and guess how the fellow spelt "Cat." You could not guess in a year?
Answer.—"Kat," No. "Catt," No. "Katt," No. Give it up? Yes. "Cat."

Why is a cow's tail like a swan's bosom? Because it grows down.

When is a horse's head where it's tail
should be?
When his tail is towards the manger.

What should a clergyman preach about?
About half-an-hour.

Although I've neither legs not feet,
  I'm only useful when I go;
I have no tongue, but yet I tell
  What hundreds want to know.
A watch.

My sides are firmly laced about,
  Yet nothing have within;
You'll find my head is straight indeed,
  'Tis nothing else but skin.
A drum.

Repeat This With A Friend
1. I am a gold lock; 2. I am a gold key.
1. I am a silver lock; 2. I am a silver key.
1. I am a brass lock; 2. I am a brass key.
1. I am a lead lock; 2. I am a lead key.
1. I am a monk lock; 2. I am a monk key.

Mind Your Punctuation

King Charles 1. spoke half-an-hour after
his head was cut off.

Every lady in this land
Has twenty nails upon each hand
Five and twenty hands and feet
All this is true without deceit.

I saw a peacock with fiery tail
  I saw a blazing comet drop down hail
I saw a cloud wrapped with ivy round

637

I saw an oak creep upon the ground
I saw a monkey swallow up a whale
I saw the sea brimful of ale
I saw an ale glass full fifteen feet deep
I saw a well full of men's tears that
weep
I saw red eyes all of a flaming fire
I saw a house bigger than the moon and
higher
I saw the sun at twelve o'clock at night
I saw the man that saw this wondrous
sight.

The Husband's Petition

Come hither my heart's darling, come sit
upon my knee
And listen while I whisper a boon I ask of
thee.
I felt a bitter craving—a dark and deep
desire
That glows beneath my bosom like coals
of kindled fire
Nay, dearest, do not doubt me, though
madly this I speak—
I feel thine arms about me, thy tresses on
my cheek;
I know the sweet devotion that links thy
heart with mine—
I know my soul's emotion is doubly felt
by thine.

And deem not that a shadow has fallen
across my love
No, sweet, my love is shadowless as yonder heaven above.
Oh, then, do not deny me my first and
fond request,
I pray thee, by the memory of all we cherish best—
By that great vow that made thee my dar-

ling and my bride;
Thou wilt not fail nor falter, but bend thee
to the task.
*Put buttons on my shirt love—that's all the
boon I ask!*

Ten Picture Puzzles

He or She is Clever Who Discovers Nine of them, and Exceedingly
Clever Who Finds Out the Whole Ten

Here is a Jew looking out for his Brother. Where is he?

The embarrassment of the Cook. Where is the Rabbit?

Here is the Showman and his learned Dog. Where is his Wife?

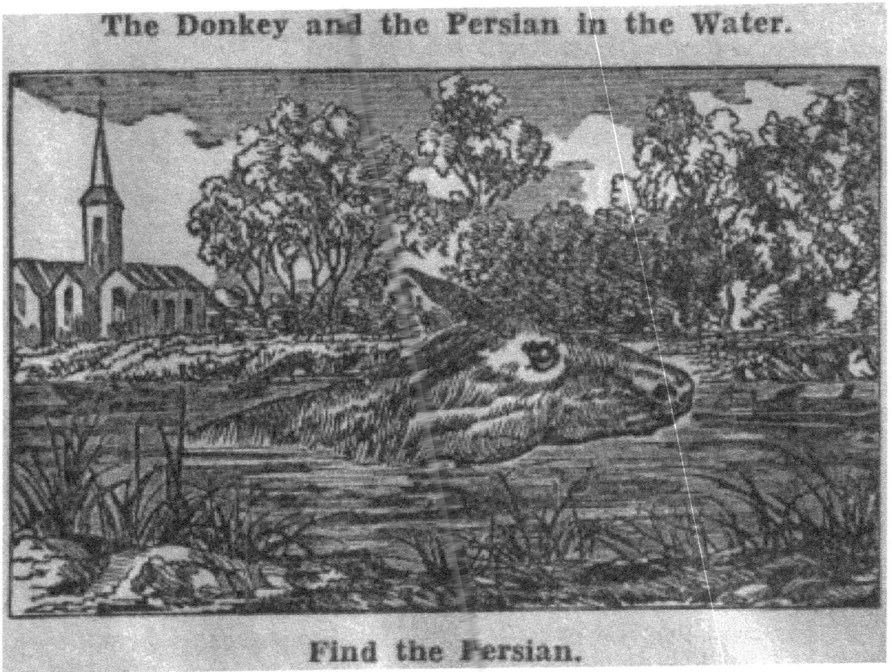

The Donkey and the Persian in the Water. Find the Persian

Brother Jonathan lamenting the loss of his wife. And she is there. Find her out.

Here is the Hunter. Where is the Game?

This is a Newfoundland Dog. Find out his Master.

You can see the Goat plainly.

Find out the Milkmaid.

You can see the goat plainly. Find out the milkmaid.

The Queen looking for the King. Where is he?

Here is a Nurse looking for the Patient. Find him out.

Here is the Cat. Where are the Rats?

Here is the Ox. Where is the Dog?

Here is the Monkey, Where is the Owl?

Here is the M∷nkey. Where is the Owl?

Here is the Lion. Where is the Lamb? It could be seen a few minutes ago.

Here is a Cruel Turk. Where is the Poor Greek?

Here are the Rats. Where is the Cat?

Some of the wild animals have got loose. Where is the Bear?

Here is Little Red Riding Hood. Where is the Wolf?

Find her Landlord.

Find their Father.

Find the Other Five Children.

Old Mother Hubbard. Find the Baker.

Find the Schoolmaster and Schoolmistress.

Attack on a United States Mail Coach by Indians.

Puzzle: Find the Cowboys.

Indian War Dance.

Puzzle: Find the Scout.

Old Mother Hubbard. Find the Publican.

Old Mother Hubbard. Find the Undertaker.

Old Mother Hubbard. Find the Hatter.

Old Mother Hubbard. Find the Tailor.

Old Mother Hubbard.—Find the Hosier.

Old Mother Hubbard. Find the Hosier.

Old Mother Hubbard.—Find the Shoemaker.

Old Mother Hubbard. Find the Shoemaker.

B one day drove a flock of geese,
And met with Farmer A:
Says Farmer A, "How much a piece
For the flock did you pay?"
Says B "I paid for all I drive
Just six pounds and a crown;
And I'm going to sell them, all but five,
At yonder market town;
When fifteen pence a head I'll charge
Above what they cost me,
And thus obtain a sum as large
As I gave for all you see."

How many geese did B buy? How much
did he give for each? and What price did
he ask?

He bought 25 geese at 5s each, and meant
to ask 6s 3d each.

Oft sought in the country, much prized in the town?
Like a king, above a , I can boast of a crown;
If not found in the palace, I grace the chateau;
Both the peer and the peasant my usefulness know.
When I've not seen six months I am said to be old;
Though exalted by nobles, I'm bought and I'm sold.
Though ne'er in a sermon, I take part in all chat;
Yet I'm ne'er found in this, but I'm always in that.
I'm seen in most colours, am brown, black, or white,
But am rarely found red and, when good, I am light;
In demand with both sexes, selected with care,
I'm prized by most men and add grace to the fair.
Of no use to my owner when kept in his sight,
I attend him by day, and oft serve him by night;
As his slave I am passive; yet, strange it may sound,
To keep me in order, I'm frequently bound.
My fetters are silken; I'm useless at home,

Though a constant companion whenever you roam;
And, though no enchantment within me doth dwell,
Pray tell me my name—for in that lies a spell!

A Hat.

'Twas born in anguish, 'twas cradled by care,
And has lived ever since in the depths of despair.
It dwells in the valley, 't glides on the wave,
It is laid with our ashes when cold in the grave.
In darkness it brightens, in sunshine it dies,
As far from the smile of enjoyment it flies.
In the rainbow it sits, in the stars it has birth,
And with angels descending it visits the earth.
With Adam it dwelt, and so to Paradise came,
But eve knew it not, though it shared in her shame.
It mingles in battle. yet still it loves peace.
It joins in the banquet, the dance, and the chase
From the dream of our childhood it ne'er can depart
And it lies, like a gem, in the core of the heart.
The traveller bears it o'er desert along;
The nightingale loves it, though strange to her song.
On the point of an arrow it cleaves through the air
Yet the pinions of birds cannot follow it there.
The bosom disowns it, yet bright through our tears,
When shed in affection, it ever appears.
The cataract fearfully hurries it on,
But, search it through billows and tempest—'tis gone.
From the joys of our mortal existence 'tis driven;
Yet finds an unchanging asylum in heaven.
With the harp of the minstrel it ever shall dwell
And it comes to my lips as I utter "Farewell".

The Letter A.

Though grief gives me birth, I'm a stranger to care.
I scorn the dull earth, and float in the air.
No lover claims me, though I revel in bliss.

665

COLE

I taste of each lip, and melt in each kiss.
I'm an egotist's pride, though in silence I reign;
And, through free from sorrow, I'm always in pain.
Though in laughter ne'er seen, in mirth I delight;
In blindness I grope, though perfect in sight.
In foolishness, Wisdom, and wit I've a place;
Though dwelling in virtue I live in disgrace.
Though frost knows me not, with winter I blend;
And always to ice I'm a capital friend.
I'm never in heat, though I live in the fire.
Though never in want, I'm in every desire.
I am I—, but the end of my paper I spy;
So I'll wind up my stave and wish you good-by.

The Letter I.

666

Buffalo Hunt on the Prairie.

Puzzle: Find the Settler

The Falls of Niagara.

Puzzle: Find Captain Webb

A Giant's Castle—Where is the Giant.

A Giant's Castle. Where is the Giant?

Old Mother Hubbard—Find the Cat.

Old Mother Hubbard. F nd the Cat.

The Giant's Father. Where is He?

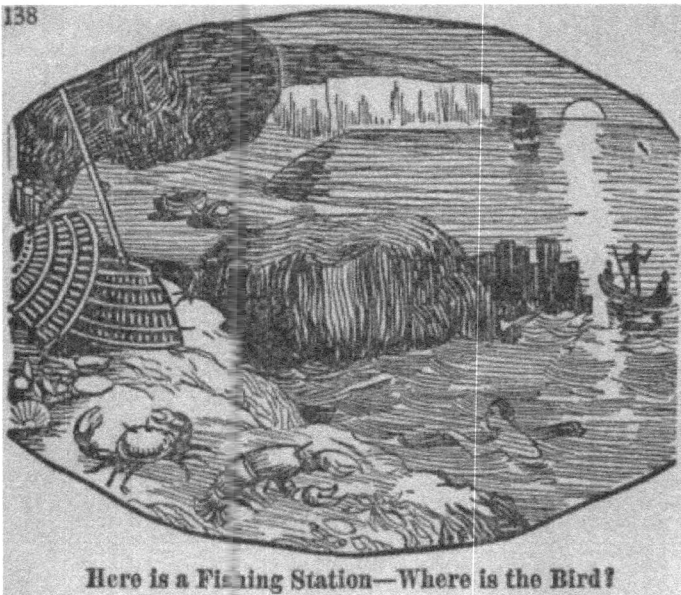

Here is the Fishing Station. Where is the Bird?

Here is a Scene in Africa—Where is the Hippopotamus?

Here is a Scene in Africa. Where is the Hippopotamus?

Here is Bluebeard and his Wife—Where is the Donkey?

Here is Bluebeard and his Wife. Where is the Donkey?

Here is a House in ̄ne Jungle. Where is John Bright?

Here is a Village. Where is the Highlandman Fishing?

Here is a lot of Furniture in a Room. Where is the Cup?

Here is a lot of Furniture in a Room. Where is the Cup?

AUSTRALIAN
PICTURE PUZZLE.

's [picture] It is [picture] town,
Of [picture] the [picture] this [picture] it has the m[picture] renown,
It was the [picture]st first [picture] t[picture] the [picture] was found;
It's [picture] the f[picture] [picture] the [picture] around.
A lovely [picture] s[picture]gn ap[picture]s above the [picture] [picture],
And 'tis the very q[picture]est s[picture]gn wa[picture] yet dis[picture]ed.
A [picture]ion, yes! a [picture]ion [picture] are [picture]d with[picture] its w[picture]s
Which [picture] [picture] n, looked at or [picture]t by anyone t[picture] c[picture].
The [picture] U wish the [picture] U w[picture] is [picture]most sure to [picture]
Found [picture]where [picture] the [picture] [picture] if U will c[picture] & C.

Don Quixote Charging the Wine Casks—Puzzle: Find the Princess.

Don Quixote Charging the Wine Casks.

Puzzle: Find the Princess.

PUZZLE:—Find the Umpire.

Puzzle: Find the Umpire

Don Quixote's Battle with the Windmill.

Puzzle: Find the Miller.

Don Quixote's last Chivalrous Battle. Puzzle: Find his Lady-love.

Don Quixoite's last Chivalrous Battle.

Puzzle: Find his lady-love.

Where's the pig?

Where's the fox?

Puzzle: Find the Drummer.

Banyan Tree Puzzle: a Mystery of the Dark Continent.

Find out Horse, Camel, Elephant, Giraffe, Kangaroo & Monkey.

This game is a kind of Magic Lantern Exhibition. It is very Interesting, always pleases the children, and is very easily learnt, and for amusing poor, sick children it is invaluable.

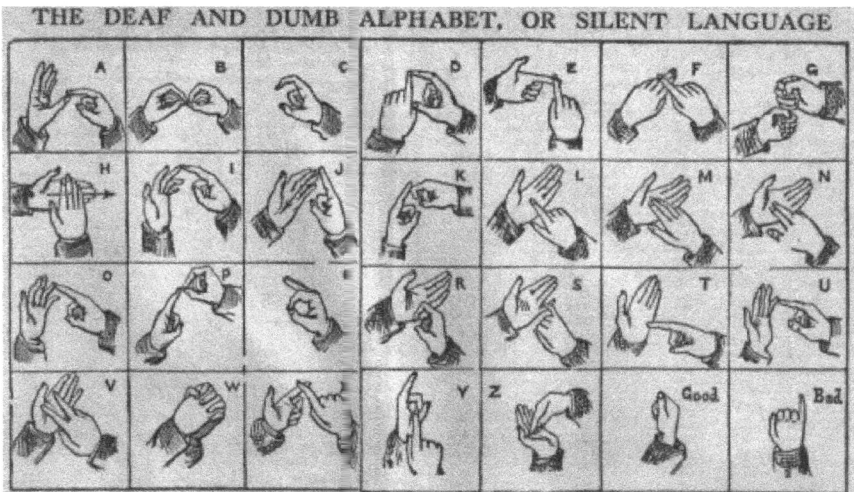

The Alphabet of HAND-SIGNS is a great blessing to deaf and dumb persons, enabling them to converse almost as efficiently as others can by the organs of speech. It is also extensively used throughout the world as a useful accomplishment by those who are not deaf and

681

dumb, and besides it has this recommendation:—It is the most easily learnt language in the world.

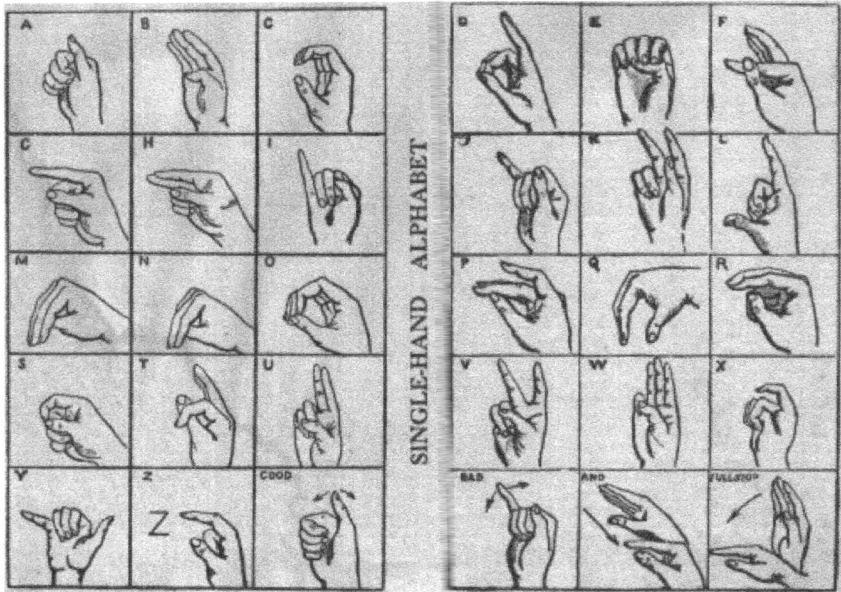

SINGLE-HAND ALPHABET

Language Of Flowers

The language of flowers in pre-eminently the language of refined and modest Courtship; millions have conveyed a message by presenting a flower which they dare not have uttered in their mother tongue.

In some countries this "LANGUAGE OF LOVE" is extremely common in the words of the poet:

> "In Eastern lands, amic fragrant bowers,
> They tell the tale of Affection in Flowers."

Abatina, Fickleness
Abecedary, Volubility
Acacia, Friendship
Acacia, Rose, Elegance
Acacia, Yellow, Secret Love
Acanthus, The Fine Arts
Acalia, Temperance
Achillea Millefolia, War
Achimenes, Such worth is rare
Aconite, Misanthropy
Adonis, Flos, Sad memories
Agnus Castos, Coldness
Agrimony, Thankfulness
Almond (common), Indiscreet
Almond (flowering), Hope
Almond, Laurel, Perfidy
Allspice, Compassion
Aloe, Affliction
Amaranth (Globe), Immortal
Amaranth (Cockscomb), Foppery
Amaryllis, Splendid Beauty
Ambrosia, Love returned
American Elm, Patriotism
American Linden, Matrimony
Amethyst, Admiration
Andromeda, Self-sacrifice
Anemone (Garden) Forsaken
Angelica, Inspiration
Angrec, Royalty
Apricot Blossom, Doubt
Apple, Temptation
Apple Blossom, Preference
Apple, Thorn, Deceitful Character
Arbor Vitae, Live for me
Arum (Wake Robin), Zeal
Ash, Mountain, Prudence
Ash Tree, Grandeur
Aspen Tree, Lamentation
Asphodel, My Regrets Follow
Auricula, Painting
Auricula (Scarlet) Avarice

Austurtium, Splendour
Azalea, Temperance
Bachelor's Buttons, Celibacy
Balm, Sympathy
Balm (Gentle), Pleasantry
Balm of Gilead, Cure
Balsam, Yellow, Impatience
Barberry, Sharpness of temper
Basil, Hatred
Bay Berry, Instruction
Bay Leaf, I change but in death
Bay Tree, Glory
Bay Wreath, Reward of merit
Bearded Crepis, Protection
Beech Tree, Prosperity
Bee Orchis, Industry
Bee Ophrys, Error
Begonia, Deformity
Belladonna, Silence. Hush!
Bell Flower (White) Gratitude
Betony, Surprise
Bilberry, Treachery
Bindweed, Great Insinuation
Bindweed, Small, Humility
Birch, Meekness
Bittersweet, Truth
Blackthorn, Difficulty
Bladder Nut Tree, Amusement
Bluebell, Sorrowful Regret
Bonus Henricus, Goodness
Borage, Bluntness
Box Tree, Stoicism
Bramble, Lowliness
Broom, Neatness
Buckbean, Calm repose
Buglos, Falsehood
Bulrush, Indiscretion
Bundle of Reeds, Music
Burdock, Touch me not
Bur, You weary me
Buttercup, Childishness

Butterfly Orchis, Gaiety
Butterfly Weed, Let me go
Cabbage, Profit. Gain
Cacalia, Adulation
Cactus, Warmth
Calycanthus, Benevolence
Camellia, Red, Excellence
Camellia, White, Loveliness
Camomile, Energy in adversity
Carnation, Striped, Refusal
Carnation, Deep Red, Poor me
Cardamine, Paternal error
Candytuft, Indifference
Canary Grass, Perseverance
Campanula, Aspiring
Carnation, Yellow, Disdain
Cardinal Flower, Distinction
Catchfly, Selene, False love
Catchfly, Red, Youthful love
Catchfly, White, Betrayed
Cattleya, Mature charms
Cedar, Strength
Cedar of Lebanon, Incorruptible
Cedar Leaf, I love for thee
Celandine, Joys to come
Centaury, Bluebottle, Felicity
Champignon, Suspicion
Cherry Tree, Good education
Chestnut Tree Do me justice
Chinese Primrose, Lasting love
Chickweed, Rendezvous
Chicory, Frugality
China Aster, Afterthought
China Aster, Double, I agree
China Aster, Single, I will think if it
Chrysanthemum, Red, I love
Chrysanthemum, White, Truth
Chrysanthemum, Yellow, Slighted Love
Cineraria, Always delightful
Cinquefoil, Maternal Affection
Circaea, Spell

Cictus, Popular favour

Citron, Ill-natured beauty

Clematis, Mental beauty

Clematis, Evergreen, Poverty

Clianthus, Worldliness

Clotbur, Rudeness

Clover, Four-leaved, Be mine

Clover, Red, Industry

Clover, White, Think of me

Cloves, Dignity

Cobaea, Gossip

Columbine, Folly

Columbine, Red, Fearful

Convolvulus, Bonds

Convolvulus, Blue, Repose

Convolvulus, Pink, Hopeless

Coreopsis, Always Cheerful

Coriander, Hidden worth

Corn, Riches

Corn Bottle, Delicacy

Corn Cockle, Gentility

Cornel Tree, Duration

Coronella, Success to you

Cosmelia, Charm of a blush

Cowslip, Winning grace

Crab (Blossom), Ill-nature

Cranberry, Cure headache

Cress, Stability

Crocus, Cheerfulness

Crocus, Saffron, Mirth

Crown Imperial, Power

Crowsbill, Envy

Crowfoot, Ingratitude

Cuckoo Plant, Ardour

Cudweed, Remembrance

Cuscuta, Meanness

Cyclamen, Diffidence

Cypress, Death

Daffodil, Yellow, Regard

Dahlia, Instability

Daisy, Innocence

Daisy, Michaelmas, Farewell
Daisy, Variegated, Beauty
Daisy, Wild, Will think of it
Dandelion, Love's oracle
Daphne, Glory
Dew Plant, A serenade
Dianthus, Make haste
Dipteracanthus, Fortitude
Diplademia, You are too bold
Dittany, Pink, Birth
Dittany, White, Passion
Dock, Patience
Dodder of Thyme. Baseness
Dogsbane, Falsehood
Dogwood, Durability
Dragon Plant, Snare
Dragonwort, Horror
Dried Flax, Usefulness
Ebony, Blackness
Echites, Be Warned in Time
Elder, Zeal
Elm, Dignity
Endive, Frugality
Escholzia, Do Not Refuse Me
Eupatorium, Delay
Evergreen Thorn, Solace
Fern, Flowering, Magic
Fern, Sincerity
Fever Root, Delay
Fig, Argument
Fig Marigold, Idleness
Fig Tree, Prolific
Filbert, Reconciliation
Fir, Time
Fir, Birch, Elevation
Flax, I Feel Your Kindness
Fleur-de-lis, I burn
Fleur-de-Luce, Fire
Fly Orchis, Error
Flytrap, Deceit
Fools Parsley, Silliness

Forget-me-not, Forget-me-not
Foxglove, Insincerity
Foxtail, Grass, Sporting
Frog Ophrys, Disgust
Fumitory, Spleen
Fuchsia, Scarlet, Taste
Furze, Love for all Seasons
Garden Chervil, Sincerity
Gardenia, Refinement
Geranium, Dark, Melancholy
Geranium, Horse-shoe Leaf, Stupidity
Geranium, Ivy, Bridal Favour
Geranium, Lemon, Unexpected Meeting
Geranium, Nutmeg, Expected Meeting
Geranium, Oak-leaved, True Friendship
Geranium, Variegated, Ingenuity
Geranium, Rose-scented, Preference
Geranium, Scarlet, Comforting, Kindness
Geranium, Silver-leaved, Recall
Geranium, Wild, Steadfast Piety
Gladioli, Ready Armed
Glory Flower, Glorious Beauty
Goat's Rue, Reason
Golden Rod, Encouragement
Goosefoot, Goodness
Gooseberry, Anticipation
Gourd, Extent, Bulk
Grape, Wild, Rural Felicity
Grass, Utility
Hand Flower Tree, Warning
Harebell, Submission
Hawkweed, Quicksightedness
Hawthorn, Hope
Hazel, Reconciliation
Heart's-ease, Thought
Heath, Solitude
Helenium, Tears
Heliotrope, I Turn to Thee
Hellebore, Scandal
Hemlock, You will be my death
Hemp, Fate

Henbane, Imperfection
Hepatica, Confidence
Hibiscus, Delicate Beauty
Holly, Foresight
Holy Herb, Enchantment
Hollyhock, Fecundity
Honesty, Honesty
Honey Flower, Love, Sweet
Honeysuckle, Affection
Hop, Injustice
Horehound, Fire
Hornbeam, Ornament
Horse, Chestnut, Luxury
Hortensia, You are Cold
Houseleek, Vivacity
Houstonia, Content
Humble Plant, Despondency
Hyacinth, Sport, Game, Play
Hyacinth, Purple, Adversity
Hyacinth, Blue, Constancy
Hydrangea, A Boaster
Hyssop, Cleanliness
Iceland Moss, Health
Ice Plant, You Freeze Me
Imbricata, Uprightness
Imperial Montague, Power
Indian Cress, Warlike Trophy
Indian Jasmine, Attachment
Iris, Common, Message
Iris, German, Flame
Ivy, Marriage
Jacob's Ladder, Come Down
Jasmine, White, Amiability
Jasmine, Cape, Too Happy
Jasmine, Carolina, Separation
Jasmine, Spanish, Sensuality
Jasmine, Yellow, Grace
Judas Tree, Betrayal
Juniper, Succour
Justicia, Perfection
Kennedia, Mental Beauty

Kingcups, Desire of Riches
Laburnum, Pensive Beauty
Lady's Slipper, Win Me
Lagerstroemia, Eloquence
Lantana, Rigour
Larch, Audacity
Larkspur, Lightness, Levity
Larkspur, Double, Happiness
Larkspur, Pink, Fickleness
Larkspur, Purple, Haughtiness
Laurel, Glory
Laurel, Common, Perfidy
Laurel, Ground, Perseverance
Laurel, Mountain, Ambition
Lavender, Distrust
Leaves, Dead, Sadness
Lemon, Zest
Lemon Blossom, Fidelity
Lettuce, Cold-heartedness
Lichen, Dejection
Lilac, Field, Humility
Lilac, White, Innocence
Lily, Day, Coquetry
Lily, Imperial, Majesty
Lily, White, Purity
Lily, Yellow, Falsehood
Linden, Conjugal Love
Lint, I feel my obligations
Liverwort, Confidence
Lobelia, Malevolence
Locust, True, Elegance
London, Pride, Frivolity
Lote Tree, Concord
Lotus, Eloquence
Lotus Flower, Estranged Love
Lotus Leaf, Recantation
Love in a Mist, Perplexity
Love Lies Bleeding, Desertion
Lucurn, Life
Lupine, Voraciousness
Madder, Calumny

Magnolia, Love of Nature
Maiden Hair, Secrecy
Mallow, Wildness
Mallow, Marsh, Beneficence
Marrow, Syrian, Persuasion
Manchineal Tree, Duplicity
Mandrake, Rarity
Maple, Reserve
Marianthus, Hope for Better
Marigold, Grief, Chagrin
Marigold, French, Jealousy
Marigold and Cyprus, Despair
Marjoram, Blushes
Marvel of Peru, Timidity
Meadow Lychnis. Wit
Meadowsweet, Uselessness
Mercury, Goodness
Mesembryanthemum, Idleness
Mezereon, I Desire to Please
Mignonette, You are Good
Milfoil, War
Milkwort, Hermitage
Mint, Virtue
Mistletoe, I Surmount
Mock Orange, Counterfeit
Monkshood, Deadly Foe Near
Moonwort, Forgetfulness
Morning Glory, Affectation
Moschatel, Weakness
Moss, Maternal Love
Mosses, Ennui
Motherwort, Concealed Love
Moving Plant, Agitation
Mulberry, White, Wisdom
Mushroom, I Can't Trust You
Musk Plant, Weakness
Myrobalan, Privation
Myrrh, Gladness
Myrtle, Love
Narcissus, Egotism
Nasturtium, Patriotism

Nemophila, Success
Nettle, Stinging, You Spiteful
Nettle Burning Slander
Nettle Tree, Conceit
Night Convolvulus, Night
Nightshade, Dark Thoughts
Oak (Live), Liberty
Oak Leaves (Dead) Bravery
Oats, Harmony
Oleander, Beware
Olive, Peace
Orange Blossoms, Purity
Orange Flowers, Chastity
Orange Tree, Generosity
Orchis, Common, a Beauty
Osier, Frankness
Osmunda, Dreams
Ox-eye, Patience
Palm, Victory
Pansy, I think of you
Parsley, Festivity, Feasting
Passion Flower, Superstition
Pea, Common, Respect
Pea, Everlasting, A meeting
Peach, Matchess Charms
Peach Blossom, Your Captive
Pear, Affection
Pear Tree, Comfort
Pennyroyal, Flee away
Peony, Shame, Bashfulness
Peppermint, Warm Feeling
Periwinkle, Early Friendship
Persicaria, Restoration
Peruvian Heliotrope, Devotion
Petunia, Keep your Promise
Pheasant's Eye, Remembrance
Phlox, Unanimity
Pigeon Berry, Indifference
Pimpernel, Change
Pine, Black, Pity
Pine-apple, You are perfect

Pine, Pitch, Philosophy
Pink, Boldness
Pink, Indian, Always lovely
Pink, Indian, S. Aversion
Pink, Mountain, Aspiring
Pink, Red, Single, Pure Love
Pink, Variegated, Refusal
Pink, White, Ingeniousness
Pink, Yellow, Disdain
Plantain, What Man's Footstep
Plane Tree, Genius
Plum, Indian, Privation
Plum Tree, Fidelity
Plum, Wild, Independence
Polyanthus, Pride of Riches
Polyanthus, Crimson, Mystery
Pomegranate, Foolishness
Pomegranate, Flower, Elegance
Poor Robin, Compensation
Poplar, Black, Courage
Poplar, White, Time
Poppy, Red, Consolation
Poppy, Scarlet, Fantastic Folly
Poppy, White, Sleep—My Bane
Potato, Benevolence
Prickly Pear, Satire
Pride of China, Dissension
Primrose, Early Youth
Primrose, Evening, Inconstance
Primrose, Red, Unpatronized
Privet, Prohibition
Purple Clover, Provident
Pyrus Japonica, Fairies' Fire
Quaking Grass, Agitation
Quamoclit, Busybody
Queen's Rocket, Fashion
Quince, Temptation
Ragged Robin, Wit
Ranunculus, Are Charming
Ranunculus, Wild, Ingratitude
Raspberry, Remorse

Ray-Grass, Vice
Reed, Complaisance
Reed, Split, Indiscretion
Rhododendron, Danger
Rhubarb, Advice
Rocket, Rivalry
Rose, Love
Rose, Australian, All that is Lovely
Rose, Bridal, Happy Love
Rose, Burgundy, Unconscious Beauty
Rose, Cabbage, Ambassador of Love
Rose, Campion, Deserve my Love
Rose, Carolina, Love is dangerous
Rose, China, Beauty Unfading
Rose, Daily, I Aspire to thy Smile
Rose, Damask, Beautiful Complexion
Rose, Deep Red, Bashful Modesty
Rose, Dog, Pleasure and Pain
Rose, Guelder, Age
Rose, Hundred-Leaved, Pride, Dignity
Rose, Japan, Beauty only
Rose, Maiden Blush, Show me Love
Rose, Multiflora, Grace
Rose, Moss, Superior Merit
Rose, Mundi, Variety, Uncertain
Rose, Musk, Capricious Beauty
Rose, Musk, Cluster, Charming
Rose, Thornless, Happy Union
Rose, Unique, Call me not beautiful
Rose, White, I am Worthy of You
Rose, White, Withered, Infidelity
Rose, Xmas, Relieve my anxiety
Rose, Yellow, Jealousy
Rose, York and Lancaster, War
Rose, White & Red together, Unity
Roses, Crown of, Reward of
Rosebud, Red, Pure & Lovely
Rosebud, White, Girlhood
Rosebud, Moss, Confession of love
Rosemary, You ever Revive
Rudbeckia, Justice

Rue, Scorn, Despite
Rush, Docility
Rye-grass, Changeable
Saffron, Shun Excess
Sage, Domestic Virtue
Sainfoin, Agitation
St. John's Wort, Animosity
Salvia, Blue, Wisdom
Salvia, Red, Energy
Saxifrage, Mossy, Affection
Scabious, Unfortunate Love
Scabious, Sweet, Widowhood
Scarlet Lychnis, Brilliant Eye
Shinus, Religious Enthusiasm
Sensitive Plant, Sensitiveness
Senvy, Indifference
Shamrock, Light-heartedness
Snakesfoot, Horror
Snapdragon, "No."
Snowball, Bound
Snowdrop, Hope
Sorrel, Wild, Wit Ill-timed
Sorrel, Wood, Joy
Sothernwood, Jest, Bantering
Spearmint, Warm, Sentiment
Speedwell, Female Fidelity
Speedwell, Spiked, Semblance
Spider, Ophrys, Adroitness
Spiderwort, Esteem, not Love
Star of Bethelhem, Guidance
Starwort, Afterthought
Stock, Lasting Beauty
Stock, Ten-week, Promptness
Stonecrop, Peace
Straw, Broken, Quarrel
Straw, Whole, Union
Strawberry Blossom Perfect
Strawberry Tree, Esteem, not Love
Sultan, Lilac, I Forgive You
Sultan, White, Sweetness
Sultan, Yellow, Contempt

Sumach, Venice, Intellectual
Sunflower, Dwarf, Adoration
Sunflower, Tall, Haughtiness
Swallow-wort, Cure Heartache
Sweet Basil, Good Wishes
Sweetbrier, I wound, but love
Sweet Flag, Yellow, Fitness
Sweet Pea, Delicate Pleasures
Sweet Sultan, Felicity
Sweet William, Gallantry
Sycamore, Curiosity
Syringa, Memory
Tamarisk, Crime
Tansy, I war against you
Teasel, Misanthropy
Thistle, Common, Austerity
Thistle, Fuller's, Misanthropy
Thistle, Scotch, Retaliation
Thorns, Branch of, Severity
Thrift, Mutual Sensibility
Throatwort, Neglected Beauty
Thyme, Activity
Toothwort, Secret Love
Traveller's Joy, Safety
Tree of Life, Old Age
Trefoil, Revenge
Tremella Nestoc, Resistance
Trillium Pictum, Modest Beauty
Truffle Surprise
Trumpet, Flower, Fame
Tuberose, Dangerous Pleasure
Tulip, Red, Declaration of Love
Tulip, Tree, Fame
Tulip, Variegated, Beautiful Love
Tulip, Yellow, Hopeless Love
Turnip, Charity
Valerian, I Wish to Please
Valerian, Greek, Rupture
Venus's Car, Fly with Me
Venus's Looking Glass, Flattery
Venus's Trap, Artifice

Verbena, Pink, Family Union
Verbena, Purple, I Weep for You
Verbena, Scarlet, Unite Against Evil
Verbena, Sweet-scented, Sensibility
Verbena, White Pray for Me
Vernal Grass, Poor but Happy
Veronica, Fidelity
Veronica, Speciosa, I Dare Not
Vetch, Shyness
Vine, Intoxication
Violet, Blue, Faithfulness
Violet, Dame, Watchfulness
Violet, Purple, Ever in My Mind
Violet, White, Modesty
Violet, Yellow, rural happiness
Virginia Creeper, I cling to you
Virgin's Bower Filial Love
Viscaria oculata, dance with me
Volkamenia, may you be happy
Walnut, Intellect
Wall-flower, Fidelity
Water Lily, Purity of Heart
Water Melon, Bulkiness
Wax Plant, Susceptibility
Wheat Stalks, Riches
Whin, Anger
Whortleberry, Treason
Willow, creeping, Love forsaken
Willow, Water, Freedom
Willow, Weeping, Mourning
Willow Herb, Pretension
Woodbine, Fraternal Love
Wormwood, Absence
Xanthium, Pertinacity
Yew, Sorrow

Flowers smell the sweetest and look the loveliest of all earthly things, and most men and woman throughout the World dearly love them, and hope to dwell beyond the grave where "Everlasting Spring abides, and NEVER WITHERING FLOWERS".

Animals

Kindness To Animals

Power of Kindness to Animals

Thousands of pathetic tales could be told of the sufferings of poor dumb animals and the sympathy of some kind human souls for them. The following one is from the Secretary of a Humane Society:—

The wife of a small country farmer wrote to me: "I can't bear sending the cattle to market. I always keep out of the way, for every animal on the place knows me, and they look at me so sadly, and, knowing what they're going to, I feel sometimes that I'd rather give the whole thing up, than go on rearing them to be knocked about and killed.

"I went to the market once myself to see a young beast being sold, but I'll never go again. I had fed it with my own hands every day, till it was like a child. I went to the market-town by train, and the young bullock was driven by road. I walked a little way out to meet it, and at last met it coming tramping along, and the drover told me he had had the greatest difficulty to get it along the last few miles; it had become so tired. You see it had not had much exercise, as when you are fattening things, it does not do to let them run about too much, or they'll 'run all the meat off their bones' again, as the saying is.

"When I went to Smithfield, I was ready to faint as I saw the men shouting and swearing, and slashing away with thick sticks. The poor things were so confused and knocked about that they didn't know what to do, and I went up to the man who seemed to be in charge of the pens that our auctioneer was going to sell from, and asked him if he would be kind to my poor bullock when it came. He only cursed it an laughed a mocking laugh, and said, 'Oh, yes, ---- it, I'll be gentle with it. You wait, missis, and see! Do you think I'm here to coddle any ---- beasts? If you do, you're ---- well mistaken.'

"I couldn't bear to see what would happen. I couldn't stand it, so I went away, and then the men (dealers) simply stood and talked, and haggled with the farmers; and the drovers shouted and yelled, and hooted, and knocked the things about, and hit them on the nose and over the eyes, and poked and prodded them with sharp pointed sticks; and the dogs yapped and barked, and I never heard a single word of pity, or saw a sign of pity for the poor, tired, bruised, panting, and terrified creatures.

"It was a terribly hot day, and I wandered about the town all the afternoon, able to think of little else than of my poor bullock, and of what had become of it, when, as I was going to the station to my train, I met three or four cattle coming driven along Suddenly one of them caught sight of me, and in spite of all the men could do came rushing up towards me. It was my poor bullock; but, oh, so terribly altered. I should hardly have known it.

"It seemed beside itself with joy to see me, and stood by me lowing so pitifully, as much as to say, 'Oh, I'm so glad I've found you! I know I'm safe now, and you won't let these awful men carry me off again'.

"At last they managed to get it to move on by flogging it savagely, and, heart-sick and conscience-smitten, I went to the station; and when I got the money that it was sold for it seemed to me like 'the price of blood.' But what can I do?

"I suppose the proper thing is to get hardened and to think nothing about it, like other people; but it is so dreadful that I can never go to market to see another of my poor beasts sold."

Kind Miss Cobbe

Miss Frances Power Cobbe gave herself, heart and soul, to the defence of the animals, not because she loved them more than human beings but because she could not bear to see the men acting so wickedly towards them, nor to hear the groans of the helpless victims.

In the account of her life, written by herself, she says: "It is not the four legs nor the silky or shaggy coat of a dog which should prevent us from discerning his inner nature of thought and love; limited thought, it is true, but an unlimited love. That he is dumb, is to me only another claim (as it would be in a human child) on my consideration... Another dog, whom I sent away at one year old to live in the country, was returned to me eight years afterwards old and diseased. The poor beast knew me again after a few moments' eager examination, and uttered *an actual scream of joy* when I called her by name, exhibiting every token of tender affection for me ever afterwards."

In her books entitled "Dogs whom I Have Met," she says: "The dog who really loves his master delights in mere propinquity, likes to lie down on the floor resting against his feet, better than on a cushion a yard away, and after a warm interchange of caresses for two or three minutes asks no more, and subsides into perfect contentment. That a short tender touch of the dog's tongue to hand or face corresponds exactly, as an expression of his feelings, to our kisses of affection, there can be no sort of doubt. All dogs kiss the people they love."

Tennyson, when on a visit to Miss Cobbe, bade her go bravely on as she had begun, and "fight the good fight," by which he meant the warfare against cruelty in which she was engaged. After his death it was sad to hear the wail of three dogs, a collie, a Scotch terrier, and a Russian wolf-hound, constant companions and friends of the poet. Thousands of dogs have pined, and died of

701

grief, for their loved masters.

At a Bull Fight

The following is a pathetic narrative entitled "El Moro."

A Cadiz letter says: "Notice had been posted on all the public places that on a certain day the bull called 'El Moro' would be introduced into the arena, and that, when he should have been goaded to the utmost fury, a young girl would appear and reduce the animal to quiet subjection. The people of Cadiz had heard of 'El Moro' as the most magnificent bull ever brought into the city, and it soon became known that the girl just advertised was a peasant girl of Espara, who had petted the bull, and fed it and cared for it during the years of it's growth. On the appointed day the vast amphitheatre was filled with an anxious, eager crowd. Several bulls had been killed and dragged away, and then the flourish of trumpets announced the coming of the hero of the day. With a deep, terrific roar, 'El Moro' entered upon the scene. He was truly magnificent; a bovine monarch, black and glossy, with eyes of fire, dilating nostrils, and wicked-looking horns. The picadores attacked him warily, hurling their banderillos (small, dart-like javelins ornamented with ribbons, and intended to jade and infuriate). The bull had killed three horses offhand, and had received eight banderillos in his neck and shoulders, when, upon a given signal, the picadores and matadores suddenly withdrew leaving the infuriated beast alone in his wild paroxysm of wrath. Presently a soft musical note, like the piping of a lark, was heard, and directly afterwards a girl of not more than fifteen years of age, an the tasteful garb of an Andalusian peasant, and with a pretty face, sprang lightly into the arena, approaching the bull fearlessly, at the same time calling his name— 'Moro! Moro! Va voy!' At the first sound of the sweet voice the animal ceased his fury, and turned towards the place whence it came, and, when he saw the girl, he plainly manifested pleasure. She came to his head, and put forth her hand, which he licked with his tongue.

Then she sang a low, sweet song, at the same time caressing the animal by patting him on the forehead, and, while she sang, the suffering monarch kneeled at her feet. Then she stooped and gently removed the cruel banderillos, after which, with her arms around 'El Moro's' neck, she led him towards the gate of the torril."

Funny Australian Natives

Kangaroo

The Kangaroo is the largest native animal in Australia. He is about 5 feet high when he sits up, he has a head somewhat like a rabbit's, his hands or fore feet are small but his hind feet are large, and he has a very thick tail. He can kick and tear with his sharp hind claws in a very dangerous manner. He frequently kills dogs with his claws, but, when he is chased by dogs, if he is near water he makes for it and often drowns the dogs if they come into the water after him. He leaps or hops about 15 feet at a time and goes very fast. The mother carries her young in a pouch, as seen in the picture, and when the baby kangaroos are frightened they run at once into their mother's pouch for safety, like any other babies running

703

to their mother.

Australian Native Cat

It is a wild Cat, generally brown or black with many large and small white spots on it. It lives on small animals, including birds and their eggs, and is a great pest to farmers, killing their poultry.

Emu

The Emu lives upon vegetable food such as fruits, roots, and grass. It has a great curiosity and is easily tamed. It is very inoffensive except when violently attacked; then it kicks like a horse. It is said that its kick will break a man's leg. Its flesh is eaten by the natives and is said to look and taste like beef. It can run very fast. It lays from 6 to 12 dark green coloured eggs and its young are pretty little striped things as in the above picture. It is, next to the Ostrich, the largest bird in the world, being 5 or 6 feet high, its colour is a mixture of grey and brown, and its voice has a low booming sound. It is generally coupled with the Kangaroo in the Australian Arms.

Platypus

The Platypus is sometimes called the Water Mole. It is, perhaps, the most wonderful animal in the world in its combination, being part bird, part beast, part fish. It has a bill like a duck; five toes with claws and webbed feet; it is covered with thick glossy fur like a seal; it has cheek pouches like a monkey to keep it's food in; it lays two eggs, its voice resembles that of a young puppy, and the young platypuses play like puppies; it lives in rivers and makes burrows often 20 or 30 feet long; it feeds upon water insects, shell fish, etc.

Native Bear

The Australian Native Bear is a dear little harmless fellow, and is easily tamed. He lives in the gum trees, feeds upon gum leaves, and loves his mother who carries him on her back and is very fond of him. He has a thick fluffy coat, big bushy ears, and no tail. He cries like a child if he misses his mother. The cry very pathetically if they are wounded, which they frequently are in the bush, by cruel wicked boys and men who think it is sport to shoot at the poor harmless creatures.

Bower Bird

The Australian Bower Bird is an extensive builder; it not only builds its nest in a tree but it builds a palace on the ground in the shape of a bower hut, furnishes it with nick-nacks such as shells, bones, pieces of mineral, metals, bright parrots' feathers and other trifles. What the English magpie would steal and hide away the Bower Bird openly decorates his pavilion with. Often several birds collect together and play like children, running in, out, and around their wonderful bower-palace as shown in our picture

Lyre Bird

The Australian Lyre Bird is a most beautiful crea-ture, said to be a variety of the Bird of Paradise. It runs very quickly, and springs very high, and calls very loudly. It lays but one egg a year and, consequently, only has one baby per annum. It is a great mimic. Mr.

Metcalfe in his "Australian Zoology", describing it, says: "It is a consummate mimic and ventriloquist. It imitates to perfection the notes of all other birds, the united voices of a flock of parrakeets, the barking of dogs, the sawing of timber and the clink of the wood-man's axe. This it has earned for itself the title of the Australian Mocking Bird."

Our Seven Funny Australian Natives

The Kangaroo says, whenever I jump,
I always come down with a great big thump.

The Emu can give a nasty kick;
Which is worse than getting a hit with a brick.

I'm but a funny wild, little, spotted Native Cat,
With claws and tail like a squirrel and a nose like a rat.

Common people call me simply Mr. PLATYPUS,
Learned people call me Mr. OR-NI-THO-RINK-KUS.

I'm bit a little Native Bear, and am so happy and bright,
I sleep and dream in a tree by day, and climb about at night.

The clever Bower Bird builds his nest up a tree,
And his beautiful palace down on the lea.

Here we see a pretty bird, of its voice you will never tire,
But tho' it mocks the sounds it hears the bird is still a Lyre.

(By a Company of Three Particularly Poor Poets.)

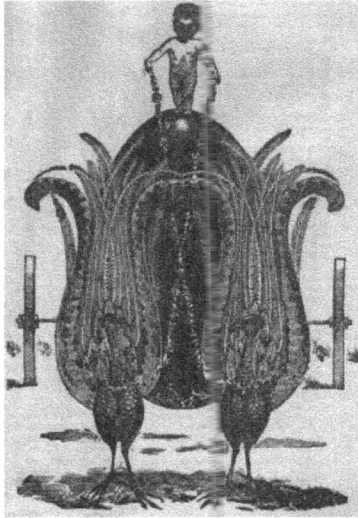

Cat Stories

Puss in the Well

Ding dong dell, pussy's in the well!
Who put her in?—little Tommy Lin.
Who pulled her out?—dog with long snout.
What a naughty boy was that
To drown poor pussy cat.
Who never did any harm
But kill'd the mice in his father's barn.

The Singing Cat

A cat came fiddling out of a barn,
With a pair of bagpipes under her arm;
She could sing nothing but fiddle cum fee,

The mouse has married the bumble-bee.
Pipe cat—dance mouse,
We'll have a wedding at our good house.

Puss in London

Pussy-cat, pussy-cat, where have you been?
I've been to London to visit the Queen.
Pussy-cat, pussy-cat, what did you there?
I frighten'd a little mouse under the chair.

Pussy-Cat and Mousey

Pussy-Cat lives in the servant's hall,
  She can set up her back and purr;
The little mice live in a crack in the wall,
  But they hardly dare venture to stir;
For whenever they think of taking the air,
  Or filling their little maws,
The Pussy-cat says, "Come out if you dare;
  I will catch you all with my claws."
Scramble, scramble, scramble, went all the little Mice,
  For they smelt the Cheshire cheese,
The Pussy-Cat said, "It smells very nice,
  Now do come out, if you please."
"Squeak," said the little Mouse; "squeak, squeak, squeak,"
  Said all the little ones too;
"We never creep out when cats are about,
  Because we're afraid of you."
So the cunning old Cat lay down on a mat
  By the fire in the servants' hall:
"If the little Mice peep, they'll think I'm asleep;"
  So she rolled herself up like a ball.
"Squeak," said the little Mouse, "we'll creep out
  And eat some Cheshire cheese,
That silly old Cat is asleep on the mat,

And we may sup at our ease.
Nibble, nibble, nibble went all the little mice,
  And they licked their little paws;
Then the cunning old Cat sprang up from the mat,
  And caught them all with her claws.

Puss in the Pantry

Hie, hie, says Anthony, puss in the pantry
Gnawing, gnawing a mutton, mutton-bone;
See now she tumbles it, see now she mumbles it,
See how she tosses the mutton, mutton-bone,

Dick killed Puss

Do look at the cat! why, what is she at?
She's catching a rat that's hid in Dick's hat.
Dick ran for a bat to knock him down flat,
But, crossing the mat the foolish young brat
Tripped up and fell flat, He half killed the cat
Instead of the rat, Hal cried out that that
Was just tit for tat.

Puss and the Monkey

Says Mr. Monkey, giving a wink;
"It would be exceedingly funny, I think,
To catch the cat, and give her a drink,
Out of a great big bottle of ink."

So, suiting the action to word,
He caught up Puss, but she demurred;
And made such a noise you never heard,
And said it 'twas worse than eating a bird.

The Puss she didn' like ink at all!
She didn't like bottles great or small;
Ink to her was worse than gall,
And so she did nothing but spit, mew, and squall.
    And that's all!

Sing Sing

Sing, sing, what shall I sing?
The cat has ate the pudding-string!
Do, do, wha shall I do?
The cat has bit it quite in two.

Good Puss

Poor Puss, dear, lovely pretty puss,
    Content at home to stay;
Thy pleasure's shown in gambol tricks
    And loves to skip and play.

Grateful for every sup of milk,
    And for every bit of meat;
Gives lively proof of gratitude

713

By singing while you eat.

See, how she cleans her sleeky skin!
  A soil would prove a flow;
She licks her neck, her sides and back,
  And don't forget her paw.

Mary's Puss Drowned

Mary had a little cat.
  With long snow-white hair.
Such a merry little cat,
  Jumping everywhere.

When Mary went to take a walk,
  Pussy ran to meet her,
Rubbed its head against her frock
  And said, 'Purr, purr,' to greet her.

Once, when Mary was at school,
  Some cruel bad boys found it,
And in a pond beside the road,
  Oh, sad to tell, they drowned it!

Poor Mary's face was wet with tears,
  When she found Pussy lying:—
I would not be a cruel boy,
  To set poor Mary crying.

My Pussy

I love little Pussy, her coat is so warm;
And if I don't hurt her, she'll do me no harm,
So I'll not pull her tail, nor drive her away,
But Pussy and I very gently will play.
She'll sit by my side, and I'll give her some food;

And Pussy will love me, because I am good.
Oh! here is Miss Pussy, she's drinking her milk;
Her coat is as soft and as glossy as silk.
She sips the milk up with her little lap-lap;
Then, wiping her whiskers, lies down for a nap.
My kitty is gentle, she loves me right well;
How funny her play is I'm sure I can't tell.
Now under the sofa, now under the table.
She runs and plays bopeep as well as she's able.
Oh! dearly I love her! you never did see
Two happier playmates than kitty and me.

Dame Trot

Dame Trot once went to a neighbouring fair.
And what do you think she bought herself there?
A pussy! the prettiest ever was seen;
No cat was so gentle, so clever and clean.

Each dear little paw was as black as a sloe,
The rest of her fur was white as the snow,
Her eyes were bright green, and her sweet little face
Was pretty and meek, full of innocent grace.

Dame Trot hurried home with this beautiful cat;
Went upstairs to take off her cloak and her hat;
And when she came down she was astonished to see
That Pussy was busy preparing the tea.

"Oh, what a strange cat!" thought poor little Dame Trot,
"She'll break my best china and upset the pot."
But no harm befell them; the velvety paws
Were quite sure; the Dame for alarm had no cause.

Next morning when little Dame Trot came downstairs,
To attend as usual, to household affairs,

She found that the kitchen was swept up as clean
As if Puss a regular servant had been.

The tea stood to draw, and the toast was done brown;
The Dame very pleased to her breakfast sat down;
While Puss by her side on an armchair sat up,
And lapped her warm milk from a nice china cup.

Now Spot, the old house-dog, looked on in amaze,
He'd never been used to such queer cattish ways,
But Puss mewed so sweetly, and moved with such grace,
That Spot at last liked her, and licked her white face.

Poor little Dame Trot had no money to spare,
And only too often her cupboard was bare;
Then kind Mrs Pussy would catch a nice fish,
And serve it for dinner upon a clean dish.

The rats and the mice, who wished Pussy to please,
Were now never seen at the butter and cheese;
The Dame daily found that their numbers grew thinner,
For Puss ate a mouse every day for her dinner.

If Puss had a weakness, I need but confess
'Twas a girl of the period's fancy for dress,
Her greatest desire a high chignon and hat,
And a very short dress *a la mode* for a cat.

So one day when Dame Trot had gone out to dine,
Puss dressed herself up, as she thought, very fine,
And coaxed kind old Spot, who looked at her with pride,
To play pony for her, and give her a ride.

Now Spot, who to welcome his mistress desired,
And to "company manners" had never aspired,
Jumped up to fawn on her—and down came the cat,
And crushed, in her tumble, her feather and hat.

"Oh, puss!" said Dame Trot, "what a very sad mess!
You'd best have remained in your natural dress;

The graces which Nature so kindly bestows
Are more often hid than improved by fine clothes.

Mistress Puss and Doggy

A little dog said, and he looked very wise,
  "I think, Mistress Pus,
  You make a great fuss
With your back and your great green eyes
  And you, Madam Duck,
  You waddle and cluck,
Till it gives one the fidgets to hear you;
  You'd better run off
  To the old pig's trough,
Where none but the pigs, ma'am, are near you."

The duck was good-natured, and she ran away;
  But old pussy-cat
  With her back up sat,
And said she intended to stay;
  And she showed him her paws,
  With her sharp long claws,
So the dog was afraid to come near,
  For Puss if she pleases,
  When a little dog teases
Can give him a box on the ear.

Don't Hurt Puss

I like little pussy, her coat is so warm,
And if I don't hurt her she'll do me no harm;
So I'll not pull her tail, nor drive her away,
But Pussy and I very gently will play.

717

Head In The Milk Jug

Ho! Master, Mistress, Mary, run,
  Your Tabby is in grief;
This broken jug caught hold of me
  As though I were a thief.

Cat Up The Plum Tree

Diddledy, diddledy, dumpty,
The cat ran up the plum tree
  I lay you a crown
  I'll fetch her down;
So diddledy, diddledy, dumpty.

Pussy-Cat Mole

Pussy Cat Mole
  Jumped over a coal,
And in her best petticoat burnt a great hole

718

Poor Pussy is weeping, she'll have no more milk
Until her best petticoat's mended with silk.

The Three Little Kittens

Three little kittens they lost their mittens,
  And they began to cry,
"Oh! mammy dear, we sadly fear,
  Our mittens we have lost."
  "What! lost your mittens,
  You naughty kittens,
  Then you shall have no pie."
    Miew, miew miew, miew.

The three Little kittens had need of mittens:
  The winter was now nigh.
"Oh! mammy dear, we fear, we fear,
  Our mittens we shall need."
  "Go, seek your mittens,
  You silly kittens;
  There's a tempest in the sky."
    Miew, miew, miew, miew.

The three little kittens, in seeking their mittens,
  Upset the table high.
"Oh! mammy dear, we doubt and fear,
  The house is tumbling down,"
  "You foolish kittens,
  Go find your mittens,
  And do not make things fly."
    Miew, miew, miew, miew.

The three little kittens they found their mittens,
  And they began to cry,
"Oh! mammy dear, see here, see here,
  Our mittens we have found."
  "What! found your mittens,
  You little kittens;

Then you shall have some pie."
  Purr, purr, purr, purr.

The three little kittens put on their mittens,
  And soon ate up the pie;
"Oh! mammy dear, we greatly fear,
  Our mittens we have soiled."
  "What! soiled your mittens,
  You naughty kittens!"
Then they began to sigh.
  Miew, miew, miew, miew.

The three little kittens they washed their mittens,
  And hung them up to dry.
"Oh! mammy dear, look here, look here,
  Our mittens we have washed,"
"What! washed your mittens,
  You darling kittens!—
  But I smell a rat close by!
  Hush! Hush!" Miew, miew.

The three little kittens put off their mittens,
  A hunting match to try.
"Oh! mammy dear, his hole is here:
  Our mittens down we fling."
  Both cat and kittens
  Flung down their mittens;
When—whisk!—the rat ran by.
  Miew, miew, miew, miew.

The Dunce of a Kitten

Come, Pussy, will you learn to read?
  I've got a pretty book:
Nay, turn this way, you must indeed,
  Fie, there's a sulky look!

Here's a pretty picture, see

An apple with a great A;
How stupid you will ever be
If you do nought but play!

Come, A B C, an easy task,
  What anyone can do,
I will do anything you ask,
  For dearly I love you.

No, no, your lesson is not done,
  You have not learnt it half;
You'll grow a downright simpleton,
  And make the people laugh.

Old Daddy Hubbard and His Cat

Old Daddy Hubbard
Went to the cupboard,
  To get poor Puss some meat;
But when he got there,
I do declare,
  There was nothing but two pig's feet.

Daddy went to the fish shop
  To get Puss a sprat,
And when he came back,
  She was watching a rat.

Daddy went to the carpenter's
  To get Puss a house,
And when he came back
  She was catching a mouse.

Daddy went to the miller's
  To get Puss some meal,
And when he came back
  She was skinning an eel.

Daddy went to a meadow
  To get milk from a cow,
And when he came back,
  Puss cried: "Me-ow, Me-ow."

Daddy went to the crockery shop
  To get Puss a dish,
And when he came back
  She had caught Ma's goldfish.

Daddy went to the dairy
  To get Puss some curd,
And when he came back
  She'd ate Ma's pet bird.

Daddy went to the brewer's
  To get Puss some beer,
And when he came back
  She's a flea in her ear.

Daddy went for some water,
  To give Puss some souse,
And when he came back
  Puss was top of the house.

Daddy went to the iron-monger's
  To get Puss a saw,
And when he came back
  She had scalded her paw.

Daddy went to the photographer's
  To get Puss some pictures,
And when he came back,
  She had burnt off her whiskers.

Daddy went to the garden
  To get Puss a snail,
And when he came back
  She'd a bottle-brush tail.

Daddy went tc the grocer's
  To get Puss some tea,
And when he came back
  She had run up a tree.

Daddy went tc the draper's
  To buy Puss some mittens,
And when he came back
  She was licking her kittens.

Daddy went tc the stable
  To get Puss a donkey,
And when he got back
  She was teaching the monkey.

Daddy went tc the confectioner's
  To buy Puss a lollie,
And when he came back
  She was nursing the dolly.

Daddy went tc get clothes
  To make Puss a lady,
And when he came back
  She was kissing the baby.

Daddy took Cole's balloon
  And got Puss a cloud,
But Puss when she saw it
  Laughed right out loud.

Daddy went to the store
  To get Puss a herring,
And when he came back
  She kept loving and purring

Daddy went to the furrier's
  To get Puss a muff,
And when he came back
  She was taking some snuff.

Daddy went to the baker's
  To get Puss a bun,
And when he came back
  She was beating a drum.

Daddy went to the dressmaker's
  To buy Puss a frock,
And when he came back
  She was winding the clock.

Daddy went to the jeweller's

To get Puss a brooch,
And when he came back
  She'd caught a cockroach.

Daddy went to Cole's Book Arcade
  Some cheap music to buy,
And when he came back
  Puss had made a mud pie.

Daddy went to Cole's Book Arcade
  To buy Puss some pens,
And when he came back
  She was feeding some hens.

Daddy went to Cole's Book Arcade
  To buy Puss a slate,
And when he came back
  She opened the gate.

Daddy went to Cole's Book Arcade
  To buy Puss some ink,
And when he came back
  She gave him a wink.

Daddy went to Cole's Book Arcade
  For an exercise book,
And when he came back
  Puss gave a wise look.

Daddy went to Cole's Book Arcade
  To buy Puss a purse,
And when he came back
  She was singing a verse.

Daddy went to Cole's Book Arcade
  And Oh me! Oh my!
And when he came back
  Puss had swallowed a fly.

Daddy went to Cole's Book Arcade

COLE

> Some paper to buy,
> And when he came back
> Puss thought she would die.
>
> Daddy went to the doctor's
> To get Puss a pill,
> And when he came back
> She still looked very ill.
>
> Daddy went to the auction sale
> To buy Puss a bed,
> And when he came back
> Puss Shammed to be dead.

This was a very wise, knowing Puss, she could read and write, and liked books very, very much, and didn't want to die and be buried, and leave all the mice, and milk, and sausages, and nice books; so she made haste and got better, and when

> Daddy went to the cemetery
> To dig her a grave,
> Puss rushed off at once
> Into Cole's Book Arcade.

And that is the present residence of Miss Puss.

The Story of a Little Mouse:
Or, Our Happy Family.

Once there was a little mouse,
  Who came to live in our house;
She came because she was terribly frighten'd
  To stay outside as it thunder'd and lighten'd.

When she came in 'twas nearly dark,
  And Ponto he began to bark;
But she ran round at a rapid rate,
  Then darted in behind the grate.

Ponto smelt, and sniff'd, and bark'd and scratch'd,
  But Mousey was safe and couldn't be catch'd;
So Ponto, when tired laid down to sleep,
  And Mousey quite quiet determined to keep.

Mousey stayed there a month as she thought it was better,
  And Ponto could smell her, but never could get her,
But every morning when Ponto went out,
  Miss Mousey crept forth, and for crumbs looked about.

Now one day as Ponto came into the house,
  Thinks he, I'll be KIND to that poor little mouse;
"So come out Miss Mousey," our Ponto he said,
  "And if anyone hurts you I'll bite off his head."

So the poor little mouse came out of the grate,
  And ate with our Ponto out of his plate,
And always when Ponto laid down on the mat,
  Beside him Miss Mousey in her little chair sat.

But one rainy night as Miss Mousey sat still,
  A thing called a bat, came over the hill;
But Ponto says to him, "You are not wanted here,"
  And sent the bat off with a flea in his ear.

The very same night as they lay on the mat,
  What should come rushing in but a great big rat;

Up jumped Mr. Ponto and gave a loud bark,
  And that rat scampered off out into the dark.

They had just got rid of the bat and the rat,
  And what should come in but a GREAT TOM CAT;
Came jumping, springing, and bounding along,
  And frightened Miss Mousey more than a gong.

He raced after mousey, around, in and out,
  Through the house and the yard, and all round about;
To the East, to the West, to the North, to the South,
  And at last caught her up in his great big mouth.

He squeezed her back hard and frighten'd her so,
  She scarcely could say, "O, please let me go!"
But Tom spoke and said, "Mouse is very good meat,
  And as I feel hungry, why, it's you I shall eat."

Tom let her go once, but caught her afresh,
  Although Mousey made a most desperate dash;
And again Mousey pleaded, "Oh, please let me go";
  But Tom only answered, "Decidedly No!"

But as luck should now have it, our Ponto came in,
  And asked Mr. Puss, "What's this horrible din?"
Says Puss to our Ponto, "I've caught this sly thief,
  And now I intend to bring her to grief."

Says Ponto to Puss, "The mouse is my friend,
  And if you would hurt her, why I must defend
That nice little, kind little, good little mouse,
  As long as she ever remains in this house."

Says Pussy to Ponto, "I pray you don't fret;
  I'll love and I'll cherish your poor little pet;
She shall sleep on the mat, and we'll find her in food,
  Because she is nice and because she is good."

So the nice little mouse, the dog and the cat,
  all three ate together, and slept on the mat;

They sung, danc'd and romp'd with joy and merry laughter,
And as the old take says, 'Lived happy ever after."

History of Mr. Tom Puss And The Rats

Mrs. Puss stayed at home, minded and played with young Master John Puss, Miss Mary Puss, and Baby Puss, while Mr. Puss went out to get them something to eat. He went into a barn, tied a piece of cheese to the tip of his tail, and put it through a hole in a door, thinking that he would catch a rat that way. Some very knowing rats on the other side of the door got a piece of string, tied it to his tail, pulled all together, and made Mr. Puss me-ow very loud, and he found that instead of his catching a rat, the rats had caught him. Mrs. Puss, finding that Mr. Puss did not come home, put little John Puss and Mary Puss to bed without any supper, and then sang little deaf Baby Puss off to sleep by means of the ear trumpet. The rats ate their supper off Mr. Puss's tail, and then let him go. You see what a fine long tail he had when he put it through the hole to catch rats in that foolish manner; and look at his short tail now, in the corner of the page.

Wasn't He A Foolish Puss!!!

Puss In Boots

Once upon a time there was a miller who had three

sons. When he was dying he left each of them a legacy. To his eldest son he lef his mill; to his second his ass; and to his youngest his cat. The poor boy was very sad when he found that he had nothing belonging to him but a cat; but, to his great surprise, puss jumped on the table and said in a friendly manner: "Do not be sad, my dear master, only buy me a pair of boots and a bag and I'll provide for you and myself." So the miller's son, who had a shilling or two in his pocket, bought a smart little pair of boots and a bag, and gave them to puss, who put some bran and sow-thistles into his bag, opened the mouth of it, and lay down in a rabbit warren. A foolish young rabbit jumped into it; puss drew the string and soon killed it. He went immediately to the palace with it. He found the king and queen sitting on the throne, and, bowing low, he laid the rabbit at the king's feet, saying: "Please, your majesty, my master, the Marquis de Carabas, has sent you a rabbit from his warren, as a mark of respect." "I am much obliged to the Marquis," said the king, and he ordered the rabbit to be taken to the cook, and a piece of money to be given to the cat.

During two or three months the cat continued to carry game every now and then to the king, which was supposed to be the produce of his master's sport. One day when he happened o hear the king was going to take a drive on the banks of the river, in company with his daughter, who was the most beautiful princess in the world, puss desired the master to go and bathe in the river at the spot that he should point out, and leave the rest to him. The Marquis of Carabas did as his cat advised him. Just as he was bathing the king came past, when the cat bawled out as loud as he could—"Help! help! or the Marquis of Carabas will be drowned!" On hearing this, the king looked out of the carriage window, and recognising the cat, ordered his bodyguards to fly to the assistance of my Lord Marquis of Carabas. As the poor Marquis was being fished out of the river, the cat informed his majesty that while his master was bathing, some robbers had stolen his clothes. The king immediately ordered the gentlemen of his wardrobe to fetch one of his most sumptuous dresses. No sooner had this been done and the Marquis suitably attired, then he looked to such advantage that the king took him to be a very fine gentleman; while the princess was so struck with his appearance, that at once she became head and ears in love with him.

The king insisted that the Marquis should get into the carriage. The cat, highly delighted at the turn thinks were taking, now ran on before, and having reached a meadow where there were some peasants, he thus accosted them; "I say, good folks, if you do not tell the king that this field belongs to the Marquis of Carabas, you shall all be chopped as fine as mince-meat." The king did not fail to inquire of the peasants to whom the meadow belonged? "To the Marquis of Carabas, please your majesty," said they in a breath.

And the cat kept running on before the carriage, and repeating the same instructions to all the labourers he met with, so that the king was astonished at the vast possessions of the Marquis of Carabas.

At length the cat reached a magnificent castle belonging to a giant who was immensely rich. The cat having inquired what sort of person the giant might be, and what he was able to do, sent in a message to request leave to speak with him.

The giant received him civilly. "I have been told," said the cat, "that you have the power of transforming yourself into all sorts of animals." "So I have," replied the giant, "and to prove the truth of what I say you shall see me become a lion." When the cat beheld a lion standing before him, and saw the monster quietly light his pipe, he was seized with such a panic that he clambered up to the roof. After a time, the cat perceiving that the giant had returned to his natural shape, came down again.

"And do you possess the power of assuming the shape of the smallest animals likewise?" "You shall see;" and the giant immediately assumed the shape of a mouse, when the cat pounced upon him and ate him up.

By this time the king had reached the gates of the Giant's magnificent castle, and expressed a wish to enter so splendid a building. The cat ran out to meet the king, saying—"Your majesty s welcome to the Marquis of Carabas's castle."

The king was so delighted with the Marquis of Carabas, that he accepted him as a son-in-law, and that very same day he was married to the princess.

The cat became a great lord, and ever after hunted mice only for his own amusement.

Monkey And The Cats

Two hungry cats having stolen some cheese, could not agree between themselves how to divide their booty; therefore they went to the law, and a cunning monkey was to decide their case.

"Let us see," said the judge (with as arch a look as could be); "ay, ay, this slice truly outweighs the other;" and with this he bit off a large piece, on order, as he told them, to make a fair balance.

The other scale had now become too heavy, which gave this upright judge a pretence to make free with a second mouthful.

"Hold, hold!" cried the two cats; give each of us our share of what is left and we will be content.

"If you are content," said the monkey, "justice is not; the law, my friends, must have it's course."

Upon this he ribbled first one piece and then the other, till the poor cats, seeing their cheese in a fair way to be all eaten up, most humbly begged him not to put himself to any further trouble, to give them what still remained.

"Ha! ha! ha! not so fast, I beseech you, good ladies," said the monkey; "we owe justice to ourselves as well as to you: and what remains is due to me as the lawyer." Upon this he crammed the whole into his mouth at once, and very gravely broke up the court.

This fable teaches us that it is better to put up with a trifling loss, than to run the risk of losing all we have by going to the law.

Dick Whittington And His Cat

There was once a Lord Mayor of London, whose name was Sir Richard Whittington. He rose to that office from being a poor orphan, living in a distant village. Dick was a sharp boy, and was always picking up knowledge from some of the villagers. Dick heard of the great City of London; he often heard it said that the streets were paved all over with gold.

One day seeing a waggon and team of horses on the road to London; he took courage and asked the waggoner to let him walk by his side. Having gained permission, they set off together. When Dick got to London, he was very eager to see the fine streets paved all over with gold, but the poor boy saw nothing but dirt

instead of gold, so he crouched down at the door of one
Mr. Fitzwarren, a great merchant. Here he was soon
found by an ill-tempered cook, who ordered him to go
about his business. But just at this moment Mr. Fitzwarren himself came home, and finding that the poor boy
was willing to work, he took him into his house, and
said that he should be kept to do what dirty work he was
able for the cook. The cook was always scolding him
from morning till night, and was very cruel to him. Poor
Dick had another hardship. His bed was places in a garret where there were great numbers of rats and mice,
which ran over his face, and made a great noise. Dick at
last bought a cat which was famous for being an excellent mouser.

Soon after this, the merchant, who had a ship
ready to sail, asked his servants if they would send any
goods abroad. All the servants mentioned something
they were willing to venture but poor Whittington, who
said he had nothing but a cat which was his companion.

"Fetch thy cat, boy," said Mr. Fitzwarren, "and
let her go." Dick hesitated for some time; at last he
brought poor Puss, and delivered her to the captain with
tears in his eyes. The cook continued to be so cruel to
him that the unhappy fellow determined to leave his
place. He accordingly packed up his few things, and
travelled as far as Holloway, and there sat down on a
stone. While he was there musing, Bow-bells began to
ring; and it seemed to him that their sound said:

"Turn again Whittington,
Lord Mayor of London."

So back went Dick, and got into the house before
the cook came down stairs.

The ship with Dick's cat on board happened to be
driven by contrary winds on a part of the coast of Bar-
bary, inhabited by Moors, who showed great eagerness
to purchase the things with which the ship was laden.
The captain seeing this, took patterns of the choicest
articles he had to the King of the Moors. While he was
showing them to him, dinner was brought in, and at once
lots of rats and mice came in and ate up all the dainties.
The captain was astonished when the King told him that

this often happened. The captain rushed off at once to the ship, and brought Puss to the palace. The second dinner had been brought in, and, as usual, in came the rats and mice; Pussy at the sight of them sprang out of the captain's arms and killed lots of them, and the rest ran off to their holes. The King was greatly pleased with the wonderful Puss, and gave two sackfuls of gold for the cat, and the captain at once sailed for London. When Mr. Fitzwarren heard the news, he ordered Dick Whittington to be called, and showed him all the riches which the captain had brought in exchange for his cat. Dick was now a rich man, and soon after married the merchant's daughter, at the very church whose bells seemed to call him back to London. He grew richer and richer, became Sheriff, and at length Lord Mayor of London.

Our Kate Washing our Kitties.

Weighing our Puss against our Doggy

The White Kitten

My little white kitten's
  Asleep on my knee;
As white as snow
  Or the lily is she,
    She wakes up with a purr
    When I stroke her soft fur;
  Was there ever another
    White kitten like her?

My little white kitten
  Now wants to go out
And frolic, with no one
  To watch her about:
    "Little kitten," I say,
    "Just an hour you may stay;
  And be careful in choosing
    Your places to play."

But night has come down,
  And I hear a loud "mew";
I open the door, and my

739

Kitten comes through;
  My white kitten! ah me!
Oh! can it be she—
This sad looking beggar-like
  Cat that I see?

What ugly grey marks
  On her side and her back!
Her nose, once as pink
  As a rosebud is black!
  Oh! I very well know,
  Though she does not say so,
She has been where white kittens
  Ought never to go.

If little good children
  Would wish to do right,
If little white kittens
  Would keep themselves white,
  It is needful that they
  In their houses should stay,
Or be careful in choosing
  Their places to play.

Kitty

Pretty little Kitty
  Sat upon a stile,
Sang a little ditty
  To herself for a while,
Watching how the sparrows—
  Seeking grain to eat—
Dart about like arrows
  In among the wheat.

Pretty little Kitty
  Liked the birds to see!
Though it was a pity

They were wild and free.
So she stopped her singing—
　Left the stile forlorn;
And went gaily springing
　In among the corn.

Pretty little Kitty
　Fond of country things,
Cares not for the city
　Where no birdie sings.

Our Jacko, our Jessie, our Jemmy.

Our Pansies riding Horseback.

Our naughty Kitten caught stealing jam.

Naughty Pussy

"Oh, for shame,
 Baby Cat.
Mother's pet
 Her cupboard at.

"With a spoon
 Eating Jam
Quite ashamed
 Of you I am.

"If she comes
 And catches you
You'll be punished
 Rightly too.

"She will send you
 Straight to bed,
With for supper
 Plain dry bread."

Our naughty Kitten caught in trying to
catch the Goldfish.

Little Pussy

I love little Pussy,
  Her coat is so warm;
And if I don't tease her,
  She'll do me no harm.

I'll not pull her tail,
  Nor drive her away,
But Pussy and I
  Very gently will play.

She'll be gentle with me,
  If I'm gentle with her,
And if I speak kindly,
  I know she will purr.

She shall sit by my side,
  And I'll give her some food
And Pussy will love me
  Because I am good.

It's true, if I tease her,
  Her claws she will show;
But Pussy knows well
  That I never do so.

Puss and the Crab

"I wonder," says puss,
  "If a thing like that
Would presume to bite
  A respectable cat?

'Tis the queerest thing
  That ever I saw;
I'll hit it a slap

With my strong forepaw.

No! No! On the whole
  I had better not;
But what curious claws
  The creature has got!

I'll just step up
  And quietly ask it
How it got out
  Of that market-basket.

I'll play with the animal,
  Just to see
If it wants to do
  Any harm to me.

No! I thank I had better
  Get out of its way,
And I surely am safer
  Not even to p ay.

For I'll get into trouble,
  And horribly wail,
If that thing with the claws
  Takes a grip on my tail."

Rev. A. Taylor

Little Pussies

Three little pussies,
  All in a row,
Ranged on the table,
  Two down below.

Five little pussies
  Dressed all in silk,

Waiting for sugar,
Waiting for milk.

Dear little pussies,
If you would thrive,
Breakfast at nine o'clock,
Take tea at five.

Our Loving Doggy and Pussy.

Our Smartly-dressed Friends.

Puss in the Corner

You are a naughty pussy-cat;
I think it right to mention that
For all who see your picture here—
'Twas you who broke my bunny dear.

An hour ago, as you can tell,
I left him here, alive and well;
And now he's dead, and, what is more
You've broke his leg I'm pretty sure.

For you, my puss, I'l never care,
No—never, never, never—there!
And you are in disgrace, you know,
And in the corner you must go.

What, crying? Then I must cry too,
And I can't bear to punish you;
Perhaps you've only stunned his head.

And though I'm sure you broke his leg,
It may be mended with a peg;
And though he's very, very funny,
My bunny's not a real bunny;
And I'll forgive and tell you that
You are my precious pussy-cat.

Robert Mack

Tabby

Tabby was a kitten,
Tabby was a thief.
Tabby tried to steal the cream,
And so she came to grief.

Jumping on the table

747

(Nobody was nigh),
On the pretty cream-jug
Tabby cast her eye:

Wondered what was in it;
Thought she'd like to see;
Crept a little nearer,
Slyly as could be.

Cream was very low down;
Jug was very high;
"Must have some," said Tabby.
"Even if I die!"

Then into the cream-jug
Popped her naughty nose;
Just what happened after,
Only Tabby knows.

This is how we found her,
Naughty little cat!
Did she get a whipping,
Think you, after that?

Tabby was a kitten,
Tabby was a thief,
Tabby tried to steal the cream,
And so she came to grief.

Old Puss

Don't hurt the poor old cat,
There can be no fun in that;
And it would be cruel too—
She never tried to injure you.

She, for years, has kept the house
Free from thievish rat and mouse;

748

Puss has always faithful been,
And has kept herself so clean.

True, she now is getting old,
Though she once was strong and bold;
At her prey she cannot leap,
And, if caught, can scarcely keep.

Poor old puss! 'Twould be a shame
Thee for uselessness to blame;
When though canst not active be—
Useless through infirmity.

In the Park

I'm a rich little kitten:
    I live at my ease,

I keep my own carriage,
    I go where I please;

My turn-out is stylish,
    I nothing neglect,

And often I notice
    That all recollect

That a rich little kitten
    Deserves much respect.

Our Kitten in her Perambulator.

Our Puss and her Dog Carriage.

Our Puss and her Chicken Coach.

The Dead Kitten

Don't talk to me of parties, Nan;
  I really cannot go;
When folks are in affliction
  They don't go out, you know.
I have a new brown sash, too;
  It seems a pity—eh?
That such a dreadful trial
  Should have come just yesterday!

The play-house blinds are all pulled down
  As dark as it can be;
It looks so very solemn
  And so proper, don't you see?
And I have a piece of crape
  Pinned on my dolly's hat,
Tom says it is ridiculous
  For only just a cat.

But boys are all so horrid!
  They always, every one,
Delight in teasing little girls
  And kitties, "just for fun."
The way he used to pull her tail—
  It makes me angry now—
And scat her up the cherry tree,

751

To make the darling "meow!"

I've had her all the summer.
  One day, away last spring,
I heard a frightful barking,
  And I saw the little thing
In the corner of a fence;
  'T would have made you laugh outright
To see how every hair stood out,
  And how she tried to fight.

I shooed the dog away,
  And she jumped upon my arm;
The pretty creature knew
  I wouldn't do her any harm;
I hugged her close, and carried her
  To mamma, and she said
She should be my own wee kitty,
  If I'd see that she was fed.

A cunning little dot she was,
  With silky, soft, grey fur;
She'd lie for hours on my lap,
  And I could hear her purr;
And then she'd frolic after
  When I pulled a string about,
Or try to catch her tail,
  Or roll a marble in and out.

Such comfort she has been to me
  I'm sure no one could tell,
Unless some other little girl
  Who loves her pussy well.
I've heard about a Maltese cross;
  But my dear little kit
Was always sweet and amiable,
  And never cross a bit!

But oh, last week I missed her!
  I hunted all around;

My darling little pussy-cat
  Was nowhere to be found.
I knelt and whispered softly,
  When nobody could see:
"Take care of little kitty, please,
  And bring her back to me."

I found her lying yesterday
  Behind the lower shed;
I thought my heart was broken
  When I found that she was dead.
Tom promised me another one;
  But even he can see
No other kitty ever will be
  Just the same to me.

I can't go to your party Nannie,
  Maccaroons, you say?
And ice-cream? I know
  I ought to try and not give way;
And I feel it would be doing wrong
  To disappoint you so.
Well, if I'm equal to it
  By to-morrow, I may go!

Sydney Dayre

The Monkey and the Nuts

A monkey, being fond of nuts,
  Thought he would have some roasted;
But how was he to get them done,
  Not liking to be toasted?
A poor young cat was passing by,
  And innocently watches;
The wicked monkey saw her stop,
  And at his victim snatches.

"Dear pussy, you are just the one
  That I've been looking out for;
How beautiful you look to-day,
  But tell me what you pout for!
Upon my word I long have had
  For you a fond affection;
Now you shall stay and dine with me,
  Or take some slight refection."

"Twas no use for poor puss to speak,
  Or offer to deny him,
The monkey had her in his grasp,
  And she could not deny him.
So he began to laugh and chat,
  And show a few grimaces;
Oh! if you had but seen, like me,
  The contrast of their faces.

He put some nuts into her paw,
  And he the fire approaches,
As if a salamander she.
  Or made of young cockroaches.
The poor cat now began to squall,
  Her face the fire attacking;
And sadly too, her paw was burnt,
  The while the nuts were cracking.

The monkey having feasted well
  Began to snarl and grumble,
That he should be so taken in
  With nuts he scarce could mumble.
"Dear me," he said, "how they are burnt,"
  And at poor pussy looking,
"I cannot think how I could bear
  Such miserable cooking.

And what a fuss you make about
  A little bit of warning;
I've often done the thing myself—
  There's nothing so alarming.

Now take this for yourself," he said,
   "And next time be less squalling:"
Then gave the cat a hearty cuff,
   Which sent the poor thing sprawling.

"Now let me give you his advice,
   For I am one of letters:
Leave off your rude, obstreperous way,
   When you are with your betters.
And think yourself well off," he said,
   "That I had mercy on you;
For many would have sent you home
   Without a dress upon you."

Mrs. W. Taylor

My Own Puss

I wish you could just see my cat:
She's a darling, there's no doubt of that:
So soft, and so sleek, and so fat.

Her eyes are a beautiful green,
The brightest that ever were seen:
Of cats she is truly the queen.

She loves to lie stretched in the sun
But as soon as my lessons are done,
She is ready for frolic and fun.

My kitty has two sets of claws,
Tucked away in those velvety paws:
She can use them, too, when there is cause.

I cannot thin what I should do,
If, my pussy, I ever lost you:
We're so happy together, we two!

I call her my bundle of fur:
Hark! now she's beginning to purr:
Kit loves me, and oh, I love her!

The Frolicsome Kitten

Dear kitten, do be still, I say,
  How much I want you to be quiet,
Instead of scampering away,
  And always making such a riot.

There, only see! you've torn my frock,
  And poor mamma must put a patch in;
I'll give you a right earnest knock,
  To cure you of this trick of scratching.

Nay, do not scold your little cat,
  She does not know what 'tis you're saying;
And every time you give a pat,
  She thinks you mean it all for playing.

But if your pussy understood

The lesson that you want to teach her,
And did not choose to be so good,
She'd be, indeed, a naughty creature.

Putting Kitty to Bed

Kitty, Kitty, go to sleep,
Shut your eyes, and don't you peep.
Sing with me your little song,
We will not make it very long.

Hurry Kitty for to see
Mamma soon will come for me,
And I must see you safe in bed
All covered up except your head.

And while I rock you in my chair,
You must purr your little prayer,
Altho' you say it soft an low,
'Twill all be just the same you know.

Mamma makes me bend my knee,
But Kitty dear, you can't, you see,
For you're too little yet to try—
See! I'm so big, and tall, and high.

And then you can't say any words,
No more than chicks, or little birds.
But I've heard the Bible tell
That even birds are cared for well.

M. E. S.

Our Puss and her Shoe Coach.

Our Doggy and Pussy growling at each other.

Our Pussies' Party.

Old Mother Hubbard and Her Dog

Old Mother Hubbard
Went to the cupboard
  To get her poor Dog a bone;
But when she got there
The cupboard was bare,
  And so the poor Dog had none.

She went to the baker's
  To buy him some bread,
And when she came back
  The poor Dog looked dead.

She went to the joiner's
  To buy him a coffin,
But when she came back
  The poor Dog was laughing.

She took a clean dish
  To get him some tripe,
But when she came back
  He was smoking a pipe.

She went to the ale-house
  To get him some beer,
But when she came back
  The Dog sat on a chair.

She went to the hatter's
  To buy him a hat.
But when she came back
  He was feeding the cat.

She went to the barber's
  To buy him a wig.
But when she came back
  He was dancing a jig.

759

COLE

She went to the fruiterer's
  To buy him some fruit,
But when she came back
  He was playing the flute.

She went to the tailor's,
  To buy him a coat,
But when she came back
  He was riding a goat.

She went to the seamstress
  To buy him some linen,
But when she came back
  The Dog was a-spinning.

She went to the hosier's
  To buy him some hose,
But when she came back
  He was dressed in his clothes.

She went to the cobbler's
  To buy him some shoes,
But when she came back
  He was reading the news.

She went to the hotel
  To get him some ale,
But when she came back,
  He was wagging his tail.

She went to the tavern
  For white wine and red,
But when she came back
  The Dog stood on his head.

The dame made a curtsey,
  The Dog made a bow;
The dame said "Your servant,"
  The Dog said "Bow-wow."

This wonderful Dog
  Was Dame Hubbard's delight;
He could sing, he could dance,
  He could read, he could write.

She went to Cole's Book Arcade
  To buy him a book,
And when she came back
  He at once took a look.

She went to Cole's Book Arcade
  To buy him book two,
And when she came back

COLE

He was tying his shoe.

She went to Cole's Book Arcade
To buy him book three,
And when she came back
He getting his tea.

She went to Cole's Book Arcade
To buy him book four,
And when she came back
He sat at the door.

She went to Cole's Book Arcade
To buy him book five,
And when she came back
He was out for a drive.

She went to Cole's Book Arcade
To buy him book six
And when she came back
He was picking up sticks.

She went to Cole's Book Arcade
To buy him book seven,
And when she came back
He was brewing some leaves.

She went to Cole's Book Arcade
To buy him book eight,
And when she came back
He was baking a cake.

She went to Cole's Book Arcade
To buy him book nine,
And when she came back
He said it was fine.

She went to Cole's Book Arcade
To buy him book ten,
And when she came back

He took it an then

She went to Cole's Book Arcade
To buy him book eleven,
And when she came back
He had gone up to heaven.

To Parents And Schoolmasters

I have been blamed for printing and distributing "Mother Hubbard." My answer is:—"Old Mother Hubbard" has done more towards the education of young children than perhaps any piece of reading in existence. Amongst the hundreds of millions of English speaking people in all parts of the earth, there are very few but can repeat a part or the whole of "Mother Hubbard," and I have seen it somewhat asserted that it is to be found in almost every home in the civilised world. Its rude style of poetry tells nothing against it. The child knows nothing of correct metre: as long as there is a jingling rhyme it is satisfied. The dog is the domestic animal in millions of families, and in numberless cases is actually a more loved companion then brothers and sisters. A simple rhyme, therefore, about this attached, playful, and constant companion is sure to fascinate the young, and it has fascinated more than a thousand millions of the little dears. I firmly believe that it would produce grand results if a pretty illustrated edition of the principal nursery rhymes were made a text-book in infant schools. You may try, and try, and try again, to drive an ordinary dry school-book lesson into the infant mind, and make very little progress—it is up-hill work. But take an illustrated edition of a nursery rhyme, say the "Death of Cock Robin," or "Mother Hubbard," and call the little one to you, begin to teach it—how eagerly, how intently does it begin to learn now! What animation in its little eyes! What music in its little, joyous, interested voice! It learns this lesson ten times as fast as the other one, and gives you ten times the pleasure in teaching it, and this

763

kind of teaching gradually and insensibly leads the child into a love of learning: it interests and sets the young inquiring mind at work. We all know how much easier it is to do a work we are interested in than a work we are not. It is just so with the child, and for that reason I would commence to teach the infant mind with that which pleased it best, and so gradually create a love for reading. For years I have allowed numbers of little children, of their own accord, to stand and read nursery rhymes to themselves, and to teach other youths to read interesting and instructive fiction, gratis, in the Book Arcade; and I hold that, by its enticingly creating a love for reading, which will lead to something higher, time is one of the best and most effective schools in the country.

—E. W. Cole

Tom Tinker's Dog

Bow, wow, wow, whose dog art tho?
I'm Tom Tinker's dog, and I'll bite you.

Puppy

There was an Old Man of Leghorn,
The smallest as ever was born;
But quickly snapt up he
Was once by a puppy,
Who devoured that Old Man of Leghorn.

Doggy

The cat sat asleep by the side of the fire,
The mistress snored loud as a pig;

Jack took up his fiddle by doggy's desire,
And struck up a bit of a jig.

Hark, the Dogs bark

Hark, hark, the dogs do bark,
   Beggars are coming to town;
Some in jags, some in rags,
   And some in velvet gown.

Poor Dog Bright

Poor dog Bright
Ran off with all his might,
Because the cat was after him:
Poor dog Bright.

Dog Blue Bell

I had a little dog, and his name was Blue Bell,
I gave him some work, and he did it very well;
I sent him up stairs to pick up a pin,
He stepped into the coal-scuttle up to the chin;
I sent him to the garden to pick some sage,
He tumbled down and fell in a rage;
I sent him to the cellar to draw a pot of beer,
He came up again and said there was none there.

Little Dog Buff

I had a little Dog, and they called him buff,
I sent him to the shop for a hap'orth of snuff;

But he lost the bag and spilled the snuff.
So take that cuff, and that's enough.

Dog Burnt his Tail

Ding, dong, darrow,
The cat and the sparrow;
The little dog has burnt his tail,
And he shall be hang'd to-morrow.

Thievish dog Fan

Thievish dog Fan, to yell aloud began,
She burnt her mouth through stealing tripe:
Thievish dog Fan.

The Quarrelsome Dogs

Old Tray and rough Growler are having a fight,
So let us get out of their way;
They snarl, and they growl, and they bite,
Oh dear, what a terrible fray!

Good Little Dog

I will not hurt my little dog,
But stroke and pat his head;
I like to see him wag his tail,
I like to see him fed.

Poor little thing, how very good,

And very useful too.
For don't you know that he will mind
  What he is bid to do?

Then I will never hurt my dog,
  Nor ever give him pain;
But treat him kindly every day,
  And he'll love me again.

Puss And Rover

Our Pussy she is white
  Our Rover he is black,
And yet he licks Pussy's face
  While she stands on his back.

Our Pussy she is little,
  Our Rover he is big,
And yet he likes the Pussy
  Much better than the pig.

Our Pussy she is young
  And Rover he is old,
And yet he likes the Pussy

More than ons of gold.

Our Pussy she is good,
  And so is Rover too,
So Pussy says, "Ta, ta." "Good-bye,"
  And Rover says "Adieu."

Don't Tease Dogs

Foolish Edward runs away,
  From the large dog with the bone;
If we do not tease or chide,
  Dogs will leave us quite alone.

No Breakfast for Growler

No, naughty Growler, get away,
  You shall not have a bit;
Now when I speak, how dare you stay?
I can't spare any, Sir, I say,
  And so you need not sit.

Poor Growler! do not make him go,
  But recollect, before,
That he has never served you so,
For you have given him many a blow,
  That patiently he bore.

Poor growler! if he could but speak,
  He'd tell (as well as he might)
How he would bear with many a freak,
And wag his tail, and look so meek,
  And neither bark nor bite.

Upon his back he lets you ride,
  All round and round the yard;

And now, while sitting by your side,
To have a bit of bread denied,
  Is really very hard.

And all your little tricks he'll bear,
  And never seem to mind;
And yet you say you cannot spare
One bit of breakfast for his share,
  Although he is so kind.

Good Dog Tray

Good Dog Tray
  Watched Tommy t'other day,
In the garden fast asleep:
  Good Dog Tray.

Poor Old Tray

See, here is poor old Tray;
  Good dog to run so fast,
To meet my sister May and me,
  Now school is o'er at last.

Oh! how I love you, Tray,
  You are so kind to me
You run beside me in my walks,
  You sit by me at tea.

'Tis true that I give you bits
  Of cake and bread and meat;
But I'm sure you'd love as well
  If you had nought to eat.

For faithful, true, and kind
  Is our old darling Tray

He guards our dwelling all the night,
And plays with us by day.

Doggy minds the House

"Come hither, little puppy dog,
I'll give you a nice new collar,
If you will learn to read your book
And be a clever scholar."

"No, no!" replied the puppy dog,
"I've other fish to fry,
"For I must learn to guard your house,
And bark when thieves come nigh."

O'Grady's Goat

O'Grady lived in shanty row,
  The neighbours often said
They wished that Tim would move away

Or that his goat was dead.
He kept the neighbourhood in fear,
  And the children always vexed;
They couldn't tell jist whin or where
  The goat would pop up nexht.

Ould Missis Casey stood wan day
  The dirty clothes to rub
Upon the washboard, when she dived
  Head foremost o'er the tub;
She lit upon her back an yelled,
  As she was lying flat:
"Go git your goon an' kil the bashte."
  O'Grady's goat did that.

Pat Doolan's woife hung out the wash,
  Upon the line to dry.
She wint to take it in at night,
  But stopped to have a cry.
The sleeves av two red flannel shirts,
  Tat once was worn by Pat,
Were chewed off almost to the neck.
  O'Grady's goat doon that.

They had a party at McCune's,
  And they were having foon,
Whin suddinly there was a crash
  An' ivrybody roon.
The iseter soup fell on the floor
  An' nearly drowned the cat;
The stove was knocked to smithereens.
  O'Grady's goat doon that

O'Hoolerhan brought home a keg
  Ave dannymite wan day
To blow a cistern in his yad
  An' hid the stuff away.
But suddinly an airthquake coom,
  O'Hoolerhan, house an' hat,
And ivrything in sight wint up,

COLE

O'Grady's goat doon that.

Will S. Hays

The Goat and the Swing

A little story with a moral
For the young folks who are prone to quarrel.
Old folks are wise, and do not need it,
Of course they therefore, will not read it.

A vicious goat, one day, had found
His way into forbidden ground
When coming to the garden-swing,
He spied a most prodigious thing,—
A ram, a monster, to his mind,
With head before and head behind!

Its shape was odd—no hoofs were seen,
But, without legs, it stood between
Two uprights, lofty posts of oak,
With forehead ready for a stroke.

Though but a harmless ornament

Carved of the seat, it seemed intent
On barring the intruder's way;
While he, advancing, seemed to say,
"Who is this surly fellow here,
Two heads, no tail—its mighty queer!
A most insulting countenance!"

With stamp of foot and angry glance
He curbed he threatening neck and stood
Before the passive thing of wood.
"You winked as I was going by!
You did not? What! tell me I lie?
Take that!" And at the swing he sprung.

A sounding thump! It backward swung,
And set in motion by the blow,
Swayed menacingly to and fro.
"Ha! you will fight! A quarrelsome chap,
I knew you were! You'll get a rap!
I'll crack your skull!" A headlong jump;
Another and a louder bump!

The swing, as with kindling wrath,
Came rushing back along the path.
The goat, astonished shook his head,
Winked hard, turned round, grew mad, and said,
"Villain! I'll teach you who I am!"
(Or seemed to say,)—"you rascal ram,
To pick a fight with me, when I
So quietly am passing by!
Your head or mine!" A thundering stroke—
The cracking horns met crashing oak!

Then came a dull and muffled sound,
And something rolled along the ground,
Got up, looked sad—appeared to say,
"Your head's too hard!"—and limped away
Quite humbly, in a rumpled coat—
A dustier and a wiser goat!

J. T. Throwbridge

MEDDLESOME JACKO.

The Adventures of Meddlesome "Jacko"

These pictures we hope
Will our little folks please,
And also to each one
This moral convey:

"Be contented and happy,
  Whatever your lot,
And don't try, as some do,
  To have your own way."

Master Jacko, you see,
  Had a very snug home,
With plenty to eat
  That was wholesome and good;
But still he did not,
  We are sorry to say,
Behave in a way
  That a pet monkey should.

For one day he said,
  "Come, I don't like at all
The life that I lead,
  And I cannot see why
I should not live just
  As my own master does;
This chain is not strong,
  Can I break it? I'l try."

After some little time
  Jacko snapped it in two;
Said he to himself,
  "Well, now where shall I go?
To the larder, I think;
  For my appetite's good,
And I'm sure to find
  Something to eat there, I know."

He entered, and as he
  Was looking about
A lobster just brought
  From the shop seized his tail,
And pinched him, and nipped him,
  Until our young friend
Jumped about, and set up

A most piteous wail.

Next he went to the kitchen,
  And there he espied
A bottle of something—
  "Ha, ha, I must taste!"
But he found it was curry,
  Which burnt his poor throat,
So he let drop the bottle,
  And he ran off in haste.

To the dining-room the
  He repaired, and he said,
"Into master's tea-pot
  The hot water I'll pour;"
But he upset the kettle,
  And scalded himself,
And loudly screamed out
  As he rolled on the floor.

Quoth Jacko "the house
  Doesn't suit me at all,
I had better go back
  To the garden again,
And gather some peaches,
  Or grapes, or some plums,
And try to forget
  All my trouble and pain."

In the corner the rogue
  Saw a bee-hive—"Why, here
Must be honey! Delicious!"
  Said he; "Just the thing!"
So he put in his hand,
  But he brought out the bees,
And they punished poor Jacko
  With many a sting.

Pinched, scalded, and stung,
  To his home he returned.

Reasoned he, "My past folly
  I shall not regret;
For I'm sure the misfortunes
  I've gone through to-day
Have taught me a lesson
  I ne'er shall forget."

A Fruitless Sorrow

A little monkey,
  Dusky, ugly, sad,
Sat hopeless, curled
  Within his narrow cage;
Dark was the stifling room,
  No joy he had;
The sick air rang
  With tones of pain and rage.

From many a prisoned
  Creature held for sale,
Stolen from the happy
  Freedom of its life:
Dull drooping birds,
  That uttered shriek and wail,
And beast and reptile
  Full of woe and strife.

Into the place
  A cheerful presence came,
And kind eyes lighted
  On the monkey small;
Straightway the weary
  World was not the same
Such fortune did
  The little thing befall.

Safe in a basket
  Fastened, he was sent

Across the city,
 Trembling and afraid.
But once he saw his new home,
 What sweet content
Was his, while petted
 And caressed, he played.

A week of bliss,
 Alas! that it should end!
He had forgotten
 Darkness, pain, and all;
But there were monkeys
 Finer than our friend,
His master's eyes
 On such a one must fall!

So fate had ordered,
 And the frisky sprite,
Dun-coloured, grey,
 And streaked with cinnamon,
Born in far bright Brazil,
 Was bought at sight,
And all the first
 Poor pet's fortune won.

They brought into
 The bright and cheerful room
The basket small
 In which he had been borne
To such a happy life.
 He saw his doom
At once, the misery
 Of his lot forlorn.

The moment that
 The basket met his sight,
He dropped his head,
 And hid his sorrowing eyes
Against his arm,
 Nor looked to left nor right,

As any thinking
  Human creature wise.

They took him back
  Into his noisome den,
His tiny face
  Concealed as if he wept,
So helpless to resist.
  Heroic men
Might such despairing
  Patient calm have kept.

Poor little thing!
  And if he lingers yet,
Or death has ended
  Life so hard to bear
I know not;
  But I never can forget
His brief rejoicing
  And his mute despair.

Our Own Jacko

779

The Horse

The horse, the brave.
The gallant Horse—
Fit theme for the minstrel's song!
He hath good claim
To praise and fame;
As the fleet, the kind, the strong.

Behold him free
In his native strength,
Looking fit for the sun-god's car;
With a skin as sleek
As a maiden's cheek,
And an eye like a Polar star.

Who wonders not
Such limbs can deign
To brook the fettering firth;
As we see him fly
The ringing plain,
And paw the crumbling earth?

His nostrils are wide
With snorting pride,
His fiery veins expand;

And yet he'll be led
 With s silken thread,
Or soothed by and infant's hand.

 He owns the lion's
 Spirit and migh,
But the voice he has learnt to love
 Needs only be heard,
 And he'll turn to the word,
As gentle as a dove.

 The Arab is wise
 Who learns to prize
His barb before all gold;
 But us his barb
 More fair than ours,
More generous, fast or bold?

 A song for the steed,
 The gallant steed—
Oh! grant him a leaf of bay;
 For we owe much more
 To his strength and speed,
Than man can ever repay.

 Whatever his place—
 The yoke, the chase,
The war-field, road, or course,
 One of Creation's
 Brightest and best
Is the Horse, the noble Horse!

Eliza Cook

The Wonderful Horse

I've a tale to relate.
 Such a wonderful tale

That really I fear
  My description must fail;
'Tis about a fine horse
  Who had powers so amazing.
He lived without eating,
  Or drinking, or grazing;
In fact this fine horse
  Was so "awfully" clever.
That left to himself
  He'd have lived on forever.

He stood in a room,
  With his nose in the air,
And his wide staring eyes
  Looking no one knows where.
His tail undisturbed
  By the sting of a fly
One foot slightly raised
  As if kicking he'd try,
This wonderful horse
  Never slept or yet dozed,
At least if he did so,
  His eyes never closed.

"Come, gee up, old Dobbin.
  Look sharp, con't you see
I want to be there
  And get back before tea?"
But this obstinate horse
  Never offered to prance,
Or made an attempt
  At the slightest advance;
Harry slashed him so hard.
  That he slashed off one ear,
Then his mane tumbled off,
  And poor Dobbin looked queer.

With spur, and with whip,
  And with terrible blows,
He soon was deprived
  Of one eye, and his nose,

While his slightly-raised foot
  Found a place on the floor.
The tail once so handsome
  Was handsome no more,
And Harry, the tears
  Raining down as he stood,
Cried, "Bother the horse,
  It is nothing but wood!"

The Pony

Oh, Brownie, our pony,
  A gallant young steed,
Will carry us gaily
  O'er hill, dale, and mead.

So sure is his foot,
  And so steady his eye.
That even our baby
  To mount him might try.

We haste to his stable
  To see him each day,
And feed him with oats
  And the sweetest of hay.

We pat his rough coat,
  And we deck him with flowers,
Oh, never was seen
  Such a pony as ours.

The Horse

No one deserves to have a horse
  Who takes delight to beat him:
The wise will choose a better course,

And very kindly treat him.

If ever it should be my lot—
  To have, for use or pleasure,
One who could safely walk or trot
  The horse would be a treasure.

He soon would learn my voice to know
  And I would gladly lead him;
And should he to the stable go,
  I'd keep him clean and feed him.

I'd teach my horse a steady pace.
  Because, if he should stumble
Upon a rough or stony place,
  We might both have a tumble.

Should he grow aged, I would still
  My poor old servant cherish;
I could not see him weak or ill,
  And leave my horse to perish.

For should he get too weak to be
  My servant any longer,
I'll send him out to grass quite free,
  And get another stronger.

Good Dobbin

Oh! thank you, good Dobbin,
  You've been a long track,
And have carried papa
  All the way on your back;
You shall have some nice oats,
  Faithful Dobbin, indeed,
For you've brought papa home
  To his darling with speed.

The howling wind blew,
  And the pelting rain beat,
And the thick mud has covered
  His legs and his feet,
But yet on he galloped
  In spite of the rain,
And has brought papa home,
  To his darling again.

The sun it was setting
  A long while ago,
And papa could not see
  The road where he should go,
But Dobbin kept on
  Through the desolate wild,
And has brought papa home
  Again safe to his child.

Now go to the stable,
  The night is so raw,
Go, Dobbin, and rest
  Your old bones on the straw:
Don't stand any longer
  Out here in the rain,
For you've brought papa home
  To his darling again.

A Horse's Petition to his Master

Up the hill, whip me not;
Down the hill, hurry me not;
In the stable, forget me not;
Of hay and corn, rob me not;
With sponge and brush, neglect me not;
Of soft, dry bed, deprive me not;
If sick or cold, chill me not;
With bit and reins, oh! jerk me not;
And when you are angry, strike me not.

Mane measures 1 feet and tail 11 feet.

Scotchman Carrying Jessie's Pony

Work-Horses in a Park on Sunday

'Tis Sabbath-day, the poor man walks
  Blithe from his cottage door,
And to his parting young ones talks
  As they skip on before.

The father is a man of joy,
  From his week's toil released;
And jocund is each little boy

To see his father pleased.

But, looking to a field at hand,
  Where the grass grows rich and high,
A no less merry Sabbath band
  Of horses met my eye.

Poor skinny beasts, that go all week
  With loads of earth and stones,
Bearing, with aspect dull and meek,
  Hard work, and cudgel'd bones.

But now let loose to roam athwart
  The farmer's clover-lea
With whisking tails, and jump and snort,
  They speak a clumsy glee.

Lolling across each other's necks,
  Some look like brother's dear;
Other's are full of f ings and kicks—
  Antics uncouth and queer.

Superannuated Horse to His Master,
who has Sentenced him to Die

And hast thou sealed my doom, sweet master, say?
  And wilt thou kill thy servant old and poor?
A little longer let me live I pray;
  A little longer hobble round the door.

For much it glads me to behold this place—
  And house me in this hospitable shed;
It glads me more to see my master's face,
  And linger on the spot where I was bred.

For oh! to think of what we have enjoyed,
  In my life's prime, e'er I was old and poor!
Then from the jocund morn to eve employed,

787

COLE

My gracious master or my back I bore.

Thrice ten years have danced on down along,
  Since first to thee these way-born limbs I gave;
Sweet smiling years! When both of was were young—
  The kindest master and the happiest slave.

Ah! years sweet smiling now for ever flown,
  Ten years, thrice fold, alas! are as a day.
Yet as together we are aged grown,
  Together let us wear that age away.

And hast thou fixed my doom, sweet master, say?
  And wilt thou kill thy servant old and poor?
A little longer let me live, I pray,
  A little longer hobble round thy door.

But oh! Kind Nature, take thy victim's life!
  And thou a servant feeb e, old, and poor;
So shalt thou save me from the uplifted knife,
  And gently stretch me at my master's door.

The Arab and His Horse

Come, my beauty; come, my dessert darling!
  On my shoulder lay thy glossy head!
Fear not, though the barley sack be empty,
  Here's half of Hassan's scanty bread.

Thou shalt have thy share of dates, my beauty!
  And thou knowest my water skin is free;
Drink and be welcome, for the wells are distant,
  And my strength and safety lie in thee.

Bend thy forehead, now, to take my kisses!
  Lift in love thy dark and splendid eye;
Thou art glad when Hassan mounts the saddle—

Thou art proud he owns thee; so am I.

Let the Sultan bring his broadest horses,
  Prancing with their diamond-studded reins;
They, my darling, shall not match thy fleetness,
  When they course with thee the desert plains.

We have seen Damascus, O my beauty!
  And the splendour of the pachas there;
What's their pomp and riches? Why, I would not
  Take them for a handful of they hair.

The Cab Horse

Pity the sorrows of a poor cab horse,
  Whose jaded limbs have many a mile to go.
Whose weary days are drawing to a close,
  And but in death will he a rest e'er know.

When the cold winds of dreary winter rage,
  And snow and hail come down in blinding sheet,
And people refuge see 'neath roof or arch,
  The cab-horse stands unsheltered in the street.

Though worn and weary with useful life,
  In patient service to his master—man;
No fair retirement waits his failing years,
  He yet must do the utmost work he can.

His legs are stiff, his shoulders rubbed and sore,
  His knees are broken and his sight is dim,
But no physician comes his wounds to heal,
  The lash is all the cure that's given him.

Ye kindly hearts that spare the whip, and stroke,
  Just now and then, with kindly hand, his mane;
Or pat his sides, or give a pleasant word,

Your tender-heartedness is not in vain.

He has not many friends to plead his cause;
  He has not speech his own wrongs to outpour.
Pity the sorrows of a poor cab-horse;
  Give him relief, and Heaven will bless your store.

Dobbin Saving Puss From a Dog

Clever Horses

Farmer John

Home from his journey Farmer John
  Arrived this morning safe and sound,
His black coat off, and his old clothes on:
"Now I'm myself," says Farmer John.
  And he thinks, "I'll look around!"
Up leaps the dog: "Get down, you pup,
  Are you so glad you would eat me up?"
The old cow lows at the gate to greet him.
  The horses prick up their ears, to meet him.
    Well, well, old Bay!
    Ha, ha, old Grey!
Do you get good food when I'm away?"

"You haven't a rib!" says Farmer John:
"The cattle are looking round and sleek;
The colt is going to be a roan,
And a beauty too, how he has grown!
  We'll wean the calf, next week."
Says Farmer John, when I've been off,
To call you again about the trough,
And watch you, and pet you, while you drink,
Is a greater comfort than you can think."
    And he pats old Bay,
    And he slaps old Grey,
"Ah, this is the comfort of going away."

"For after all," says Farmer John,
"The best of the journey is getting home!
"I've seen great sights, but would I give
This spot, and the peaceful life I live,
  For all their Paris and Rome?
These hills for the City's stifled air,
And big hotels, all bustle and glare,
Lands all horses, and roads all stones,
That deafen your ears and batter your bones,
  Would you, old Bay?

Would you, old Grey?
That's what one gets by going away."

"I've found out this," says Farmer John,
"That happiness is not bought and sold
And clutched in a life of waste and hurry,
In nights of pleasure and days of worry,
  And wealth isn't all in gold,
Mortgage and stocks and ten per cent.,
But in simple ways of sweet content.
Few wants pure hopes, and noble ends,
Some land to till and a few good friends,
   Like you, old Bay,
   And you, old Grey.
That's what I've learned by going away.

And a happy man is Farmer John,
  Oh! a rich and happy man is he;
He sees the peas and pumpkins growing,
The corn in tassel, and buckwheat blowing;
  And fruit on vine and tree.
The large kind oxen look their thanks,
As he rubs their foreheads and strokes their flanks,
The doves light round him, and strut and coo;
Says Farmer John: "I'll take you too,
   And you, old Bay,
   And you, old Grey,
The next time I travel so far away."

The Horse

A horse, long us'd to bit and bridle,
But always much disposed to idle,
Had often wished that he was able
To steal unnotic'd from the stable.

He panted from his utmost soul,
To be at nobody's control;

Go his own pace, slower or faster.
In short, do nothing—like his master.

But yet he ne'er had got at large,
If Jack (who had him in his charge)
Had not, as many have before,
Forgot to shut the stable door.

Dobbin, with expectation swelling,
Now rose to quit he present dwelling,
But first peep'd out with cautious fear,
T' examine if the coast was clear.

At length he ventured from his station,
And with extreme self-approbation,
As if delivered from a load,
He gallop'd to the public road.

And here he stood awhile debating,
(Till he was almost tired of waiting)
Which way he'd please to bend his course,
Now there was nobody to force.

At last, unchecked by bit or rein,
He saunter'd down a pleasant lane,
And neigh'd forth many a jocund song
In triumph, as he pass'd along.

But when dark nights began t'appear,
In vain he sought some shelter near,
And well he knew he could not bear
To sleep out in the open air.

The grass felt damp and raw,
Much colder than his master's straw,
Yet on it he was forc'd to stretch,
A poor, cold, melancholy wretch.

The night was dark, the country hilly,
Poor Dobbin felt extremely chilly;

Perhaps a feeling like remorse
Just now might sting this truant horse.

As soon as day began to dawn,
Dobbin, with long and weary yawn,
Arose from this his sleepless night,
But in low spirits and bad plight.

"If this" (thought he) "is all I get,
A bed unwholesome, cold and wet,
And thus forlorn about to roam,
I think I'd better be at home."

'Twas long ere Dobbin could decide
Betwixt his wishes and his pride,
Whether to live in all this danger,
Or go back sneaking to the manger.

At last his struggling pride gave way,
To thought of savoury oats and hay
To hungry stomach, was a reason
Unanswerable at this season.

So off he set, with look profound,
Right glad that he was homeward bound;
And, trotting fast as he was able,
Soon gain'd once more his master's stable.

Now Dobbin, after his disaster,
Never again forsook his master,
Convinc'd he'd better let him mount.
Than travel on his own account.

Jane Taylor

Doggie Feeding Gee Gee

OH! WHAT A LONG DONKEY

The Cottage -'s Donkey

No wonder the Cottager
  Looks with Pride
On the well-fed donkey
  That stands at his side;

For he works, and he lives
  As hard as he,
And a creature more useful
  There cannot be.

He knows the Cottager's
  Wife and child,
And he loves to play
  With that dog so wild;
And though sometimes
  So staid and still,
He can roll in the meadow
  With right good will.

He knows the road
  To the market well,
Where garden vegetables
  He goes to sell:
And though it is hilly,
  And far, and rough,
He thinks—for a donkey,
  It's well enough.

So he trudges along,
  And little he cares
How hard he works,
  Or how ill he fares!
Content when his home
  Appears in sight,
If his kindly master
  Smiles at night.

S. V. Dodds

The Donkey

Poor Donkey! I'll give him
  A handful of grass;
I'm sure he's an honest,
  Though stupid, old ass.
He trots to the market
  To carry the sack,
And lets me ride all the
  Way home on his back;
And only just stops
  By the ditch for a minute,
To see if there's any
  Fresh grass for him in it.

'Tis true, now and then
  He has got a bad trick
Of standing stock-still,
  And just trying to kick:
But then, poor old fellow!
  You know he can't tell
That standing stock-still
  Is not using me well;
For it never comes into
  His head, I dare say,
To do his work first,
  And then afterwards play.

No, no, my good donkey!
  I'll give you some grass,
For you know no better,
  Because you're an ass;
But what little donkeys
  Some children must look,
Who stand, very like you,
  Stock-still at their book,
And waste every moment
  Of time as it passes—
A great deal more stupid
  And silly than asses!

The Ride

Up and down on Neddy's back,
  Taking turns they go,
Part the time with trot so fast,
  Part with pace so slow.

Little sisters side by side,
Sharing each the fun and ride.
Neddy thinks "it can't hurt me,
But gives the children fun, you see."
And so he leads himself that they
May happy be this pleasant day.

Old Jack, the Donkey

Old Jack was as sleek
  And well looking an ass
As ever on common
  Munched thistle or grass;
And—though 'twas not gaudy,
  That jacket of brown—
Was the pet of the young
  And the pride of the town.

And indeed he might well
  Look so comely and trim,
When his young master, Joe,
  Was so gentle to him;
For never did child
  More affection beget
Than was felt by young Joe
  For his four-footed pet.

Joe groomed him and fed him,
  And, each market day,

798

Would talk to his darling
  The whole of the way;
And Jack before dawn
  Would be pushing the door,
As though he would say,
  "Up Joe; slumber no more."

One day Jack was wandering
  Along the roadside,
When an urchin the donkey
  Maliciously eyed;
And aiming too surely
  At Jack a sharp stone,
It struck the poor beast
  Just below the shin bone.

Joe soothed and caressed him
  And coaxed him until
They came to a stream
  By the side of the hill;
And with cool water
  He washed the swoll'n limb,
And after this fashion
  Kept talking to him:—

"Poor Jack did they pelt him—
  The cowards, so sly!
I wish I'd been there,
  With my stick, standing by:
It doesn't bleed now—
  'Twill be well in a trice;
There, let me just wash it—
  Now isn't that nice?"

And Jack nestled down
  With his soft velvet nose,
And close as he could,
  Under Joe's ragged clothes
And he looked at his master
  As though he would say—

"I'm sure I can never
Your kindness repay."

S. W. P.

The Donkey's Song

"Please, Mr Donkey, Sing a song,"
 A black-bird said, one day.
The don-key o-pened wide his mouth,
 The black-bird flew a-way.

The Ass

The Ass, when treated well by man,
To pleas him will do all he can;
But if his master uses him ill,
He will not work, but stand stock-still,

To market he will carry peas,
And coals, or any thing you please;
He is not over-nice with meat,
For thorns and thistles he will eat.

He drinks no water but what's clean;
His nose he puts not in the stream;
His feet he does not like to wet,
But out of dirty roads will get.

Poor Donkey's Epitaph

Down in this ditch poor donkey lies,
 Who jogg'd with many a load;
And till the day death clos'd his eyes,

Brows'd up and down this road.

No shelter had he for his head,
  Whatever winds might blow;
A neighb'ring commons was his bed,
  Tho' drest in sheets of snow.

In this green ditch he often stray'd
  To nip the dainty grass;
And friendly invitations bray'd
  To some more hungry ass

Each market-day he jogg'd along
  Beneath the gard'ner's load,
And snor'd out many a donkey's song
  To friends upon the road.

A tuft of grass, a thistle green,
  Or cabbage-leaf so sweet,
Were all the dainties, he was seen
  For twenty years to eat.

And as for sport, the sober soul
  Was such a steady Jack,
He only now and then would roll,
  Heels upward, on his back.

But all his sport, and dainties too,
  And labours now are o'er.
Last night so bleak a tempest blew,
  He could withstand no more.

He felt his feeble limbs grow cold,
  His blood was freezing slow,
And presently you might behold
  Him dead upon the snow.

Poor donkey! travellers passing by,
  Thy cold remains shall view
And 'twould be well if all who die

To du~/ were as true.

Anne Taylor

OH M I WHAT AN AWFUL LONG COW.

The Cow and The Ass

Beside a green meadow
  A stream us'd to flow,
So clear one might see
  The white pebbles below;
To this cooling brook
  The warm cattle would stray,
To stand in the shade,
  On a hot summer's day.

A cow, quite oppress'd
  With the heat of the sun,
Came here to refresh
  As she often had done,
And standing quite still,
  Leaning over the stream,
Was musing, perhaps;
  Or perhaps she might dream.

But soon a brown ass,

802

Of respectable look
Came trotting up also,
　To taste of the brook,
And to nibble a few
　Of the daisies and grass.
"How d'ye do?" said the cow:
　"How d'ye do?" said the ass.

"Take a seat," cried the cow,
　Gently waving her hand.
"By no means, dear madam,"
　Said he, "while you stand."
Then stooping to drink,
　With a complaisant bow.
"Ma'am, your health." said the ass;
　"Thank you, sir," said the cow.

When a few of these compliments
　More had been pass'd,
They laid themselves down
　On the herbage at last;
And waited politely
　(As gentlemen must),
The ass held his tongue,
　That the cow might speak first.

Then, with a deep sigh,
　She directly began,
"Don't you think, Mr. Ass,
　We are injured by man?
'Tis a subject that lies
　With a weight on my mind:
We certainly are much
　Oppress'd by mankind.

"Now what is the reason
　(I see none at all)
That I always must go
　When Suke pleases to cal ?
Whatever I'm doing

('Tis certainly hard),
I'm forc'd to leave off
  To be milked in the yard.

"I've no will of my own,
  But must do as they please,
And give them my milk
  To make butter and cheese;
I've often a great mind
  To kick down the pail,
Or give Suke a box
  On the ears with my tail."

"But ma'am," said the ass,
  "Not presuming to teach—
O dear, I beg pardon—
  Pray finish your speech;
I thought you had finish'd,
  Indeed," said the swain,
"Go on, and I'll not
  Interrupt you again."

"Why, sir, I was only
  Just going to observe,
I'm resolved that these tyrants
  No longer I'll serve;
But leave them for ever
  To do as they please,
And look somewhere else
  For their butter and cheese."

Ass waited a moment,
  To see if she'd done,
And then, "Not presuming
  To teach," he begun.
"With submission, dear madam,
  To your better wit,
I own I am not quite
  Convinced by it yet.

"That you're of great service
  To them is quite true,
But surely they are
  Of some service to you.
'Tis their pleasant meadow
  In which you regale;
They feed you in winter,
  When grass and weeds fail.

"And then a warm cover
  They always provide,
Dear madam, to shelter
  Your delicate hide,
For my own part, I know
  I receive much from man,
And for him, in return,
  I do all I can."

The cow, upon this,
  Cast her eyes on the grass,
Not pleas'd at thus being
  Reproved by an ass,
Yet, thought she, "I'm determined
  I'll benefit by't,
For I really believe
  That the fellow is right."

Jane Taylor

The Cow

Come, children, listen to me now,
And you will hear about the cow;
You'll find her useful, alive or dead,
Whether she's black, or white, or red.

When milkmaids milk her morn and night
She gives them milk so fresh and white,

And this we, little children, think
Is very nice for us to drink.

The curdled milk they press and squeeze,
And so they make it into cheese;
The cream they skim and shake in churns,
And then it soon to butter turns.

And when she's dead, her flesh is good,
For beef is a very wholesome food,
But though 'twill make us brave and strong,
To eat too much, you know, is wrong.

Her skin, with lime and bark together,
The tanner tans, and makes into leather,
And without that, what should we do
For soles of every boot and shoe?

The shoemaker cuts it with his knife
And bound the tops are by his wife;
And so they nail them to the last,
And then they stitch them tight and fast.

The hair that grows upon her back
Is taken, whether white or black,
And mix'd with plaster, short or long,
Which makes it very firm and strong.

And, last of all, if cut with care,
Her horns make combs to comb our hair;
And so we learn—thanks to our teachers—
That cows are very useful creatures.

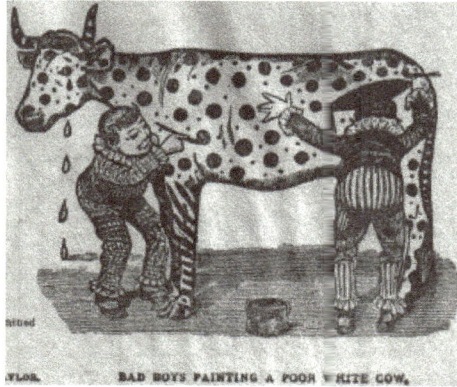

BAD BOYS PAINTING A POOR WHITE COW.

THE DANCING COW

The Cowboy's Song

"Mooly cow, mooly cow,
  Home from the wood
They sent me to fetch you
  As fast as I could.
The sun has gone down—
  It is time to go home,
Mooly cow, mooly cow,
  Why don't you come?
Your udders are full,
  And the milkmaid is there.

807

And the children are all waiting,
  Their suppers to share.
I have let the long bars down—
  Why don't you pass thro'"
The mooly cow only said, "Moo-o-o!"

"Mooly cow, mooly cow,
  Have you not been
Regaling all day
  Where the pastures are green?
No doubt it was pleasant,
  Dear Mooly, to see
The clear running brook
  And the wide-spreading tree,
The clover to crop,
  And the streamlet to wade,
To drink the cool water
  And lie in the shade;
But now it is night—
  They are waiting for you."
The mooly cow only said, "Moo-o-o!"

"Mooly cow, mooly cow,
  Where do you go
When all the green pastures
  Are covered in with snow?
You can go to the barn,
  And we feed you with hay,
And the maid goes to milk
  You there, every day;
She pats you, she loves you,
  She strokes your sleek hide,
She speaks to you kindly,
  And sits by your side:
Then come along home,
  Pretty Mooly cow, do."
The mooly cow only said, "Moo-o-o!"

"Mooly cow, mooly cow,
  Whisking your tail
The milkmaid is waiting,

I say, with her pail;
She tucks up her petticoat,
  Tidy and neat,
And places the three-legged
  Stool for her seat.
What can you be staring a,
  Mooly? You know
That we ought to have gore
  Home an hour ago.
How dark it is growing!
  O, what shall I do?"
The mooly cow only said, "Moo-o-o!"

That Calf

To the yard, by the barn,
Came the farmer one morn,
  And calling the cattle, he said,
While they trembled with fright:
"Now which of you, last night,
  Shut the barn door while I was abed?"
  Each one of them all shook his head.

Now the little calf Spot,
She was down in the lot,
  And the way the rest talked wa a shame;
For no one, night before,
Saw her shut up the door;
  But they said that she did, all the same,
  For they always made her take the blame.

Said the horse (dapple gray),
"I was not up that way
  Last night, as I recollect;"
And the bull, passing by,
Tossed his horns very high,
  And said, "Let who may be her object,

I say this, that calf I suspect.

Then out spoke the cow,
"It is terrible now,
  To accuse honest folks of such tricks."
Said the cock in the tree,
"I'm sure 'twasn't me;"
  And the sheep all cried, "Bah! (there were six)
  Now that calf's got herself in a fix."

"Why, of course we all knew
'Twas the wrong thing to do,"
  Said the chickens. "Of course," said the cat.
"I suppose," cried the mule,
Some folks think me a fool,
  But I'm not quite as simple as that;
  The poor calf never knows what she's at."

Just that moment, the calf,
Who was always the laugh
  And the jest of the yard, came in sight.
"Did you shut my barn door?"
Asked the farmer once more,
  "I did, sir, I closed it last night,"
  Said the calf; "and I thought that was right."

Then each one shook his head,
"She will catch it," they cried,
  "Serves her right for her meddlesome ways."
Said the farmer, "Come here,
Little bossy, my dear,
  You have done what I cannot repay,
  And your fortune is made from to-day.

"For a wonder, last night,
I forgot the door quite,
  And if you had not shut it so neat,
All my colts had slipped in,
And gone right to the bin,
  And got what they ought not to eat,

They'd have founded themselves on wheat."

The each hoof of them
All began to loudly to bawl,
   The very mule smiled, the cock crew;
"Little Spotty, my dear,
You're a favourite here,"
   They cried, "we all said it was you,
   We were so glad to give you your due."
   And the calf answered knowingly, "Boo!"

Phoebe Cary

THE SEA-COW WALKING.

811

The Lost Lamb

Storm upon the mountain,
  Rain torrents beating,
And the little snow-white lamb,
  Bleating, ever bleating!
Storm upon the mountain,
  Night upon its throne,
And the little snow-white lamb,
  Left alone, alone!

Down the glen the shepherd
  Drives his flock afar;
Through the murky mist and cloud,
  Shines no beacon star.
Fast he hurries onward,
  Never hears the moan
Of the pretty snow-white lamb,
  Left alone, alone!

Up the glen he races,
  Breasts the bitter wind,
Scours across the plain, and leaves
  Wood and wold behind;—
Storm upon the mountain,
  Night upon its throne—
There he finds the little lamb,
  Left alone, alone!

Struggling, panting, sobbing,
  Kneeling on the ground,
Round the pretty creature's neck
  Both his arms were wound;
Soon within his bosom,
  All its bleatings done,
Home he bears the little lamb,
  Left alone, alone!

Oh! the happy faces,
  By the shepherd's fire!

High without the tempest roars,
  But the laugh rings higher,
Young and old together
  Make that joy their own—
In their midst the little lamb,
  Left alone, alone!

T. Westwood

The Pet Lamb

The dew was falling fast,
  The stars began to blink;
I heard a voice; it said,
  "Drink, pretty creature, drink!"
And looking o'er the hedge
  Before me I espied
A snow-white mountain lamb,
  With a maiden by its side.

Nor sheep nor kine were near;
  The lamb was all alone,
And by a slender cord
  Was tethered to a stone;
With one knee on the grass
  Did the little maiden kneel,
While to this mountain lamb.
  She gave its evening meal.

"What ails thee, young one, what?
  Why pull so at thy cord?
Is it not well with thee?
  Well both for bed and board?
Thy plot of grass is soft,
  And green as grass can be,
Rest, little young one, rest;
  What is't that aileth thee?

813

"What is it thou would'st seek?
  What is wanting to thy heart?
Thy limbs, are they not strong?
  And beautiful thou art.
This grass is tender grass;
  These flowers they have no peers;
And that green corn all day long
  Is rustling in they ears!

"Rest little young one, rest;
  Hast thou forgot the day
Why my father found the first
  In places far away;
Many flocks were on the hills,
  But thou wert owned by none,
And thy mother from thy side
  For evermore was gone.

"He took thee in his arms,
  And in pity brought thee home;
Oh! blessed day for thee!
  Then whither would'st thou roam?
A faithful nurse thou hast;
  The dam that did the yean
Upon the mountain top
  No kinder could have been.

"Thou know'st that thrice a day
  I have brought thee in this can
Fresh water from the brook,
  As clear as ever ran.
And twice, too, in the day,
  When the ground is wet with dew,
I bring thee draughts of milk—
  Warm milk it is, and new.

"Here, then, thou need'st not dread
  The raven in the sky;
Night and day thou'rt safe;
  Our cottage is hard by.

Why bleat so after me?
 Why pull so at thy chain?
Sleep, and at break of day
 I will come to thee again "

Wordsworth

A Visit to the Lambs

Mother, let's go and see the lambs;
 This warm and sunny day
I think must make them very glad,
 And full of fun and play.

Ah, there they are. You pretty things!
 Now, don't you run away;
I'm come on purpose, that I am,
 To see you this fine day.

What pretty little heads you've got,
 And such good-natured eyes!
And ruff of wool all round your necks—
 How nicely curl'd it lies!

Come here, my little lambkin, come,
 And lick my hand—now do!
How silly to be so afraid!
 Indeed I won't hurt you.

Just put your hand upon its back,
 Mother, how nice and warm!
There, pretty lamb, you see I don't
 Intend to do you harm.

Easy Poetry

815

The Pet Lamb

Once on a time, a shepherd lived
  Within a cottage small;
The grey thatched roof was shaded by
  An elm-tree dark and tall;
While all around, stretched far away,
  A wild and lonesome moor,
Except a little daisied field
  Before the trellised door.

Now, it was on a cold March day,
  When on the moorland wide
The shepherd found a trembling lamb
  By its mother's side;
And so pitiful it bleated,
  As with the cold it shook,
He wrapped it up beneath his coat,
  And home the poor lamb took.

He placed it by the warm fireside,
  And then his children fed
This little lamb, whose mother died,
  With milk and sweet brown bread,
Until it ran about the floor,
  Or at the door would stand;
And grew so tame, it ate its food
  From out the children's hand.

It followed them where'er they went,
  Came ever at their call,
And dearly was this pretty lamb
  Beloved by them all.
And often on a market-day,
  When cotters crossed the moor,
They stopped to praise the snow-white lamb,
  Beside the cottage door;

They patted it upon its head,
  And stroked it with the hand,
And vowed it was the prettiest lamb
  They'd seen in all the land.

Now, this kind shepherd was as ill,
  As ill as he could be,
And kept his bed for many a week,
  And nothing earned he;
And when he had got well again,
  He to his wife did say,
"The doctor wants his money, and

I haven't it to pay.

"What shal we do, what can we do?
  The doctor made me well,
There's only one thing can be done,
  We must the pet lamb sell;
We've nearly eaten all the bread,
  And how can we get more,
Unless you call the butcher in
  When he rides by the door?"

"Oh, do not sell my white pet lamb,"
  Then little Mary said,
"And every night I'll go up stairs
  Without my tea to bed;
Oh! do not sell my sweet pet lamb;
  And if you let it live,
The best half of my bread and milk
  I will unto it give."

The doctor at that very time
  Entered the cottage door,
As, with her arms around her lamb,
  She sat upon the floor.
"For if the butcher buys my lamb,
  He'll take away its life,
And make its pretty white throat bleed
  With his sharp cruel knife;

"And never in the morning light
  Again it will me meet,
Nor come again to lick my hand,
  Look up upon me and bleat."
"Why do you weep, my pretty girl?"
  The doctor then did say.
"Because I love my little lamb,
  Which must be sold to-day;

It lies beside my bed at night,
  And, oh, it is so still,

It never made a bit of noise
  When father was so ill.
"Oh do not let them sell my lamb,
  And then I'll go to bed,
And never ask for aught to eat

  But a small piece of bread."
"I'll buy the lamb and give it you,"
  The kind, good doctor said,
"And with the money that I pay
  Your father can buy bread.
"As for the bill, that can remain
  Until another year."
He paid the money down, and said,
  "The lamb is yours, my dear:

You have a kind and gentle heart,
  And God, who made us all,
He loveth well those who are kind
  To creatures great and small;
"And while I live, my little girl
  Your lamb shall not be sold,
But play with you upon the moor,
  And sleep within the fold."

And so the white pet lamb was saved,
  And played upon the moor,
And after little Mary ran
  About the cottage-floor.
It fed upon cowslips tall,
  And ate the grass so sweet,
And on the little garden-walk
  Pattered its pretty feet;

And with its head upon her lap
  The little lamb would lay
Asleep beneath the elm-tree's shade,
  Upon the summer's day,
While she twined the flowers around its neck,

And called it her, "Sweet May."

Thomas Miller

Mary after two years' absence does not
know her own Pet Lamb

The Pig, He is a Gentleman

The pig, he is a gentleman,
 And never goes to work;
He eats the very best of food

Without knife or fork.

The pig, he is a gentleman,
  And drinks the best of milk;
His clothes are good, and thick, and strong
  And wear as well as silk.

The pig he, is a gentleman,
  And covers up his head,
And looks at you with one eye,
  And grunts beneath his bed.

He eats, and drinks, and sleeps all day
  Just like his lady mother,
His father, uncle, and his aunt
  His sister, and his brother.

E. W. Cole

The Pigs

"Do look at those pigs, as they lie in the straw,"
  Little Richard said to papa;
"They keep eating longer than ever I saw,
  What nasty fat gluttons they are!"

"I see they are feasting," his father replied,
  "They ear a great deal, I allow;
But let us remember, before we deride,
  'Tis the nature, my dear, of a sow.

"But when a great boy, such as you my dear Dick,
  Does nothing but eat all the day,
And keeps sucking good things till he makes himself sick,
  What a glutton, indeed, we may say.

"When plumcake and sugar for ever he picks,
  And sweetmeats, and comfits, and figs;

Pray let him get rid of his own nasty tricks,
And then he may laugh at the pigs."

J. T.

Five Little Pigs

Five lit-tle fingers
And five lit-tle pigs,
  Of each I've a story to tell;
Look at their faces
And fun-ny curl-ed tails,
  And hear what each one be-fell.

Ring-tail that stead-y
And good lit-tle pig,
  To mar-ket set off at a trot;
And brought him his bas-ket
Quite full of nice things,
  Con-tent-ed and pleas-ed with his lot.

Young Smil-er, the next,
Was a stay at home pig,
  Lik-ed his pipe, and to sit at his ease;
He fell fast a-sleep,
Burned his nose with his pipe,
  And a-woke with a ve-ry loud sneeze.

Num-ber three was young Long-snout
Who ate up the beef.
  He was both greed-y and fat;
He made him-self ill
By eat-ing too much,
  And then he was sor-ry for that.

And poor lit-tle Grun-ter—
You know he had none—
  A pig-gy so hun-gry and sad!

He si-lent-ly wiped
The salt tears from his eyes,
 I think it was real-ly too bad.

Young Squeak-er cried, "Wee, wee, wee,"
All the way home,
 A pig-gy so fret-ful was he;
He got a good whip-ping,
Was sent off to bed,
 And de-served it, I think you must see.

Oh, these five lit-tle pigs,
How they've made child-ren laugh
 In ages and ages now past!
And they'll be quite as fun-ny
In years yet to come,
 While small toes and small fing-ers last.

The Self-willed Pig

It happened one day,
 As the other pigs tell,
In the course of their walk
 They drew near to a well
So wide and so deep,
 With so smooth a wall round,
That a pig tumbling in
 Was sure to be drowned.

But a perverse little brother,
 Foolish as ever,
Still boasting himself
 Very cunning and clever,
Now made up his mind
 That, whatever befell,
He would run on before
 And jump over the well.

823

Then away he ran fast
　To one side of the well,
Climbed up on the wall,
　Slipped, and headlong he fell;
And now from the bottom
　His pitiful shout
Was, "Oh mother! I'm in;
　Pray do help me out!"

She ran to the side
　When she heard his complaint,
And she then saw him struggling,
　Weakly and faint,
Yet no help could she give!
　But "My children," cried she,
"How often I've feared
　A sad end his would be!"

"Oh, mother, dear mother;"
　The drowning pig cried,
"I see all this comes
　Of my folly and pride!"
He could not speak more,
　But he sank down and died,
Whilst his mother and brothers
　Wept round the well-side!

PIG GOING TO MARKET.

SCHOOL BOY PIGS

Three Naughty Pigs

Three naughty pigs,
All in one pen,
Drank up the milk
Left by the men,

Then all the three
  Fast as they could,
Dug their way out
  To find something good.

Out in the garden
  A maiden fair
Had set some flowers
  Of beauty rare.

Out in the garden
  A merry boy
Had planted seeds,
  With childish joy,

One naughty pig
  Ran to the bed;
Soon lay the flowers
  Drooping and dead.

To naughty pigs
  Dug up the seeds,
And left, for the boy,
  Not even weeds.

Three naughty pigs,
  Back in the pen,
Never could do
  Such digging again.

For, in their noses,
  Something would hurt
Whenever they tried
  To dig in the dirt.

Little Biddy

Little Biddy O'Toole, on her three-legged stool,
  Was 'atin' her praties so hot;
  Whin up stepped the pig,
  Wid his appetite big,
And Biddy got down like a shot

The Spectre Pig

It was the stalwart butcher man
  That knit his swarthy brow,
And said the gentle pig must die,
  And sealed it with a vow.

And oh! it was the gentle pig
  Lay stretched upon the ground,
And ah! it was the cruel knife
  His little heart that found.

They took him then those wicked men,
  They trailed him all along;
They put a stick between his lips,
  And through his heels a thong

And round and round an oaken beam
  A hempen cord they flung,
And like a mighty pendulum
  All solemnly he swung.

Now say thy prayers, thou sinful man
  And think what thou hast done,
And read thy catechism well,
  Thou sanguinary one.

For if its sprite should walk by night
  It better were for thee,
That thou were mouldering in the ground,

Or bleaching in the sea.

It was the savage butcher then
  That made a mock of sin,
And swore a very wicked oath,
  He did not care a pin.

It was the butcher's youngest son,
  His voice was broke with sighs,
And with his pocket handkerchief
  He wiped his little eyes.

All young and ignorant was he,
  But innocent and mild,
And, in his soft simplicity,
  Out spoke the tender child—

"Oh! father, father, list to me;
  The pig is deadly sick,
And men have hung him by his heels,
  And fed him with a stick."

It was the naughty butcher then
  That laughed as he would die,
Yet did he soothe the sorrowing child
  And bid him not to cry.

"Oh! Nathan, Nathan, what's a pig,
  That thou shouldst weep and wail?
Come bear thee like a butcher's child,
  And thou shalt have his tail."

It was the butcher's daughter then,
  So slender and so fair,
That sobbed as if her heart would break
  And tore her yellow hair.

And thus she spoke in thrilling tone—
  Fell fast the tear-drops big:
"Ah! woe to me! Alas! alas!

The pig! the pig! the pig!"

Then did her wicked father's lips
  Make merry wit her woe,
And call her many a naughty name,
  Because she whimpered so.

Ye need not weep, ye gentle ones,
  In vain your tears are shed,
Ye cannot wash the crimson hand,
  Ye cannot sooth the dead.

The bright sun folded on his breast,
  His robes of rosey flame,
And softly over all the west
  The shades of evening came.

He slept, and troops of murdered pigs
  Were busy in his dreams;
Loud rang their wild, unearthly shrieks,
  Wide yawned their mortal seams.

The clock struck twelve; the dead hath heard;
  He opened both his eyes,
And sullenly he shook his tail
  To lash the feeding flies.

One quiver of the hempen corc—
  One struggle and one bound—
With stiffened limb and leaded eye,
  The pig was on the ground.

And straight towards the sleeper's house
  His fearful way he wended;
And hooting owl, and hovering bat,
  On midnight wing attended.

Back flew the bolt, uprose the latch,
  And open swung the door,
And little mincing feet were heard

Pat, pat, along the floor.

Two hoofs upon the sanded floor,
  And two upon the bed;
And they are breathing side by side,
  The living and the dead.

"Now wake, now wake, thou butcher man!
  What makes your cheeks so pale?
Take hold! take hold! thou dost not fear
  To clasp a spectre's tail?"

Untwisted every winding coil;
  The shuddering wretch took hold,
Till like an icicle it seemed,
  So tapering and so cold.

"Thou com'st with me, thou butcher man!"
  He strives to loose his grasp,
But, faster than the clinging vine,
  Those twining spirals clasp.

And open, open, swung the door,
  And fleeter than the wind,
The shadowy spectre swept before,
  The butcher trailed behind.

Fast fled the darkness of the night,
  And morn rose faint and dim;
They called full loud, they knocked full long
  They did not waken him.

Straight, straight towards that oaken beam,
  A trampled pathway ran;
A ghastly shape was swinging there—
  It was the butcher man.

O. W. Holmes

Little Dame Crump

Little Dame Crump,
  With her little hair broom,
One morning was sweeping
  Her little bedroom,
When, casting he little
  Grey eyes on the ground,
In a sly little corner
  A penny she found.

"Dear me!" cried the Dame,
  While she started with surprise,
"How lucky I am
  To find such a prize!
To market I'll go,
  And a pig I will buy,
And little John Grubbins
  Shall make him a sty."

So she washed her face clean,
  And put on her gown,
And locked up the house,
  And set off for town.
Then to market she went
  And a purchase she made
Of a little white pig,
  And a penny she paid.

Having purchased the pig,
  She was puzzled to know
How they both should get home;
  So fearing least piggie
Should play her a trick,
  She drove him along
With a little crab stick.

Piggie ran till they came
  To the foot of a hill,
Where a little bridge stood

831

O'er the stream of a mill;
Piggie grunted and squeaked,
  But not further would go:
Oh, fie! Piggie, fie!
  To serve little Dame so.

She went to the mill,
  And she borrowed a sack
To put the pig in,
  And take him on her back:
Piggie squeaked to get out,
  But the little Dame said,
"If you won't go of yourself,
  You then must be made."

At last when the end
  Of her journey had come,
She was awfully glad
  She had got the pig home:
She carried him straight
  To his nice little sty,
And gave him some hay
  And some straw, nice and dry.

With a handful of peas
  Then Piggie she fed,
And put on her night-cap,
  And got into bed:
Having first said her prayers,
  And put out the light;
And being quite tired,
  We'll wish her good night.

The Chinese Pig

Old Madam Grumph, the pig, had got
  A pig-sty of her own;
She is a most un-com-mon pig,

And likes to live alone.

A red-tiled roofing covers in
  The one half of her sty;
And, half sur-round-ed by a wall,
  Is open to the sky.

There stands the trough, they keep it fill'd
  With pig-wash and with parings;
And all the other pigs declare
  Dame Grumph has dainty farings.

They like to see what she's about,
  And poke their noses through
A great hole in the pig-sty door,
  From whence they get a view.

The pigs, that run about the yard,
  Are very lean and tall,
With long hind legs—but Madam Grumph
  Is round as any ball.

One autumn day, when she awoke
  ('Twas very cold and raw),
She found a litter of young pigs
  Half buried in the straw.

"Humph," said the dame, "now let me see
  How many have I got."
She counted, "Six and four are ten,—
  Two dead ones in the lot.

"Eight—That's a nice round family;
  A black one and two white;
The rest are spotted like myself,
  With prick ears—that's all right.

"What's to be done with those dead things,
  They'd better be thrown out,"
Said she, and packed the litter round

The others with her snout.

"What's that, old Grumphy?" said a pig,
  Whose snout peeped through the door;
"There's something moving in the straw
  I never saw before."

"I wish you'd mind your own affairs,"
  Said she, and stepp'd between
The young pigs and the pig-sty door,
  Not wishing to be seen.

"I hope you slept well," said the pig,
  "The wind was very high;
You are most comfortably lodged—
  A most con-ve-ni-ent sty."

"I thought I told you once before
  To mind your own affairs,"
Said she, and bristling up her back,
  She bit the lean pig's ears.

"Squeak,' said the bitten pig, "sque-e-ak,
  Old Grumphy's biting hard;"
And all the lean pigs scamp-ed'd up
  From all sides of the yard.

They grumbled and they grunted loud,
  The squeak'd in every key;
At last another pig peep'd through,
  To see what he could see.

Dame Grumph was standing by her pigs,
  And looking very proud,
And all the little piggy-wigs
  Were squeaking very loud.

"These lovely creatures," said old Grumph,
  "These lovely pigs are mine;
There're fat and pink like human babes,

Most pro-mi-sing young swine."

"Indeed," ex-claim'd the peeping pig,
  "I never should have thought,
They were so very promising "
  Old Grumphy gave a snort.

"They're of a most dis-tin-guished race;
  My mother and her brother
Were both im-por-ted from Pekin,—
  My pigs are like my mother.

"They never shall as-so-ci-ate
  With long-legged pigs like you."
Said she, ad-dress-ing the lean pig,
  Whose snout was peeping through.

"Begging your pardon, ma'am
  I really think," said he,
"The dif-fer-ence is not so great
  As it appears to be.

"If you and I were bacon, ma'am
  The dif-fer-ence between
An Irish and a Chinese pig
  Would hardly then be seen.

"Give me your comfortable sty,
  And some of your nice food
Our little fa-mi-lies might prove
  In-dif-fer-ent-ly good."

Aunt Effie's Rhymes

835

Madam Grump and Her Babies

The Old Woman and Her Pig

Once an old woman was sweeping her house, and found a crooked sixpence, and went to market to buy a pig. As she was coming home she came to a stile, and the pig would not get over it: so she went a little farther and met a dog, and said to the dog:—

"Dog, dog, bite pig;
Piggy won't get over the stile,
And I shan't get home to-night."
But the dog would not.

She went a little farther and met a stick, and said:
"Stick, stick, beat dog; dog won't bite pig,
Piggy won't get over the stile,
And I shan't get home to-night."
But the stick would not.

She went a little farther and met a fire, and said:
"Fire, fire, burn stick; stick won't beat dog,
Dog won't bite pig,
Piggy won't get over the stile,
And I shan't get home to-night."
But the fire would not.

She went a little farther and met some water, and said:
"Water, water, quench fire,
Fire won't burn stick,

Stick won't beat dog, dog won't bite pig,
Piggy won't get over the stile,
And I shan't get home to-night."
  But the water would not.
She went a little farther and met an ox, and said:
"Ox, ox, drink water,
Water won't quench fire, fire won't burn stick,
Stick won't beat dog, dog won't bite pig,
Piggy won't get over the stile,
And I shan't get home to-night.'
  But the ox would not.
She went a little farther and met a butcher, and
said:
"Butcher, butcher, kill ox,
Ox won't drink water,
Water won't quench fire, fire won't burn stick,
Stick won't beat dog, dog won't bite pig,
Piggy won't get over the stile,
And I shan't get home to-night.'
  But the butcher would not.
She went a little farther and met a rope, and said:
"Rope, rope, hang butcher.
Butcher won't kill ox, ox won't drink water,
Water won't quench fire, fire won't burn stick,
Stick won't beat dog, dog won't bite pig,
Piggy won't get over the stile,
And I shan't get home to-night."
  But the butcher would not.
She went a little farther and met a rat, and said:
"Rat, rat, gnaw rope;
Rope won't hang butcher,
Butcher won't kill ox, ox won't drink water,
Water won't quench fire, fire won't burn stick,
Stick won't beat dog, dog won't bite pig,
Piggy won't get over the stile,
And I shan't get home to-night."
  But the rat would not.
She went a little farther and met a cat, and said:
"Cat, cat, kill rat; rat won't gnaw rope,
Rope won't hang butcher,
Butcher won't kill ox, ox won't drink water,

Water won't quench fire, fire won't burn stick,
Stick won't beat dog, dog won't bite pig,
Piggy won't get over the stile,
And I shan't get home to-night."

But the cat said to her, "If you will go to yonder cow, and fetch me a saucer of milk, I will kill the rat." So away went the old woman to the cow, and said:

"Cow, cow, give me some milk, cat won't kill rat,
Rat won't gnaw rope, rope won't hang butcher,
Butcher won't kill ox, ox won't drink water,
Water won't quench fire, fire won't burn stick,
Stick won't beat dog, dog won't bite pig,
Piggy won't get over the stile,
And I shan't get home to-night."

But the cow said to her, "If you will go to yonder haymakers and fetch me a wisp of hay, I'll give you the milk."

So away the old woman went to the haymakers and said:

"Haymakers, give me a wisp of hay;
Cow won't give me milk, cat won't kill rat,
Rat won't gnaw rope, rope won't hang butcher,
Butcher won't kill ox, ox won't drink water,
Water won't quench fire, fire won't burn stick,
Stick won't beat dog, dog won't bite pig,
Piggy won't get over the stile,
And I shan't get home to-night."

But the haymakers said to her, "If you will go and fetch us a bucket of water, we'll give you the hay." So away the old woman went; but she found the bucket was full of holes. So she covered the bottom with pebbles, and then filled the bucket with water, and away she went back with it to the haymakers; and they gave her a wisp of hay.

As soon as the cow had eaten the hay, she gave the old woman the milk; and away she went with it in a saucer to the cat. As soon as the cat had drank the milk, the cat began to kill the rat, the rat began to gnaw the rope, the rope began to hang the butcher, the butcher began to kill the ox, the ox began to drink the water, the water began to quench the fire, the fire began to burn the stick,

838

the stick began to beat the dog, the dog began to bite to pig, the pig in a great fright jumped over the stile, and so the old woman got home that night in time to boil some apple dumplings for her husband's supper.

The Flying Pig

The Flying Pig

Dickery, dickery dare,
The pig flew up in the air,
But Patrick Brown soon brought him down,
Dickery, dickery, dare.

The Story of the Three Little Pigs

Once there was an old pig, who had three little pigs, and sent them out to seek their fortune. The first one went and built a house with straw, and soon after a wolf came and knocked at the door and said, "Little pig,

839

let me come in. But the little pig said, "No, no by the hair of my chin." The wolf then said, "I'll huff, and I'll puff, and I'll blow your house in." So he huffed, and he puffed, and blew the house in, and ate up the little pig.

The next little pig built a house with sticks, and the old wolf came along and called out, "Little pig, let me come in." And the little pig answered, "No, no, by the hair of my chin." "Then," says the wolf, "I'll huff, and I'll puff, and I'll blow your house in." So he huffed and he puffed, and blew the house down, and ate up the little pig also.

The third little pig built a house with bricks. Just after along came the old wolf, and said, "Little pig, let me come in." The little pig said, "No, no, by the hair of my chin." "Then I'll huff and I'll puff, and I'll blow your house down." Well, he huffed and he puffed, and he huffed and he puffed, and he puffed and he huffed; but he could not get the house down.

When he found he could not, with all his huffing and puffing, blow the house down, he said "Little pig, I know where there is a nice field of turnips." "Where?" said the little pig. "Oh, in Mr. Smith's home field, and if you will be ready to-morrow morning I will call for you, and we will go together, and get some for dinner."

"Very well," said the little pig, "I will be ready. What time do you mean to go?" "Oh, at six o'clock." Well, the little pig got up at five, and got the turnips before the wolf came, which he did about six, and said, "Little pig, are you ready?" The little pig said, "Ready; I've been and come back again and got a nice potful for dinner."

The wolf felt very angry at this, but thought that he would be up to the little pig somehow or other, so he said, "Little pig, I know where there is a nice apple tree." "Where?" said the little pig. "Down at Merry Garden," replied the wolf, "and if you will not deceive me I will come for you at five o'clock to-morrow, and we will go together and get some apples."

Well, the pig bustled up the next morning at four o'clock, and went off for the apples, hoping to get back before the wolf came; but he had further to go, and had to climb the tree, so that just as he was coming down from it he saw the wolf coming, which, as you may suppose, frightened him very much. When the wolf came up he said, "Little pig, what; are you here before me? Are they nice apples?"

"Yes, very," said the little pig, "I will throw you down one." And he threw it so far that, while the wolf was gone to pick it up, the little pig jumped down and ran home. The next day the wolf came again, and said "Little pig, there is a fair at Shanklin this afternoon, will you go?" Oh, yes," said the pig, "I will go: what time shall you be ready?" "At three," said the wolf.

So the little pig went off before the time as usual, got to the fair, and bought a butter-churn, which he was going home with, when he saw the wolf coming. Then he could not tell what to do. So he got into the churn to hide, and by doing so turned it around, and it rolled down the hill with the pig in it, which frightened the wolf so much that he ran home without going to the fair. He went to the little pig's house and told him how frightened he had been by a great round thing which came down the hill past him.

Then the little pig said "Ha! I frightened you, then. I had been to the fair and bought a butter-churn, and when I saw you I got into it and rolled down the hill." Then the wolf was very angry indeed, and declared he would eat up the little pig, and that he would get down the chimney after him.

When the little pig saw what he was about, he hung onto the pot full of water, and made up a blazing fire, and just as the wolf was coming down, took off the cover, and in fell the wolf; so the little pig put on the cover again in an instant, boiled him up, and ate him for supper, and lived happy ever afterwards.

Gentlemen Rabbits.

The Wild Rabbits

Among the sand-hills,
Near by the sea,
Wild young rabbits
Were seen by me.

They live in burrows
With winding-ways,
And there they shelter
On rainy days.

The mother rabbits
Make cosy nests,
With hairy linings
From their breasts.

The tender young ones
Are nursed and fed,
And safely hidden
In this warm bed.

And when they are older,

They all come out
Upon the sand-hills
And frisk about.

They play and nibble
The long, dry grass
But scamper away
Whenever you pass.

Disobedient Bunny

A pert little rabbit,
Once lived in a hole,
And just did whatever he pleased;
His ways were so funny,
His antics so droll,
That his parents were terribly teased.

"Now, dear," said his mother
"You'd best stay at home,
And try to be patient and good."
But No! he was fully
Determined to roam
Through the green and beautiful wood.

So what did he do?
On a fine summer day,
When mother was not to be seen,
He took to his heels,
And scampered away
Right over the meadow so green.

He shook his long ears,
And he whisked up his tail,
His eyes dancing with glee,
As onward he ran
Through a beautiful vale,

843

And oh! how delighted was he!

'Twas not very long
Till he found a haystack,
Where of course there was shelter and food.
Said he to himself,
"Now, I' never go back
To my stupid old home in the wood.

"I'll dig myself a nice den
For myself in the hay;
How warm it will be and how nice!
Why in my old burrow
Full many a day
I've often felt colder than ice!"

So bunny soon dug him
A nice little hole,
And made it as round as an O;
And really he looked
So exceedingly droll,
You'd have laughed had you seen him, I know.

But evening drew on,
It was lonely and dark,
So Bunny lay down in his den;
Said he to himself,
"I'll get up with the lark,
And won't I be ravenous then!

"For really this hay,
Though it does for a nest,
Is somewhat too dry for my food;
At home there is clover,
The thing I love best,
And lettuce and carrots so good.

"I wish I had some
At this moment! but then
I'm out on my travels just now,

And I greatly prefer
To reside in this den,
Than at home where there's often a row!

"Ah, well! I feel sleepy,
I'd best go to bed—
But what is that noise that I hear?
There seems to be someone
Right over my head,
I hope that no wild beasts are near!"

Meanwhile an old fox
With a great bushy tail
Was prowling about and around
But poor little Bunny
Was hidden so well
That never a bit was he found!

When morning had come,
And the fox disappeared,
Then Bunny came forth to the light,
Said he to himself,
"It was just as I feared,
A fox has been here through the night.

"I think I had better
Go scampering home
To the dear little home in the wood,
And never, oh never
Again will I roam,
Or leave my dear mother so good."

Away then he ran,
Without once looking back,
Till he saw the dear home he loved best.
And mother came hopping
Along the hard track
To welcome him home to the nest.

And, oh! such a breakfast

Before him there lay,
Such clover and grass from the wood;
And always I've heard,
From that terrible day,
That Bunny is patient and good.

E. R. McKean

The Pet Rabbit

I have a little Bunny
  With his coat as soft as down,
And nearly all of him is white
  Except one bit of brown.
The first thing in the morning,
  When I get out of bed,
I wonder if my bunny's still
  Safe in his shed.

And then the next thing that I do,
  I daresay you have guessed;
It's at once to go and see him,
  When I am washed and dressed.
And every day I see him,
  I like him more and more,
And each day he is bigger
  Than he was the day before.

I feed him in the morning
  With bran and bits of bread.
And every night I take some straw
  To make his little bed.
What with carrots in the morning
  And turnip-tops for tea,
If a bunny can be happy,
  I'm sure he ought to be.

Then when it's nearly bed-time

I go down to his shed,
And say "Good-night, you bunny!"
  Before I go to bed,
I think there's only one thing
  That would make me happy quite,
If I could take my bunny dear
  With me to bed at night.

Robert Mack

A Working Rabbit.

The Little Hare

Beyond the palings of the park
  A Hare had made her form,
Beneath a drooping fern, that made
  A shelter snug and warm.

She slept until the daylight came,
  And all thinks were awake,
And then the Hare, with noiseless steps,
  Crept softly from the brake.

She stroked her whiskers with her paws,
  Looked timidly around
With open eyes and ears erect
  That caught the smallest sound.

The Field-Mouse rustled in the grass,
  The Squirrel in the trees,
But Puss was not at all afraid
  Of common sounds like these.

She frisked and gambolled with delight,
  And cropped a leaf or two
Of clover and of tender grass,
  That glistened in the dew.

What was it, then, that made her start,
  And run away so fast?
She heard the distant sound of hounds,
  She heard the huntsman's blast.

Tally-ho!-hoy tally-ho!
  The hounds are in full cry;
Ehew! ehew—in scarlet coats
  The men are sweeping by.

So off she set with a spring and a bound,
Over the meadows and open ground,
Faster than hunter and faster than hound

And on—and on—till she lost the sound,
And away went the little Hare.

Aunt Effie

Peter and the Hare

Thoughtless little Peter,
  With his little gun,
Went out by the woodside
  For a little fun;
Saw a happy little hare,
  Who on clover fed—
With his little gun took aim
  And shot him in the head.

Thoughtful little Peter,
  Sad for what he'd done,
Sat down on a stump, and there
  By it laid his gun;
Wished that he could bring to life
  That little hare so still;
"Never more," said he, "will I
  A harmless creature kill "

Epitaph on a Hare

Here lies whom hound did ne'er pursue,
  Nor swifter greyhound follow,
Whose foot ne'er tainted morning dew
  Nor ear heard huntsman's halloo.

Old Tiney, surliest of his kind,
  Who, nursed with tender care,
And to domestic bounds confined,

Was sti_ a wild Jack-hare.

Though duly from my hand he took
　His pittance every night,
He did it with a jealous look,
　And when he could he would bite.

On twigs of hawthorn he regaled,
　On pippin's russet peel;
And when his juicy salads fail'd,
　Sliced carrot pleased him well.

A Turkey carpet was his lawn,
　Whereon he loved to bound,
To skip and gambol like a fawn,
　And swing himself around.

His frisking was at evening hours
　For then he'd lost his fear!
But most before approaching showers,
　Or when a storm drew near.

Eight years and five round-rolling moons
　He thus saw steal away,
Dozing out all his idle noons
　And every night at play.

I kept him for his humour's sake,
　For he would oft beguile
My heart of thoughts that made it ache,
　And force me to a smile.

But now beneath this walnut shade,
　He finds his long last home,
And wants, in snug concealment laid
　Till gentler puss shall come.

He, still more aged, feels the shocks
　From which no care can save;
And partner once of Tiney's box,

Must soon partake his grave.

William Cowper

Punch's Appeal for the Hunted Hare

All on the bare and bleak hills de,
One night this merry Christmastide,
A shivering hunted hare did hide;
     Poor Pussy!

Though we had hunted puss all day,
The wind had blown her scent away,
And balked the dogs, so there she lay,
     Poor Pussy!

There to the earth she humbly crept,
There brooding o'er her lot she wept,
There, on her empty stomach she slept.
     Poor Pussy!

And there, while frozen fell the dew,
She dreamt an ugly dream or two,
As starved, wet folk are apt to do,
     Did Pussy!

Loud hungry hounds of subtle ken,
And thundering steeds, and hard-eyed men,
Are fast on Pussy's trail again,
     Poor Pussy!

Onwards she strains, on, as they tear
Foremost amongst the foremost there,
Are ruthless women's faces fair;
     Poor Pussy!

One moment's check, to left, to right,
In vain she spends her little might,

851

Some yokel's eyes have marked her flight,
    Poor Pussy!

What use her fine small wits to rack!
Closer, and faster on her track
Hurries the hydra-headed pack,
    Lost Pussy!

"For pity's sake, kind huntsman, stop!
Call off the dogs before I drop,
And kill me with your heavy crop."
    Shrieks Pussy!

With shuddering start and stifled scream,
She wakes!—She finds it all a dream;
How kind the cold, cold earth doth seem
    To Pussy!

The Hare and the Tortoise

A Gentleman Rat

The Pied Piper of Hamelin
—or—
The Vanished Children

Hamelin Town's in Brunswick
By famous Hanover city;
The river Weser, deep and wide
Washes its wall on the southern side.
A pleasanter spot you never spied;
But, when begins my ditty,
Almost five hundred years ago,
To see the townsfolk suffer so
From vermin was a pity.

Rats!
They fought the dogs and killed the cats,
And bit the babies in the cradles
And ate the cheeses out of the vats,
And licked the soup from the cook's own ladles,
Split open the kegs of salted sprats,
Made nests inside men's Sunday hats,
And even spoiled the women's chats,
By drowning their speaking,

With shrieking and squeaking
In fifty different sharps and flats.

At last the people in a body
  To the Town Hall came flocking:
"'Tis clear," cried they, "our Mayor's a noddy;
  And as for our Corporation—shocking
To think we buy gowns lined with ermine
For dolts that can't or won't determine
What's best to rid us of our vermin!

The mayor and Town Councillors were greatly perplexed what to do, when there entered a strange-looking
piper, and offered to charm away all the rats for a thousand guilders. The council joyfully agreed to this, and at
once:—

Into the street the Piper swept,
  Smiling first a little smile,
As if he knew what magic slept
  In his quiet pipe the while:
Then, like a musical adept,
To blow the pipe his lips he wrinkled,
And green and blue his sharp eyes twinkled
Like a candle flame where salt is sprinkled;
And ere three shrill notes the pipe uttered,
You heard as if an army muttered;
And the muttering grew to a grumbling;
And out of the houses the rats came tumbling.

Great rats, small rats, lean rats, brawny rats,
Brown rats, black rats, grey rats, tawny rats,
Grave old plodders, gay young friskers,
  Fathers, mothers, uncles, cousins,
Cocking tails and pricking whiskers,
  Families by tens and dozens,
Brothers, sisters, husbands wives—
Followed the Piper for their lives.
From street to street he piped advancing,
Until they came to river Weser
Wherein all plunged and perished
—Save one.

You should have heard the Hamelin people
Ringing the bells till they rocked the steeple.
"Go," cried the Mayor, "and get ong poles!
Poke out the nests and block up the holes!
Consult with carpenters and builders,
And leave in our town not even a trace
Of the rats!"—when suddenly up the face
Of the Piper perked in the market-place,
With a "First, if you please, my thousand guilders!"

The mayor and Councillors abused the Piper, refused to pay him the thousand guilders, and offered him fifty and a drink, he refused to take less than they had offered, and said:
"Folks who put me in a passion
May find me pipe to another fashion,"
"How?" cried the Mayor, "d'ye think I'll brook
Being worse treated than a crook?
Insulted by a lazy ribald
With idle pipe and vesture piebald?
You threaten us, fellow? Do your worst,
Blow your pipe there till you burst!"
Once more he stept into the street:
And to his lips again
Laid his long pipe of smooth straight cane;
And ere he blew three notes (such sweet
Soft notes as yet musicians cunning
Never gave the enraptured air),
There was a rustling, that seemed like a bustling
Of merry crowds pustling, at pitching and hustling,
Small feet were pattering, wooden shoes clattering,
Little hands clapping, and little tongues chattering,
And like fowls in a farmyard when barley is scattering,
Out came the children running,
All the little boys and girls,
With rosy cheeks and flaxen curls,
And sparkling eyes and teeth like pearls,
Tripping and skipping, ran merrily after
The wonderful music with shouting laughter.

The Mayor was dumb, and the Council stood
As if they were carved into blocks of wood,

855

Unable to move a step, or cry
To the children merrily skipping by—
And could only follow with the eye
That joyous crowd at the Piper's back.
But how the Mayor was on the rack,
And the wretched Council's bosoms beat,
As the Piper turned from the High street
To where the Weser rolled its waters
Right in the way of their sons and daughters!
However he turned from South to West,
And to Koppelberg Hill his steps addressed,
And after him the children pressed;
Great was the joy in every breast.

"He never can cross that mighty top!
He's forced to let the piping drop,
And we shall see out children stop!"
When lo! as they reached the mountain's side,
A wondrous portal opened wide,
As if a cavern was suddenly hollowed
And the Piper advanced and the children followed.
And when all were in to the very last,
The door in the mountain-side shut fast,
Did I say all? No! one was lame,
And could not dance the whole of the way!

And in after years, if you would blame
His sadness, he was used to say—
"It's dull in our town since my playmates left;
I can't forget that I'm bereft
Of all they pleasant sights they see,
Which the Piper also promised me;
For he led us, he said, to a joyous land,
Joining the town and just at hand,
Where waters gushed and fruit trees grew,
And flowers put forth a fairer hue.

And everything was strange and new;

The sparrows were brighter than peacocks here,
And their dogs outran our fellow deer,
And honey-bees had lost their stings;
And horses were born with eagles' wings,
And just as I became assured
My lame foot would be speedily cured,
The music stopped, and I stood still,
And found myself outside the Hill,
Left alone against my will,
To go now limping as before,
And never hear of that country more!"
Alas, alas for Hamelin!
  There came into many a burgher's pate
  A text which says. that Heaven's Gate
  Opens to the Rich at as easy rate
As the needle's eye takes a camel in!

The mayor sent East, West, North and South,
To offer the Piper by word of mouth,
  Wherever it was men's lot to find him,
Silver and gold to his heart's content,
If he'd only return the way he went,
  And bring the children all behind him.
But at length they saw 'twas a lost endeavour,
For Piper and dancers were gone for ever.

    Browning

The Wicked Bishop Hatto

The summer and autumn had been so wet
That in winter the corn was growing yet;
'Twas a piteous sight to see all around
The grain lie rotting on the ground.

Every day the starving poor
Crowded around Bishop Hatto's door,
For all the neighbourhood could tell

His granaries were furnished well.

At last Bishop Hatto appointed a day
To quiet the poor without delay:
He bade them to his great Barn repair
And they should have food for the winter there.

Rejoiced such tidings good to hear,
The poor folk flocked from far and near;
So the great Barn was full as it could hold
Of women and children, and young and old.

Then when he saw it could hold no more,
Bishop Hatto he made fast the door;
And while for mercy with shrieks they call,
He set fire to the Barn and burnt them all,

"A rare and excellent bonfire!" quoth he,
"And the country is greatly obliged to me,
For ridding it in these times forlorn
Of Rats that only consume the corn."

So then to his palace returned he,
And he sat down to supper merrily,
And he slept that night like an innocent man;—
But Bishop Hatto never slept again.

In the morning as he entered the hall,
Where his picture hung against the wall,
A sweat like death all over him came,
For the Rats had eaten it out of the frame.

As he looked, there came a man from his farm,
He had a countenance white with alarm;—
"I opened your granaries this morn,
And the Rats had eaten all the corn."

Another came running presently,
And he was pale as pale could be;—
"Fly! my Lord Bishop, without delay,

Ten thousand rats are coming this way."

"I'll go to my tower on the Rhine," quoth he,
"'Tis the safest place in Germany;
The walls are high and the shores are steep,
And the stream is long and the water deep."

Bishop Hatto fearfully hastened away,
And he crossed the Rhine without delay,
And reached his tower, and barred with care
All the windows, doors, and loopholes there.

He laid him down, and closed his eyes.
But soon a scream made him arise:
He started, and saw two eyes of flame
On his pillow, from whence the screaming came.

He listened, and looked—it was only the cat;
But the Bishop grew more fearful for that,
For she sat screaming, mad with fear
At the army of rats that were drawing near.

For they have swum over the river so deep,
And they have climed the shores so steep,
And up the tower their way is bent,
To do the work for which they were sent.

They are not to be told by the dozen or score—
By the thousands they come, and by myriads, and more;
Such numbers have never been heard of before,
Such a judgement had never been witnessed of yore.

Down on his knees the Bishop fell,
And faster and faster his beads did tell,
As louder and louder, drawing near,
The gnawing by their teeth he could hear.

And in at the windows, and in at the door,
And through the walls helter-skelter they pour,
And down from the ceiling, and up from the floor,

859

From the right and the left, from behind and before,
From within and without, from above and below;
And all at once to the Bishop they go.

They have whetted their teeth against the stones,
And now they pick the Bishop's bones;
They gnawed the flesh from every limb,
For they were sent to do judgement on him.

R. Southey

What became of them!

He was a rat, and she was a rat,
  And down in one hole they did dwell,
And both were as black as a witch's cat,
  And they loved one another well.

He had a tail, and she had a tail,
  Both long and curling and fine,
And each said, "Yours is the finest tail
  In the world, excepting mine."

He smelt the cheese, and she smelt the cheese,
  And they both pronounced it good;
And both remarked it would greatly add
  To the charms of their daily food.

So he ventured out, and she ventured out,
  And I saw them go with pain;
But what befel them I never can tell,
  For they never came back again.

RATS CARRYING HOME AN EGG

The Gingerbread Cat

A baby-girl, on Christmas night
Had filled her little apron white
With all a happy child could take
Of Christmas toys and Christmas cake;

But on the stairway she let fall
The chiefest treasure of them all—
A little cat of gingerbread
All frosted white from tail to head.

Now in the moonlit midnight time,
When merry mice do run and climb,
A plump gray mouse come down the stair

861

And saw the Christmas cake-cat there.

She stood still in her cruel fright
And gazed upon the monster white
Who seemed to feel as great surprise,
And stared with both his raisin eyes.

Poor mousie dared not, could not stir!
Her little brain was in a whirr!
Five minutes—ten—but not a paw
Had puss put forth! "I never saw

A cat like this!" the poor mouse said.
A brave bold thought came in her head—
Her wee heart beating pit-a-pat,
She moved her own paw—touched the cat—

Then sprang upon it with a squeal
And made a most delicious meal
"Ho! ho!" she cried, "Sugar! spice!
And everything that's good and nice—

That's what cats are made of,
The cats that we're afraid of!"
Then up the stairs she madly pranced,
And o'er the attic floor she danced

And then she stood upon her head
And to her 'stonished friends she said,
"O, joy to every mouse and rat,
For I have eaten up the cat!"

The Mice

The mice are in their holes,
   And there they hide by day;
But when 'tis still at night,

They all come out to play.

They climb up on the shelves,
  And taste of all they please;
They drink the milk and cream,
  And eat the bread and cheese.

But if they hear the cat,
  At once they stop their fun;
In fright they seek their holes
  As fast as they can run

Three Mice

Three Mice went into
  A hole to spin,
Puss came by,
  Puss peeped in;
What are you doing,
  My little old men?
We're weaving coats
  For gentlemen.
Shall I come and help you
  To wind up your threads?
Oh, no, Mrs. Pussy,
  You'd bite off our heads!

Says Pussy, "You are
  So wondrous wise
I love your whiskers
  And round black eyes;
Your house is the prettiest
  House I see.
And I think there is room
  For you and me."
The mice were so pleased

That they opened the door,
And Pussy soon laid them
All dead on the floor.

"Run Mousey, Run!"

I am sitting by the fireside,
  Reading, and very still,
There comes a little sharp-eyed mouse,
  And run about he will.

He flies along the mantelpiece
  He darts beneath the fender;
It's just as well that Jane's not here,
  Or into fits he'd send her.

And now he's nibbling at some cake
  She left upon the table.
He seems to think I'm somebody
  To hurt a mouse unable.

Run, mousey, run! I hear the cat,
  She's scratching at the door,
Once she comes in, you'll have no chance
  Beneath her savage claw.

Run, mousey, run! I hear Jane's foot,
  She's coming up to bed,
If puss but makes a spring at you,
  Poor mousey, you'll be dead!

A Mouse Caught in a Cage

I'm only a poor little mouse, ma'am!
I live in the wall of your house, ma'am!
With a fragment of cheese, and a very few peas,

I was having a little carouse, ma'am!

No mischief at all I intend, ma'am!
I hope you will act as my friend, ma'am!
If my life you should take, many hearts it would break,
And the trouble would be without end, ma'am!

My wife lives in there in the crack, ma'am!
She's waiting foe me to come back, ma'am!
She hoped I might find a bit of rind,
Or the children their dinner will lack, ma'am!

I never was given to strife, ma'am!
(Don't look at that terrible knife, ma'am!)
The noise overhead that disturbs you in bed,
'T is the rats, I will venture my life, ma'am!

In your eyes I see mercy I'm sure, ma'am!
Oh, there's no need to open the door, ma'am!
I'll slip through the crack, and I'll never come back,
Oh I'll never come back any more, ma'am!

The Foolish Mouse

In a crack, near the cupboard,
  With dainties provided,
A certain young mouse
  With her mother resided;
So securely they lived,
  In that snug, quiet spot,
Any mouse in the land
  Might have envied their lot

But one day the young mouse,
  Which was given to roam,
Having made an excursion
  Some way from her home,
On a sudden returned,

With such joy in her eyes,
That her grey, sedate parent
Expressed some surprise,

"Oh mother," said she,
"The good folks of this house
I'm convinced, have not any
Ill-will to a mouse;
And those tales can't be true
You always are telling,
For they've been at such pains
To construct us a dwelling.

"The floor is of wood,
And the walls are of wires
Exactly the size that
One's comfort requires;
And I'm sure that we there
Shall have nothing to fear,
If ten cats, with kittens,
At once should appear.

"And then they have made
Such nice holes in the wall,
One could slip in and out,
With no trouble at all;
But forcing one through
Such rough crannies as these,
Always gives one's poor ribs
A most terrible squeeze.

"But the best of all is,
They've provided, as well,
A large piece of cheese,
Of most exquisite smell;
'Twas so nice, I had put
In my head to go through,
When I thought it my duty
To come and fetch you."

"Ah, child," said the mother,
  "Believe, I entreat,
Both the cage and the cheese
  Are a terrible cheat;
Do not think all that trouble
  They took for our good,
They would catch us and kill us
  All there if they could.

"Thus they've caught and killed scores,
  And I never could learn,
That a mouse who once entered
  Did ever return."
Let young people mind
  What the old people say.
And, when danger is near them,
  Keep out of the way.

HELPING THEIR COMRADE OUT

A Clever and Good Mother Mouse

One Summer day the sun shone bright,
  Mid sweet flowers roved the bee,
And I wandered in a garden old
  Beside the deep blue sea.

But close at hand, a shady path,
  Beneath some beech trees wound,

COLE

And there. that sultry summer day,
  A pleasant seat I found.

Suddenly, just beside my chair,
  A little sound I heard;
A scratch upon the gravel path,
  As of a mouse or bird.

I turned my head; there, on the path,
  What strange sight did I see!
A little mouse, and in her mouth
  Another still more wee.

Softly she crept across the path,
  And then, her journey done,
In a hole beneath the green grass verge
  She laid her little one.

And back and forth from side to side,
  I watched her carry five
Sweet little mice, her own dear brood,
  Long tailed, and all alive.

She never wearied in her work,
  Yet oh so small was she!
And thus, that bright, hot summer day
  She moved her nursery.

Dear mother mouse! My verse has told
  Your patient loving deed;
Methinks our boys and girls may learn
  Some lessons as they read.

Francis E. Cooke

The True History of a Poor Little Mouse

A poor little mouse
 Had once made him a nest,
 And he fancied, the warmest,
 And safest, and best,
That a poor little mouse could enjoy;
 So snug and convenient,
 So out of the way.
 This poor little mouse
 And his family lay,
They fear'd neither pussy nor boy.

It was in a store
 That was seldom in use,
 Where shavings and papers
 Were scattered in loose,
That this poor little mouse made his hole,
 But alas! Master Johnny
 Had seen him one day,
 As in a great fright
 He had scampered away,
With a piece of plum pudding he stole.

As soon as young Johnny
 (Who, wicked and bad,
 No pitiful thoughts
 For dumb animals had)
Descried the poor fellow's retreat,
 He crept to the shavings
 And set them alight,
 And, before the poor mouse
 Could run off in its fright,
It was smother'd to death in the heat!

Poor mouse! how it squeak'd
 I can't bear to relate,
 Nor how its poor little
 Ones hopp'd in the grate,
And died, one by one, in the flame!

I should not much wonder
To hear, that, some night,
This wicked boy's bed-curtains
Catching alight,
He suffered exactly the same.

Ann Taylor

The Mouse's Call

A little mouse crept out one day,
  When all was still about;
To dollie's house he took his way,
  The lady being out.

He skipped about with bead-bright eyes
  From table down to chair;
He thought the house was just the size
  For him to settle there.

He found some jelly cake so nice,
  This naughty little mouse;
He nibbled first, then in a trice
  'Twas gone from dollie's house.

He curl'd himself upon the floor,
  To have a little nap,
When suddenly upon the floor
  There came a fearful rap.

The mouse who had not left a crumb,
  With fear began to shake,
For dollie's mistress back had come
  To get her piece of cake.

She opened wide the little house,
  Her doll lay on her arm,
And when she spied the trembling mouse

She cried out with alarm.

She tumbled back upon the ground,
  Her dear doll falling too,
While the mouse went rushing round,
  Not knowing what to do.

At last he tumbled down the stair,
  Then to his hole he flew;
And which did most the other scare
  They never, never knew.

A KIND HUSBAND.

COLE

The Foolish Frog

In a tank at the foot of the hill
  Lived Mr. and Mrs. Frog,
At the head of the sparkling rill,
  By the side of a queachy bog;
And they had children ten—
  All froggies as yellow as gold,
Who loved to play on the fen,
  But they often were over-bold.

Now it fell out one bright day,
  As it never had done before,
When Father Frog was away
  A stickleback sailed to the door.
"Oh! Mrs. Frog," said he,
  "Your sister is very ill;
And much she wants to see
  You down at the water mill."

Then Mother frog showed her grief
  In such tears as you never saw;
And, having no handkerchief,
  She wiped her eyes with a paw.
Said she, "Now, froggies dear,
  You must not go to the fen:
There is no danger here,
  And I'll soon come back again!"

But the naughty little froggies,
Disobeyed their mother and went.

Then a duck, which had lazily swum
  For hours in a reedy pool,
Seeing the shadows come,
  And feeling the air grow cool.
With a "Quack, quack, quack," came out
  She meant, "It is time to sup!"
So finding the froggies about,

She gobbled them quickly up.

So Mr. and Mrs. Frog,
  By the peeping stars made bold,
Came back by the queachy bog,
  To their froggies all yellow as gold.
They never saw them again—
  Alas! that it should be so.
They were told not to go to the fen;
  But the did not obey, you know.

"Early Days"

Marriage of Mr. Froggie

There was a Frog
Lived in a bog—
A Frog of high degree—
A stylish youth,
And yet, forsooth,
A bachelor was he.

He had not wed
Because, he said,
He'd ne'er in all his life
Seen in the bog
A pollywog
He cared to make his wife.

But one fine day,
When drest up gay,
He passed a pretty house,
And there beside
The window spied
A most attractive mouse.

He raised his hat,
And gazing at

873

Miss Mouse, in suit of gray,
  He made a bow,
  Likewise a vow
To marry her straightway.

  When he was drest
  In scarlet vest,
And coat of velvet sheen
  With frills of lace,
  And sword in place,
His like was nowhere seen.

  His smile was bland,
  His style so grand,
He said with pride, "I know
  Miss Mouse so fair,
  Can find nowhere
So suitable a beau!

  "If she'll agree
  To live with me,
And be my faithful wife,
  Oh, she shall dine
  On dishes fine,
And lead an easy life."

  When he went by,
  Miss Mouse so shy,
Would hide her blushing face;
  But truth to tell
  Could see quite well
Through curtains of thin lace.

  And from her nook,
  Ah! many a look
She gave, with heart a-stir;
  And oft did she
  Confess that he
Was just the beau for her.

At last so blue
Poor froggie grew,
He went up to the house
And rang the bell,
In haste to tell
His love for Mistress Mouse.

He passed the door,
And on the floor
He knelt and kissed her hand,
"Wilt marry me?"
He asked, while she
Her burning blushes fanned.

She answered "Yes,"
As you may guess,
To Mister Frog's delight;
His arm he placed
Around her waist,
And joy was at its height.

The wedding-day
Was set straightway,
The town was all agog;
And gifts, not few,
Were sent unto
Miss Mouse and Mister Frog.

And never yet
Was banquet set,
In country or in town,
With fare more rich
Than that to which
The wedding guests sat down.

And, after all,
There was the ball,
For which the band was hired,
And frogs and mice
Were up in a trice,

And canced till their toes were tired.

Frogs at School

Twenty froggies went to school,
Down beside a rushy pool;
Twenty little coats of green,
Twenty vests all white and clean,
"We must be in time," said they;
"First we study, then we play;
That is how we keep the rule
When we froggies go to school."

Master Bullfrog, grave and stern,
Called the classes in their turn;
Taught them how to nobly strive,
Likewise how to leap and dive;
From his seat upon the log
Showed them how to say, "Ker-chog!"
Also, how to dodge a blow
From the sticks which bad boys throw.

Twenty froggies grew up fast;
Bullfrogs they became at last;
Not one dunce among the lot,
Not one lesson they forgot.
Polished in a high degree,
As each froggie ought to be,
Now they sit on other logs,
Teaching other little frogs.

FLYING FROG.

Mouse that Lost her Tail

Once upon a time a Cat and Mouse were playing together, when, quite by accident, the cat bit off the Mouse's tail.

It was very strange that the Cat did not bite off the Mouse's head. But this Mouse was a good Mouse, and never stole any cheese; and so the Cat only bit off her tail. Mousey was very much vexed to see that her tail was gone, so she said to Pussy—

"Oh, dear Pussy! do give me my tail again."

"No, that I will not," said Pussy, "till you get me some milk for my breakfast."

"Oh, the Cow will give me some," said the Mouse.

So she frisked and jumped, and hen she ran

Till she came to the Cow, and thus began:—

"Please, Cow, give me some milk. I want to give Pussy milk, and Pussy will give me my own tail again."

"So I will, Mousey, if you will get me some hay for my breakfast." said the Cow.

"Oh, the Farmer will give me some," said the Mouse.

So she frisked and jumped, and hen she ran

Till she came to the Farmer, and thus began:—

877

"Please, Mr. Farmer, give me some hay; I want to give
the Cow hay The Cow will give me some milk; I will
give Pussy milk; and Pussy will give me my own tail
again."
"So I will, Mousey, if you get me some bread for my
breakfast," said the Farmer.
"Oh, the Baker will give me some," said the Mouse.
     So she frisked and jumped, and then she ran
     Till she came to the Baker, and thus began:—
"Please, Mr. Baker, give me some bread; I want to give
the Farmer bread. The Farmer will give me some hay; I
will give the Cow hay, the Cow will give me some milk;
I will give Pussy milk; and Pussy will give me my own
tail again."
"So I will, Mousey, if you get me some meat for my
breakfast," said the baker.
"Oh, the Butcher will give me some," said the Mouse.
     So she frisked and jumped, and then she ran
     Till she came to the Butcher, and thus began:—
"Please, Mr. Butcher, give me some meat. I want to give
the Baker meat. The Baker will give me some bread; I
will give the Farmer bread. The Farmer will give me
some hay; I will give the Cow hay, the Cow will give
me some milk; I will give Pussy milk; and Pussy will
give me my own tail again."
"So I will, Mousey, if you will eat up the crumbs that
have fallen at my breakfast," said the Butcher.
"Oh, that I will," said the Mouse, and she soon cleared
the floor of every crumb.
     Then the Butcher gave the Mouse some meat, and
the Mouse gave the Baker the meat, and the Baker gave
the Mouse some bread, and the Mouse gave the Farmer
the bread, and the Farmer gave the Mouse some hay,
and the Mouse gave the Cow the hay, and the Cow gave
the Mouse some milk, and the Mouse gave Pussy the
milk, and then Pussy gave poor little Mousey her own
tail again.
     So she frisked and jumped, and away she ran
     And cried out to Pussy, "Catch me if you can!"

Mouse Gruel

There was an Old Person of Ewell,
Who chiefly subsisted on gruel
But to make it taste nice, he inserted some mice,
Which refreshed that Old Person of Ewell.

Wise Mice

Some little mice sat in a barn to spin,
Pussy came by and she popped her head in.
"Shall I come in and cut your threads off?"
"Oh, no, kind sir, you will bite our heads off!"

Mouse Ran up the Clock

Hickory, diccory dock,
The mouse ran up the clock,
The clock struck one, the mouse ran down,
Hickory, diccory, dock.

A Frog he would a-Wooing Go

A Frog he would a-wooing go,
Whether his mother would have it or no;
So off he set with his nice new hat,
And on the road he met a rat.

"Pray, Mr. Rat, will you go with me,
Kind Mrs. Mousey for to see!"
When they came to the door of Mousey's hall,
They gave a loud knock, and gave a loud call.

"Pray, Mrs. Mouse, are you within?"
"Oh, yes, kind sirs, I'm sitting to spin."
"Pray, Mrs. Mouse, Will you give us some beer?
For Froggy and I are fond of good cheer."

"Pray, Mr. Frog, will you give us a song—
But let it be something that's not very long!"
"Indeed, Mrs. Mouse," replied the Frog,
"A cold has made me as hoarse as a dog."

"Since you have a cold, Mr. Frog," Mousey said,
"I'll sing you a song that I have just made."
But while they were all a merry-making,
A cat and her kittens came tumbling in.

The cat she seized the rat by the crown;
The kittens they pulled the little mouse down.
This put Mr. Frog in a terrible fright:
He took up his hat, and wished them good-night.
But as Froggy was crossing over a brook,
A lily-white duck came and gobbled him up,
So there was an end of one, two, and three.
The Rat, the Mouse, and the little Frog-ee.

Man that Caught a Mouse

The Little priest of Felton,
The little priest of Felton
He killed a mouse within his house,
And ne'er a one to help him.

Three Blind Mice

Three blind mice! three blind mice!
See how they run! see how they run!
They all ran after the farmer's wife,
They cut off their tails with a carving knife;
Did you ever see such a thing in your life
As three blind mice?

The Three Unfortunate Mice

Three little dogs were basking in the cinders;
Three little cats were playing in the windows;
Three little mice hopped out of a hole,
And a piece of cheese they stole;
The three little cats jumped down in a trice,
And cracked the bones of the three little mice.

The Foolish Mouse

In a crack near the cupboard, with dainties provided,
A certain young mouse with her mother resided;
So securely they lived in that snug, quiet spot,
Any mouse in the land might have envied their lot.

But one day the young mouse, which was given to roam,
Having made an excursion some way from her home,
On a sudden returned, with such joy in her eyes,
That her grey, sedate parent expressed some surprise.

"O mother," said she, "The good folks of this house,
I'm convinced, have not any ill-will to a mouse;
And those tales can't be true you always are telling,
For they've been at such pains to construct us a dwelling.

"The floor is of wood, and the walls are of wires,
Exactly the size that one's comfort requires;
And I'm sure that we there shall have nothing to fear,
If ten cats, with kittens, at once should appear.

"And then they have made such nice holes in the wall,
One could slip in and out, with no trouble at all;
But forcing one through such rough crannies as these,
Always gives one's poor ribs a most terrible squeeze.

"But the best of all is, they've provided, as well,
A large piece of cheese, of most exquisite smell;
'T was so nice, I had put in my head to go through,
When I thought it my duty to come and fetch you."

"Ah, child," said the mother, "believe, I entreat,
Both the cage and the cheese are a terrible cheat;
Do not think all that trouble they took for our good,
They would catch us and kill us there if they could.

"Thus they've caught and killed scores, and I never could learn,
That a mouse who once entered did ever return."
Let young people mind what the old people say,
And, when danger is near them keep out of the way.

The Fox and the Cat

The fox and the cat as they travelled one day,
With moral discourses cut shorter on the way:
"'Tis great," says the fox, "to make justice our guide!"
"How godlike is mercy!" Grimalkin replied.

Whilst thus they proceeded, a wolf from the wood,
Impatient of hunger, and thirsting for blood,
Rushed forth—as he saw the dull shepherd asleep—
And seized for his supper an innocent sheep.

"In vain, wretched victim, for mercy you bleat;
When mutton's at hand," says the wolf, "I must eat."
Grimalkin's astonished—the fox stood aghast,
To see the fell beast at his bloody repast.

"What a wretch!" says the cat—"'tis the vilest of brutes;
Does he feed upon flesh when there's herbage and roots?"
Cries the fox, "While our oaks give us acorns so good,
What a tyrant is this to spill innocent blood!"

883

Well, onward they marched, and they moralised still.
Till they came where some poultry picked chaff by a mill.
Sly Reynard surveyed the them with gluttonous eyes,
And made, spite of morals, a pullet his prize!
A mouse, too, that chanced from her covert to stray,
The greedy Grimalkin secured as her prey!

A spider that sat in her web on the wall,
Perceived the poor victims, and pitied their fall;
She cried, "Of such murders how guiltless am I!"
So ran to regale on a new-taken fly!

Sour Grapes

A fox was trotting one day,
  And just above his head
He spied a vine of luscious grapes,
  Rich, ripe, and purple-red.

Eager he tried to snatch the fruit,
  But, ah! it was too high;
Poor Reynard had to give it up,
  And, leaving a deep sigh,

He curled his nose and said, "Dear me!
  I would not waste an hour
Upon such mean and common fruit—
  I'm sure those grapes are sour!"

'Tis thus we often wish thro' life,
  When seeking wealth and pow'r
And when we fall, say, like the fox,
  We're "sure the grapes are sour!"

The Fox and the Mask

A fox walked round a toyman's shop
  (How he came there, pray do not ask),
But soon he made a sudden stop,
  To look and wonder at a mask.

The mask was beautiful and fair,
  A perfect mask as e'er was made;
At which a lady meant to wear
  At the ensuing masquerade.

He turned it round with much surprise,
  To find it prove so light and thin;
"How strange!" astonished Renard cries,
  "Here's mouth and nose, and eyes and chin.

"And cheeks and lips, extreme y pretty;
  And yet, one thing there still remains
To make it perfect—what a pity,
  So fine a head should have no brains!"

Thus, to some boy or maiden pretty;
  Who to get learning takes no pains,
May we exclaim, "Ah! what a pity,
  So fine a head should have no brains!"

The Fox and Crow

  In a dairy a crow,
  Having ventured to go,
Some food for her young ones to seek,
  Flew up in the trees
  With a fine piece of cheese
Which she joyfuly held in her beak.

  A fox who lived by,
  To the tree saw her fly,

885

And to share in the prize he made a vow,
  For, having just dined,
  He for cheese felt inclined,
So he went and sat under the bough.

  She was cunning he knew,
  But so was he, too,
And with flattery adapted his plan;
  For he knew if she'd speak,
  It must fall from his beak,
So, bowing politely, began:

  "'Tis a very fine day,"
  (Not a word did she say),
"The wind, I believe, ma'am, is south:
  A fine harvest for peas;"
  He then looked at the cheese,
But the crow did not open her mouth.

  Sly Reynard, not tired,
  He plumage admired:
"How charming! how brilliant its hue!
  The voice must be fine
  Of a bird so divine,
Ah, let me hear it, pray do.

  Believe me I long
  To hear a sweet song;"
The silly crow foolishly tries;
  She scarce gave one squall,
  When the cheese she let fall,
And the fox ran away with the prize.

    Jane Taylor

The Blind Men and the Elephant
(A Hindoo Fable)

It was six men of Indostan
  To learning much inclined,
Who went to see an elephant,
  (Though all of them were blind),
That each by observation
  Might satisfy his mind.

The FIRST approached the Elephant,
  And happening to fall
Against his broad and sturdy side,
  At once began to bawl:
"God bless me!—but the Elephant
  Is very like a wall!"

The SECOND feeling of the tusk,
  Cried: "Ho! what have we here
So very round and smooth and sharp!
  To me 'tis mighty clear
This wonder of an Elephant
  Is very like a spear!"

The THIRD approached the animal,
  And happening to take
The squirming trunk within his hands,
  This boldly up and spake:
"I see," quoth he, "The Elephant
  Is very like a snake!"

The FOURTH reached out his eager hand,
  And felt about the knee,
"What most this wondrous beast is like
  Is mighty plain," quoth he.
"'Tis clear enough the Elephant
  Is very like a tree!"

The FIFTH, who chanced to touch the ear,
  Said: "E'n the blindest man

Can tell what this resembles most,
  Deny the fact who can,
This marvel of an Elephant
  Is very like a fan."

The SIXTH no sooner had begun
  About the beast to grope,
Than, seizing on the swinging tail
  That fell within his scope,
"I see," quoth he, "the Elephant
  Is very like a rope!"

And so these men of Indostan
  Disputed loud and long,
Each in his own opinion
  Exceeding stiff and strong,
Though each was partly in the right,
  And all were in the wrong.

An Address to a Mouse

Sly little, cowering, timorous beastie!
Oh what a panic's in thy breastie!
You need not start away so hasty,
  With bickering speed:
I should be loth to run and chase thee
  I should indeed!

I'm truly sorry man's dominion
Hath broken Nature's social union,
And justifies that ill opinion
  Which makes thee startle
At me, thy poor earth-born companion,
  And fellow mortal.

Sometimes, I doubt not, thou dost thieve;
What then? poor beastie, thou must live;
A little barley in the shieve
  Is small request;
And all thou tak'st, I do believe,
  Will ne'er be missed.

   R. Burns

Song of the Toad

I am an honest toad,
Living here by the road,
Beneath a stone I dwell
In a snug little cell.

When the rain patters down,
I let it wet my crown;
And now and then I sip
A drop with my lip.

And now a catch a fly,

And now I wink my eye,
And now I take a hop,
And now and then I stop.

And this is all I do,
And yet they sat it's true
That the toad's face is sad,
And his bite is very bad.

Oh! naughty folks they be
Who tell such tales of me!
For I'm an honest toad
Just living by the road,
   Hip, hip, hop.

Mosquito Song

In a summer's night I take my flight
  To where the maidens repose;
And while they are slumbering sweet and sound,
  I bite them on the nose;
The warm red blood that tints their cheeks,
  To me is precious dear,
For 'tis my delight to buzz and bite
  In the season of the year.

When I get my fill, I wipe my bill,
  And sound my tiny horn;
And off I fly to mountain high
  Ere breaks the golden morn;
But at eve I sally forth again
  To tickle the sleeper's ear;
For 'tis my delight to buzz and bite
  In the season of the year.

On the chamber wall about I crawl,
  Till landlord goes to bed;
Then my bugle I blow, and down I go

To light upon his head.
Oh, I love to see the fellow slap,
    And regret to hear him swear;
For 'tis my delight to buzz and bite
    In the season of the year.

The Nightingale and Glow-worm

A Nightingale, that all day long
Had cheered the village with his song,
Nor yet at eve his note suspended,
Nor yet when eventide was ended,
Began to feel—as well he m ght—
The keen demands of appetite;
When looking eagerly around,
He spied, far off, upon the ground,
A something shining in the dark,
And knew the glow-worm by his spark;
So; stooping down, from hawthorn top,
He thought to put him in his crop
The worm, aware of his intent,
Harangued him this, quite eloquent—
"Did you admire my lamp," quoth he,
"As much as I your minstrelsy?
You would abhor to do me wrong,
As much as I to spoil your song;
For 'twas the self-same power divine
Taught you to sing, and me to shine:
That you with music, I with light,
Might beautify and cheer the night."
The songster heard his short oration,
And, warbling out his approbation,
Released him as my story tels,
And found a supper somewhere else.

Cowper

891

The Glow-worm

Beneath this hedge, or near the stream,
  A worm is known to stray,
That shows by night a lucid stream
  That disappears by day.

Disputes have been, and still prevail,
  From whence his rays proceed;
Some give the honor to his tail,
  And others to his head;

But this is sure—the hand of might
  That kindles up the skies,
Gives him a modicum of light,
  Proportion'd to his size.

Perhaps indulgent Nature meant,
  By such a lamp bestow'd,
To bid the traveller as he went,
  Be careful where he trod.

                    Cowper

Happiness of the Grasshopper

Happy insect! what can be
In happiness compared with thee!
Fed with nourishment divine,
The dewy morning's gentle wine;
Nature waits upon thee still,
And thy verdant cup does fill.
All the fields which thou dost see,
All the plants belong to thee:
All that summer hours produce,
Fertile made with easy juice;

The country hinds with gladness hear,
Prophet of the ripened year!

Cowley

The Whale

Warm and buoyant, in his oily mail,
Gambols on seas of ice th' unwieldily whale;
Wide waving fins round boating islands urge
His bulk gigantic through the troubled surge;
With hideous yawn, the flying shoals he seeks,
Or clasps with fringe of horn his massy cheeks;
Lifts o'er the tossing wave his nostril bare,
And spouts the watery columns into air;
The silvery arches catch the setting beams,
And transient rainbows tremble o'er the streams.

Darwin

The wasp and the Bee

A wasp met a bee that was just buzzing by,
And he said "Little Cousin, can you tell me why
You are loved so much better by people than I.

"My back shines as bright, and as ye low as gold
And my shape is most elegant too to behold,
And yet nobody likes me for that, I am told,"
  Bz.

"Ah! Cousin," the bee said, "'tis all very true,
But if I were half as much mischief to do,
Then I'm sure they would love me no better than you.
  Bz.

"You have a fine shape and a delicate wing,
And they say you are handsome; but then there's one thing
They never can put up with; and that is your sting.
   Bz.

"My coat is quite homely and plain, as you see,
But yet no one is angry or scolding at me,
Just because I'm a harmless and busy bee."
   Bz.

From this little story let people beware,
For if, like the cross wasp, ill-natured they are,
They will never be loved, though they're ever so fair.

My Pets

I bring my little doggies milk;
  I bring my rabbits hay;
I feed and tend, and love them well—
  Such helpless things are they!
See! now in soft and cozy bed
  They roll about and play;
They've milk and bones, and all they want—
  Such happy pets are they!

The Squirrel

I'm a merry, merry squirrel,
All day I leap and whirl
Through my home in the old beech-tree
If you chase me I will run
In the shade and in the sun;
But you never, never can catch me

For round a bough I'll creep,
  Playing hide and seek so sly;
Or through the leaves bo-peep,
  With my little shining eye.

Up and down I run and frisk,
With my bushy tail to whisk
All who mope in the old beech-trees.
  How droll to see the owl
  As I make him wink and growl,
While his sleepy, sleepy head I tease!
  And I waken up the bat,
    Who flies off with a scream,
  For he thinks that I'm the cat
    Pouncing on him, in his dream.

Through all the summer long
I never want a song
From birds in the old beech-trees
  I have singers all the night,
  And with the morning bright
Come my busy, humming, fat, brown bees.
  When I've nothing else to do
    With the nursing birds I sit;
  And we laugh at the cuckoo
    A-coo-cooing to her tit!

When winter comes with snow
An its cruel tempests blow
All my leaves from the old beech-trees,
  Then beside the wren and mouse
  I furnish up a house,
Where, like a prince, I live at ease.
  What care I for hail or sleet,
    With my cozy cap and coat;
  And my tail about my feet,
    Or wrapped about my throat?

Norman Macleod

Ducks and Ducklings

One little white duck,
  One little grey,
Six little black ducks
  Running out to play;
One white lady-duck,
  Motherly and trim,
Eight little baby ducks
  Bound for a swim.

One little white duck
  Running from the water,
One very fat duck—
  Pretty little daughter—
One little grey duck
  Holding up its wings.
One little bobbing duck
  Making water rings.

One little black duck
  Standing on a stone,
One little grey duck
  Swimming all alone,
One little grey duck
  Holding down it's head.
One sleepy little duck,
  It has gone to bed!

One little what duck
  Running to its mother,
Look among the water-reeds,
  May be there's another.
One hungry little duck
  Going out to dine,
Two dainty little ducks,
  Snowy-white and fine.

Merry little brown eyes
  O'er the picture linger,
Point all the ducks out,
  Chubby little finger;
Make the picture musical,
  Merry little shout;
Now where's that other duck?
  What is he about?

I thank that other duck
  Is the nicest duck of all,
He hasn't any feathers,
  And his mouth is sweet and small;
He runs with a light step
  And jumps upon my knee,
And though he cannot swim
  He is very dear to me.

One white lady-duck,
  Motherly and trim,
Eight little baby ducks
  Bound for a swim;
One sleepy little duck
  Taking quite a nap,
One precious little duck
  Here on mother's lap.

A. L.

The Squirrel

The pretty red squirrel
  Lives up in a tree,
A little blithe creature
  As ever can be;
He dwells in the boughs
  Where the stock-dove broods,
Far in the shades

Of the green summer woods;

His food is the young
  Juicy cones of the pine,
And the milky beech-nut
  Is his bread and his wine.
In the joy of his nature
  He frisks with a bound
To the topmost twigs,
  And then down to the ground.

Then up again like
  A winged thing,
And from tree to tree
  With a vaulting spring;
Then he sits up aloft,
  And looks ragged and queer,
As if he would say:
  "Ay, follow me here!"

And then he grows pettish,
  And stamps his foot,
And then with a chatter,
  He cracks his nut;
And thus he lives
  All the long summer through,
Without either a care
  Or a thought of rue.

The Mountain and the Squirrel

The mountain and the squirrel
  Had a quarrel,
And the former called the latter "Little Prig;"
  Bun replied,
"You are doubtless very big,
But all sorts of things and weather
Must be taken together

To make up a year,
  And a sphere.
And I think it no disgrace
To occupy my place.
If I'm not so large as you,
You are not so small as I.
And not half so spry;
I'll not deny you make
A very pretty squirrel track.
Talents differ; all is well and wisely put;
If I cannot carry forests on my back,
Neither can you crack an nut!"

R. W. Emerson

AN INTELLIGENT TAME RACOON.

Wonderful Birds' Nests

At the Age of 40.

EDWARD WILLIAM COLE—Aged 80.

Cole's Own Portrait, at
the age of 41.

*(He bought it amongst some
old Books, thus it became
his own Portrait.)*

What Books Do For Mankind

1.

Books should be found in every house,
To form and feed the mind;
They are the best of luxuries
To happify mankind.

2.

For all good books throughout the world
Are man's most precious treasure;
They make him wise, and bring him
His best, his choicest pleasure.

903

3.

Books make his time pass happily,
Relieve his weary hours;
Amuse, compose, instruct his mind;
Enlarge his mental powers.

4.

Books teach the boys and girls of earth
In quite ten million schools;
Books make the difference between
Earth's learned and its fools.

5.

Books teach earth's teeming artisans
The proper way to take,
To find, to plan, to build, to mix,
And every product make.

6.

Books teach schoolmasters, clergymen,
Of every rank and grade;
And doctors, lawyers, judges, too—
Books are their tools of trade.

* * * * * *

128.

Books thus, by print, and pictures, bring
The whole world into view,
And show what all men think about,
And everything they do.

129.

Books give to man the history
Of each and every land;
Books show him human actions past,

The bad, the good, the grand.

130.

Books show him human arts and laws
Of every time and place;
Books show the learnings and the faiths
Of all the human race.

131.

Books give the best and greatest thoughts
Of all the good and wise;
Books treasure human knowledge up,
And thus it never dies.

132.

Books show men all that men have done,
Have thought, have sung, have said,
Books show the deeds and wisdom of
The living and the dead.

133.

Books show that mankind's leading faiths,
In morals are the same;
That in their main essentials
They differ but in name.

134.

Books show that virtue, goodness love,
Exist in every land;
That some with kindly sympathies
Are found on every strand.

135.

Books show the joys, griefs, hopes and fears,

Of every race and clan;
Books show, by unity of thought,
The brotherhood of man.

136.

Books thus will cause the flag of peace
Through earth to be unfurled—
Produce "the parliament of man,"
And federate the world.

137.

Books give the reader vast delight,
The bookless never know;
Books give him pleasure, day and night,
Wherever he may go.

138.

Books show narcotics, toxicants,
Of each and every kind;
Insidious destroyers all,
Of body and of mind.

139.

Books, like strong drink, will drowns man's cares
But do not waste his wealth;
Books leave him better, drink the worse,
In character and health.

140.

Books teach and please him when a child,
In youth and in his prime;
Books give him soothing pleasure when
His health and strength decline.

141.

Books teach, from their beginning, of
Higher beings than man;
That One Almighty Goodness was
Before the world began.

142.

Books give us hope beyond the grave,
Of an immortal life;
Books teach that right, and truth, and love,
Shall banish every strife.

143.

Books therefore are, of all we own,
The choicest things on earth;
Books have, of all our worldly goods,
The most intrinsic worth.

144.

Books are the greatest blessing brought,
The grandest thing we sell;
Books bring more joy,
Books do more good,
Than mortal tongue can tell.

Our serious thumbs, who never laughed before, on reading a piece in Cole's Fun Doctor slightly smiled, as you see. On reading the Second Piece. On reading the Third Piece. On reading the Fourth Piece. On reading the Fifth Piece. On reading Sixth piece. He was about to read the Seventh Piece, but his medical adviser interfered, and told him not to do so, as he would not be responsible for the consequences.

Cole's Comic Advertiser
(Or Fun Doctor's Assistant)
Laughter as a Medicine.

"The physician tells us of the physical benefits of laughing. There is not the remotest corner or little inlet of the minute blood-vessels of the human body that does not feel some wavelet from the convulsion occasioned by good hearty laughter. The life principle, or the central man, is shaken to the innermost depths, sending new tided of life and strength to the surface, thus materially tending to insure good health to persons who indulge therein. The blood moves more rapidly, and conveys a different impression to all the organs of the body, as it visits them on that particular mystic journey when the man is laughing, from what it does at other times. For this reason every good, hearty laugh in which a person indulges lengthens his life, conveying as it does a new and distinct stimulus to the vital forces."

"Fun is worth more than
physic, and whoever
invents or discovers a new
supply deserves the name
of public benefactor."

Man Made to Laugh, not to Morn.

Man warnt made tew mourn, man waz made tew laff. He iz the onla creeter or thing that God made tew laff out loud. It iz true he knows how to mourn, do duz animills know how, the birds kan tell their sorrows, and the flowers kan hang their pretty heds. Man was made tew smile, tew laff, to haw! tew throw up his hat, and sing halleluger. Man was made tew praze God, and he can't dew it by mourning. Awl the mourning there iz in this wurld was introduced bi man; man warnt made tew mourn any more than he was made to crawl. Tharfore i sa tew awl men and women, stop crying and go tew laffing, you will last longer, and git fatter, and stand just as good a chanse tew git tew heaven with a smile on your countenance as yu will with yure face leaking at every pore.—*Josh Billings*

Josh Billing's Prayer.

"From a wife who don't
luv us, from fluky mutton,
and tite butes, and from
folks who won't laff, good
Lord deliver us."

909

**Testimonials to the astonishing Curing Power of
Cole's Fun Doctor.**

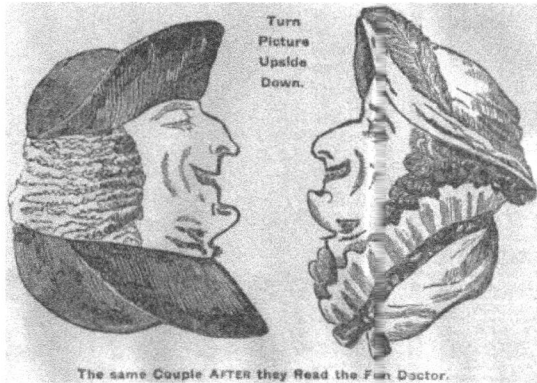

The same Couple AFTER they Read the Fun Doctor.

Most Astonishing Cure of the Age

Dear Sir—Many years ago it was my misfortune to be jilted in love by a cruel-hearted woman. I pined away, and fell into a bad state of health, and was advised by my friends to take some physic. I never took a single dose except somebody told me that it was exactly what I wanted to make me well—but it all did me no good. I only got worse until I came across the right thing, which I will presently describe. I find, in looking over my paid bills, the following are the kinds and quantities of physic I have used during my illness:— Holloway's Pills, 227 boxes; Cockle's Pills, 121 boxes, Beecham's Pills, 80 boxes; Parr's Life Pills, 76 boxes, Blue Pills, 849 boxes. One friend advised me to give up Pills and take some good old-fashioned physic. I took of Jalap, 37 pounds; Caster Oil; 180 bottles, Salts and Senna, 800 doses; Rhubarb and Magnesia, 300 doses; Brimstone and Treacle, 800 doses—but this did me no good. Another friend advised me to take some world-fames patent medicines, so I took of Eno's Fruit Salt 190 bottles, Warner's Safe Cure, 200 bottles; Townsend's Sarsaparilla, 120 bottles; Hop Bitters, 180 bottles; Dandelion Ale, two hogsheads. I took Hayter's Nerve Tonic, Hayter's Blood purifier, Hayter's Invigorator, and Hayter's Pick-Me-Up, of each

911

100 bottles; and Wolfe's Schnapps, 630 bottles— but I felt no better. Another friend came along, and said for my complaint it was no use taking medicines internally, and I must use the "Rub On Remedies," so I rubbed on Holloway's Ointment, 241 boxes; Davis's Pain Killer, 70 bottles; Moulton's Pain Paint, 60 bottles; St. Jacob's oil, Weston's Wizard Oil, and Croton Oil, of each 100 bottles: and of Eucalyptus Oil, 900 quart bottles—but I felt no better. Another friend advised the Herb Cure, so I took strong decoctions of Chamomile, Pennyroyal, Peppermint, Rue, Tansy, Quassia, Horehound, Wormwood, Aconite, Belladonna, Hemlock, Nux Vomica, Lungwort, Liverwort, Moonwort, Sneezewort, and Snakeweed— altogether I took about 1700 quarts of these horrid decoctions—but I felt no better. Another friend told me my stomach was out of order, and required cleansing, so I took of Ipecacuanha Wine 139 quarts—but this did not cure me. Another friend said all diseases come from insects, and I had insects in me, and must take special medicine for them, so I took of Keating's insecticide 730 packets—but got no better. Another friend advised me to try Homoeopathy. I took 111 tubes of pilules and 80 bottles of tinctures—but they did me no good. Another friend advised me to try the water cure. I took cold baths, warm baths, tepid baths, and Turkish baths in hundreds, and drank about twenty hogsheads of mineral waters—but it did me no good. Another friend advised the Acid Cure, so I took Acetic Acid, Muriatic Acid, Nitric Acid, Sulphuric Acid, Oxalic Acid, and Prussic Acid, of each about twenty quarts—but got no better. Another friend advised Soothing Medicines, so I took over 400 of Steedman's Soothing powders, and 130 bottles of Mother Winslow's Soothing Syrup—but I was still irritable and nervous. My last course of medicine consisted of Steel Drops, Balm of Gilead, Turpentine, Chloroform, Cod Liver Oil, Assafoetida, Spanish Flies, and Cayenne Pepper—about fifteen pounds of each— but it all did me no good. I simply got worse and worse, and was reduced to a mere shadow of skin and bone, but, as luck would have it, another friend came along—a true friend this time—and suggested Cole's FUN

912

DOCTOR. I got it, and was well and stout in a Week, at a cost of 1s 6d.

Sworn at Temple Court, and Signed in Everlasting Gratitude,
Government House, Melbourne
JOHN SMITH

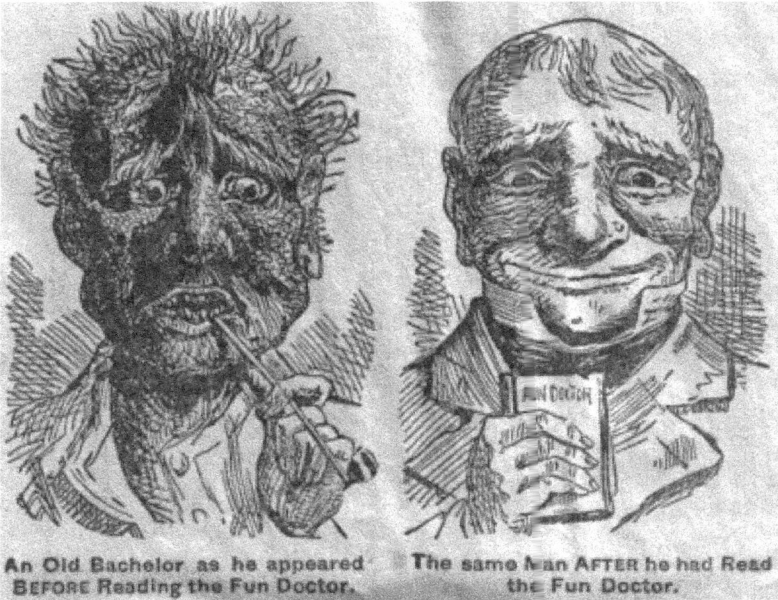

An Old Bachelor as he appeared BEFORE Reading the Fun Doctor.

The same Man AFTER he had Read the Fun Doctor.

VOCAL SOLO

A man on a train was heard to groan so frightfully that the passengers took pity on him, and one of them gave him a drink out of a whisky flask. "Do you feel better?" asked the giver. "I do," said he who had groaned. "What ailed you anyway?" "Ailed me?" "Yes; what made you groan so?" "Groan! Great Land o'Goshen! I was singing!" The generous man will never quite cease to regret the loss of that drink of whisky.

TRIO—"Come into the Garden, Maud!"

DUET.

This gentlemanly musician is very tall when he stands up and puts his hat on.

QUARTETTE.

Cole's Book Arcade, Cole's Book Arcade, it is in Melbourne town,
Of all the book stores in this land, it has the most renown.

Cole's Book Arcade. Cole's Book Arcade,
  it is in Melbourne town,
Of all the book stores in this land,
  it has the most renown.

Full Band and Choir.

TUNE: All the Tunes there are mixed.

TUNE: All the Tunes there are mixed.

Going To Cole's Book Arcade, Melbourne

All the way from Persia on this bicycle.

Why are these two nice children like thousands of knowledge-loving individuals? Because they frequently visit Cole's Book Arcade.

Guess where this young gentleman is going?
To Cole's book arcade. Right. You're a Witch.

The Sea-Serpent as a Carrier

The world-renowned sea-serpent has been specially chartered to bring a fresh supply of books every week from England to Cole's Book Arcade, Melbourne; and also to show upon the coils of his body 2000 rainbows, being so many copies of that establishment. The sea-

920

serpent, upon being communicated with, demanded a heavy price for his services, but Mr. Cole agreed to his terms, as he considered that 2000 of his rainbow signs travelling round the world on the sides of the famous sea-serpent would be a good advertisement for the Book Arcade.

The Sea-Serpent as a Carrier

THE world-renowned sea-serpent has been specially chartered to bring a fresh supply of books every week from England to Cole's Book Arcade, Melbourne; and also to show upon the coils of his body 2000 rainbows, being so many copies of the beautiful sign of that establishment. The sea-serpent, upon being communicated with, demanded a heavy price for his services, but Mr. Cole agreed to the terms, as he considered that 2000 of his rainbow signs travelling round the world on the sides of the famous sea-serpent would be a good advertisement for the Book Arcade.

True History of the Great Sea Serpent

John Smith, the sea-serpent, was born in a swamp near Sydney, about 5000 years ago. He was hatched by a female Bunyip from an immense three cornered egg, which is supposed to have fallen out of the moon, and he is the only sea-serpent that ever existed. He never had relations, and is the only being in the world of whom the verse is true. He never had a father. He never had a mother. He never had a sister. He never had a brother. He also never had a wife. He is of a very shy disposition, and many fascinating mermaids have made love to him, and practiced all their well-known wiles upon him—but in vain: he is a bachelor still. Like some other

921

animals mentioned in history, he thinks and talks like a man. He is exceedingly intelligent, and seems to have as much sense as 10,000 ordinary men or 21,000 women. He can sing with a voice of tremendous compass, from the sweet piping of a nightingale down to far below the deepest tones of the largest organ, or the noise made by discharges of artillery. Sometimes when he sings it shakes the ground for miles around, and if at sea causes a storm. His favourite songs are "A Life on the Ocean Wave," "What are the Wild Waves Saying," "Down by the Deep Sad Sea," and such like. He plays all the musical instruments in the world. His whistle can be heard a distance of 100 miles, his shout 50 miles, and his whisper 10 miles. Of course, in an active life of 5000 years, a life almost as long as some Hindoo patriarchs, he has seen and heard, and done, many astonishing things. He relates that he once rescued a travelling menagerie at sea, he swallowed the whole lot of animals, and the woman in charge of them, let them roam about inside of him and enjoy themselves, and then landed them safely on dry land at the end of 48 hours. He says that he was in Arabia, and saw that remarkable occurrence of the moon coming down and going into Mahomet's sleeves, and there and then he objected to the whole proceeding. The sea-serpent is 15 miles long and 50 feet in diameter, his skin is of a horny nature, but harder than steel, and about 5 feet thick. He travels at the rate of 200 miles per hour, and can carry 120 times as much as the "Great Eastern." If he was coming up to the Queen's Wharf, Melbourne, when his head was at the wharf, his body would reach right down the River Yarra out in the Bay past Williamstown, and the Traffic would have to be stopped in the river whilst he was unloading. The sea-serpent is rather a large eater. Since he reached full growth, namely, for the last 4000 years, he has swallowed a whole whale every morning for breakfast except once. The reason of his going without his breakfast that once is explained in the following manner:—

The reader will remember the account of Jonah and the Whale in the Talmud. It states that when Jonah was in the whale's belly, it went out of the Mediterranean right around Africa into the Red Sea, and that Jonah looked out through the eyes of the whale and saw the place where the children of Israel crossed the Red Sea. The sea-serpent states that he can corroborate this piece of history, as he happened to be after that very whale for breakfast when he saw Jonah looking out through its eyes. He says he did not swallow that whale, as he had found that the whales which he had previously swallowed with prophets inside of them did not agree with him, and consequently he had to go that morning without his breakfast, the first time in 4000 years. Those who want any further information about the famous sea-serpent can acquire it at Cole's Book Arcade, Melbourne, or come and interview and question the sea-serpent himself when he arrives.

P.S.—Some people don't believe in the existence of the sea-serpent, but if he did not exist how could we have got his likeness and his history? That's a question for the unbelievers to answer.

Fashion

A Servant Girl dressed in four absurdities of fashion—a Tight Corset, Tight High-heeled Boots, a Bustle Improver, and Fifteen-button Gloves.

She appears very conceited, but with her tight-lacing must feel very uncomfortable and unwell, and wall sensible people must feel that she is very silly, and with her absurd boots her feet must pain her almost as much as the Chinese woman's shown above [right] pained her when first compressed.

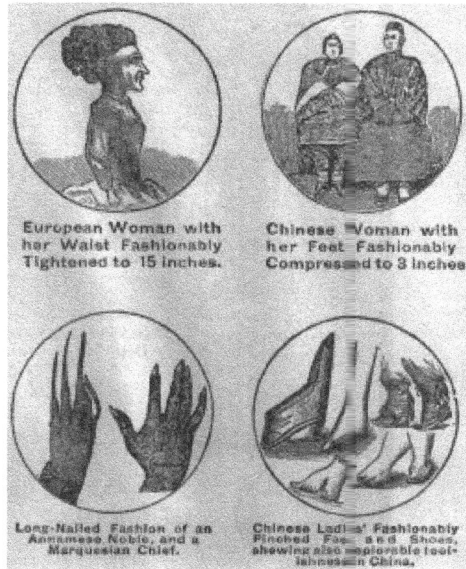

European Woman with her Waist Fashionably Tightened to 15 inches.

Chinese Woman with her Feet Fashionably Compressed to 3 inches

Long-Nailed Fashion of an Annamese Noble, and a Marquesian Chief.

Chinese Ladies' Fashionably Pinched Feet and Shoes, shewing also deplorable foolishness in China.

European Woman with her Waist Fashionably Tightened to 15 inches. Chinese Woman with her Feet Fashionably Compressed to 3 inches. Long-Nailed Fashion of an Annamese Noble, and a Marquesian Chief. Chinese Ladies' Fashionable Pinched Feet and Shoes, shewing also deplorable foolishness in China.

Old English Fashions, showing our ancestors were as foolish as we are.

Old English Fashions, showing our ancestors were as foolish as we are.

Costume of an Ancient Greek Youth, very easy, elegant and suitable for a Lady's Reform Dress. This is a much more sensible dress than the one opposite it [servant girl] and the two below it—look at them.

Crinoline, 1859.
The Dog has got through all right,
but how will the lady manage.

Crinoline, 1859.
Coach licensed to carry four. The coachman and the
horse are both wondering how it can be done.

927

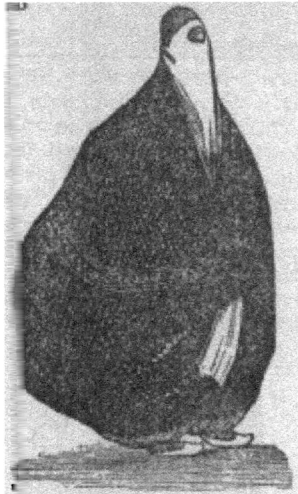

Persian Lady in Out-door
Costume.

French Costume.

Costume, beginning of
the 19th Century

A German Crinoline Frame.

Indians of the Rio Colorado.

Roumanian Costume.

An English and French
Costume.

A North American
Indian Maiden.

931

Reformed American Costume, leaving the Limbs free to Walk, Run, Skate, or Play.

The Gorget Costume.

Turkish Out-door Costume.

Ancient English Costume.

A British Lady and the Chinese Ambassador's Wife and Daughter at the Queen's First Drawing Room, Buckingham Palace, 1893.

**A British Lady and the Chinese Ambassador's Wife
and Daughter
at the Queen's First Drawing Room, Buckingham
Palace, 1893.**

The Chinese ladies are dressed more rationally, but the have such fashionably small feet that they have to lean against the table to enable them to stand with safety. The European lady and the Asiatic ladies are each alike martyrs to foolish fashion, one with the waist and the other with the feet.

Old Alsatian Costume.

bad kind of dress to run, and jump, and play in.

Too much material in the train and too little on the shoulders

935

COLE

"Mother, do put on a shawl, please, before you go down."
"Why, Sonnie?"
"Oh, because some one's is sure to see you if you go down like that!"

The Physical Exercise
Costume, designed by
Mrs. Genness Miller.

Jewess of Tunis.

Reform Costume, 1892.

A Reform Dress for
Travelling, 1894.

Bloomer Costume.

An Afghan Lady.

Syrian Costume.

Mountain Climbing Costume.
1892.

The Maharajah of Jodhpore.

Japanese Court Dress.

Chinese laborer, dressed in bamboo leaves.

Gentleman, 1314.

941

King Munza of Central Africa.

An Ancient Fop.

Ashamed to show his face. A few frivolous fops and other foolish men still wear corsets.

English Costume of
the era of Wickliffe.

A Canadian Indian.

A Zulu Kaffir.

A Kaffir.

A Mandan Chief,   A Gen
1833.   of t

A Gentleman, beginning
of the 19th Century.

Social Ills

Boy's First Smoke.
Enjoying the Tobacco Poison.

Shortly Afterwards.
Suffering from the Tobacco Poison.

A Youth stunted,
wasted and wasting by
Cigarette Smoking.

947

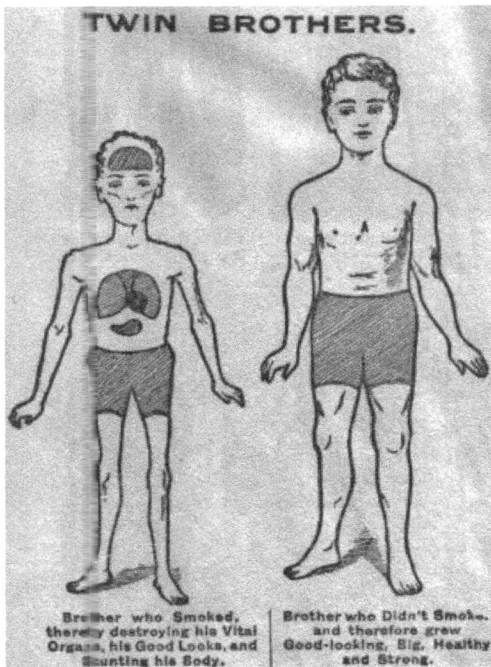

Twin Brothers.

Brother who Smoked,
thereby destroying his Vital
Organs, his Good Looks, and
Stunting his Body.

Brother who Didn't Smoke,
and therefore grew
Good-Looking, Big, Healthy
and Strong.

Multitudes of Employers, both in England and America, will not employ Boy Smokers, and publicly announce the same.

[From the "Social Gazette," also from the "Australian War Cry."]

The following statements show some of the large establishments that are
closed against cigarette smokers in America:—

"Swift & Co. (Packing House, Chicago), and other Chicago business
houses, employing hundreds of boys, have issued this announcement,
or similar ones—*So impressed with the danger of Cigarette using
that we do not employ a Cigarette user.*
Marshall Field, the Mammoth Universal Provider, gave similar
notice.

Montgomery, Ward and Co., the universal providers, say, "We will
not employ cigarette users."

"Morgan and Wright Tyre company, large employers, announce,
"No
cigarettes can be smoked by our employees."

"At John Wanamakers.—The application blank to be filled out by
boys applying for a position reads: 'Do you use tobacco or
cigarettes?' A negative answer is expected, and is favourable to
their acceptance as employes."

"Heath and Milligan, Chicago, bar cigarette users."

"Carson, Pirie and Scott, Chicago, bar cigarette smokers as

employes."

Ayer's Sarsparille Company, Lovell, employs hundreds of boys. —"March 1, 1902—Believing that the smoking of cigarettes is injurious to both mind and body, thereby unfitting young men for their best work—therefore after this date we will not employ any young man under twenty-one years of age who smokes cigarettes."

"I've got a boy for you, sir." Glad of it; who is he?" asked the master workman of a large establishment. The man told the boy's name and where he lived. "Don't want him," said the master workman, "he has got a bad mark." "A bad mark, sir; what?" "I meet him every day with a cigar in his mouth; I don't want smokers!"

"The Lehigh Valley Railroad bars cigarette smokers."

"The Chicago, Rock Island, and Pacific Railroad bars cigarette smoking."

"The New York, New Haven, and Hartford Railroad bars employes who
smoke cigarettes."

"The Central Railroad, Georgia, forbids cigarette smoking."

"The Union Pacific Railroad forbids cigarette smoking."

The following is a public notice: "The Western Union Telegraph Company will discharge from their messenger service boys who persist in smoking cigarettes."

A Telephone Company.—Order: "You are directed to serve notice
that the use of cigarettes after August 1 will be prohibited; and you are further instructed to, in the future, refuse to employ anyone who is addicted to the habit."—Leland Hume, Assistant General Manager of the Cumberland Telephone and Telegraph Company.

"In the United States Weather Bureau.—'Chief of United States Weather Bureau, Willis M. Moore, has placed the ban on cigarettes in this department of Government service'."

Smoking Does Some Good, but More Evil

Smoking soothes and comforts millions of the worried and the weary, and brings much pleasure to the habitual smoker, but it always more or less injures the health of the smoker and sometimes kills him. The vast majority of the medical fraternity condemn smoking, especially by the young.

Smoking injures multitudes of boys in many respects.

Smoking often leads to boys into bad company.

Smoking often makes them precocious, undutiful, impudent and callous.

Smoking often ruins the health.

Smoking generally stunts their growth.

Smoking generally sallows their complexion.

Smoking often leads them to lying.

Smoking often leads them to stealing

Smoking often leads them to drinking.

Smoking degenerates the boy physically, mentally, and morally.

Smokers cannot excel in athletic sports, such as boating, cricket, cycling.

Smokers are always at the bottom of the class in school and college, and backward at all kinds of study.

Excessive smoking causes mental and physical laziness in boys and men.

The following organs, fluids, functions, etc., of the body, especially of the young, are frequently more or less affected by the use of tobacco:—The blood, the heart, the nerves, the brain, the liver, the lungs, the stomach, the throat, the saliva, the taste, the voice, the eyes, the ears, the nose, the mouth, the tongue, the palate, the pancreas, the lips, the teeth, the bones, the skin.

Medical men and observing experts affirm many diseases are caused or accelerated by the use of tobacco, among which are the following:— Heart disease, consumption, cancer, ulceration, asthma, bronchitis, neuralgia, paralysis, palsy, apoplexy, indigestion, dysentery, diarrhoea, constipation, sleeplessness, melancholia, delirium tremens, insanity.

Smoking frequently leads to prolonged suffering.

Smoking often destroys the appetite.

Smoking sometimes weakens the will power.

Smoking sometimes leads to loss of memory.

Smoking often leads to despondency.

Smoking sometimes leads to suicide.

Smoking frequently leads to loss—loss by bad health

and waste of valuable time—direct loss in money required for other purposes, and immense loss through reckless, thoughtless, or unfortunate smokers being the cause of partial or total destruction by fire of buildings, ships, factories homesteads, crops, stores, and property of many kinds also loss of life and property by explosions in mines. explosive factories, powder magazines, explosive stores, etc.

Tobacco using is an unclean habit, and offensive habit, an enslaving habit, often it is an intensely selfish habit.

Tobacco fumes, especially in small and poorly-ventilated houses or rooms, injure or destroy the health of multitudes of wives, and injure the health of multitudes of infants and children.

Tobacco using injures the unborn child by giving it a puny body and an imperfect start in life.

Tobacco using is fast degenerating the race.

A third of the recruits for the Army are disqualified through smoking.

The following Governments have passes laws against juvenile smoking: Germany, Switzerland, Norway, Japan, Canada, Nova Scotia, New Brunswick, Prince Edward Island, British Columbia, the North West Territories, Cape Colony, New South Wales, Victoria, South Australia Tasmania, and about 48 of the States and Territories out of 53; and so terrible and deplorable an effect has juvenile smoking upon the race that most other Governments are considering the advisability of passing laws against it.

The insidious influence of cigarette smoking by boys is shown in these examples of handwriting, taken from a London Country Council health report. The first was written by a boy when he was a victim of the habit; the second is the same boy's writing when he had given it up, ten months later.

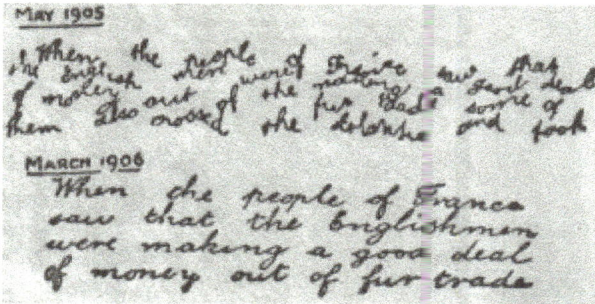

Narcotics and Intoxicants

In most parts of the word man has found out some way of stimulating, soothing, or deadening his animal system by means of plants or drugs. Hundreds of these stimulating, intoxicating, soothing, and stupefying substances have been discovered and used in various countries, chief amongst which may be mentioned—

Opium, Tobacco, Indian Hemp, Betel Nut, and Alcohol; and others are used in a less degree, such as Coca, Kola Nut, Thorn Apple, Cocculus Indicus, Intoxicating Toadstool, Deadly Nightshade, Henbane, Rhododendron, Azalea, Emetic Holly, Bearded Darnel, etc. The first five among those human pleasers and human destroyers are—

1. Alcohol, now drank in the shape of spirits, wine, beer, or some
    other form probably by 500,000,000 persons.
2. Opium, smoked, inhaled, drank or swallowed by probably
    100,000,000.
3. Tobacco, now smoked, chewed, and snuffed by probably 300,000,000
4. Haschish, made from Indian Hemp, now smoked, chewed, or
    swallowed by probably 150,000,000.

953

5. Betel Nut, chewed probably by 50,000,000.

These five narcotising and intoxicating poisons are used, more or less, by half the people in the world, giving some considerable pleasure at times, but destroying, more or less, the health of all who use them, and gradually stunting the form and otherwise undermining the well-being of the entire human race.

Chemistry also produces many things which are taken in the same way and for the same purpose, such as Laudanum, Morphia, Cocaine, Chloral, Chloroform, Ether, &c., and many so-called patent medicines. These all tend to form habits which soothe and please for a time, but they all damage or destroy in the end.

The great bulk of easy-going, unreflecting people have no idea what an amount of mischief and misery the habit of using these things inflict upon poor humanity.

> *Books show* **narcotics, toxicants,**
> *Of each and every kind;*
> *Insidious destroyers all,*
> *Of body and of mind.*

These four pages show at a glance the effects of the three most fascinating and seductive Drugs in the world—Tobacco, Opium, and Alcohol, and which physically, mentally, and morally injure or ruin the greatest number of mankind.

Virginian Tobacco

A good-looking young man soothing, comforting, poisoning, and gradually destroying himself with Tobacco

A good-looking young man soothing,
comforting, poisoning, and gradually
destroying himself with Tobacco.

Chinese Smoking Opium.

Chinese Smoking Opium.

955

The Poppy Plant, from which Opium is made.

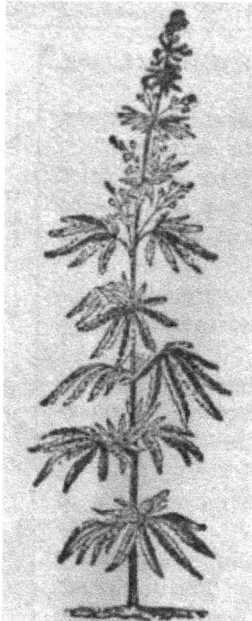

Indian Hemp Plant, from which Hasheesh is made.

First Shoeblack—What yer doin', Bill
Second Shoeblack—Learnin' to Smoke.

First Shoeblack—What yer dcin', Bill?
Second Shoeblack—Learnin' o Smoke.

The Drink Craving

Probably the best use a man can make of his leisure time is to read good books and to follow their advice, and the worst use he can make of it is to indulge in intoxicating liquor, and to go where that will lead or take him.

It is said that "Dipsomania," "Alcoholism," or the "Craving-for-Drink" disease can be cured in most persons by certain remedies an proper management, and the time has come now when the lovers of human progress everywhere feel that this fearful curse must be grappled with, and, if possible, stamped out like the smallpox, or any other terrible disease. One writer sums up the evils of drinking as follows:—

"It injures the health.
It shortens life.
It originates hereditary disease.
It ruins the character of thousands.
It destroys the peace of families and of individuals.
It causes husbands and wives to neglect each other, their children,

and their homes.
It makes wives widows, and children orphans.
It bereaves parents of their children.
It reduces families to penury.
It hinders the amelioration of the poorer classes of society.
It makes time hard and trade bad.
It is a cause of quarrels, robberies, and murders.
It is a cause of suicide.
It fills our prisons.
It fills our poorhouses.
It fills our hospitals
It fills our madhouses."

Books, like strong drink, will drown a man's cares
  But do not waste his wealth,
Books leave him better, drink the worse,
  In character and health.

Two talented men soothing, comforting,
and gradually poisoning themselves
with Brandy and Tobacco.

Pipes of the World
Showing one of Cole's "Similarities of Mankind"

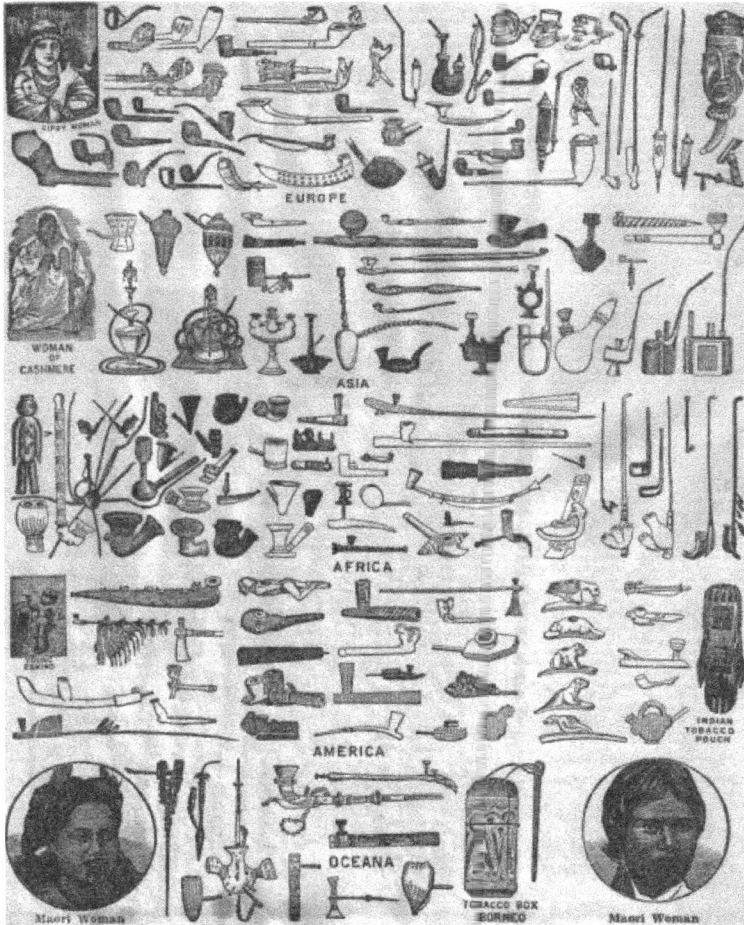

GOD

Go to the top of a mountain so that you can see 50 miles in all directions; you then observe a space 100 miles in diameter. Now the *world* contains 25,000 such areas as that. Our world is amazingly vast, but our sun is a million times as large; yet we see rolling in space thousands as large as our own, which probably have accompanying worlds. And again, beyond this the telescope and astral-photography reveal to us that *to the right, and to the left, before and behind, above and below, and to every point of the heavens, and at immense distances,* millions and millions again of enormous stellar bodies exist, roll, revolve and travel through space. Multitudes of these suns and worlds around us in every direction are at such immense distances that a person travelling with the speed of light, namely, 200,000 miles, or 8 times round our earth, in a *second,* world take *1000,000 years* to reach them. Nor can we imagine an end to this stupendous universe, or an end to space, for is we try to do so the question immediately occurs, *what is still outside and beyond that?* And so on to incomprehensible and overwhelming infinite. And these many millions of suns and worlds and systems and all their parts are clearly working together, like the most exquisitely designed clockwork. Look at the marvellous mechanism of the human brain, the human eye, the human hand, the human heart, and in fact the whole human structure and composition; they all prove the truth of the affirmation that man is "fearfully and wonderfully made." Nay further, examine carefully every object in existence, however stupendously large or, as shown by the microscope, infinitesimally small, and they each and all appear equally perfect for their purpose. Can we see all this, and think on it, and not imagine a Designer and Controller of infinite attributes? It always appeared to me that there must be in this vast, illimitable, and beautiful universe, myriads of beings, superior to our weak mortal selves, and at the head of all and over all, an immortal Being of infinite perfections, which thinking men in all countries and ages have called GOD. And shall not we, immortal souls, increase in knowledge and wisdom, and as the ages roll on, more and more perceive and understand this mighty universe and its Author? I firmly believe we shall, and that as yet we are only beginning to live and think and understand and appreciate.

The Supreme Being was believed in, praised and worshipped by all the ancient peoples and is now believed in, praised and worshipped by the vast majority of the people of the world—it is true under different names, but still it is the same idea—a Being without beginning and without end—Infinite in Wisdom—Infinite in Goodness —Infinite in Power—Infinite in Action and, at all times, everywhere and present.

E. W. Cole

The Ancients' Idea of God

God extends from eternity to eternity.—*Aristotle.*

Nothing is more ancient than God, for He was never created; nothing more beautiful than the world, it is the work of that same God.—*Thales.*

Nature herself has imprinted on the minds of all the idea of a God; for what nation or race of men is there that has not, even without being taught, some idea of a God.—*Cicero.*

There is one God; Him the Christians, Him the Jews, Him all the

Gentile people worship.—*Emperor Adrian.*

Amid so much war, contest, and variety of opinion, you will find one consenting conviction in every land that there is one God, the King and Father of all.—*Maximus Tyrius.*

If we suppose a God, to Him there can be nothing mean and nothing great. The most trivial things must be equal under His regard as the most august. All-powerful, omniscient, and omnipresent, He must encompass all things, and pervade all things. Ignorant of nothing, forgetting nothing, despising nothing, He must direct the operations of the universe with perfect skill, and sustain every part in consummate order.—*Plato.*

What land or what sea will man find without God? Into what part of the earth wilt thou descend and hide thyself, O unhappy wretch! where thou canst escape from God?—*Plutarch.*

Thine, O Lord, is the greatness, and the power, and the glory, and the victory, and the majesty; for all that is in the heaven and in the earth, is Thine. Thine is the kingdom, O Lord, and Thou art exalted as head above all.—*David.*

He is God, the Great, the Mighty, the Tremendous, the Merciful, the Gracious, the Benign, the Wise, the Faithful, the Just, and the Virtuous; Omniscience, Omnipresence, Omnipotence, are His alone, whose Being knew no beginning, and can know no end.—*The Mishna Torah.*

The Name of God in 48 Languages

"Aeolian and Doric—Ilos. Arabic—Allah. Armorian—
Teuti. Assyrian —Eleah. Celtic and Gallic—Diu. Chal-
daic—Eilah. Chinese—Prussa. Coromandel—Brama.
Cretan—Thios. Danish and Swedish—Gut. Dutch—
Godt. English and Old Saxon—God. Finch—Jumala.
Flemish—Goed. French—Dieu. German and Swiss—
Gott. Greek—Theos. Hebrew— Elohim, Eloha. Hin-

dostanee—Rain. Irish—Dia. Italian—Do. Japanese—
Goezur. Lapp—Jubinal. Latin—Deus. Low Breton—
Done. Low Latin—Diex. Madagascar—Zannar. Ma-
lay—Alla. Modern Egyptian —Teun. Norwegian—Gud.
Olalu Tongue—Deu. Old Egyptian—Teut. Old Ger-
man—Diet. Pannonian—Istu. Persian—Siie. Peruvian—
Puchecammae. Pollaacca—Bung. Portuguese—Deos.
Provencal—Diou. Runic—As. Slav—Buch. Spanish—
Dios. Syriac and Turkish—Alah. Tartar—Magatal. Teu-
tonic—Goth. Zemblain—Fetiza."

The Moderns' Idea of God

Father of ALL! in every age,
 In every clime adored,
 By saint, by savage and by sage,
 Jehovah, Jove, or Lord.—*Pope.*

The Supreme Being whom we call God, is a necessary, self-existent,
eternal, immense, omnipotent, omniscient, and best Being; and
therefore also a Being who is and ought to be esteemed most sacred
of holy.—*N. Grew.*

What an immense workman is God! in miniature as well as in the
great. With the one hand, perhaps, He is making a ring of one
hundred thousand miles in diameter, to revolve round a planet like
Saturn, and with the other as forming a tooth in the ray of a
feather of a humming-bird, or a point in the claw of the foot of a
microscopic insect. When he works in miniature, everything is
gilded, polished, and perfect, but whatever is made by human art,
as a needle, etc., when viewed by a microscope, appears rough, and
coarse, and bungling.—*Bishop Law.*

Nothing is easier than to say the word—*universe*, and yet it
would take us millions of millions of years to bestow one hasty
glance upon the surface of that small portion of it which lies
within the range of our glasses. But what are all the suns, comets,
earths, moons, atmospheres, seas, rivers, mountains, valleys,
plains, woods, cattle, wild beasts, fish, fowl, grasses, plants,

shrubs, minerals, and metals, compared with the meaning of the one name—God!—*Pulford.*

The whole evolution of times and ages, from everlasting to everlasting, is, collectedly an presentifickly represented to God at once, as if all things and actions were at this very instant really present and existent before Him.—*Sir T. More.*

Who taught the bird to build her nest,
  Of wool and hay and moss?
Who taught her how to weave it best,
  And lay the twigs across?
Who taught the busy bee to fly
  Among the sweetest flowers—
And lay her store of honey by,
  To eat in winter hours?
Who taught the little ants the way
  Their narrow holes to bore,
And through the pleasant summer's day
  To gather up their store?

—

There's not a tint that paints the rose,
  Or decks the lily fair,
Or marks the humblest flower that grows
  But God has placed it there.
There's not of grass a simple blade,
  Or leaf of lowliest mien,
Where heav'nly skill is not displayed,
  And heav'nly goodness seen.
There's not a star whose twinkling light
  Illumes the distant earth,
And cheers the solemn gleam of night,
  But mercy gave it birth.
There's not a cloud whose dews distil
  Upon the parching clod,
And clothe with verdure vale and hill,
  That is not sent by God.
There's not a place on earth's vast round,
  In ocean deep, or air,

964

Where skill and wisdom are not found,
  For God is everywhere.
Around, beneath, below, above,
  Wherever space extends,
There Heaven displays its boundless love,
  And power with mercy blends.—*Wallace.*

Eternal Goodness

I dimly guess from blessings known,
  Of greater out of sight,
And, with the chastised Psalmist, own
  His judgements, too, are right.

I know not what the future hath
  Of marvel or surprise,
Assured alone that life and death
  His mercy underlies.

I know not where His islands lift
I only know I cannot drift
  Their fronded palms in air;
  Beyond His love and care.

Also from Benediction Books ...

Wandering Between Two Worlds: Essays on Faith and Art
Anita Mathias
Benediction Books, 2007
152 pages
ISBN: 0955373700

Available from www.amazon.com, www.amazon.co.uk

In these wide-ranging lyrical essays, Anita Mathias writes, in lush, lovely prose, of her naughty Catholic childhood in Jamshedpur, India; her large, eccentric family in Mangalore, a sea-coast town converted by the Portuguese in the sixteenth century; her rebellion and atheism as a teenager in her Himalayan boarding school, run by German missionary nuns, St. Mary's Convent, Nainital; and her abrupt religious conversion after which she entered Mother Teresa's convent in Calcutta as a novice. Later rich, elegant essays explore the dualities of her life as a writer, mother and Christian in the United States-- Domesticity and Art, Writing and Prayer, and the experience of being "an alien and stranger" as an immigrant in America, sensing the need for roots.

About the Author

Anita Mathias is the author of *Wandering Between Two Worlds: Essays on Faith and Art.* She has a B.A. and M.A. in English from Somerville College, Oxford University, and an M.A. in Creative Writing from the Ohio State University, USA. Anita won a National Endowment of the Arts fellowship in Creative Nonfiction in 1997. She lives in Oxford, England with her husband, Roy, and her daughters, Zoe and Irene.

Visit Anita at http://www.anitamathias.com, and on http://theoxfordchristian.blogspot.com, her Christian blog; http://wanderingbetweentwoworlds.blogspot.com/, her personal blog, and http://thegoodbooksblog.blogspot.com, her literary and writing blog.

The Church That Had Too Much
Anita Mathias
Benediction Books, 2010
52 pages
ISBN: 9781849026567

Available from www.amazon.com, www.amazon.co.uk

The Church That Had Too Much was very well-intentioned. She wanted to love God, she wanted to love people, but she was both hampered by her muchness and the abundance of her possessions, and beset by ambition, power struggles and snobbery. Read about the surprising way The Church That Had Too Much began to resolve her problems in this deceptively simple and enchanting fable.

About the Author

Anita Mathias is the author of *Wandering Between Two Worlds: Essays on Faith and Art.* She has a B.A. and M.A. in English from Somerville College, Oxford University, and an M.A. in Creative Writing from the Ohio State University, USA. Anita won a National Endowment of the Arts fellowship in Creative Nonfiction in 1997. She lives in Oxford, England with her husband, Roy, and her daughters, Zoe and Irene.

Visit Anita at http://www.anitamathias.com, and on http://theoxfordchristian.blogspot.com, her Christian blog; http://wanderingbetweentwoworlds.blogspot.com/, her personal blog, and http://thegoodbooksblog.blogspot.com, her literary and writing blog.

www.ingramcontent.com/pod-product-compliance
Lightning Source LLC
Chambersburg PA
CBHW020409100426
42812CB00001B/266